LIBRARY OF LATIN AMERICAN
HISTORY AND CULTURE

GENERAL EDITOR:
DR. A. CURTIS WILGUS

THE SPANISH DEPENDENCIES
IN SOUTH AMERICA

THE
SPANISH DEPENDENCIES
IN SOUTH AMERICA

AN INTRODUCTION TO THE HISTORY
OF THEIR CIVILISATION

BY

BERNARD MOSES, Ph.D., LL.D.

PROFESSOR IN THE UNIVERSITY OF CALIFORNIA
HONORARY PROFESSOR IN THE UNIVERSITY OF CHILE

IN TWO VOLUMES   VOL. II

COOPER SQUARE PUBLISHERS, INC.
NEW YORK
1965

980
M85
V. 2

Published 1965 by
Cooper Square Publishers, Inc.
59 Fourth Avenue, New York, N. Y. 10003

Library of Congress Catalog Card Number: 65-21908

Printed in the United States of America

CONTENTS

CONTENTS

PAGE

CHAPTER IX

I. Bishop Trejo, founder of the University. II. The organisation of the University. III. The studies. IV. Degrees and graduation. V. The University after the expulsion of the Jesuits.

CHAPTER X

I. Earthquakes and Spanish faith. II. The mines of Laicacota. III. Indians and the *obrages*. IV. The Maynas missions. V. Henry Morgan. VI. Castellar and the viceroy-archbishop.

CHAPTER XI

I. The distress of the Indians and efforts for their relief. II. The hostility of the archbishop. III. The earthquake of 1687. IV. The walls of Lima. V. Peru under the Count of Monclova.

CHAPTER XII

I. The royal patronage. II. The beginnings of the ecclesiastical organisation in America. III. The great power of the king in ecclesiastical affairs. IV. The general organisation of the Church.

CHAPTER XIII

Chilean affairs civil and ecclesiastical in the beginning of the century. II. The Franciscans and the Mercedarios. III. The Dominicans and the Jesuits. IV. The Augustinians. V. Schools in other towns than Santiago. VI. Instruction in the universities.

CONTENTS

PAGE

CHAPTER XVIII

CHAPTER XIX

CHAPTER XX

THE SPANISH DEPENDENCIES
IN SOUTH AMERICA

CHAPTER I

A MINING TOWN IN UPPER PERU

I. Discovery of the mines of Potosi. II. The Imperial City. III. Wealth and extravagance. IV. Fights and fiestas. V. Abdication and death of Charles the Fifth. VI. Governmental changes. VII. The case of Ordaz. VIII. Viceroy Toledo in Potosi.

I

THE towns of Upper Peru, which were called into existence by the exploitation of mines, presented social conditions, a knowledge of which helps one to appreciate the history of this part of South America in the sixteenth and seventeenth centuries. In most cases these communities flourished and declined with the mines, leaving no adequate record of their peculiar society. Much light, however, is thrown on one of these towns, in some respects the most important, by the *Anales de la Villa Imperial de Potosi*, by Bartolomé Martinez y Vela. Vicente G. Quesada has made use of this chronicle and a vast mass of other material in his attractive book called *Crónicas Potosinas : Costumbres de la Edad medieval Hispano-Americana*. The sources of information concerning Potosi are sufficient to afford a more or less clear view of the social career of this remarkable community.

The only reason for the existence of this city is found in the wealth of the mines of the famous hill of Potosi.

The legends of the Indians affirm that the Inca Huaina Capac suspected the presence of precious metals here, and that, returning from a campaign against certain revolted towns, he halted at Cantumarca, in the valley of Tarapaia, and sent to the mines of Porco, six or seven leagues away, for Indians to seek for the ore that was supposed to be concealed in the hill ; but, when they began to dig, they heard a terrible noise and a mysterious voice which gave this command in Quichua : " Take no silver from this hill which is destined for other owners." Whether the mysterious voice had any influence or not, it appears to be a fact that no silver was taken from the hill until after the arrival of the other owners.

This cold and inhospitable region, lying between thirteen and fourteen thousand feet above the level of the sea, was used by the Indians chiefly for grazing and mining. Whatever agricultural products were consumed here were raised in the lower valleys. The life of the Indians, even under the far-famed empire of the Incas, was not merely simple ; it was a low and mean form of existence. The precious metals which the mines yielded brought them little or no amelioration, for the ordinary Indians had no opportunity to transmute them into means for personal enjoyment or social advancement. They were wrought into the forms of plants, trees, animals, and flowers, which were used to adorn the temples. They were for the Sun and the monarch. There was thus no temptation to steal them, no object in possessing them, and no incentive to search for them.

After centuries of isolation the Indians were suddenly startled and terrified by the coming of the Spaniards. Atahualpa was murdered, the temples were pillaged, and the inhabitants of the conquered regions were distributed among the invaders. In a few years the old social system was destroyed, and the imagination of this present generation is unable to picture the barbarities of the new order of things.

The first mines exploited by the Spaniards were those that had been worked by the Incas. Those of Porco were taken in 1543. They seem to have fallen into the hands of three Spaniards : Captain Juan de Villarroel, Captain Diego Centeno, and Captain Santardia. Some of the Indians allotted to these men were employed in the mines, and others attended the herds of animals that grazed in this region. Qualca was in the service of Villarroel. His flocks were accustomed to feed about the base of the hill of Potosi, and to him is attributed the accidental discovery of the veins of silver which, through their attraction, made this desolate spot the site of the Imperial City of Potosi. This discovery was made in January 1545.[1]

[1] In his *Crónicas Potosinas*, i. 25–7, Dr. Vicente G. Quesada has included three versions of the story of the discovery :

" 1. It is said that after having gone with his llamas the distance from Porco to Potosi, with the slow pace of these animals, Gualca arrived in the evening at the latter place fatigued from the journey. As the night was dark, he did not dare to go on to the huts of the shepherds of Cantumarca ; and then, in order to secure the llamas, he tied them to some shrubs of *lichu* and there passed the night in the open air. The next day the llamas, by the efforts they made to graze, pulled up by the roots the *lichu*, and disclosed a valuable vein of metal, the richness of which the Indian, with the knowledge he possessed as a miner of Porco, was able to appreciate.

"2. Others say that Gualca went from the place already referred to in search of the llama that had gone astray. Skilful in following the tracks which animals make in the soil, he followed this one to Potosi, where he arrived at night. The cold was intense, and it soon became very dark, so that in order to secure the animal that had been lost he tied him to a bush of *queñua*, gathered some dry grass, cut some branches from the neighbouring shrubs, made a fire with the stroke of a flint, and passed the cold night in light and warmth. The next day the fire had melted the metal on the surface, which ran in little streams of pure silver. As a skilful miner, he knew the immense richness of the vein.

" 3. Still others affirm that Gualca followed a deer or a llama up the hill, and, while the animal was climbing along the slope and sharp cliff, he, wishing to seize it, was on the point of slipping and falling over the precipice. Then, to avoid the accident, he grasped the branch of a *queñua*, and by the force which he exerted to hold himself, he pulled the bush up by the roots. He saw with surprise, laid bare in the hole left by the roots of the plant, the rich vein of a silver mine

From time to time Gualca extracted small quantities
of ore for his own use, and for a month kept his secret.
But it became evident to the other Indians with whom
he was associated that he had some unusual source from
which he got silver.   One Guanca, as an intimate friend,
obtained the secret in confidence.   Then Villarroel knew
it, and then all the world.   Villarroel and Guanca together
registered the first claim.   This was the vein called the
Centeno, April 21, 1545.   Gualca was treacherously left
out ; later Guanca mysteriously disappeared, and Villarroel remained the sole proprietor.

In a few days Porco was almost entirely abandoned,
nearly the whole population having gone to the site of
the new mine.   A little later the vein called *Estaño* was
found, and information of these discoveries soon reached
Chuquisaca.   Then the rush to Potosi began.   The
Spaniards brought their Indian dependents, but in the
beginning they all lived exposed to the rigours of this
mountain climate rather than take the time to construct
houses.   The support of this increasing population was
derived from the products of the neighbouring valleys
cultivated by the Indians.   When it became absolutely
necessary, on account of the number of inhabitants and
the storms of winter to have houses, the Indians of Cantumarca were brought in to build them.   But this forceful
conscription of labourers involved the risk of neglecting
the harvests of the lower lands, thus causing a dangerous

the finding of which filled him with delight.   Having a knowledge of
the method of melting the metal by *guayras*, he took some pieces,
built a fire, and, having convinced himself of the richness of the ore,
carried away several pieces to repeat the experiment."

The method referred to was that used by the Indians of this region.
It involved the use of portable furnaces of clay, *guayras*, in which the
metals were placed and melted (Quesada, *Crónicas Potosinas*, i. 90).
This attractive work is based on the *Anales de la Villa Imperial de
Potosi*, by Don Bartolomé Martinez y Vela, which was printed, in
1872, in *Archivo Boliviano*, vol. i. 283–487 ; Diego Fernandez refers
to the manner in which the mines were discovered in his *Historia del
Perú*, lib. ii. cap. xi. ; Cieza de Leon, *La Crónica del Perú*, cap. cix.

scarcity of provisions. It, moreover, aroused hostility among the Indians, and led those engaged in making *adobes* to form a conspiracy to punish the invaders. The Spaniards, who were not well armed, undertook to enter into negotiations. But the Indians had learned of the injustice done the discoverer of the mine, and demanded as a basis for the establishment of peace that those persons in possession of the hill should abandon it, and turn it over to Gualca. The Spaniards had no mind to accept these terms, but, having sent to Porco for arms, prepared to resist the Indians who had gathered a few miles from the mine, and were advancing to take possession of it. The fight that ensued lasted two hours. Fifty Indians and twenty-five Spaniards were killed, besides many wounded in both parties. In consequence of this conflict, many Indians who had had no part in it fled from Cantumarca and other adjacent villages. The surviving Spaniards remained in control of the mine, and continued their efforts to found here a town.

II

A sloping plain of a few square leagues, thirteen or fourteen thousand feet above the sea ; a barren hill of many colours, about three leagues in circumference, rising two thousand feet above the plain ; a horizon of broken mountain peaks ; a climate of thin air rigid in the extreme, frequently varied by icy winds and terrific storms : these were the characteristics of the site and the environment of the city of Potosi.

The building of the town was begun in December 1545. In a short time all the inhabitants had roofs to shelter them, either those of the new houses or those of the cabins made vacant by the withdrawal of the Indians. Early in the next year they laid the foundations of the church. A certain part of the site of the town was swampy, and the rapid growth of the population made artificial drainage necessary. This part had also to be filled to prepare it for buildings. At first the houses were built here and there without regard to order or street lines, but in later decades this irregularity was corrected. At the end of eighteen months two thousand five hundred houses had been erected, and the number of the inhabitants was fourteen thousand. The fame of the mines was extended throughout Peru, and Potosi became the chief point of attraction in America.

Throughout the colonial period Potosi was known as the Imperial City. It was given this designation in honour of the emperor, Charles V. In 1546 Captain Villarroel, the owner of the first mine put on record, had accumulated an immense fortune, and wished to acquire the distinction he might attain with the title of discoverer and founder. With this object in view, he applied to the emperor. He sent to him a description of the discovery and ninety-six thousand ounces of silver. The silver was sent on account of the royal fifths. The emperor confirmed the title sought by Villarroel, conferred upon him the order of Santiago, decreed arms for the city and established its title as the Imperial City. The first census of Potosi was taken under the order of Francisco de Toledo, who was viceroy of Peru from 1569–81. It showed one hundred and twenty thousand inhabitants. A subsequent enumeration made under the order of the viceroy Montesclaros in 1611, indicated a population of one hundred and fourteen thousand. Of these sixty-five thousand were Indians, forty-two thousand were Spaniards and creoles, and the balance were negroes and mulattoes. In 1650 the population was one hundred and sixty thousand. In 1825 it was eight thousand. The abundance of silver and this large increase of inhabitants in a region ill adapted to the production of food made prices very high. The prices of the ordinary articles of consumption in Potosi for a long period might be compared with those of California in 1849. The improved means of communication in the middle of the nineteenth century soon made the prices in California normal. California, moreover, possessed the most favourable conditions for raising food ; while the region about Potosi was a mountain desert, relieved only by a few small and poorly cultivated valleys. Many persons who had made fortunes at the mines in California found it agreeable to continue to live in this region ; but the bleak tableland of Upper Peru offered few attractions to those whose wealth enabled them to choose freely the place of their permanent residence. The country, moreover, had few or no other sources of wealth adequate to support a large population when the mines failed. But while the mines continued to pour out their abundant riches the towns increased, and society assumed there many of the features of civilisation. It matured early. For a period the mining region of Upper Peru might claim superiority in cultivation and in the perfection of its institutions over the low lands of other parts of the continent that were later to outstrip it.

Under the system of the *mita* the owners of the mines of Potosi drew into their service, earlier or later, a large part of the Indian population of the town and the surrounding country. The *mita* as here employed was a form of conscription, under which a certain number of Indians between the ages of eighteen and fifty were forced to work in the mines. Those liable to this service were arraigned in seven divisions, and each group drawn worked for six months, and were then, under the rule, free for two years. But the severity of the labour and the unfavourable conditions were such that eighty per cent., or four out of every five, died the first year. It is affirmed that under this system eight millions of Indians perished in the mines of Peru.

III

The employment of forced labour made possible a very rapid accumulation of wealth in the hands of the dominant class. A certain evidence of this wealth may be seen in the enormous sums spent by the city in public works and celebrations. In 1556, eleven years after the founding of the town, the inhabitants celebrated the accession of Philip II to the throne of Spain. The city spent on this occasion eight million dollars. The funeral ceremonies of the emperor, Charles V, in 1559, involved an expenditure of one hundred and forty thousand dollars. In 1577, three million dollars were spent on waterworks. The fortunes of the dominant class, in 1580, ranged from a minimum of $300,000 or $400,000 to $2,000,000 or $6,000,000. On the death of Philip II, a funeral service was held costing one hundred and thirty thousand dollars. Prior to 1593, the royal fifth had been paid on three hundred and ninety-six millions of silver. There had been deposited for safety in the royal treasury and in the Augustinian and Dominican monasteries in 1624, jewels and money belonging to the residents of the town amounting in value to forty-two million dollars.

Other statistics show that the treasure known to be held by the inhabitants, in 1650, amounted to thirty-six million dollars. This leaves out of account that which was concealed from the persons who had been ordered to take the census. It goes without saying that in a city of one hundred and fifty or one hundred and sixty thousand inhabitants, there were numerous traders of all sorts. There were fourteen dancing-schools, thirty-six gambling houses, and one theatre, to which the price of admission ranged from forty to fifty dollars. The luxury in dress was in keeping with the enormous incomes received. Touching this point, the writer of the *Crónicas Potosinas* says : " The ladies of Potosi had jewels and dresses for each *fiesta* which were worth from twelve to fourteen thousand dollars ; one lady spent five hundred dollars merely for pearls for her embroidered overshoes. The mestizas wore sandals (*alpargatas*) and belts of silk and gold, with pearls and rubies, skirts and jackets of fine cloth of silver, pendants and chains of gold, and other rich jewels." [1]

Other evidence of the wealth and extravagance of Potosi may be found in the life of Doña Clara, the gayest, the most beautiful, the most accomplished, and the most elegant woman of the Imperial City : the first in wealth, the most superb in her Oriental ostentation, the one, in a word, whose jewels had no rivals either for their price or for their variety.[2] Her house was the centre of the worldly society of the most powerful miners, who were zealous rivals for the first place in the good graces of its attractive mistress. Sober historians have found the details of her life worthy of their attention. According to Martinez y Vela, " she had as many chemises of fine cambric and Dutch linen as there are days in the year, and a change was made every night ; four rich bedsteads of wood and bronze, with feather-beds and draperies of beautiful cloths ; and she changed from one to another every three months. In a word, she was the most affluent woman in Potosi." " She had a large number of slaves, encomiendas of Indians, and white servants whom she paid very liberally. Her treasure of gold, silver, jewels, precious stones, pearls, and ornaments was immense. Her table service was all of silver and gold ; filigree with emeralds and rubies was abundant among her ornaments. The silversmiths were continually occupied with her orders." " Her reception-room was magnificent. The Venetian mirrors had frames of burnished silver ; her furniture was adorned with gold and mother-of-pearl,

---

[1] Quesada, *Crónicas Potosinas*, i. 66.
[2] *Archivo Boliviano*, i. 465.

upholstered with cloth of gold and silver from Milan ;
figures of gold taken from Quichuan antiquities adorned
her tables." [1] Her writing-desk was of ebony and ivory ;
her floors were covered with rugs from Cairo, Persia, and
Turkey. Her pride did not permit her to allow anyone
to rival her in the splendour of her ornaments or in the
extent of her expenditures. In the games at her house
the rich miners took delight in staking sums equivalent
to a modern fortune.

IV

For many years Potosi was the scene of great disorder.
There were duels between individual persons, and fights
between social groups. Medieval anarchy found here an
excellent illustration. The local government was incompetent to preserve order. The Europeans with their easily
acquired riches, and the poor Indians dependent on them
under the law of encomiendas, constituted the elements
of a feudal society. The *fiestas*, the gambling, the intrigues, the antagonism of Europeans and creoles, and the
rivalries for the favours of women, produced ever re-
curring conflicts ; and when the lords followed by their
dependents quarrelled, there was civil war. Fighting
became a pastime, a social function. The parties to a duel
" sometimes fought in trousers and shirt, sometimes naked
to the waist, scorning the use of a shield ; and again they
were dressed in trousers and shirt of crimson tafety, so
that the blood from the wounds might not be seen and
they might not lose courage." [2] Sometimes, moreover,
they fought kneeling. In every case the challenge indicated the etiquette of the duel and the weapons to be
used.

In January 1552, the chronicler relates that Potosi
was full of life and movement. A multitude of gentlemen,

[1] *Archivo Boliviano*, i. 465; Quesada, *Crónicas Potosinas*, i. 180.
[2] *Ibid.*, 189.

carrying all kinds of weapons, pressed along the streets. Before five o'clock in the morning of the day to which he makes special reference, the whole population was abroad. They were on foot, on horseback, in *carramatas*, and in litters, as if going on a pilgrimage. There were men and women, mestizos and negroes, Indians and Spaniards. Everywhere rose the peculiar murmur of an interested crowd. There was to be fought a duel on horseback and with lances. It was a medieval crowd, with a wealth of colour and variety of dress that no other city could present. Knowledge of the publicity of these combats at Potosi had been spread to all parts of America ; and a distinguished champion had come from Cuzco to add to his laurels by a victory in the Imperial City. On his arrival Montejo had found that Doña Clara was the most noted woman in Potosi ; and at her house he had met Godinez, whose prestige as a fighter he hoped to dispute. From the quarrel which had been bred here arose the joust that was moving half the population. Even before the beginning of the battle Montejo had made one conquest ; he had awakened a new emotion in the heart of Doña Clara.

The chronicler, Bartolomé Martinez y Vela, has described the event of this combat, with all the details that might be expected in an account of the Field of the Cloth of Gold. The crowd, the arrival of the mounted contestants, their fine horses, their gorgeous costumes and waving plumes, their spears and shields, the onset, the shock, the first wounds, and the final fall of Montejo make a picture we are not accustomed to think of as formed on a background of America in the sixteenth century.

The death of Montejo was the beginning of the end of Doña Clara's glory. Recovering from a distressing illness which followed this event, she found a number of her servants had fled, carrying off her jewels and a large part of her treasure ; her Indians had deserted ; and hereafter in mourning costume she divided her time between the solitude of her home and prayers at the church.

The years following the death of Montejo were filled with treachery, rebellions, and assassinations, in which Godinez had a leading part. He was, however, finally arrested and placed in irons in the prison of La Plata. Tried before Alonzo de Alvarado, whom he had intended to assassinate, he was condemned to be quartered ; in the words of Garcilaso de la Vega, he was condemned " as a traitor to God, to the king, and to his friends." One after another the individual actors played out their rôles, and Doña Clara with the rest ; but the drama of public disorder and crime went on. Many years later, " on a day that was comparatively warm for the rigid climate of Potosi, an old woman of ninety-two years entered the church of Merced. She was poorly clothed, for she was accustomed to beg and lived from charity. She knelt and heard mass with great devotion, and prayed for a long time. This beggar was the splendid Doña Clara." [1] Martinez y Vela wrote : " Finalmente pagó en esta vida los desórdenes de la pasada y sufrió con admirable paciencia sus trabajos, desengañando á los avaros y ricos soberbios con razones de experiencia, y asi murió muy pobre de bienes corporales, pero muy rica de virtudes. Entarráronla de limosna los piodosos y nobles vecinos. Pongo este caso para desengaño y enmienda de los que se hallan muy asegurados de sus temporales bienes." [2]

V

The fact of the abdication of Charles V was known at Potosi in October 1556. The sentiment of surprise at the retirement of the emperor was followed by public rejoicing over the accession of Philip II. This was a new experience for Potosi ; for Charles V was on the throne

[1] Quesada, *Crónicas Potosinas*, i. 231.   [2] *Archivo Boliviano*, i. 466.

when the city was founded. The inhabitants immediately began preparations for their remarkable celebration, which lasted twenty-four days, and consisted of almost every form of public rejoicing then known.[1]

But while Potosi was celebrating the accession of Philip II, Peru was in a state of political turmoil. The civil war had left the country full of restless and adventurous spirits. The Imperial City was not exempt from their influence, and the streets sometimes witnessed bloody conflicts. These things, however, disturbed the viceroy less than the fact that Potosi had dared to celebrate the accession of the king without first applying for and receiving his viceregal permission. As soon as he had heard what had been done at Potosi, he sent a special messenger to convey his reprimand and vigorous threats to the inhabitants for their audacity. His personal dignity appears to have been slighted, and this apparently moved him more, and was regarded as a greater social offence than brigandage, treason, or rebellion.

Irritated by the independent action of the authorities of Potosi, and provoked by letters he had received casting doubt on the loyalty of certain prominent residents of that city, the viceroy determined to make an example of General Robles. He, therefore, sent to Potosi one of the judges of the audiencia, with express orders that he should have Robles garroted. Robles, aware of the coming of the messenger, but not knowing the purpose of his mission, went out to meet him and to extend to him an honourable welcome to the city. The reason of Robles' failure to return was for a time veiled in mystery ; later it transpired that he was murdered by the direct command of the viceroy. This barbarous act aroused the inhabitants

---

[1] Martinez y Vela says : " Se solemnizaron con generales aplausos, tanta vanidad y competencia de fiestas, costosas galas, máscaras, torneos, cañas, toros, justas, sortijos, saraos, comedias, banquetes soberbios, y otros ingeniosas invenciones de las mayores que se habian visto en este reino ; " see Quesada, i. 239.

of Potosi, and put them in a mood to take vengeance on the pusillanimous judge, who found it advisable to seek the protection of the authorities. He wished to excuse himself by showing his instructions, and by making it appear that he had acted under a specific command issued by the viceroy. The fact that a high officer of the colonial government was willing to obey a command in a field of action to which the orders of a superior cannot properly reach is an indication of the length the political system had gone in suppressing the independence of individual character.

With all the extravagance and display of wealth which the unparalleled richness of the mines made possible, there was still, in 1557, little provision for agreeable living. The great storm of that year showed how ill-prepared the city was to meet an emergency of that kind. The snow continued to fall for seven days without ceasing. It was piled up like mountains in the plazas, the streets were blocked, and all ways leading to the city were impassable. The temperature fell to a point where it was almost unendurable. The houses were comfortless. There were no means of heating them except the braziers; and the little fire which they ordinarily contained, made with wood and charcoal, filled the room with smoke and gas, leaving the occupant in doubt whether his end would come by choking, asphyxiation, or freezing. At first the inhabitants, driven from the streets, gathered about the family brazier; but as the town was supplied with wood and charcoal from day to day by the Indians, the store was necessarily limited, and was soon exhausted; for the snow prevented the Indians from coming to the city. Many perished in the attempt, and, in the city itself, many persons whose hold on life had been weakened by age were cut off.

Two years later another event of public importance excited general interest in the city. Towards the end of the year 1559, a special messenger from the viceroy at

Lima brought to Potosi information of the death of Charles V. A communication announcing this event was read in public, together with an order fixing twenty days as the official period of mourning. A committee of the most distinguished citizens took charge of the preparations for a formal funeral ceremony, which was held in the church of San Francisco. Within the church a temple-like structure was erected, and appropriately draped. All classes were disposed to unite in honouring the memory of the emperor ; even the Indians wished to have part in the public demonstration, and they respectfully asked the privilege of appearing in their ancient national costume. Their petition was at first refused ; but when the effect of this refusal on the Indians was observed, there was somebody wise enough to see that, in disregarding this profound sentiment of the Indians, the authorities had blundered. The decision was then modified : the Indians might wear their national costume, but they were expressly required to submit to the order of the ceremonial as fixed by the Spaniards.

The function in the church lasted from two o'clock in the afternoon until seven o'clock in the evening, and it was repeated the following day. Around the newly constructed funeral temple, on the altars, and in the chapels, were distributed fifteen hundred candles, which the chronicler informs us contained two thousand pounds of white wax valued at eight dollars a pound, making a total of sixteen thousand dollars for this item of expenditure. But the most remarkable features of the meetings were the crowds and unprecedented richness and variety of the costumes. The rich miners vied with the nobles, the nobles with the members of the orders of Calatrava and Santiago ; and more noticeable than all the rest were the quaint and original costumes of the Indians.

VI

An important change made at this time in public affairs was the establishment, at Chuquisaca, of an audiencia, or supreme court, which, like the audiencias established elsewhere, exercised not only judicial, but also administrative powers. This was needed to strengthen the government and to prevent the population from falling into complete anarchy. Hitherto the chief official had been the corregidor of the district, whose jurisdiction embraced not only the Imperial City, but also Chuquisaca, or La Plata. During this time he had resided six months of each year in Chuquisaca, and six months in Potosi. In the absence of the corregidor, the administration was necessarily inefficient under a deputy, or a lieutenant, corregidor. After this change the corregidor resided permanently at Potosi, which thus became an important centre of local government. In the brief period of fifteen years the desolate spot at the foot of the hill of Potosi had become the site of a rich city and a local capital, the seat of a petty governor, or corregidor, in the Spanish colonial system.

Potosi was not founded in accordance with any established rules, or methods of proceeding determined by Spanish legislation. The inhabitants, called together by the discovery of the mines, made a city without previous governmental authorisation and without a prearranged plan. In fact, during the civil wars that had unsettled affairs in Peru, in the middle of the sixteenth century, it was not easy to find a person whose pretensions to authority were not questioned. The failure of the founder to follow the legal formula was a sufficient excuse for Chuquisaca to maintain that Potosi was properly under its jurisdiction. In order to confirm this view, the cabildo of Chuquisaca appealed to the audiencia, and that body acting as the supreme authority in this region ordered the founders of Potosi to obey the magistrate who might be appointed by the corregidor of the dominant city. The official appointed by Chuquisaca under this decision was the deputy, or lieutenant, corregidor. If Villarroel as the founder had followed the prescribed rules for establishing a municipal government, the town might have enjoyed the usual independence of a municipality from the beginning. As it was, the corregidor of Chuquisaca and three regidores went to Potosi and established a municipal government, and at the same time fixed the dependence of Potosi on the neighbouring city. Under the regulations adopted at this time, six regidores were to be appointed from the residents of Potosi, who should manage the ordinary affairs of the town ; but in matters of grave importance the regidores of Chuquisaca should be summoned, and the presence of one of them would be sufficient to legalise such a meeting of the cabildo.

The drama of municipal government in Potosi was not wanting in action. The members of the council attended the meetings armed with swords and pistols, and in coats of mail. The discussions often ended in fights, as the chronicler observes, " in the place consecrated to the consideration of the interests of the community, and neither the audiencias nor the viceroys were able to stop them." [1] In fact, the persistence of this form of disorder made it sometimes necessary to suspend the meetings for long periods. The dependence on Chuquisaca was a fruitful source of conflicts. Potosi wished to be independent, and in the election of alcaldes, members of the council, who were residents of that city, were naturally zealous for their own candidates. In the election of 1563, the two parties were vigorously opposed to one another. Each wished the election of its candidates. Juan Lucero Cigali, the senior regidor from Chuquisaca, presided. In the hall of the ayuntamiento the disputes very early

[1] Quesada, *Crónicas Potosinas*, i. 387.

passed beyond the control of the presiding officer. Shouts, insults, and threats filled the air ; and in the next scene we find the whole company in the plaza engaged in a very noisy battle, with the presiding officer as the central object of attack. During the confusion which attended his death, his partisans had the good fortune to escape by flight.

It was evident the union could not be maintained in peace. Potosi appealed to the superior government at Lima for emancipation ; while Chuquisaca defended the existing order. The authorities at Lima were disposed to uphold the claims of Chuquisaca. Not finding the desired satisfaction in the courts, Potosi resorted to her wealth, and offered the regidores of Chuquisaca thirty thousand dollars. The offer was accepted and Potosi was emancipated ; but it does not appear that this sum went to the private accounts of the regidores, for it is reported that the city hall of Chuquisaca was built with this money. The new position of Potosi was recognised in 1565, by Philip II, who granted the city, by a royal decree, " the same liberties, dignities, and privileges as were held by the ayuntamiento of Seville." [1] Under this decree the city might have twenty-four regidores, but it became customary to have only twelve. The corregidor as governor of the district embracing the city presided at meetings of the council. In addition to the twelve regidores, the corregidor, and the two alcaldes, there were a number of other officials, making the whole number twenty-six.

The corregidor's removal from Chuquisaca to Potosi, in 1564, was not solely for the purpose of improving the political administration. He was attracted by the prospect of receiving some part of the increasing wealth of the city. Exercising his practically absolute power, he ordered that all those persons who held Indians in encomiendas should present them the first of each month for a personal review, and should pay at this time for

[1] Quesada, *Crónicas Potosinas*, i. 392.

each Indian the amount of two marks of silver, or sixteen ounces. For failure to meet this requirement, a fine of four thousand dollars was fixed for the first offence, and double this amount for the second; and for the third failure the penalty was loss of Indians and confiscation of property. It might have been urged that the object of this monthly review was to ensure to the Indians the payment of their wages and their proper treatment by their masters; but the real object was exploitation for the benefit of the corregidor. In four months he received somewhat more than two hundred and fifty thousand ounces of silver, which the encomenderos thought should have tempered his avarice. Therefore, at the end of this period, they presented to him a vigorous protest against the further prosecution of his plan. Corrión, the corregidor, refused to modify his procedure, and there arose a contest that promised to develop into a civil war. Don Julian de Cupide proposed that his Indians should not be presented, and when a messenger arrived to enjoin compliance with the order, Don Julian killed him and threw his body into the street. Then followed a fight at the house of Don Julian, in which Corrión was wounded. Later he fled to Chuquisaca, and instituted criminal proceedings against Don Julian and his followers. But these brought little satisfaction to either party, and the corregidor, drawn back to Potosi by his great financial opportunities, was finally assassinated.

VII

The state of affairs in Potosi showed the need of reform. In 1568 one Ordaz, as treasurer and royal judge, arrived, commissioned to examine the condition of the administration and make such improvements as were necessary. As the chronicler presents him, he does not appear especially attractive. " He was tall, thin, with a high forehead and little hair, an aquiline nose, a big mouth, and thin pale lips. He was, in spite of his leanness, one of those who often commit the sin of gluttony. A glutton, garrulous, and arrogant, he had the capital defect of an irritable temper, which surely did not make him very agreeable in intimate association. His appearance was, moreover, rough and dry. He always spoke dogmatically, and could not bear contradiction, an evident proof of bad habits in childhood and a vicious education. He dressed in black velvet, with the cape and sword of the hidalgo, with a white and well-fitting collar. His emaciated figure and his penetrating look had something analogous to the appearance of a bird of prey lying in wait for its prize." His first two decrees related to the order and form of collecting the royal fifths and to regulating the work of the Indians. Afterwards he increased the *alcabala* from two to six per cent. Then there was trouble. The merchants resolved not to comply with the decree, alleging that the royal authorities had previously fixed the rate, and that the increase, which violated their interests, was unreasonable and unjust. They also enumerated extensive contributions to the public funds ; but Ordaz was not persuaded. He was only irritated, and informed them that if they did not pay the six per cent., he would impose double that amount as a penalty. Then, if they still refused, he would declare them disloyal and embezzlers of the royal funds, and would exile them from the city. The reply of the merchants did not indicate any disposition to give up their position. " Señor Licenciado, your honour is unjust, and we are disposed to give twelve millions which we have in clothing and money, in order to have the pleasure of taking the life of your honour with a thousand stabs. Consider yourself warned and be prepared."

Ordaz was advised to settle the matter by compromising with the merchants. But he was in no mood to take this course. He assembled a hundred Spaniards and four hundred Indians and proceeded to the houses where the merchants were gathered and prepared for resistance. On the arrival of the forces of Ordaz, the merchants prepared for the conflict, occupying the tops of the houses and such rooms as would enable them to discharge their weapons upon the enemy through the windows. But before the fight was over it became a hand-to-hand engagement with swords and spears. The forces of Ordaz were routed and scattered, while Ordaz himself was caught and dragged by the hair to the plaza, where his clothes were stripped off and his rawboned form was beaten with clubs. At this stage of the negotiations a number of priests and friars appeared and asked that the life of the unfortunate man might be spared. They carried him away dressed only in his shirt, amid the shouts and derision of the populace. When he had recovered from the beating he had received, he went back to Chuquisaca, and sent to the authorities at Lima an account of what had happened.[1]

When the messenger sent by Ordaz returned, he brought instructions from the superior authority in Lima to the audiencia and the corregidor. Under these instructions the audiencia and the corregidor were to carry out the decrees that had been issued with respect to the merchants of Potosi. The merchants in the meantime had not been expecting a peaceful settlement. Many of them had retired to the agreeable and fruitful valleys of Mataca, where, in contrast with the desolate region of Potosi, were to be found in abundance the products of temperate and semi-tropical lands. Here they gathered arms, and prepared to make war on the local government, which they considered unjust and oppressive. In April 1569 they found an additional excuse for their attitude in the arrival of General Avendaño, who had been appointed corregidor of the district embracing the Imperial City. He was commissioned to administer justice, pro-

---

[1] Quesada, *Crónicas Potosinas*, i. 421–9.

mote the good government of the Indians of the repartimientos, who worked in the mines, and to introduce such
reforms as were indispensable. He arrived at Potosi
attended by twenty horsemen and some of his friends.
Whatever favourable reputation he brought was soon
smirched by his " contemning the nobles and his abusive
treatment of the lower classes." Almost immediately on
taking up the duties of his office he caused the arrest of
a large number of persons for having been implicated in
former uprisings. These arrests and the subsequent confiscation of property caused a notable increase in the ranks
of the insurgents in the valleys of Mataca, who began
active hostilities by interrupting the communication between the city and the neighbouring valleys, from which
the supplies for the city had been drawn. Owing to this
interruption the inhabitants of Potosi began almost immediately to experience the scarcity and want of a besieged
city. The merchants, on the other hand, were abundantly provided with money, food, and arms, and the
force at their command, counting Spaniards, Indians, and
negroes, embraced somewhat more than five hundred
men. The troops gathered in the city went out to meet
them, but in the hand-to-hand battle that ensued the
merchants were victorious, and continued to dominate
the approaches to Potosi. Hoping to put an end to the
conflict by the removal of Avendaño, they sent agents
into the city to assassinate him, who broke into his house
and killed one or two members of his household ; but
Avendaño escaped by jumping out of a window into
another street. They shot at him, but failed to kill him.
He was, however, seriously wounded by his fall, and was
afterwards a miserable hunchbacked cripple, instead of
the dashing and gallant official who had come to govern
the city, and who had been a central figure in this episode
in the unquiet life of the region.

VIII

In 1572 the viceroy, Don Francisco de Toledo, visited Potosi. He came to study the conditions with a view of issuing such decrees as would promote the peace and prosperity of the city. Fifteen days were given over to the celebration of this important event ; and then, after having given some attention to the condition of the mines, he turned to the task of improving the appearance of the city. It had been built without regard to any systematic plan ; and it had become necessary to broaden and straighten the streets and to form a central plaza. Provision was also made for the construction of important public buildings, such as the prison, the city hall, and the mint. Not the least of his improvements was the introduction of the use of mercury in reducing the silver ore, with the purpose of avoiding the losses that had attended the method borrowed from the Indians, and hitherto employed. In the ordinances which he issued relating to the affairs of the city, he confirmed the repartimientos of the Indians. Whatever beneficent design may have been entertained in constructing this system, it became here as elsewhere an oppressive form of tyranny.

A city of one hundred and twenty thousand inhabitants was not properly equipped in the sixteenth century without its traditions of miracles and its wonder-working figures. Toledo gave his assistance in this matter also. He examined the box which contained the *Santo Cristo de la Vera Cruz de Potosi*, as it had been deposited at the entrance of the church, and was persuaded that it was " a divine gift, a holy relic, with which no one should concern himself except with profound veneration." And thus the city became possessed of a miraculous image, before which sinners were said to tremble and to repent of their sins. The Franciscan fathers sometimes cut its

beard, but it grew again. They combed it every year
after a procession, and distributed the hairs that came
out among the faithful, but still its hair never grew thin.
In the belief of the viceroy, " the *Santo Cristo* was a gift
sent by angels to protect the city, and to support those
who pray with faith, or turn away from sin." [1]

That there was need of repentance in a large number
of cases appears to be evident even from the meagre information which the chroniclers have given us. Glimpses
of lives that would have been improved by a moral awakening may be had in the gay gallants, the rich miners, and
the unscrupulous gamblers who made up the circle of
Doña Clara or the company that was attracted by the
beauty, the wit, and the gaiety of Claudia. Claudia was
of the world worldly. " She was versatile, light-hearted,
and amused herself in awakening passions and desires,
only to break the idol of to-day on the altar of the idol
of to-morrow." But at last she fell under a spell like
that which she had been accustomed to exercise over
others, and conceived a profound and serious passion for a
distinguished official in the royal service. But the ambition of Claudia had overleaped itself, and she found
herself in the position of a woman scorned. Then she
determined to destroy the confidence of the official in his
faithful and devoted wife. Here is the argument of the
tragedy that followed. Claudia sent an anonymous letter
to him while he was in Cuzco in the performance of his
official duties. He returned to Potosi to free himself from
the doubt that tormented him. On the evening of his
arrival he was made to see persons dressed as gentlemen
of rank, in costumes furnished by Claudia, coming from
his wife's apartments, and was then unaware that these
persons were servants in disguise. What was expected
to follow did follow : anger that would not reason, murder,
and at last, when it was too late, a revelation of the whole
series of events as a scheme arranged by Claudia to re-

[1] Quesada, *Crónicas Potosinas*, ii. 16–17.

move the person whom she vainly fancied was the only obstacle to the realisation of her ambition.

The temporary prominence attained by a Doña Clara or a Claudia was due to the large number of homeless adventurers in the population, to the relatively small number of European women, and to the very limited influence exercised by wives and mothers, either in the home or in society in general. In a community kept turbulent by the passions of greed and avarice, and by expectations of extraordinary wealth, homely pleasures and homely virtues appeared too tame and colourless to be attractive. The women who broke down the barriers that surrounded the narrow life of the household, who threw virtue and all the forms of social restraint to the winds, and who spent their gains in personal adornment and luxurious living did not want for admirers and champions in the brief periods of their worldly glory. But a notable phase of the society supercharged with violent emotions was a series of horrible crimes, in which women had an active part. Jealousy, vengeance, and the desire to redress a wrong were effective motives to acts in which the hands of women were often smirched with blood.

In this society, agitated and torn by conflicting passions, there was only a feeble undertone of unworldliness. Men and women suffered here the ordinary ills of human existence, disappointment, loss of property, treachery of pretended friends ; and a few sought to escape from these ills by retiring behind the walls of religious houses. But the great majority of the inhabitants were not woman-hearted. The civil wars that raged in Peru brought individual evils as well as public disaster. But in these early decades, the Spanish colonist manifested a virility that commends him to those who admire the heroic qualities of men.[1]

[1] Groot, *Historia de Nueva Granada*, i. 253 ; Lorente refers to Potosi as the "ásilo de todos los perdidos" (*Historia del Perú*, 1598–1700, 60). In his *Crónica moralizada del orden de S. Agustín*, Antonio de la

Calancha made use of the astrological wisdom of his time " to presage the fortune and explain the customs of not a few cities and towns of the two divisions of Peru." Some notion of his astrological explanations may be derived from his reference to Potosi :

" Predominan en Potosi (que está en veinte un grado, i poco más de veinte minutos) los signos de Libra i Venus, i así son los más que inclinan á los que allí abitan á ser codiciosos, amigos de música i festines, i trabajadores por adquirir riquezas, i algo dados á gustos venereos ; sus Planetas son Iupiter i Mercurio ; este inclina á que sean sabios, prudentes e inteligentes en sus comercios i contrataciones, i por Iupiter magnanimos, i de animos liberales." Quoted by René-Moreno, *Bolivia y Perú*, 45. For an account of Calancha, see René-Moreno, *Bolivia y Perú*, 1–84.

Viceroy Luis de Velasco (1596–1604), in *Relacion* given to his successor, the Count of Monterey ; " Entre las grandes cosas que contiene ansí esta provincia, lo es mucho y la más principal el Cerro del Potosi, porque dél sale la sustancia de que todo el Perú se mantiene. La grosedad del comercio con España, los muchos y forzosos gastos que aqui se hacen, y el tesoro que cada año se envia á S. M. para socorro de sus necesidades, todo esto sale de las entrañas del Cerro ; porque, aunque, hay otros miembros de Real Hacienda, no bastan para mucho que se gasta," *Doc. inéd.*, iv. 406 ; for other observation on Potosi, see the rest of the *Relacion*, ibid., iv. 407–39.

CHAPTER II

THE BEGINNINGS OF TUCUMAN

I. Aguirre's successors in Tucuman. II. Tucuman separated from Chile, and Aguirre's second term as governor. III. Aguirre's trial for heresy. IV. The audiencia of Charcas and the governors in the last decades of the century.

I

DURING the early decades of Potosi's noteworthy history, the internal province of Tucuman was beginning its tardy and slow development. After the departure of Aguirre, who went to seek the governorship of Chile, the chief command of the few soldiers or colonists who remained in the province fell into the hands of Juan Gregorio Bazan. For several years the colony continued a weak and precarious existence, torn by discord and afflicted by crime. But, with an increase in the number of the inhabitants through immigration from Chile and Peru, Juan Pérez de Zurita at the head of the government was able to bring to the settlers of this region a larger measure of prosperity than they had previously enjoyed. Captain Zurita, who had been sent from Chile by Governor García Hurtado de Mendoza, arrived in Santiago del Estero in May 1558. He was accepted by all parties, who were doubtless more or less influenced by the fact that Governor Mendoza, who had sent him, was a son of the viceroy of Peru. He was not disposed, like some of his predecessors, to be a partisan, but to treat the members of all parties with equal justice. Zurita changed the name of the province to New England (Neuva Inglaterra), in honour of the union of Philip II and Queen Mary. He

27

also founded three towns : London, Cañete, and Cordova. The last was destined to be the principal centre of intellectual life in this part of the continent for two hundred and fifty years. Zurita's principal task was that which his predecessors had faced, the task of subjugating or pacifying the Indians.

Diego Lopez de Zuñiga, who arrived in Peru in 1560, to succeed Mendoza in the office of viceroy, determined to make the province of Tucuman independent, except as subordinated to the viceroy. This proposed change provoked a revolt on the part of those who preferred to maintain the connection with Chile. The inhabitants of London were the leaders in this movement, but they were reinforced by the garrison of the town, who went over to the insurgents. The uprising was, however, suppressed, and two of the captains of the revolted garrison were hanged.

The opposition aroused by Zurita finally persuaded the governor of Chile that it was desirable to transfer the affairs of the province of Tucuman to other hands. Gregorio Castañeda was, therefore, sent to supersede Zurita. He assumed authority under circumstances where greater ability and a more robust courage than he possessed were needed for the successful government of the province. The Indians under a chief known as Juan de Calchaqui had apparently determined to put an end to Spanish domination in their territory. They destroyed the three recently established towns of Cordova, Cañete, and London. The siege and overthrow of Cordova was attended by outrageous cruelties ; and after the depopulation of these towns, the barbarians who surrounded the town of Nieva appeared determined to follow the example of Calchaqui, and imitate his achievements. Captain Pedro de Zárate, the commander of the little garrison, was unable to resist the assaults of the Indians, and the inhabitants were at length obliged to abandon the town. After these losses, Spanish occu-

pancy was reduced to the city of Santiago. This was all
that remained to them after ten years of labour, war,
and sacrifices of every sort. As Funes remarks, the province was in the position in which General Juan Nuñez
de Prado had left it. If there was any change in the state
of affairs, it was that the Indians had been converted
into uncompromising enemies, and at the same time they
had learned that the Spaniards were not invincible.[1]

II

The connection of Tucuman with Chile had been attended with serious inconveniences, not the least of which
arose out of the great distance, and the barrier of the
Andes, which separated them. The inhabitants thought
that many of these inconveniences would be set aside by
withdrawing the province from its political union with
Chile, and bringing it within the jurisdiction of the audiencia of Chuquisaca. This was provisionally decreed in
1562, and Francisco de Aguirre, for the second time, was
appointed governor of Tucuman.

In August 1563, Philip II approved the viceroy's
decree separating Tucuman from Chile, and confirmed
the appointment of Aguirre as governor. When Aguirre
received official information of his appointment, he was
living on his Chilean estate, where, after his return from
Lima, he had led the life of a feudal landlord. It was
the season in which the passes of the mountains were
closed, and he had to postpone taking possession of his
province until the return of spring. The intervening
months were spent in enlisting a little troop of soldiers,
and making other preparations for his expedition. In
November 1563, he began his journey over the mountains,
taking with him his family and a considerable number of

[1] Funes, *Ensayo de la Historia civil de Buenos Aires, Paraguay y
Tucuman*, i. 148. For an account of the Indian wars under Castañeda,
see *ibid.*, i. 139–48.

other relatives and friends.   He now proposed to establish himself permanently in Tucuman, and the prospect of practically absolute rule over the vast region still dominated from the capital of Tucuman, was sufficient to assuage his hitherto disappointed ambition.

The state of the colony on the arrival of Aguirre was deplorable.   The administration of the preceding governors had been unsatisfactory.   The Indians had reduced the smaller towns to masses of charred ruins, and, made bold by their victories, were in revolt throughout the province.   They were even besieging Santiago del Estero, in which the Spaniards from the region round about had taken refuge.   In the few years that had passed since Aguirre's first term as governor, the Indians had not forgotten him, and some report of his campaigns in Chile had doubtless entered into the traditions of the natives on both sides of the mountains.   The terror which his name inspired was a factor in restoring peace.

The early events of Aguirre's administration led Lope García de Castro, the governor of Upper Peru, to send an expedition to Santiago del Estero.   The avowed object of the expedition was the pacification of the Indian tribes south of Tarija.   Captain Martin de Almendras was the leader, and Captain Jerónimo de Alanis was the second in command.   The march towards Tucuman was begun in September 1565.   The Indians about Santiago del Estero were in revolt, but they laid aside their hostility on the arrival of the forces of Almendras.   Alanis was in command when the expedition reached Santiago del Estero.   He spent about two months here ; on returning to Upper Peru he turned over to Aguirre the bulk of his troops and supplies.   He found the plans of the governor worthy of commendation, and his report to his superior concerning the general results of the expedition was rather favourable than prejudicial to Aguirre.

III

The rest of Aguirre's career was marked by severe afflictions, which appeared to proceed in great part from the enmity of Pedro Ramirez de Quiñones, president of the audiencia of Charcas. While returning from a campaign which he had made toward the south, the soldiers whom he had received from Alanis mutinied, the leaders affirming at first that they were acting under the orders of the president of the audiencia, and later that they took this step by order of the Inquisition. What gave ground for accepting one or both of these affirmations as true, was the fact that the expedition of Almendras and Alanis was attended by Jerónimo de Holguin and the ecclesiastic Julian Martinez, the purposes of both of whom were somewhat mysterious. They were suspected of seeking to undermine Aguirre and to prepare for his overthrow by the president of the audiencia. The mutineers took Aguirre prisoner, carried him to Santiago del Estero, and finally to La Plata (Chuquisaca), where he was tried for heresy.

In the accusation on which Aguirre was tried, it was affirmed that he believed faith was sufficient for salvation; that it was not necessary to hear mass, but only to commend one's self to God in contrition of spirit; that he had said he had not much confidence in prayer, since he had known a man who had prayed much and had remained in hell, and an apostate who had gone to heaven; that if there were a blacksmith and a priest in a commonwealth, and he had to banish one or the other of them, he would prefer to banish the priest; and that he had absolved the Indians so that they might work on feastdays. The accusation set forth a long list of other remarks attributed to the governor, indicating his unwillingness to acknowledge the claims of the clergy, and

showing little respect for their pretensions.[1] At La
Plata he was obliged to wait while the business of his
trial was carried through the slow processes of the Inquisition. The bishop, who was authorised to pronounce
the decision in this case, was in Lima, and everything
seemed to contribute to delay, so that, as Aguirre observed with bitterness, " what might have been finished
in an hour was made to detain me about three years, and
subject me to an expense of thirty thousand dollars."

In his view, the judges who caused these delays were
not judges, but tyrants, who wished to stir up the country
rather than to serve the king.   Finally, when it was not
possible to prolong the delay, the delegates of the bishops
pronounced the governor's sentence, which in its essential
part was as follows :

" Having considered the records and merits of this
case, and all other things touching it which it was necessary to consider, we decide, that, for the offence which
stands against him, we ought to condemn him, and do
condemn him, to two years' imprisonment over and above
what he has had, which we declare to have been just and
given as punishment : and besides, we condemn him,
after he shall have been released from the prison where
he is at present, and taken to the city of Santiago del
Estero, province of Tucuman, to hear high mass on the
first or second Sunday in the parochial church, in person,
standing uncovered from the beginning to the end of it,
with a lighted candle in his hand, and at the time of the
offertory he shall repeat the propositions which he acknow-
ledges in a loud voice, so that those who may be in the
church may be able to hear him, and he shall declare them
in the form and manner in which they shall be given to
him, written and signed by the ordinary and by his notary ;
and he shall say this on account of the liberty which

[1] A part of this document is printed by Medina in his *Inquisición
en Chile*, i. 115 ; Lea, *The Inquisition in the Spanish Dependencies*,
322–4.

he has had and taken as governor and supreme judge of that province, and with arrogance and temerity, he said and affirmed the aforesaid propositions in ignorance, which have scandalised by their bad example those who may be edified by the humility, obedience, and reverence entertained for the Holy Mother Church : this penance is imposed upon him, that he shall send to the ordinary of this bishopric testimony of the *Vicario* in the said city of Santiago, by the first person coming thence to this kingdom, under the order that in case he shall not do this or send this evidence, he shall be proceeded against as one proceeds against an impenitent person. Moreover, we impose upon him a fine of fifteen hundred dollars of standard silver, to be applied in the following manner : seven hundred and fifty dollars to aid in paying for vestments of brocade which this Holy Church has purchased, and the other seven hundred and fifty dollars for the expenses of justice, at the disposal of the ordinary. Furthermore, we condemn him to give to the parochial church of Santiago del Estero a bell which shall weigh more than fifty pounds. Furthermore, we condemn him to pay the costs of this case, the appraisement of which is reserved to the ordinary ; all of which shall be observed, complied with, and paid before he is released from the prison where he is now confined; and after he shall have complied with this and made payment, we command him to absolve himself from any censure and excommunication under which he has fallen on account of the proceedings in this case ; and we command him to redeem from sequestration whatever property may have been sequestered in the course of this case." [1]

[1] The delegates of the bishop who rendered this decision were Fernando Palacio Alvarado, archdeacon, provisor, and vicar-general of the bishopric ; the licenciate, Baltisar de Villalobos ; Friar Marcos Xufré, guardian of the Franciscan monastery at La Plata ; and Bartolomé Alonso, vicar of the imperial city of Potosi. The text of the decision is found in Medina's *Historia de la Inquisición en Chile*, i. 118–21 ; *Documentos inéditos*, xxv. 373–6.

This sentence was subsequently modified so as to provide for the reading of the retraction, or abjuration, by the vicar-general, instead of by Aguirre. In this manner the abjuration was offered on the 1st of April, 1569, in the city of La Plata.[1]

When Aguirre returned to his province in October 1569, to take up the duties of his office for the third time, he found it in a sleepy and unprogressive state. Among the inhabitants there were only about two hundred Europeans. Some of these were at Santiago del Estero, some on the farms and cattle ranges, and others at recently established towns. They had few or no facilities for commercial intercourse with places that might demand their products, or from which they could obtain needed articles ; and in this isolation of the frontier they had fallen into a stagnant and semi-barbarous state of existence. During the imprisonment of Aguirre in Chuquisaca, Diego Pacheco had acted as provisional governor. When Aguirre resumed his duties, he banished from the province all persons who had been involved in the movement for his arrest in 1566, and the decree of expulsion provided that they should not return except under penalty of death. He hurled his reproaches against everybody concerned in his imprisonment and trial, and, if one may judge from his measures for personal defence, he expected only hostility in return. He constructed for himself a house like a fort, mounted on it a cannon brought from

[1] The retraction, or abjuration, was a carefully written document of seventeen hundred words ; see Medina's *Inquisición en Chile*, i. 122–8; *Doc. inéd.*, xxv. 362–85. Friar Domingo Santo Tomás, under whose authority this trial was held, was born in Seville, and went to Peru in the early days of the conquest. He was appointed prior of the monastery of Rosario in Lima in 1545 ; vicar-general, in 1552 ; and provincial, in 1553. In 1560 he caused to be printed in Valladolid a *Gramatica, or Arte de la lengua general de los indios de los reynos del Perú*. This was the first book written on the Quichua language. He had been made a bishop before the beginning of the trial of Aguirre, and during this trial he was in Lima to attend the second of the councils held in that city. Medina, *El Tribunal del Santo Oficio de la Inquisición en las provincias del Plata*, cap. ii.

Chile, collected provisions that might support him during a siege, and organised a guard to defend himself and his capital against encroachments by his enemies. Under these circumstances, a large number of persons, friends of preceding governors and supporters of Aguirre's enemies in Chuquisaca, naturally conspired to effect his ruin ; and the newly established Tribunal of the Inquisition was thought to furnish an effective instrument. Accusations in great numbers were sent to the office of the Inquisition, and in the autumn of 1570 Aguirre was arrested, and taken to the capital. The long overland journey, lasting about seven months, including delays by the way, was in itself a severe undertaking for a man of over seventy years. He was placed in the prison of the Inquisition at Lima, in May 1571.

The charge against Aguirre included a variety of items : he had said he was the vicar-general in the spiritual as well as in the temporal sphere, and that he did not fear excommunication ; he had permitted his pages to eat meat in Lent ; he had struck a priest ; he had believed in the efficacy of certain incantations in relieving one from, or curing, disease ; he had affirmed the pope could not excommunicate him ; he had maintained that mass celebrated by a certain vicar was valueless, that the mass was not necessary, for God considered only the heart, and that the tithes and first-fruits paid to the vicar should be paid to him as vicar-general in both spiritual and temporal matters. These, and a few other equally important charges, together with items added by Cerezuela, formed the basis of the action against the governor.

The trial itself had its principal motive in temporal rather than spiritual interests ; and in it the viceroy made use of the Tribunal to effect the removal of Aguirre from his position as governor of Tucuman. The proceedings against Aguirre lasted about five years, and as a result of the trial he was removed from the government of Tucuman. As Medina says : " Old, disillusioned, broken in health, and without income, he retired to the city of Serena, which he had founded.   In the meantime he had lost three of his four sons, a son-in-law, a brother, and three nephews, all of whom had died in the service of the king ; and after having spent in the royal service, as he said, more than three hundred thousand dollars, he found himself in such want and with so many debts that ' he was not able to appear before His Majesty to ask for grace and compensation for his many services and expenses.' " [1]

One of the penalties imposed upon Aguirre was that of perpetual exile from the province of Tucuman.   He was now seventy-six years old, and he may not be supposed to have had any very strong desire to return to scenes which had been associated with defeated expectations, persistent hostility, and losses of property.   He went back to Chile to occupy his house in Serena, from which he had been absent thirteen years, and his principal care henceforth was to put his estates in such a condition that they might furnish support for his family.   The northern, as well as the southern settlements of Chile, appeared to be in a state of stagnation or decay.   Serena was " a miserable village, in which resided seven encomenderos, from eighty to one hundred Spaniards, and eight hundred Indians who paid tribute."   The southern part of Chile was embroiled in the hopeless war with the Araucanians.   The fields went uncultivated, and the population was declining and the soldiers deserting. Santiago was inhabited at this time " only by old men, invalids, women, and children." [2]   The last warlike adventure of Aguirre was to defeat and drive back to their ship a company of Drake's pirates, who had sacked Valparaiso, and who had landed to repeat the exploit with Serena.   This was in December 1578.

[1] *Inquisición en Chile*, i. 257 ;   Medina, *La inquisición en el Rio de la Plata*, cap. iv.
[2] Lezaeta, 245.

His remaining days were devoted to the care of his lands and his mines ; but near the end he still felt the weight of his numerous debts, and appealed to the king for relief. The king's reply, however, came too late. Aguirre died in 1581. The attention of the Chilean chroniclers was not now directed toward Serena, but to the Araucanian war ; and for this reason the day of the old warrior's death passed unnoted.

Francisco de Aguirre was not as conspicuous a figure in the history of Spanish colonisation as many of his contemporaries. He had some of those defects which are attributed to many of them. He was uncompromising, ambitious, and at times, cruel. But he was loyal in friendship, courageous in all relations of life, and had a higher degree of cultivation than most of his associates.

IV

The audiencia of Charcas was established at La Plata by Philip II in 1559. The district placed under its jurisdiction was then a part of the viceroyalty of Peru, and extended from the Pacific at Arica on the west to Brazil and the Atlantic on the east. On the north it was limited by the district subject to the audiencia of Lima, and on the south-west by the territory under the jurisdiction of the audiencia of Santiago de Chile. Its authority extended over the vast region claimed by the governments of Tucuman, Buenos Aires, and Paraguay.[1]

In 1570, Diego de Arana appeared in the province authorised by Viceroy Toledo to supersede Aguirre. He was apparently unwilling to perform the duties of his office, and there is reason to suppose that he was sent simply to arrest Aguirre and conduct him to Lima.

[1] René-Moreno, *La Audiencia de Charcas*, 1559–1809, in *Bolivia y Perú*, 201–325. In this essay, the author discusses, among other things, the relation of the audiencia to the viceroy. *Leyes de Indias*, lib. ii. tit. xv. leyes 9, 14, 15 ; *Doc. inéd.*, xviii. 18, 28, 101.

Miguel de Ardiles, who had been appointed to succeed him, resigned in favour of Nicolas Carrizo, who became the *interim* governor, holding the office until the arrival of Jerónimo Luis de Cabrera. One of the noteworthy acts of Cabrera's brief career as governor was laying the permanent foundation of the city of Cordova, in July 1573. The peace which prevailed in the province permitted him to devote the whole of his attention to projects for internal improvements ; but before he had an opportunity to carry out his beneficent plans he was superseded by the unwise and tyrannical Gonzalo Abreu, who caused him to be executed without any sufficient reason. The only assignable ground for this act of barbarity was the jealousy, or hostility, of the audiencia. The governors of Tucuman had hitherto been appointed either by the governors of Chile or by the viceroys of Peru ; and, as Tucuman lay within the jurisdiction of the audiencia, it was in keeping with that body's desire for power to seek to break down any authority that seemed to be acting independently of its supervision within its proper district. The persistent hostility of the audiencia towards Aguirre helps to confirm this view and make manifest the spirit of the audiencia.[1]

Abreu's treatment of Cabrera was only the beginning of the crimes with which he scourged the unhappy colony. Self-respecting men avoided him, and he turned for counsel to the most depraved class. His barbarous nature seemed to find pleasure in shameful robberies, cruel imprisonments, inhuman torture, and unjust executions. Many persons fled from the province, in order to escape from impending evils. His campaigns against the Indians were for the greater part fruitless, and but for the bravery displayed by the lieutenant-governor, Gaspar de Medina, might have passed without revealing any marked traces of the heroism which characterised the acts of many of the Spaniards in the sixteenth century. From the un-

[1] Funes, *Ensayo*, i. 172.

promising conditions of life in the colony, the attention of the inhabitants was attracted by the reports concerning the city of Césares, and by the project to equip an expedition for the purpose of visiting it. Although some of these reports had been issued under oath, the expedition returned after many months, persuaded that they were the product of a diseased imagination.[1]

Perhaps the sense of justice would not have been satisfied if Abreu had gone from his office to the enjoyment of continued good fortune; but when Hernando de Lerma, who succeeded him in 1580, subjected him to torture, which he evidently hoped would kill him, the reasonable part of the colonists were persuaded that there was no justification for such extreme cruelty. Abreu did not die under torture, but he was doubtless hastened towards his death by the treatment which he received. He died in the following year, 1581.

In the first years of his administration, Lerma displayed great moderation in his dealings with the inhabitants of the province; but after the arrival of Bishop Francisco de Victoria, and Francisco Salcedo as dean charged with the government of the new church, Lerma found various occasions for opposing the ecclesiastics, particularly Salcedo. And, during his career as governor, his mood underwent a serious change. His reasonable moderation disappeared, and he became capricious and cruel. He caused Salcedo to be arrested in the monastery of the Mercedarios, and brought before the audiencia of Charcas, whose members saw in Lerma's conduct not only a violation of the law, but also a profanation of the right of asylum. The audiencia finally ordered his arrest, and this order was executed, in 1584, by Captain Francisco de Arévalo Brizeño. The fall of the governor was greeted with public rejoicing. At Chuquisaca he was brought to trial, but before a conclusion was reached, Juan Ramirez de Velasco appeared as provisional governor. He was

---

[1] Funes, *Ensayo*, i. 174; Angelis, *Colección*.

also commissioned to hold the residencia of his predecessor. The case, which had been instituted before the
audiencia, was then turned over to him. The result of
the trial under Velasco was the conviction of Lerma,
who appealed to the Council of the Indies, but he died
in prison before the case was finally determined.

On assuming the duties of his office, Velasco encountered a serious insurrection of Indians in the district of
Cordova. The province was, however, fortunate in
having in Tristan de Tejeda a leader of sufficient wisdom
and force to put down the uprising, but even his victory
did not produce a state of permanent peace. For many
years the inhabitants of the province had to face occasional hostile uprisings on the part of the natives. In
this region the Indians appear to have been especially
reluctant to surrender their independence, and become
vassals of the encomenderos. Here, in the absence of
mines, the colonists were obliged to look to agriculture
for a basis of prosperity ; and, without security for those
who worked in the fields, and a sure prospect of an undis-
turbed harvest, the conditions were decidedly unfavourable for economic progress. Such progress was opposed,
moreover, by the lack of markets. The silver of Upper
Peru might be profitably transported to a foreign market,
in spite of the long and rough mountain trails over which
it had to be carried ; but the products of agriculture, by
reason of their comparatively small value in great bulk,
could not, with profit, be taken to a foreign market, but
had to be consumed near the place of their origin. Here,
therefore, with the fertile soil and the delicious climate,
only peace, security, and good government were needed
to ensure a slow but fortunate development of an independent society. But hitherto these had been wanting.
There were, however, signs of improvement in the government during the seven years of Velasco's rule, from 1586
to 1593, and under his successors, Fernando de Zárate
(1593-5), and Pedro de Mercado Peñalosa (1595-1600),

who conducted the administration of the province during the remaining years of the century. Several new towns, Salta, Tujuy, and Rioja, were established, and the inhabitants, less disturbed by hostile Indians, gradually gathered about themselves the conditions and appliances of civilised life. In the beginning of the following century, Cordova became the seat of the third university established on the American continent.

CHAPTER III

THE ENCOMENDEROS AND THEIR VASSALS IN CHILE

1. The feudal oath. II. Occupations in Chile. III. Provisions relating to the treatment of the Indians. IV. The *demora* of work in the mines. V. Governor Mendoza's campaign. VI. Movement for emancipation. VII. Rules of Santillan and Pedro de Villagra. VIII. Tribute. IX. Governor Sotomayor.

I

THE relation of the Indians to the Europeans in Tucuman was not exceptional. Everywhere under Spanish rule in America the Indian problem was always present and always unsolved. It was magnified and made more difficult by Spain's plan to adopt the Indians as a constituent part of Spanish-American society. The English colonists reduced their relations to the aborigines to their lowest terms by holding them aloof from the new communities. For them the only Indian question was the question of defence. The Spaniards, on the other hand, by forming a social alliance with the Indians, encountered a multitude of difficulties. The social equality of the Spaniards and the Indians was out of the question, and this point having been determined, the way was open to the establishment of any one of a large variety of possible relations. In spite of the fact that feudalism was never an important feature of society in Spain, some characteristics of European feudalism appeared under the Spaniards in the New World. The Indian lacked the knowledge and the cultivation required for independence in civilised society, and this fact marked him either for disappearance, as under the English régime, or for serfdom or for some other form of servitude under Spanish rule. The system of encomiendas, particularly as applied in Chile, was reminiscent of the feudalism of Europe. It was adopted to secure the dominance of the Spaniards, on the one hand, and the subjection of the Indians, on the other ; and the Indians were held as vassals, while their Spanish superiors were known as *feudatarios* or *comendadores*. On assuming authority as an encomendero over his vassals, the Spaniard took an oath,[1] in which he swore " to be a faithful and loyal vassal to our lord the king and to his successors in these and his other kingdoms, and to place himself under the royal standard whenever he might be summoned, and to defend it even to the sacrifice of his life, doing all that which a good and loyal vassal of his Majesty is obliged to do."

The main purpose of the feudal system in Chile, however, was not to provide the king with a body of loyal warriors, as in the case of European feudalism, and as implied in the oath ; but rather by this means to take possession of territory, subjecting the natives to obedience, and employing them to construct houses and fortifications, to cultivate the land, to exploit mines, and to render all kinds of service within the colony.[2]

In Europe the vassal belonged to the same race as his feudal lord, but in America he was of an alien and subjugated race. The sentiment of racial kinship helped at times to ameliorate the fate of the European vassal ; but in America the gulf which separated the two classes was so wide that the hardships or sufferings of the members of the lower class awakened in their masters, except in rare cases, no sentiments of sympathy or compassion. In establishing the system in America, it was designed that

---

[1] See the oath of Don Alonso Campofrio de Carvajal on taking possession of the encomienda of La Ligua, Amunátegui Solar, *Las Encomiendas de Indíjenas en Chile* (Santiago, 1909), i. 70 ; also *Mayorazgos i Titulos de Castilla*, iii. 398.

[2] Amunátegui Solar, *Las Encomiendas*, i. 73.

the fiefs should not be perpetually hereditary, as in Europe, but that the Indians should be bound for a specified number of generations. In practice, however, the law involving this provision was ignored, and the feudalism of Chile, and of Spanish South America generally, tended in this respect to assume the European form. A period of two lives was an ordinary term of a royal grant, or of an encomienda ; but grants for three, four, five, or even nine generations were not uncommon, and the essential characteristics of the feudal relation were continued indefinitely.

II

The work in which the Indian dependents were employed is sufficiently revealed by the nature of the industries in the early decades of the colonies. Santiago was the most important early centre of European civilisation in Chile. Serena was prosperous in the beginning, but later it suffered much from the incursions of pirates. Concepcion became prominent as the headquarters of the forces sent against the Araucanians, but after the death of Valdivia it was temporarily abandoned. In and about Santiago were developed the beginnings of Chile's industrial life, which was devoted chiefly to providing food and clothing, constructing houses, and repairing arms. Here at the foot of San Lucia was built the first mill. Here were made tiles and adobes for the roofs and walls of houses that were erected after the original buildings, which were covered with straw or grass, had been burned.

In the course of time the industries requiring more experience and skill than the Indians could readily acquire were generally conducted by persons who came from Europe. Conspicuous among the early manufacturers was Jerónimo Molina. In connection with an Italian named Anton Galan, he established a mill for making cloth. Another person engaged in a similar undertaking was Juan Jufré. The labourers in these establishments, and in those for making pottery, were chiefly Indians. The early success of the cloth mills was in large part due to the skill and facility which the Indian operators acquired. Their economic advantage was based on the fact that their products had an extended market. In spite of the prohibition of intercolonial trade, cloth from Chile was sent to Panama, Cartagena, and all the towns of Tierra Firme, as well as to Tucuman, Buenos Aires, and even to Brazil. In the last half of the sixteenth century Central Chile had several establishments for making cordage, some part of which at least was used in equipping the ships that were built at some of the southern ports, for defence and for trading along the coast.

The need of communicating with Peru by sea led to the beginning of ship-building in Chile. Antonio Nuñez began the construction of ships as early as 1554. He had acquired extensive landed estates near Santiago and Valparaiso, and established a shipyard at Concon. He built the first warehouses at Valparaiso, and carried on trade with Peru in his own ships. He organised the fishing industry, and secured certain privileges with respect to supplying fish to the city of Santiago. But the industry which especially attracted the Spaniards and excited their zeal was placer mining for gold. It is possible that the accounts given by some of the early chroniclers concerning the amount of gold obtained are greatly exaggerated ; but a distinguished Chilean writer has reached the conclusion that this was the most productive industry of the colony, and that it was made so by the gratuitous and indefatigable labour of the natives.

III

In this as in all other industries the Spaniards had, under the law of encomiendas, complete control over the labour of the Indians, and both men and women were obliged to work at this form of mining; and wherever the relation provided for by this law existed, it may be inferred from the fact itself that there would be abuses by the superiors, and cruelties of which the inferiors would be the victims.   The King of Spain apparently foresaw that evils would arise under this system of encomiendas, and, before the conquest of South America, provided by law that the Indians should be well treated by the encomenderos.   Some of these provisions were: (1) that no Indian should become the bearer of burdens, either willingly or unwillingly, with pay or without it; (2) that no encomendero should have in his house, for his service or for other purpose, Indians from the towns of the repartimiento; (3) that no person should employ the Indians for carrying goods from the seaports to any town, and if they might be willing to undertake this work they should not be permitted to do it; (4) that the provision prohibiting the enslaving of the Indians should be observed and carried out; (5) that the encomenderos should not employ the Indians of their repartimientos at the times when the Indians might wish to prepare their land and plant their crops; (6) that those who employed Indians in their mines should provide priests to teach them the Christian doctrine, and to celebrate mass for them on Sundays and holidays; (7) that they should not take the Indians from their districts, even if the Indians might be willing to be transferred.

This law was violated from the beginning.   The order relating to slavery was so far disregarded that the Indians whose services were profitable were in reality slaves, whatever they might be called.   From the beginning, moreover, the Indians were employed as carriers, as if they were beasts of burden, carrying goods in all directions, and especially over the bad trail between Santiago and the port of Valparaiso.   Disregarding the decree, the encomendero employed in his personal service all the Indians of his repartimiento, old and young, and often under conditions more unfavourable than those of slavery.

A still worse evil appeared in the encomendero's practice of renting his Indians to persons who had need of their labour. This practice was specifically condemned by royal order, but, like many other commands issued with reference to affairs in America, this order had but little effect. In spite of the illegal character of the transaction, persons did not hesitate to make a record of it in their wills.[1]

The law prohibiting the taking of Indians from their districts not having proved effective, a later decree, signed at Talavera in 1541, ordered that the Indians should not be transferred, even within their own country, from the cold region where they had been born, to the hot region, or from the hot to the cold districts. In founding Santiago, there was a direct violation of the rule which this decree sought to enforce. The Indians who had occupied the site of the existing city of Santiago were removed to other lands. Some of them were taken by Francisco de Aguirre to Serena to be employed in his placer mines.

IV

It was admitted both in Spain and America that the bulk of the manual labour in the Spanish colonies, both in mining and agriculture, was to be performed by Indians. While mining was largely absorbing the attention of the colonists, an effort was made to fix by law the period during which the Indians might be employed, the design

---

[1] Doña Marina Ortiz de Gaete's will furnishes an instance : " Item, declaro que tiene Juan de Azócar, vecino de esta ciudad, once indios de mi encomienda, alquilados por un año, en cien pesos de buen oro, i cien fanegas de trigo, i cincuenta de maiz o lo que fuese, i cincuenta de cebada, i veinte carneros, de los cuales declaro me ha dado los diez. Mando se averigüe, i que se cobre del dicho Juan de Azócar todo lo sobredicho " (Medina, *Documentos inéditos*, x. 338).

of this legislation being to release them from work in the mines for such a term as might be needed for the cultivation of the land on which they depended for their support.   The period of work in the mines was called the *demora*, and lasted six or eight months, on account of the lack of water in the summer.   In Chile, in 1555, the *demora* ended at the beginning of October.   In that year the cabildo of Santiago fixed a penalty of five hundred dollars for continuing the work in the mines beyond this period. But avarice often prevailed over law.

It was in the mines, even when the work was not continued beyond eight months in the year, that the Indians suffered their greatest hardships.   They were crowded together in great numbers, and worked from week to week and from month to month standing knee-deep in water throughout the coldest season of the year.   " Encomendero Rodrigo de Quiroga," to quote an old chronicle, " had six hundred Indians of his repartimiento in the mines, half of them men and the other half women, all from fifteen to twenty-five years of age, and all employed in washing for gold during eight months of the year, on account of having no water in the four other summer months." [1]   In 1553, Francisco de Victoria, writing to the Council of the Indies, affirms that at the mines, " there is neither Christianity nor charity, and the abominations cry to heaven.   Each encomendero puts into the mines his Indians, men and women, old and young, without giving them any rest or more food, during the eight months of the year in which they work, than a pint of maize a day ; and the person who does not produce the quantity of gold which is required of him receives blows with a club or lashes, and if any one hides a grain of gold he is punished by cutting off his nose and ears and exposing them nailed to a pole." [2]

The cruelties imposed upon the Indians in the mines

---

[1] *Historiadores de Chile*, vi. 75.

[2] Barros Arana, *Historia jeneral de Chile*, i. 412.

and the manufacturing establishments could not continue indefinitely without calling forth voices of protest. At the same time the large interests which the Spaniards had in the various means of exploitation made it certain that the existing profitable practices would be stoutly defended.

V

In the train of García Hurtado de Mendoza, on his expedition to take possession of the governorship of Chile, there were three priests, the Dominican friar, Jil Gonzalez, Juan Gallegos, and the licentiate Vallejo. Before they left Peru, Gonzalez was known for his zeal in behalf of the Indians, and he continued his propaganda in their favour as soon as he arrived in Chile. He wished to persuade the governor to put off his campaign against the Araucanians and enter into negotiations with them. He wished to persuade him, moreover, in the meantime to liberate the Indians from the severe service imposed upon them by the encomenderos. Gallegos, on the other hand, counselled war and the immediate execution of Mendoza's policy. The young governor, then only twenty-two, was eager for conquest and the distinction of a successful campaign, and was fully determined to follow the course advocated by Gallegos. At Serena he allowed the debate to proceed publicly concerning the merits or demerits of the proposed war. After they had advanced farther towards the south the governor and the two priests held a conference, which ended in a noisy controversy. Mendoza held that it would be advisable to subjugate the Indians at once, to make war on them before they could fortify themselves ; and he claimed that by this means fewer would be killed than in a campaign undertaken after long delay. Gallegos supported the views of the governor as consistent with the teachings of Saint Thomas. A noteworthy feature of this series of events was that a priest was allowed to

harangue the officers and soldiers in opposition to the
plans which the governor had determined to carry out.

Gonzalez was finally permitted to retire, and after this
event the dominant influences in the forces at the front
were not such as to favour a considerate treatment of the
Indians, either of those who were still unsubdued or of
those who had been brought into subjection to encomenderos.   In Santiago Gonzalez continued his public
protests against the cruelty of the Spaniards ; and the
opposition which he aroused threatened the support of
the monastery which he had founded.   For the purpose of
correcting some of the observed abuses, royal decrees were
published which provided that in those cases where it
was permitted to use the Indians as carriers, their burden
should never exceed fifty pounds ; that the encomenderos
should not employ more than a fifth part of their Indians
in the mines ; and that the Indians should receive, free
from all obligations, the sixth part of the gold produced.

VI

The feudalism of Chile was scarcely established before
a movement was instituted to emancipate the subjugated
class ; and the later history of the system is the history
of a controversy between the interested encomenderos
and the humanitarian champions of the serfs.   The report of Santillan, after his investigations, indicate his
views of what should be done to improve the status of
the Indians, under the encomenderos.   In order to secure
the payment of the sixth of the gold which belonged to
the Indians, and its proper investment for their profit, it
was considered advisable that there should be appointed
in Santiago and in Serena two persons, one by the cabildo
and the other by the justicia-mayor, who in agreement
with the encomenderos and priests of the encomienda,
should invest the gold in clothing, wool, cattle, and other

things of which the natives might have need. The cattle thus acquired should be placed under the care of the encomenderos, after they had been publicly registered, and the encomendero should render an account of the animals that had been delivered to him and of their increase. In order to prevent the encomenderos from diverting to their own advantage the gold taken from the mines, without paying the royal fifth, and the sixth due to the Indians, it was provided that all the gold mined should be immediately taken to the existing mints of the country; that the Spaniards might not form contracts among themselves for the payment of unminted gold; and that the merchants alone should be authorised to make sales to the natives payable in gold dust to the amount of ten dollars. Under these regulations proposed by Santillan, the encomenderos were to be permitted to employ bands of negroes in washing for gold; and the Indians were to be allowed to wash for gold on their own account, and they might also cultivate certain tracts of land in company with the encomenderos, who should furnish plows and allow the Indians a third part of the crop.[1]

The encomenderos naturally resented these and all other attempts to subject their treatment of the Indians to restrictive regulations. Juan Jufré employed Indians in his mill without wages. The Indians who worked in the ropewalk of Juan Bautista Pastene received no compensation for their labour. The proposed regulations of Santillan found more favour with the Council of the Indies than with the audiencia of Lima. The Council ordered Mendoza's successor, Governor Villagra, to cause the established regulations to be carried out, and at the same time appointed a commission consisting of Villagra, the Bishop of Santiago, and two priests to report on the advantages and disadvantages that would be produced in the country by the execution of the ordinances of Santillan. The

[1] Amunátegui Solar, *Las encomiendas*, i. 185–87.

Council, moreover, ordered the new governor to oblige the encomenderos to employ negroes in the gold mines. But this order could not be carried out on account of the lack of negroes and the poverty of those persons who were expected to purchase them.

Neither the royal decrees, nor the orders of the governors, nor the rules of Santillan put an end to the abuses of the encomenderos in their treatment of the Indians. The main reason for the ineffectiveness of these orders and rules was their revolutionary character as judged from the viewpoint of the society that was establishing itself in the Spanish colonies. The dependence and practical slavery of the Indians constituted the vital feature of this society. This relation was involved in the ideal under which Spanish American society came into existence. The Spanish settlers had not come, like the settlers in New England, to form a complete society by themselves, but rather to be one social class, a dominating class, while the Indians were expected to constitute another class, a class in some form of subjection.

At the beginning of 1562, the treasury of Spain had great need of funds, and to secure them the king proposed to have the encomiendas converted into fiefs in perpetuity, the holders of which should make to the Crown contributions proportionate to the rights they were to acquire. The views of the cabildos of the principal towns were sought concerning the proposed change ; and in reply they affirmed the advisability of giving perpetuity to the system. The governor of Chile, however, reported to Lima that it would not be desirable to make the change until the following year, 1563. But in the meantime the governor died, and the proposed plan was indefinitely postponed.

VII

The most important result of the agitation for setting aside the hardships and cruelties imposed upon the Indians by the encomenderos was the series of rules published by Pedro de Villagra, completing or supplementing those that had been previously issued by Santillan. These rules present the ideas of those persons who aimed to remove the abuses of the system of encomiendas :

" 1. Henceforth the *demora* shall be only for six months. In the jurisdictions of Santiago and Serena, embracing the cities of Mendoza and San Juan, gold shall not be mined, except in March, April, May, June, July, and August ; and in the other parts of the country in November, December, January, February, March, and April.

" 2. The rule according a sixth of the gold to the Indians shall be re-established in all its force, as also the guarantees ordered by Santillan in their favour.

" 3. In view of the evil results of the mingling of the negroes with the Indians in the work of mining, the introduction of negroes as inspectors in the repartimientos shall be prohibited ; the penalty being that the encomenderos, for the first violation of the rule, shall pay, for the benefit of the Indians, one hundred dollars in gold, and for the second two hundred dollars. Besides, each of the negroes shall receive a hundred lashes. For the third offence, the encomenderos shall lose their slaves, and shall be deprived of their repartimientos for three years.

" 4. The protector of the Indians, and the priest appointed for the purpose of teaching them the Christian doctrine, shall use the product of the sixths in acquiring sheep for their wards ; and, before an officer of the court, shall turn these animals over to the encomenderos, who shall be obliged to render an account annually of the state of the flock.

" 5. This account shall be received by the protector and the priest ' both together, and not the one without the other.' The same protector and priest were authorised to distribute among the Indians as many sheep as they thought advisable.

" 6. The protector and the priest shall make effective the responsibility of the encomenderos whenever they become delinquent, and even take from them the care of the flock, and commit it to proper persons without prejudice to the institution of judicial proceedings in the case against the delinquents.

" 7. The protector and the priest shall visit together every six months the repartimientos of the district committed to their care, and shall inform themselves concerning the treatment accorded to the Indians, and concerning the execution of the laws, and send a detailed report to the governor, to the end that justice may be done.

" 8. In each district there shall be appointed a protector and a priest. The protector shall be selected by the governor of Chile from persons of strictly Christian character ; and the priest shall be the superior of the monastery of Saint Francis, or, indeed, some other Franciscan designated by the order, in case there shall be a local establishment of the order, or, in the absence of any such establishment, then the parish priest, or a priest of prestige of another order than the Franciscan, until this order shall be established in the district.

" 9. The protector shall be given a salary fixed by the governor, which shall be paid by halves by the Indians and by the encomenderos, although it shall by preference be deducted from the product of the penalties established by this law.

" 10. Annually an account shall be taken of the manner in which the protectors shall have performed their duties, and they shall be punished if found delinquent.

" 11. In the first visit of each year the protector and the priest shall form, in connection with the encomendero, a list of the Indians of the repartimiento."

The regulations of Pedro de Villagra, the main features of which are presented in the foregoing, were expected to bring relief to the Indians at several points. The *demora* was reduced from eight to six months ; the negroes were no longer to be employed as foremen, or inspectors ; and the number of protectors was increased. An obstacle to the execution of these rules was found in the fact that they ran counter to the plans and interests of the encomenderos. Through the increase of their flocks the Indians were nominally advancing to a position of greater advantage ; but the Dominican friar, Gonzalez, scoffed at the idea that the Indians derived any real advantage from this source. If, as he assumed, " the wool and the flesh belonged to the encomenderos," the Indians were in reality owners only in name. Moreover, as opposed to the powerful encomenderos, the protectors found it practically impossible to perform their proper functions in an impartial manner.

Another difficulty in the way of a proper execution of the laws relating to the Indians was found in the disposition of the governors to ignore the decrees of their predecessors. When Quiroga became governor in 1565, he practically annulled the rules of Pedro de Villagra, and consequently those of Santillan. The governors, in their war with the Araucanians, had need of the support which the encomenderos were in a position either to give or to withhold. This circumstance naturally led the governors to overlook certain abuses which, under an impartial judgment, they would have tried to correct. In some cases where fines were imposed, the encomenderos appealed to a higher authority, with the result that no decision was rendered.

The Araucanian war, always a present danger, some-

times taxed to their limit the resources of the colony ; and
the king, as well as the colonial authorities, sought by all
possible means to weaken the enemy. Philip II favoured
sending the captured Araucanians as exiles to Peru. Governor Quiroga, however, held that those taken in war
should be transferred to the jurisdictions of Santiago and
Serena, to be employed in the mines. This plan was
ultimately approved by the king. In the campaign of
1577, Governor Quiroga captured several hundred Indians,
and in the following year he wrote to the king concerning
his treatment of the prisoners as follows :

" I issued a decree, in which I commanded that there
should be executed on these Indian prisoners the sentence
of death which I had pronounced on them and the other
rebels, which penalty I then ordered suspended ; and in
the meantime I ordered that these prisoners should be
taken to the city of Serena, and that there one foot of
each of them should be cut off, and they should be employed in the works of the gold mines, in order to contribute to the expenses of the war, and that the chiefs should
be taken to the viceroy of Peru." [1]

Gregorio Sanchez was commissioned to govern the
Indians who had been taken to the mines from the
southern frontier. In March 1578 he wrote to Toledo,
the viceroy of Peru, and gave some account of his steward-
ship :

" The governor," he wrote, " has commanded me to
take in charge and govern the Indians whom he exiled to
this city of Serena, and their earnings which may constitute a contribution to the great expenses of the war ;
and, although his lordship had ordered their feet to be
cut off, he has modified this to that which might appear
to me, as having the knowledge of one present, as the most
fitting for the service of His Majesty, and, indeed, for the
Indians. When the Indians had arrived at this city,
some of them wished to run away ; and six or seven of

---

[1] Amunátegui Solar, *Las encomiendas*, i. 235.

them were taken and hanged, and the feet of fifty others were cut off." [1]

The disposition of the encomenderos to disregard the rules already proposed and to make an unwarranted use of their power over the Indians led to the attempt to substitute a fixed tribute for personal service. Governor Martin Ruiz de Gamboa, the successor of Quiroga, urged this reform, and was supported by the Bishop of Santiago and some of the friars. The protectors of the Indians, on the other hand, instead of defending the Indians, united with the encomenderos to exploit them.

VIII

The rule respecting tribute to be paid by the Indians as published by Governor Gamboa, in 1580, provided that each Indian between the ages of seventeen and fifty should pay the sum of seven dollars, and grain, fish, fowls, or sheep to the value of two dollars, making the total annual payment nine dollars. Long accustomed to the service of the Indians without the obligation of payment, the Spaniards resisted the execution of this measure, which recognised to some extent the freedom of the Indian and his right to compensation for his services. In this, Gamboa had taken a position which could be maintained only after some centuries of progress ; and in the meantime the encomenderos used all their influence to support their ideas and their practices. In complete control of the cabildos of the municipalities, the will of the encomenderos was likely to prevail. Supporting their views, a commission was sent to Peru to petition the royal audiencia of Lima to annul the rule of Gamboa. This tribunal, however, refused to make the required decision, and referred the petition to the Council of the Indies.

The encomenderos had apparently anticipated the

[1] Printed in Amunátegui Solar, *Las encomiendas*, i. 236–37.

action of the audiencia of Lima ; for even before that body had referred the petition to the Council, they had instructed Ramiriañez Bravo de Saravia to defend their cause in Spain.   While this question was under discussion the king appointed Alonso de Sotomayor to be governor of Chile.   Whether through his friendly intercourse with Saravia, or through independent investigations, Soto- mayor appears to have left Spain already opposed to the innovations of Gamboa ; and in Chile he was intimately associated with Louis Lopez de Azócar, also a determined opponent of Gamboa's reforms.   The influences proceed- ing from these and other sources were sufficient to cause the regulations of Gamboa to be abolished.   The *demora* of eight months was re-established, and the Indians were continued in their miserable condition of bondage, from which, in fact, they had been given no practical relief under any of the projected changes.   The sixth part of the gold mined, which was nominally set apart for the Indian, never became his in reality ; and the cattle and sheep, which were said to belong to him, had no existence, except as an indistinguishable and, for him, an unrealis- able part of the property of the encomendero.   In one respect, however, the Indians of 1585 were better served than those of twenty-five or thirty years earlier ; there were more priests essaying to teach them the Christian doctrines.

IX

But the efforts of Sotomayor were not limited to pro- viding religious instruction.   He appointed his brother, Luis de Sotomayor, protector-general of all the Indians of the country ; and, in 1589, he appointed Martin de Zamora administrator-general and defender of the Indians in the province of Santiago.   With these appointments were set aside the previously existing protectors, who appear to have been, at least in many cases, unfaithful to the trust reposed in them.   In making more tolerable the condition of the Indians employed in the mines, the governor was moved by an intelligent interest, not only in the Indians but also in the encomenderos. By making more satisfactory regulations for the workers, he hoped that the incomes of the encomenderos might be increased, and that thereby they would be enabled to render him more efficient assistance in his campaigns and other undertakings.

Under the conditions then existing, the encomenderos were unable to offer the governor any very important support ; and the authorities of Spain as well as of the viceroyalty of Peru refused to give the needed assistance. Sotomayor's successor, Martin García de Oñez y Loyola, turned his attention to relieving the Indians from their tyrannical masters. Still, it is to be noted that the salaries of the general administrator and the protector of the Indians were paid from the sixth of the gold mined and other property that nominally belonged to the Indians. The fact that what was said to be a possession of the Indians could be taken without their consent for the payment of political functionaries, would seem to indicate that their rights of property were of the flimsiest sort. In fact, with the progress of the Araucanian war, and the capture and sale of the Indians, the idea that the native was a person with rights tended gradually to disappear, and the idea that he was merely a chattel, to be more widely entertained. " The territory of the bishopric of Imperial had been converted into an immense fair for the sale of human beings, where the soldiers became rich by the sale of the Araucanians, and where the encomenderos and residents of Santiago and Serena sought household servants, and renewed the personnel of their encomiendas." [1] The personal interests and avarice of the Spaniards, and not the voice of the Church or the designs of reformers were at this time giving direction to the course of social affairs, and determining the relation of the invaders to the natives.

[1] Amunátegui Solar, *Las encomiendas*, i. 287.

But there came a change in the affairs of the Araucanians; victory gave them courage for new victories; and in the course of a few years, they overthrew and laid waste the cities of Arauco, Santa Cruz, Valdivia, Imperial, Angol, Villarica, and Osorno. The remaining cities of central and northern Chile at this time, the first decade of the seventeenth century, were of little importance. Serena had only forty-six houses; Santiago, the capital, had two hundred; Chillan, fifty-two; Concepcion, seventy-six; and Castro, twelve. About three-fourths of the houses in each city were little more than rude huts, with grass or straw roofs; while one-fourth had roofs of tiles. The centre of the colony's affairs was evidently not the cities, but the encomiendas, many of which were the antecedents of the great estates of modern Chile. These produced the wealth of the colony, and the encomenderos, the lords of the soil, constituted the dominant social and political element in the country. Rules touching their affairs were not likely to be carried out, except with their consent.

CHAPTER IV

PERU IN THE FIRST HALF OF THE
SEVENTEENTH CENTURY

I. Projected Dutch invasion and other hostilities. II. Negroes and
Indians. III. The ensign-nun and Santa-Rosa. IV. The *con
sulado*. V. Esquilache's successor, the Marquis of Guadalcazar.
VI. The administration of the Count of Chinchon. VII. The
Marquis of Mancera.

I

ON the death of Philip II in 1598, the Crown of Spain
passed to the pious but inefficient Philip III. At this
time Luis de Velasco, Marquis of Salinas, was the viceroy
of Peru (1596–1604). Spain's weakness and the enormous production of the Peruvian mines incited members
of other nations to seek to acquire at least some part of
this abundant wealth. The Dutch in their conflict with
Spain had become conscious of their power ; and, confirmed in their hostility to the Spaniards, they determined to invade Peru. The fleet which they despatched
for this purpose in 1599, was, however, scattered by
storms off the southern part of the continent. A knowledge of the preparations made by the Dutch for this
expedition was a warning sufficient to move the viceroy
to undertake to put the port of Callao into a position to
resist attacks. To this end he provided four armed
vessels, one of six hundred tons, one of five hundred and
twenty tons, and two of four hundred tons each.

While attention was directed to the danger of foreign
invasion, the volcanic explosions which occurred near
Arequipa and were heard along the coast, convinced the

excited inhabitants that the enemy was already upon them. But the continuance of the agitation from week to week, attended by the crash of falling buildings, gave the citizens of Arequipa a sufficient indication of the nature of the disturbance. Some of them ran to the churches and prayed for mercy, while others wandered aimlessly about the streets, dazed with fear. Hot ashes and cinders covered the face of the country, burned up the vegetation, and destroyed the domestic animals. The villages about the volcano disappeared, and with them many of their inhabitants. The surviving part of the population appeared to be face to face with famine. Some who might have escaped, became mad with terror, and took their own lives.

The interior and eastern parts of the kingdom, that had escaped the destructive eruption of the volcano, suffered the shock of an Indian revolt, which had been produced by unjust and excessive exactions. At the same time the Araucanians resumed active hostilities. Martin de Loyola, the governor of Chile, although he had been warned from Lima of the impending danger, persisted in his project to traverse the Araucanian country with a small body of soldiers. The consequence was disastrous. Not only were the governor and his followers cut off, but also the frontier posts, that had been established with great labour and sacrifice, were swept away. In the south-eastern part of the continent, the Chiriguanas broke over their borders and carried their savage incursions into the province of Charcas. The serenity of the viceregal government was further disturbed by the coming of Portuguese Jews from Brazilian territory. The lines of demarcation, which separated Brazil from Spanish possessions were not obliterated by the union of Spain and Portugal, and it was impossible to guard the frontier of the viceroyalty in the interior of the continent. The secular authorities were powerless to hinder the invasion of the Jews, but the Inquisition, with its omnipresent spies, its secret processes, and terrible punishments, presented obstacles that were more effective than legal commands.

II

Among the inhabitants of the kingdom, the negroes had already become sufficiently numerous to constitute a disturbing element in the society. They were turbulent, corrupt, and given to drunkenness and unrestrained licentiousness. Many of the murders and robberies were traced to them. Their balls and meetings for other purposes were occasions of great disorder, and often ended in riots. The burdens of toil rested less heavily upon them than upon the miserable Indians, who continued in personal servitude, in spite of the charitable intentions of the Crown. These intentions found expression in the decree of November 24, 1601, which was designed to release the Indians from the obligations created by the system of repartimientos, and to make them free labourers, who might seek work for a stipulated compensation. Under this plan, the encomenderos might not require tribute to be paid in personal service, and no authority might impose forced labour upon the Indians as a penalty for crime. The Indian, moreover, might not be employed in the fisheries, or as beasts of burden, or in the cultivation of coca, or in factories belonging to Spaniards, or in sugar-mills or any similar establishments. For whatever work destined, they should be employed only in the region where they were accustomed to live, and they should be allowed free time sufficient to enable them to cultivate their little farms. The yanaconas should cease to be serfs bound to the soil, but should be at liberty to withdraw and seek another place of residence whenever they wished to do so. The advocates of this proposed reform did not fail to appreciate, at least in some measure, the difficulty that would be encountered

in the reluctance of the Indians to engage in any kind of
regular activity, and, therefore, provided that great care
should be taken to attract them to voluntary labour by
just and gentle means, and to make possible favourable
conditions for their subsistence. As a step towards a
further amelioration of the state of the Indians, it was proposed to abolish gradually the system of the mita, and
thus to remove the source of many grievances.

The encomenderos and many other persons considered
the provisions of this decree as part of the Crown's uto-
pian policy. In Charcas, where a corregidor proposed to
publish the decree, certain oidores protested and affirmed
that if the yanaconas were set free, the estates would be
abandoned, and the means of subsistence would be wanting.[1] In other parts of Spain's American possessions,
the repartimientos, personal service, forced labour in factories and in the fields were continued under various
pretexts ; sometimes by the connivance of the local
authorities, and sometimes on account of the inability
of those authorities to carry out the decrees of the Crown.
The viceroy was obliged to recognise that the most influential members of Peruvian society were opposed to
the projected reforms, and he was not disposed to incur
the open hostility of those persons whose support was
necessary to the maintenance of peace and orderly
government in his kingdom.

In 1615, the peace of the kingdom was disturbed by
the appearance of a Dutch squadron in the Pacific. It
was composed of six vessels, and was commanded by
George Spitberg. After attacks at various points on the
Chilian coast, it proceeded northward, and off Cañete
encountered the Peruvian squadron of eight vessels.
The superior arms and discipline of the Dutch, in spite
of their inferiority in numbers, gave them a complete
victory, which enabled them to enter the port of Callao
without meeting with further resistance. The inhabi-

[1] Lorente, *Historia del Perú*, 1598–1700, 17.

tants of Lima were panic-stricken, not merely because the enemy displayed superiority in arms, but also because they were heretics. Still, all their fears were not realised ; for after three days Spitberg left the port, took and sacked Huarmey and Paita, and then abandoned the coast of Peru.

III

Francisco de Borja y Aragon, the Prince of Esquilache, became the viceroy of Peru, succeeding the Marquis of Montesclaros, in 1616. He observed the defenceless condition of Callao, and formed a squadron for its protection, which consisted of four galeones, two tenders, and two launches, together carrying one hundred and forty-three guns. He caused thirteen heavy guns to be mounted on the shore, and organised five companies of infantry, each composed of one hundred men, doing, as he reported to his successor, whatever he was able to re-establish the credit of the military profession.[1] He found a reason for greater military preparations in the fact that by making use of the route around Cape Horn, opened in 1616 by Jacob Le Maire, Europeans might reach the Pacific, and at the same time avoid the risks which attended the passage of the Strait of Magellan. The government's need of a stronger military force was, moreover, emphasized by the continuing turbulence of the inhabitants of Potosi, among whom the daily conflicts between individual persons and the parties of Basques and Castillians made evident the need of a power competent to preserve internal order.

Among the notorious bullies of Potosi, there was a beardless ensign, with agreeable features, but of a quarrelsome disposition, impressionable as a child, yet endowed with unflinching courage, who in a few years had

[1] *Memorias de los Vireyes*, i., 111 ; Lorente, *Hist. del Perú*, 1598-1700, 67.

passed through most extraordinary and almost incredible adventures. This was Doña Catalina Erauso, who was born at San Sebastian and educated among the nuns of a convent. Before taking her vows, she left the convent and went to Peru disguised in the dress of a man. At Trujillo she entered the service of a merchant, whose wife conceived a blind passion for her. In order to escape from the embarrassment of persistent declarations, and to preserve her secret, she fled to Lima. Here she encountered new embarrassments, and became involved in duels, in which she displayed her remarkable skill with the sword. Later she joined a military expedition, and went to Chile, where, even among the trained soldiers, she maintained her reputation as a swordsman and a courageous duellist. From Chile she crossed the cordillera in the winter, and was in danger of perishing in the snow. Her adventures in Tucuman made it advisable for her to seek refuge in Potosi, where she was arrested and condemned to death, but was pardoned on her way to execution. Leaving Potosi, she went to Cuzco, and there killed in a duel the bully who called himself the new Cid. Although severely wounded in the encounter, she fled to Guamanga, where, having been again arrested, she made known her sex and her monastic education. After this she was for a time in the convent of Santa Clara, in Guamanga, then at the convent of Trinity in Lima, and later in Spain. The last scene of her strange life was laid in Mexico, where the ensign-nun, as she was called after her sex was made known, died in the manly occupation of mule-driver between the City of Mexico and Vera Cruz.[1]

Another feature of Peruvian society in the seventeenth century is suggested by the life of Santa Rosa. This young woman, who was inspired with an intense spirit of devotion and consumed by a marvellous religious

[1] *Lorente, Hist. del Perú*, 1598–1700, 70; Mendiburu, ii. 61, iii. 35–45; Markham, *Cuzco and Lima*, 65.

fervour, who, near the end of her days, saw visions that presaged " her transition to glory," was born in Lima on the 20th of April 1586. Her father was Gaspar Flores, who, in 1548, at the age of twenty-three, had gone from Porto Rico to Lima, was a member of the viceregal guard of the Marquis of Cañete. Her mother was Doña Maria de Oliva, a native of Lima. Although baptized as Isabel, it was the fancy of the mother to call her Rosa, on account of her beauty. By this name she was generally known, and later, when she was canonised, she became Santa Rosa. Like the majority of the young women of her time in South America, she received only limited instruction, and this laid emphasis on music and poetry. For two or three years after 1597, Gaspar Flores was obliged by his official duties to live in the town of Quivi, in the province of Canta, and here the child of eleven years, destined to sainthood, received confirmation at the hand of Santo Toribio, who was then Archbishop of Lima and visiting that part of the country. Tradition refers to the great amount of time which she spent in the church during her residence in Canta. In 1600 she returned to Lima with her family, and six years later, in 1606, she assumed the habit of Santo Domingo. During the next eleven years her life was marked by religious zeal and devotion, sometimes by an exaltation akin to hysteria, and by seasons of agonising penitence that threatened to wreck a physical system already suffering from the ravages of prolonged nervous excitement. In the last months of her life, she was the victim of a fatal illness, " in which," to borrow Lorente's statement, " all the members of her body were subjected to strange and most acute suffering ; a most painful agony, accepted with superhuman resignation, announced her glorious triumph." She died in 1617, at the age of thirty-one.[1] Her religious experience, her devotion to the Church, and

---

[1] *Historia del Perú*, 1598–1700, 76 ; Zegarra, Felix C., *Santa Rosa de Lima : Estudio Biog.* (Lima, 1886).

her many acts of charity and patriotism had made a powerful impréssion on her contemporaries, and the funeral of a viceroy would not have been attended with a manifestation of greater pomp and circumstance than was evoked by the celebration of the last rites over the body of Isabel Flores, who was canonised in 1671 as Santa Rosa de Santa Maria.[1]

IV

To the Spaniards of the seventeenth century the supernatural existences presented by their ecclesiastical writers were scarcely less real than the beings apprehended by the senses. They were in no sense the creatures of the constructive imagination of the race, but invisible elements of a real world. In this view, placing a city or an institution under the patronage of a saint was not the adoption of a mere conventional form ; it was submitting the city or the institution to a real protectorate. The Prince of Esquilache was acting in accordance with this belief when, in organising the commercial court known as the *consulado*, or consulate, he placed it under the immaculate Virgin, and caused the coat of arms to bear this inscription : *Maria concebida sin pecado original.*

This tribunal was called the " consulate of the university of the merchants of this city of the kings, kingdoms, and provinces of Peru, Tierra Firme, and Chile, and of those who trade and carry on commerce with persons belonging to the kingdoms of Spain and New Spain." Through the ordinance of December 20, 1619, Esquilache conferred upon the tribunal authority " to take cognisance of the affairs and controversies of commerce and the contracts between merchant and merchant, partners, factors, and encomenderos ; of

---

[1] Mendiburu, vii. 211–16, 240 ; *Fiestas que se hicieron para la Beatificación y Canonización de Santa Rosa*, in Odriozola, *Doc. lit. del Perú*, iv. 366–8 ; Markham, *Cuzco and Lima*, 293.

purchases, sales, exchanges, bankruptcies, insurance, accounts, companies, and of freighting by beasts of burden or by ships ; of the execution of contracts and other things, of payment for merchandise and for losses and damage and other controversies which might result from the foregoing ; and of those which might arise between the masters and mariners, their accounts and contracts as soldiers ; and of all of those things which might happen and appear touching the traffic and other matters which the consulates of Burgos, Seville, and Mexico might and ought to take cognisance of." [1]

The formation of this institution was one of Esquilache's notable contributions to the economic affairs of the kingdom. It acted not merely as a court of justice in cases arising from controversies concerning commercial transactions, but it also assisted the administration in the department charged with the revenues. It collected the alcabala in Lima, and had charge of the customs duties. In performing this task, it effected an increase in the amount produced from each of these sources of income. Esquilache paid special attention to the mines of Potosi and Huancavelica, since the Crown regarded these as the principal sources of the nation's wealth. The Spaniards of the seventeenth century had little appreciation of the economic revolution through which they were passing. The Cortes, seeing the rapid rise in the price of Spanish products under the importation of gold and silver, concluded this must be due to the large demand made for these products in America, and petitioned the king to prevent their exportation. Ignorant of the cause of the rising prices, in which the masses of the people seemed to see their approaching ruin, the Crown urged the viceroy to foster especially those sources of wealth which, in fact, produced the high prices that they wished to make impossible. After the barbarous expulsion of the Moriscos, the industries of Spain were moribund. It was in

---

[1] Quoted by Mendiburu, ii. 67.

a large measure foreign capital that provided the ships as well as the goods that were taken from Seville to America and appeared as Spanish commerce ; and " the wealth returned to Spain by the fleets," to borrow Lorente's phrase, " passed through the country like a desolating torrent, without fertilising the land, only causing a growth of vanity and indolence." [1]

The project to make use of the newly discovered route around Cape Horn to enlarge the commerce between Spain and Callao found little support among the merchants of Lima, who feared that their practical monopoly might be overthrown by large importations that would not have to be reshipped or carried any part of the way by land ; and the inhabitants of Panama saw in the diminution of the transisthmian commerce, which would follow the use of the Cape-Horn route, a serious interference with the basis of their prosperity.

V

When the Prince of Esquilache was appointed viceroy of Peru in 1614, he was thirty-two years of age, and, after six years of service, he was persuaded that life near the court of Spain would be more agreeable than further experience in his viceregal office. He knew, moreover, that the king, Philip III, intended to transfer to Lima the viceroy of Mexico, who at that time was Diego Fernandez de Cordova, the Marquis of Guadalcazar. Therefore, without waiting to greet his successor, in accordance with the custom, Esquilache departed for Spain before Guadalcazar's arrival in Lima. He left, however, a memorial from which his successor might learn the state of the country he was appointed to govern.[2] He was apparently anxious to avoid the annoyance of a residencia, particularly as it was generally believed that a part of the

[1] *Historia del Perú*, 1598–1700, 82.
[2] *Memorias de los Vireyes*, i. 71–145.

product of certain taxes had gone to swell the amount of his private fortune. He entered upon his journey to Spain on the 31st of December 1621, leaving the supreme authority in the kingdom to the audiencia, under the presidency of Juan Jimenez de Montalvo. King Philip III had died earlier in this year, and on the 31st of March 1621, his son, at the age of sixteen, had ascended the throne as Philip IV.

The Spanish people turned to the young king with the hope that he might eradicate the administrative corruption which absorbed the resources of the State, and that he might check the decline of Spain. But it became manifest very early that their hopes were vain : it was not within the power of the narrow-minded bigot, Philip IV, to stay the nation's downward course. The famous Castillian regiments were discredited by repeated defeats. The diplomatists had lost their cunning, and the nation was obliged to accept treaties which curtailed her power and lessened her honour. The greed of Spaniards for offices in Portugal and the disproportionate burden of taxation that rested on the Portuguese violated the sentiments of the inhabitants of that country and led them to revolt and to break the bond that had held the two nations together for sixty years. There was, moreover, trouble in Cataluña, insurrection in Spain's Italian possessions, and discontent in the Low Countries. Corruption had brought misery, and misery had intensified popular ignorance.[1]

During the brief rule of the audiencia, the attention of the authorities was directed to the social disturbances of Potosi. The enormous wealth produced by the mines had drawn together there, as already indicated, ambitious, turbulent, and reckless spirits from many quarters. No force adequate to preserve order had been provided for the local government, and, owing to the distance from the capital and the difficulties of communication, the

[1] Lorente, *Hist. del Perú*, 1598–1700, 89–91.

central government could exercise over that community only an imperfect control. The means of amusement or distraction, called forth by the presence of great wealth, furnished an extraordinary impulse to vice and violence. Even priests and missionaries, who sought to reconcile the hostile parties, were not free from the vicious attacks of the ruffians to whom they had been sent as advocates of peace and charity. The provincial of the Jesuits exhorted the hostile parties and the reckless bullies to assist in maintaining order in the community. A little later, and in the night, the leader of one of the gangs of desperadoes called out the priest under the pretext that his assistance was needed for a person desperately ill, and, having drawn him into the street, beat him with a club and left him for dead. Finding himself shunned and contemned by the community, the perpetrator of this outrage left the city, but before he went away, he urged his comrades to destroy his enemies, to spoil the rich, and to be checked by no scruples in satisfying their unrestrained desires.[1]

Those who received this counsel were willing to follow it. They defeated the force that was organised to suppress them, and treated the city as soldiers might treat the camp of a captured enemy. No life, property, or honour was exempt from their assaults. They wreaked vengeance on all persons who opposed them, and destroyed the rich for their wealth. Terror reigned throughout the city of Potosi when Guadalcazar arrived in Lima, July 25, 1622, to assume the government of the kingdom.[2]

In May 1623, the corregidor, Felipe Manrique, with three hundred men sent by the viceroy, arrived at Potosi. The Basques, who were called Vicuñas, retired to the valley of Ulti, and elected Francisco Castillo to be their general. Other troops were sent from Chuquisaca,

---

[1] Lorente, *Hist. del Perú*, 1598–1700, 95 ; Mendiburu, iii. 248–50.
[2] Lorente, *Hist. del Perú*, 1598–1700, 96 ; Mendiburu, iii. 238, 249.

Cochabamba, and Oruro. The Vicuñas of Ulti made attacks on Potosi and Chuquisaca, in which they killed many persons, and carried off whatever they could seize. The extremes to which the parties under arms were willing to go was apparently one of the causes of an early settlement ; for those who had property at stake, and those who desired to preserve whatever features of civilisation that region possessed, urged upon the combatants reasons for maintaining peace, and petitioned them to adopt measures of conciliation. Guadalcazar proclaimed a general pardon, and thus for a certain period at least quiet was restored to the troubled city. In order to confirm the peace, the viceroy expelled the Basques, and prohibited the use of firearms within sixty leagues of the city. The uprising of the Indians of Tucuman presented for the moment a common enemy, whose appearance helped to draw all factions together.[1]

The viceroy found himself in conflict with an active enemy not only in Tucuman, but also in Chile, where offensive war with the Araucanians had been resumed, and where Luis Fernandez de Cordova, a brother of the viceroy, held the post of commander-in-chief. The viceroy was more directly engaged in another military undertaking that was imposed upon him by the arrival in the Pacific of a Dutch fleet under Admiral Jacob Heremita Clerk. The fleet consisted of eleven vessels, two hundred and ninety-four guns, and an infantry force of sixteen hundred and thirty-seven men. The force for the defence of the port embraced the regular Spanish infantry, various bodies of the militia, squadrons of cavalry, and several extemporised companies of students and ecclesiastics. The enemy appeared off the port in the beginning of 1624, and anchored under the protection of the island of San Lorenzo. Admiral Clerk's forces captured certain merchant ships, and burned others in the harbour, but their attempts to gain a position of advantage on the

[1] Mendiburu, iii. 249 ; Lorente, *Hist. del Perú*, 1598–1700, 97, 98.

coast were repulsed, and before they had made any important progress towards the conquest, which they had expected would not be difficult, the admiral died of disentery, and was buried on the island of San Lorenzo.   The siege lasted five months, during which the Dutch suffered a great loss of men, and when they finally retired, they proceeded to the coast of Brazil.   For a short period they occupied Bahia de Todos Santos.

From the defence of the port of Callao, the viceroy turned to a very different undertaking.   He observed, and many persons before him had observed, that great abuses and scandals had arisen through the practice, on the part of the women, of appearing closely veiled in the streets, the churches, and other public places ; and in order that these evils might be abolished, the viceroy issued a royal ordinance, which provided that " no woman, of whatever state, quality, and condition she may be, may be veiled with a *manto* or in any other manner while going on the streets of this city, or the alameda or other public places, whether on foot or in a carriage or a sedan chair, or in balconies or windows, but that all shall be obliged to go with their faces uncovered, to the end that they may be seen and known, and the identity of each be recognised." [1]

The successful resistance offered to the attacks of the Dutch fleet was followed by popular rejoicing, but there was another consequence of this episode less agreeable to contemplate.   The fact that heretics, such as the Dutch were in the eyes of the Spaniards, had attempted to invade the country, intensified the hatred entertained by the inhabitants towards all heretics who came within the reach of their influence, and made them more than ever zealous to uphold the Inquisition, and to stimulate it to more thorough and uncompromising action.

---

[1] This document is printed by Mendiburu, iii. 242–3.

VI

The zeal of the inquisitors, moreover, was especially manifest during the reign of the Count of Chinchon (1629–1639), who succeeded the Marquis of Guadalcazar. On the 27th of February 1631, an *auto-de-fé* was held in the chapel of the Inquisition, at which twelve victims appeared.[1] In 1635 the prisons of the Inquisition were full of prisoners, and on the 17th of August an *auto-de-fé* was held to dispose of some of the accused, in order to make room for others ; for six days before the date of this *auto* nearly a hundred persons had been arrested. Three years later another *auto-de-fé* was announced for January 23, 1639, and was celebrated with eighty victims, and with more pomp and elaborate ceremonies than had been displayed on any previous occasion.[2]

The superstitious sentiments of the Peruvians were further awakened by the shock of a severe earthquake, November 27, 1630. The inhabitants of Lima attributed the fact that they were not completely destroyed to the intervention of an image of the Virgin. The monks of San Francisco affirmed that this image turned its face towards a figure of Christ with gestures of supplication, and that when the earthquake had ceased, the image of the Virgin turned back to its original position. As might very well be expected, a miracle like this, announced by pious men, was celebrated with great splendour and much rejoicing. It was also during the government of Chinchon that the Jesuits consecrated their temple and celebrated its completion with fiestas in which was displayed an extravagance unknown even in the richest cities of Spain. A few years earlier, in 1625, the cathedral was

---

[1] Medina, *Historia del Tribunal del Santo Oficio de la Inquisición de Lima*, ii. 43–5, gives the names of the victims, their offences, and the sentence of each.

[2] Medina, *Historia de la Inquisición de Lima*, ii. 110.

dedicated ; it was completed eighty-five years after the foundations were laid.

Some of the noteworthy explorations of the Amazon and its tributaries, in which members of the clergy had a principal part, were made in the decade of Chinchon's government. In 1632 five ecclesiastics left Quito to descend the Putumayo. The Indians received them in a friendly manner at first, but their only interpreter deserted them, and they were compelled to return to Quito. Two of these, Domingo Brieba and Pedro Pecador, were joined by two other priests and by four other Spaniards, and started on a journey of exploration into the region of the Amazon in the beginning of 1634. This undertaking was fruitless on account of the hostility of the natives. Another expedition of a similar character was undertaken in December 1635. One of the five ecclesiastics, Pedro Pecador, with thirty soldiers of the escort, formed a settlement, which he called San Diego de Alcalá de los Encabellados. The captain maltreated an Indian, and an insurrection followed. The prospects of the settlement were ruined, and Brieba, with one of his associates, Andrés Toledo, and six soldiers, started down the river in a boat. After almost four months, they arrived at Gurupá, where they found a Portuguese garrison under the command of Captain Juan Pereira de Cárceres. From Gurupá they passed on to Pará. Padre Toledo went to Spain to inform the king of their discoveries, while Brieba remained to conduct an expedition of seventy men, which Governor Noronha organised for the purpose of exploring the river. This expedition, under the command of Pedro de Texeira, spent eight months in ascending the stream to a point where the company landed, and from which Brieba, followed by Texeira, marched to Avila and afterwards to Quito. The soldiers remained near Avila, and waited eleven months for the return of their commander. The viceroy finally ordered Texeira to return with his men by the route he had come, and furnished him the necessary supplies. At the same time he provided that two Jesuits should accompany the expedition to Pará, on their way to Madrid. These were Cristoval de Acuña and Andrés Artieda. At the request of the commander, Padre Brieba consented to return to Pará with the expedition. From that city he went to Spain, landing at Lisbon, October 13, 1640.

It was during this period that the virtues of the famous febrifuge were made generally known to the colonists. The wife of the viceroy, the Countess of Chinchon, had suffered from an intermittent fever, which resisted all known or available remedies, but she was cured by the use of a bark sent to her by the corregidor of Loja. This bark as a remedy for fever had long been in use by the Indians, and soon after this event it became widely known among Europeans under a variety of names : as cinchona, the Countess's powders, the powders of the Cardinal de Lugo, Jesuits' bark, and Peruvian bark. But these names have been generally superseded by *quinine*, the name of an alkaloid compound derived from the bark. The name of the bark, however, immortalises the name of the countess, who died at Cartagena in 1640, returning to Spain with her husband, the viceroy.

VII

After holding the office of viceroy for nearly eleven years, the Count of Chinchon was relieved, on the 18th of December 1639, by the arrival of his successor, Pedro de Toledo y Leiva, the Marquis of Mancera. Spain at this time was suffering the consequences of the inefficient and wasteful government of Philip IV. Cataluña had risen against the Castillians ; Portugal had proclaimed her independence ; and Holland was still at war with her ancient enemy.

In view of the hostility of both Holland and Portugal, the fortifications of Callao seemed to the viceroy insufficient to protect the fort. He, therefore, built a wall about the city, and erected batteries at various points. In carrying out this purpose, he established an excise on a number of articles, required vessels in the harbour to fetch stone from the island of San Lorenzo, and caused all the slaves to work for a brief period, unless their masters should make a proper compensation in money. The revenues of the government were also increased by the introduction and use of stamped paper.

Mancera also furthered the construction of vessels of war. These were brought into use after the arrival of the Dutch on the coast of Chile, under Hendrick Brower. In November 1642, Brower left Holland with three ships : the *Amsterdam*, the *Concordia*, and the *Flesinger*. At Pernambuco, he acquired a supply ship called the *Naranjo* and the yacht *Delfin*. He passed through the strait of Le Maire, and landed in the southern part of Chile. He intended to capture and fortify Valdivia, and by forming an alliance with the Araucanian Indians, the inveterate enemies of the Spaniards, to establish a colony in this part of Chile. Brower died shortly after he had taken Valdivia, on the 7th of August 1643, leaving the command of the squadron to Elias Herckmans. At this point the Dutch encountered an insurmountable obstacle. The Indians who at first had exchanged food for firearms, withdrew and refused either to labour or furnish supplies. The invaders, seeing the impossibility of carrying out their design, abandoned their undertaking and returned to Brazil.

In the meantime, Mancera, informed of the capture of Valdivia, prepared an expedition of twelve ships, under the command of his son, General Antonio Sebastian de Toledo, and sent it to Chile to expel the enemy. But on arriving at Valdivia, Toledo discovered that the Dutch had abandoned the coast, having failed in this their third unsuccessful attempt to establish themselves in Chile. The viceregal government now took measures to strengthen the defences of the Chilean coast ; to provide against the encroachments of the Portuguese ; to place a garrison at the port of Buenos Aires ; and to furnish arms to the reductions of Paraguay, in order that the neophytes might be in a position to defend themselves against the Mamelucos.[1]

In internal affairs, the silver mines of Potosi and the mercury mine of Huancavelica continued to be important sources of wealth, but their relative importance had undergone a change before the end of the fifth decade of the century. The production of Potosi had declined, partly through the exhaustion of some of the richer veins and partly through the difficulty of obtaining the required labourers. But in spite of diminished revenues, the city of Potosi continued to be the centre of the gayest, the most extravagant, and the most reckless society in the kingdom. No other city was as rich as Potosi, but all of the principal towns began to show the social extremes which Western civilisation tends to develop. The gulf was wide between the families of distinguished birth and abundant wealth and the miserable slaves, who, abandoned by their masters, " died in the street, and, thrown to the rubbish-heaps, were devoured by dogs and vultures." [2]

The Marquis of Mancera surrendered the office of viceroy to his successor, García Sarmiento, the Count of Salvatierra, on the 20th of September 1648, and embarked for Spain. In his administration he had displayed great energy, but it was charged that in obtaining funds for his public works, he had often neglected or violated prescribed forms ; that in levying an excise on various articles, he had acted without the authority of the Crown ;

[1] Barros Arana, *Historia jeneral de Chile*, iv. 375–400 ; Mendiburu, ii. 87, viii. 75 ; Lorente, *Hist. del Perú*, 1598–1700, 125–9 ; Rolt, *A New and Accurate History of South America* (London, 1756), 189.

[2] Lorente, *Hist. del Perú*, 1598–1700, 135 ; Relación del Marqués Montesclaros, *Doc. inéd.*, vi. 232–8.

and that in many transactions which involved salaries or other financial considerations, he had not been careful to observe the requirements of the laws.[1]

The Count of Salvatierra had been the viceroy of Mexico, and in passing from that country to Peru, he embarked at the port of Acapulco. The peace which prevailed in Peru at the time of his arrival continued throughout the seven years (1648–1655) of his administration. The country was, however, seriously shaken, on the 30th of March 1650, by an earthquake which destroyed Cuzco, killed a number of the inhabitants, and ruined many of the neighbouring fields. The notion that this was a divine punishment made a powerful impression on the surviving population of the city. Processions were celebrated, and the persons who took part in them subjected themselves to barbarous acts of penance. They threw aside not only their articles of personal adornment, but also all except their simplest articles of clothing, going to extremes in their self-mortification. Some marched with ropes around their necks, gags in their mouths, and shackles on their feet. Some, borne down with heavy crosses and chains, were hardly able to walk. Some lashed themselves with iron scourges ; while others went with their arms extended, like the arms of a cross ; each apparently sought to outdo the others in self-inflicted penance.[2]

---

[1] *Cargos que en el Juicio de Residencia se hicieron al Virey Marqués de Mancera por el Juez nombrado D. Pedro Vasquez de Velasco, Oidor de Lima*, printed by Mendiburu, viii. 81–4.

[2] Lorente, *Hist. del Perú*, 1598–1700, 150.

CHAPTER V

A GENERAL VIEW OF NEW GRANADA IN THE SEVENTEENTH CENTURY

I

DURING the long vacancy of the episcopal see of Bogotá, from the death of Archbishop Zapata, January 24, 1590, until the arrival of Archbishop Lobo Guerrero, March 28, 1599, the civil authorities very naturally encroached upon the field which the archbishop assumed lay within the limits of his jurisdiction. When, therefore, Lobo Guerrero arrived and proceeded to exercise the functions of his office as he comprehended them, he inevitably found himself in conflict with the president. Complaints were then sent to the court, and this step was followed by the usual procedure of appointing a visitador, commissioned to hold a residencia of the president. But before the conclusion of this process, the president died suddenly, and the affairs of the government fell into the hands of the oidores of the audiencia. The members of the audiencia at this time were Diego Gomez de Mena, Luis Enriquez, Lorenzo de Torrones, and Alonso Vásquez de Cisneros ; and the subject which especially engaged their attention was an uprising of the Pijao Indians, who carried their depredations to Buga, Toro, Cali, Caloto, Popayan, Neiva, Almaguer, Sumapaz, Sutagaos, and even to the plains of San Juan.[1]

The raids of the Indians were marked by robbery and murder, but their attacks were not confined to Spaniards ; they were in part directed against their native enemies. The communities sent appeals for assistance to the audiencia ; the friars of Ibaqué declared that unless an armed force were placed in that town, they would abandon their monastery and go to Bogotá. Moved by the petitions received from many quarters, the audiencia ordered the formation of three companies of thirty men each ; one at Cartago, one at Tocaima, and a third at Ibaqué. But these provisions made by the audiencia for putting down the insurrection were entirely inadequate, and the governments of Popayan and Neiva informed the Council of the Indies of the obstinate character of the war. It was thought that, in an emergency like that which these settlements had to face, a single person at the head of the government would be more effective than an executive composed of a number of persons. The state of affairs, moreover, demanded the appointment of a president of military standing and experience. Juan de Borja was thought to be such a person, and, having received the appointment, he arrived in Bogotá and assumed the duties of his office, October 2, 1605.

On the president's arrival, hostilities had proceeded too far to permit him to adopt any policy but that of active war, and in pursuing this policy, he had to contend with the Pijao chief, Calarca, whose skill and fearlessness made him an enemy not to be despised. But no skill or bravery was able, in the long run, to overcome the superior advantages of the Europeans ; and although for a time fate seemed to favour the Indian forces, after the death of their leader, they were completely overthrown. Some escaped by flight, but more were captured, and these,

[1] Groot, *Historia de Nueva Granada*, i. 215.

after they had been compelled to witness the decapitation of thirty of their chiefs, were distributed among the different encomiendas.[1]

II

To this period, the end of the sixteenth and the beginning of the seventeenth century, belong a number of religious foundations in New Granada. The college of San Bartolomé was established, and was placed in charge of the Jesuits, who had arrived in the kingdom in 1598. Perhaps the most distinguished of the early instructors in the institution was Padre José Dadey, an Italian who belonged to a rich and noble family of Milan. The year in which the Jesuit college was founded witnessed the establishment of the monastery of Saint Augustine in the "Desert" of Ráquira. Especially instrumental in this work was Diego de la Puente, who sought the retirement of a solitary religious life. At first there was only a hermitage in the wilderness, but after the death of the founder it became, through funds received from various sources, an important monastery under the name of La Candelaria, and a centre of missionary influence. Its fame attracted settlers to the region, and later the valley of the "Desert" was described as "a meadow green as an emerald, occupied by perfectly cultivated farms, with fruit trees, and with herds of cattle that pastured on the plain."[2]

Among other religious houses that had their beginning at this time was the monastery in Panama, established by Juan de San Agustin, from the monastery of Bogotá. To this time also belongs the foundation of the Jesuit college of Cartagena. Archbishop Lobo Guerrero had manifested a lively interest in these foundations, and in all efforts made to extend the influence of the Church, but he was called away from this field by his promotion to the archbishopric of Lima in 1609.

[1] Groot, i. 220–3.   [2] Groot, 226.

At this time the Church in New Granada was acting under the plan which required the missionaries to learn the native language, as the instrument for teaching the Indians religion. But, as in the absence of facilities for printing, it was difficult to obtain the catechism in a sufficient number of copies, Padre Barnardo Lugo, the professor of the Indian language in the Dominican monastery, prepared a manuscript of the desired catechism, dedicated it to the president, Juan de Borja, and the provincial of the Dominicans, under whose order it had been prepared, caused it to be sent to Spain to be printed. Yet in this case, as in other cases, the task of giving the natives, through their undeveloped speech, an adequate idea of Christianity as conceived by Europeans proved insurmountable. They could be made to commit to memory certain simple statements, but they acquired no comprehension of the significance of these statements, or no real knowledge of the system of thought involved in the Christian religion.

In order that the political government might have reliable and first-hand knowledge of the condition of the country, and particularly of the Indians, it was determined by royal decree, that a member of the audiencia each year should visit some specified district to make provision for furnishing the natives whatever they might need, and whatever " might contribute to their welfare, the service of God, and the salvation of their souls." [1]

Among provisions resulting from these visits was the requirement that a church, with a *cura doctrinero*, should be maintained in each of the Indian towns ; that the cura should allow the Indians to dispose freely of their interests, as free persons ; and that on the first day of the year two of the most prudent of the inhabitants should be named as alcaldes for the year, to administer justice among the residents, and direct them in their cultivation of the soil. It was also provided that orphans

[1] Groot, i. 244.

and superannuated labourers should be brought together under the direction of the corregidor into a kind of agricultural community, the product of which should be for the support of these unfortunate persons. The encomenderos should be prohibited from carrying off the Indians to work in the mines, on account of the many deaths which had occurred in them. The taking of Indians for labour from the climate under which they had lived to a distinctly different climate was also prohibited. The wages which should be paid to the Indians who worked in the houses or on the farms should be fixed, in order that no one might deceive or abuse them, because of their ignorance. The encomenderos were strictly prohibited from making the Indians carry any burdens whatsoever on their backs, even though they themselves should offer to do it.

In view of the fact that there had been many cases where the encomenderos or their major-domos had flogged the Indians more severely than if they had been slaves, it was ordered that " the encomenderos, administrators, or overseers should not venture to whip any Indian or Indian woman, nor cause them to be whipped, nor consent that other persons should whip them, under pain, in case of encomenderos, of forfeiting their encomiendas, and five hundred dollars for the royal treasury ; and should the offending person be poor, he should receive a hundred lashes. . . . Any person who should maltreat or in any manner injure the Indians should be punished with much rigour and without grace ; with reference to this matter the royal decree of his Majesty should be observed, in which he orders that the Spaniards and other persons who shall maltreat, wound, kill, or injure the said Indians, shall be punished with the same penalties as if they had committed the said crimes against Spaniards." [1]

[1] Quoted by Groot, i. 244.

III

Between 1619 and 1623, Archbishop Fernando Arias de Ugarte made a journey which lasted somewhat more than three years, and during this time he visited many parts of the kingdom. Besides performing his apostolic duties, ordering the affairs of the churches and confirming such Indians as were found to manifest an interest in the new worship, he kept a book of notes and observations concerning all those matters which attracted his attention, and which, in the interest of good government and the welfare of the natives, seemed to demand a remedy or reform. On returning to Bogotá, he presented this book to President Juan de Borja, who derived from it a large amount of information relating to the state of affairs in the different parts of the country. Guided by this information, the president issued various regulations, correcting evils which by this means were brought to the attention of the government. This incident suggests the superior advantage of the Church, as compared with the political officials, in acquiring knowledge of the country and the inhabitants. The hierarchical organisation of the ecclesiastics, their ambition to rule, and their intimate association with the people of the different parts of the kingdom were elements of this advantage, and through them it became possible for the Church to become a rival of the civil government in the actual control of public affairs.

The information gained by the archbishop on this journey doubtless emphasized in his mind the desirability of holding a provincial council, and it was called to meet on the 6th of January 1625 in the cathedral church of Bogotá. Of the suffragan bishops, only the Bishop of Santa Marta was present. The see of Cartagena was vacant, for Bishop Francisco de Sotomayor had been promoted to the bishopric of Quito; and the Bishop of Popayan excused himself on account of his illness. The small assembly was thus composed chiefly of lower ecclesiastical officers, canons, representatives of the ecclesiastical cabildos, priors, and a number of the superior civil officials. A few days after the conclusion of this council, Archbishop Arias de Ugarte received his appointment to the archbishopric of Charcas, and the ecclesiastical historian affirms that the faithful looked upon his face for the last time through their tears and with lamentation. Ugarte died in Lima in 1638, and in consideration of his distinguished services and virtues, the Pope accorded him the title of *Praelatus praeletorum, et Episcopus Episcoporum*, which is a title that may be more appropriately applied to the pope himself rather than to a bishop or an archbishop.

IV

President Juan de Borja lent his support to the efforts of the Church to found missions among the Indians, and recognised in this work of the ecclesiastics an effective means for enlarging the area of civilisation. A recognition of this fact does not necessarily exclude the opinion that another system of civilising the natives might have been more effective ; that a knowledge of some of the real or material achievements of civilised life would, in the long run, have produced more important results than the mere contemplation of a mystery. The president, moreover, brought to an end the war with the Pijao Indians, and sought to defend and make safe the navigation of the Magdalena River by establishing presidios along its course ; and in this manner he caused a great increase in the commerce between the coast and the towns on the highlands of the interior. During Borja's rule order and peace were generally preserved throughout New Granada, and the Spanish monarch on several occasions recognised with favour the interest he had taken in the well-being of the colonists and the natives.

After the office had remained vacant for two years, Sancho Giron, the Marquis of Sofraga, arrived at Bogotá as the successor of Juan de Borja. He assumed the duties of the presidency on the 1st of February 1630. In character he presented a distinct contrast to his peace-loving and compromising predecessor. He was desirous of maintaining the prerogatives of his office, and determined to dominate all rival or opposing forces. The clergy saw very early that the policy of the new president provided that they should recognise their subordination.

When Bernardino de Almansa, the new archbishop, arrived at Facatativa, a delegation representing the ecclesiastical cabildo went out from Bogotá to receive him. At the same time two Jesuits were commissioned by the president to inform the archbishop, that when he should pass out of the cathedral on the day of his formal reception, he should present himself in the palace before going to his residence. The messengers also informed the archbishop that *señoría ilustrisima* must be accorded to the president as a title of courtesy, as it was given to the president of the council of Castile. There was needed no clearer indication of the vanity of the president, or of his determination to rule absolutely, than these early orders to the archbishop. The archbishop's courteous reply contained the statement that it was opposed to the laws of the kingdom to give to the president a title that was conceded only to the grandees of Spain and to bishops after their consecration. The breach between the president and the archbishop became so complete that at the ceremony attending the latter's reception of the pallium, the president refused to be present, and made an excursion into the country, informing his wife that she should not go to the cathedral, nor permit their children to go. Not satisfied with giving the archbishop this rebuff, Sancho Giron seized other public occasions to show his disrespect for the chief officer of the Church.

On one occasion the archbishop found it necessary to make certain repairs to the cathedral. When the labourers reached the facade, the president ordered the work stopped, on the ground that it obstructed the passage of his carriage. This order, however, was not effective, and the work was continued. But the constables, on the president's order, arrested and imprisoned the labourers. This happened as the canons were leaving the choir, and when they saw what was done, they threw off their vestments, took up the tools, and continued the work under the direction of the dean as foreman. The president then sallied forth in the uniform, and with the truncheon, of captain-general, and ordered the militia to assemble, for the purpose of overawing the town and arresting the canons and the other ecclesiastical labourers. But the captain-general had overestimated the power of his command. The citizens refused to obey. The majority of the Spaniards and creoles retired to their houses, but the Indians gathered in mutinous groups, and, armed with clubs and stones, prepared to attack and burn the president's palace. The acolytes, reinforced by the boys from the streets, carried stones into the tower of the church with the design of throwing them from the windows upon the president's men, if they should come to arrest the canons. And thus a rebellion appeared about to enter upon the active stage. At this point the archbishop, learning of the perilous position in which the president had placed himself, and wishing to avert the outbreak, ordered the ecclesiastics to retire to their houses, and, taking means to appease the multitude, saved the president's palace from destruction.

V

The president's hostility to the archbishop was carried to such an extent that it became persecution, before which the prelate saw himself obliged to flee from the capital to avoid the attacks of his enemies. The devotees among his partisans were disposed to find in the pest which broke out in Facatativa a divine chastisement of the people for their persecution of their spiritual leader. The disease, which was called *tabardillo*, was a form of typhus. In the two years of its continuance, it destroyed the majority of the towns on the plateau, and carried off four-fifths of the Indians. In contrast with the ordinary progress of epidemics, this one laid waste the country, and appeared afterwards in the city. In Bogotá nearly the whole population was attacked, and the two alcaldes were among the first victims. So many died that whole families disappeared, leaving no one to inherit their property. The notary, Santos Gil, is reported to have been the only one who dared to enter the houses of those who were stricken, to attest, or legalise, their wills. Many of these persons were the last of their families to succumb, and they very naturally, in numbers of cases, made him their heir. This threw large amounts of property into his hands, and is said to furnish an explanation of the many foundations that were made by him at his death. The part which he played in this period of general disaster was so conspicuous that the epidemic became known as the *Pest of Santos Gil*. The duration of the plague for two years caused the fields to be left uncultivated, and to the ravages of disease were added the ravages of famine, which were felt with all their terrors, especially among the poor. Men fled from the houses of the sick, for fear of contagion, and the unfortunate victims were abandoned to die alone. The members of the religious orders, in ministering to the afflicted, gave, in many instances, an illustration of Christian charity.

There is naturally no evidence that measures of sanitation were undertaken to stay the progress of the plague. There is an extensive and detailed record, however, of processions, by which the image of the Virgin was carried through the streets and, in fact, from Tunja to Bogotá. In the ignorance and indifference with respect to the real conditions which favoured the spread of the pest, and in the elaborate processions and fervent prayers for immediate divine intervention, the Spanish spirit of that age found a positive expression. Archbishop Almansa succumbed to an attack of fever, and the faithful believed that divine favour was shown to him after his death, by keeping his body from corruption ; for it is seriously reported that after three years, after it had been buried and taken up three times at intervals of a year, if was found, although not embalmed, to be in a perfect state of preservation. In 1638 it was transported to Spain. The armada which carried it, carried also the deposed President Sancho Giron, who had been subjected to the trial of residencia, and was now taken to Madrid and imprisoned.

In the period of Giron's government there was a limited revival of the spirit of exploration and adventure. Captain Juan de Carate, a resident at Tunja, proposed a new expedition for the conquest of the region beyond the mountains, known as the *Llanos*. According to the suggested *capitulaciones*, it was proposed that, the conquest having been made, the land occupied, to the extent of twenty thousand square leagues, should remain under the jurisdiction of Captain Carate during his life and that of his children, in case he had any, or that of a successor whom he might name, if he had no children. It was proposed, moreover, that, besides granting the titles of Marquis and Adelantado, there should also be conveyed to the explorer various privileges. The conquest was expected to be of great advantage to the Indians, in that it would give them a knowledge of the Christian faith.

The cause of civilisation would be advanced, moreover, by an increase of the population of the region, which would further the progress of agriculture and commerce. The documents providing for this undertaking were sent to the Spanish court for confirmation, but they were not returned, and Carate died of the pest.

VI

On the 8th of September 1635, Archbishop Cristobal de Torres arrived in Bogotá as the successor of Bernardino de Almansa. Two years later, on October 5, 1637, Martin de Saavedra y Guzman assumed his duties as president, succeeding Sancho Giron, who had been removed after his residencia. The rivalry of these officials, the chiefs of the civil and of the ecclesiastical organisations, indicates over what insignificant subjects high officials may quarrel, when brought into close relations with one another without other associations. In this case the president wished to prevent the archbishop from preaching under a throne canopy, while neither the president nor the audiencia had a canopy in the church. He was opposed to permitting the prebendaries to occupy chairs but wished them to occupy benches as did the members of the secular cabildo, since their sitting in chairs indicated pre-eminence. He urged, moreover, that when the oidores of the audiencia participated in public processions with the prebendaries, the latter should not carry parasols. These subjects were considered of sufficient importance to be brought to the attention of the Spanish Crown, where the case of the ecclesiastics was presented by Padre Francisco de Mendoza, while the wife of President Saavedra advocated the president's pretensions.

The result of this case was that a royal decree issued by Philip IV ordered that the archbishop might preach *bajo de solio ;* that only the archbishop and the president should occupy chairs, and that the oidores and the members of the exchequer should be seated on benches, as also the ecclesiastical cabildo ; and that if in any meeting chairs were placed for the members of the audiencia, they should also be placed for the canons ; and, finally, " that as the sun shone alike on the good and the bad, and heaven sent rain upon the just and the unjust, they might all carry parasols or umbrellas, except in the procession of the most holy sacrament." Thus, finally, these points of etiquette were settled by supreme authority, after they had been carried to the solemn consideration of the Council of the Indies, and then brought to the attention of the king.[1]

Near the end of Saavedra's term of service, the country was shocked by a violent earthquake, which was especially destructive at Pamplona. It occurred between five and six o'clock in the morning of January 16, 1644. The city was reduced to a mass of ruins. Many of the inhabitants were killed ; some, terrified by the catastrophe, emigrated to other districts ; and the survivors who remained found shelter in tents or straw-covered huts, either on their lots or outside the town. In response to Pamplona's appeal for assistance, the audiencia relieved the inhabitants for four years from the obligation to pay the alcabala and certain other taxes, and the president suspended for two years the excise tax on food and liquors, known as the sisa. Provisions for the relief of Pamplona were the last notable acts of Saavedra's administration. The next year, December 25, 1645, he was succeeded by Juan Fernandez de Córdova y Coalla, the Marquis of Miranda de Auta, who was promoted from the government of Ceuta to the presidency of New Granada.

As a result of the pest and other causes, the supply of Indians for agricultural labourers was insufficient to meet the demand in New Granada during the fourth and fifth decades of the seventeenth century. Many persons sent petitions to the president, asking that Indians might be

[1] Groot, i. 301.

assigned to them, some affirming that the desired labourers were required in order that they might be able to furnish the needed supplies of food for the towns. One of them, a type of many, wrote as follows :

" I, Pedro Forero, resident in this valley of Cogua, declare that I have my lands in this valley, and on them my live stock of various kinds, and with my products I contribute to the provisions of Santa Fé, and for its advantage I have need of four Indians, one for a vacquero, another for a shepherd, and two for ordinary labourers for the improvement and cultivation of the said lands." [1]

VII

The plan to provide instruction for the sons of chiefs was resumed in the beginning of the seventeenth century, and the Jesuits were charged to carry it out. The ecclesiastics were apparently the only persons especially interested in schools, who had the education requisite to conduct them. Here, therefore, as elsewhere in Spanish America, the early schools flourished in connection with religious houses. In cases where they were established by individual persons, they sometimes, as in the case of the foundation by Luis Zapata de Cárdenas, went out of existence with the death of the founder. But the religious orders were permanent institutions, and schools established under their direction were not dependent for their continuance on the efforts or the life of any individual person. Although some of the early schools were designed for the instruction of the sons of caciques, yet they do not appear to have been successful in this respect, for the records do not show the natives in attendance. It is possible that the chiefs here, as in Chile, resisted this proposed invasion of their ancient customs.

Members of the Dominican order were the first actually to undertake the work of instruction in New

[1] Printed by Groot, i. 301.

Granada. They offered courses in Latin as early as 1543, and in philosophy in 1572. It was on the fact of their early practical work in teaching that they founded their petition for authority to establish a university. A licence was granted to them in accordance with this petition, but it was contested by the Jesuits, and the case was under consideration for about twenty years. Finally, in 1627, a decision was rendered in favour of the Dominicans. The reception of the bull and the decree, putting an end to the controversy, was celebrated in Bogotá with many signs of rejoicing. The day after the formal reception of these documents by the vicar-general and the civil authorities there was a religious service, followed by literary exercises embracing an oration by Padre Farfan, and discussions by the persons who had been appointed to be professors in the new university. After this part of the celebration, there was a procession, in which both the civil and ecclesiastical officials and all the other noteworthy persons of the community participated. It passed through the principal streets of Bogotá, and returned to the church of the monastery, where the *Te Deum* was sung, and an oration was pronounced by Archbishop Torres.

When the Jesuits found themselves thus unable to monopolise the affairs of advanced instruction in the capital, they established colleges in a number of the provincial cities, in Honda, Pamplona, Tunja, Cartagena and Antioquia. At the time of their expulsion, in 1767, they were conducting thirteen colleges in the kingdom. Ten others were in the hands of the Franciscans and the Dominicans. Much of the instruction in all of these institutions was necessarily elementary. The higher instruction in Latin, theology, and philosophy was carried on most effectively in Bogotá.[1]

The first college of the Jesuits was established in the houses of the treasurer, Juan de Albis, which were pur-

[1] Vergara, *Historia de la Literatura en Nueva Granada*, 62–5.

chased by the archbishop.   The archbishop assigned five hundred pesos of his income for the support of the padres, and other sums for other purposes.   President Juan de Borja gave two thousand pesos, and provided an annual pension from the encomienda of Guatavita, which belonged to him.   The secular cabildo gave a certain amount for the maintenance of instruction in Latin, and other donations came from private persons.   This college, under the name of *Seminario de San Bartolomé*, was opened September 7, 1604, by a proclamation of the courses of study and by an oration by Padre José Dadey.[1]

This controversy, which was now decided in favour of the Dominicans, had lasted for nearly ninety years.   From 1563 the Dominicans had maintained instruction which they thought entitled to recognition under the name, and with the privileges, of a university.   They therefore petitioned the Crown for the right to confer degrees, and in 1595 they received a favourable response.   A few years later the heirs of Gaspar Nuñez proposed to give thirty thousand dollars to found a college of Santo Tomas, under the direction and administration of the Dominican fathers, together with a school for children of the poor, where they would be taught the doctrines of the Church, and also to read, write, and make use of the fundamental operations of arithmetic.   The Jesuits opposed this donation, and the procurador of the order presented a private document, in which Gaspar Nuñez promised the rector of the Society to endow with his property the college of the Jesuits in Bogotá.   And here arose the question in dispute :   whether the heirs of Nuñez were able to dispose of the property under consideration in favour of the Dominican college, in view of the fact that Gaspar Nuñez himself had expressed his will in favour of the Society of Jesus.   The Jesuits won in the hearing of the case before the audiencia, but this decision was reversed by the Council

---

[1] Borda, José Juaquin, *Historia de la Compañía de Jesus en la Nueva Granada* (Poissy, 1872), i. cap. i.

of the Indies, and the amount of the donation was adjudged to the college of Santo Tomas.[1]

After fifteen years in the office of archbishop, Cristobal de Torres determined to erect a monument that would make his name remembered and at the same time establish a source of enlightenment for the kingdom. In the pursuit of these ends, he founded in Bogotá the Colegio Mayor de Nuestra Señora del Rosario, where instruction should be given in those subjects which were then embraced in the curriculum of a university. The licence for this foundation was contained in a royal decree of December 31, 1651. The funds for the endowment of the proposed college were furnished by the archbishop. In making the gift, the archbishop recognised that since all the property which he donated to the college had been received by him from the kingdom, it was only an act of justice and gratitude to return it, in order that it might be used for the instruction of the people.[2]

At the Court, the Jesuits opposed the archbishop's plan, on the ground that the proposed college would detract from the prosperity and prestige of the Seminario de San Bartolomé, which was in their charge. Their opposition was, however, not effective, and, indeed, what they feared was not realised; for the existence of the new college stimulated the activity of the institution that had already made noteworthy progress. Later a plan for the union of the two colleges was proposed, but the persons especially interested in the college of the Rosario feared that through such a union they might become involved in the legal controversy that had attended the foundation of the Seminario de San Bartolomé.

[1] The essential part of this decision is printed by Groot, i. 305.

[2] " Reconociendo que todas las haciendas que donamos á este colegio las hemos recibido de este reino, y era un género de justicia y agradecimiento retornárselo todo para que se criasen personas nobles en las letras, tan grandes que mereciesen de justicia las garnachas y las prebendas con todas las demas mercedas de su Majestad " (Groot, i. 321).

VOL. II.   G

From these efforts to enlarge the means of public instruction, the attention of the community was turned to the resignation of President Cordova and the reception of his successor. The new president was Dionisio Pérez Manrique de Lara, Marquis of Santiago. He had been the rector of the University of Alcalá de Henares, oidor of the audiencia of Lima, and president of Charcas. He assumed his duties as president of New Granada on April 25, 1654, and was received with the usual signs of public rejoicing ; but the manifestations of joy were soon replaced by evidences of mourning for the loss of the archbishop, who, after directing the ecclesiastical affairs of the kingdom for nineteen years, died July 8, 1654. The place which the archbishop had come to occupy by the side of the president, in the middle of the seventeenth century, shows what progress had been made in this part of America towards ecclesiastical domination.

VIII

In this year, 1654, died also Padre Pedro Claver, whose labours among the slaves imported from Africa and landed at Cartagena entitle him to a place in the history of devoted lives. Born in Cataluña in the year 1585, he entered upon his novitiate for the Society of Jesus in 1602, and for his services among the slaves at Cartagena he became known as the " Apostle to the Negroes." This city had, in the seventeenth century, about four times as many inhabitants as at present. It was the port of greatest wealth and the most extensive commerce in this part of the world. The cargoes of ships arriving from Spain were deposited in its vast warehouses ; traders came from many quarters to take advantage of its stores ; and in its slave markets were gathered the wretched beings brought from Africa. The mind of these later generations is unfamiliar with the horrors of the slave-ship, which landed their cargoes at tropical ports in the seventeenth century. They were usually over-crowded ; they had an entirely insufficient supply of food and water ; they were practically without ventilation ; and at the end of the voyage the living, the moribund, and the dead were found packed in a mass of filth more foul than anything which the fancy can picture.[1]

For forty years Padre Claver devoted himself to the task of rendering more tolerable the condition of the negroes at this port. He descended into the noisome holds of the ships on their arrival, assisted the sick in finding places in the hospital, and, to those who needed no physical ministrations, he administered baptism and the consolations of the Church. It is not, however, to be supposed that these miserable wretches obtained any very clear notion of the meaning of the ecclesiastical ceremonies in which they were made to play a part ; their gain from the devotion of Padre Claver was doubtless the physical ameliorations which he supplied and the relief which they derived from this manifestation of human sympathy. Claver died in 1654 at Cartagena, where the greater part of his life had been spent.

[1] Borda, José Joaquin, *Historia de la Compañia de Jesus en la Nueva Granada* (Poissy, 1872), i. 32–5.

"On ne peut exprimer toutes les misères que ses pauvres esclaves ont à souffrir durant tout le cours de la navagation. On les entasse pêle-mêle au fond des vaisseaux, sans lit, sans vêtemens, et presque sans nourriture, toujours chargés de chaînes, et plongés dans leurs ordures. Tout cela, joint à la chaleur du lieu obscur où on les renferme, et à la mauvaise qualité des aliments qu'on leur donne, leur cause des maladies, des plaies et des ulcères qui augmentent leur infection naturelle à un tel point, que souvent ils ne la peuvent supporter eux-mêmes. Il n'est point de bêtes si maltraitées que ces malheureux ; de là vient que plusieurs tombent enfin dans le désespoir, et qu'ils aiment mieux se laisser mourir de faim, que de vivre dans un état si déplorable. Il arrive même souvent que quand la vieillesse ou l'infirmité les a mis hors d'état de travailler et de rendre service, leurs maîtres les abandonnent impitoyablement à leurs propres misères, comme des animaux devenus inutiles, sans daigner leur procurer le moindre secours" (Fleuriau, *La vie du vénérable Père Pierre Claver, de la Compagnie de Jésus* (Clermont-Ferrand, 1834), 62).

IX

Between the death of Archbishop Torres, in 1554, and the appointment of Juan de Arguinao as his successor, in 1661, Lucas Fernandez Piedrahita was vicar-general and governor of the archbishopric. Piedrahita was born in Bogotá, March 6, 1624, studied in the Seminario de San Bartolomé, and was later given the degree of doctor by the University of St. Thomas. After holding various ecclesiastical offices, he was appointed treasurer of the cathedral of Popayan ; but, before he actually took possession of this post, he was made a prebendary of the metropolitan church. Shortly after the promotion of Arguinao to the archbishopric, Piedrahita was cited to defend himself before the Council of the Indies against charges brought by the visitador Cornejo. This case was carried on slowly, but Piedrahita finally showed that the charges were unfounded. He was in Spain from 1663 to 1669, and during this period he wrote his *Historia general del Nuevo Reino de Granada*. In 1669 he returned from Spain as Bishop of Santa Marta. During his continuance in this office, as later in Panama, he gave a striking illustration of the virtue of charity by his self-denial and his devotion to the interests of the poor, often denying himself the clothing befitting his position. In 1676 he was promoted to be Bishop of Panama, but before he departed from Santa Marta that town was taken by pirates, and the bishop was tortured for the purpose of compelling him to reveal the hiding-place of the treasure which the church was supposed to have in its keeping. Carried off by the pirates and taken into the presence of Morgan, he was received and treated with great consideration by that courteous pirate, who gave him the pontifical regalia which he had stolen in Panama, and even furnished him with a ship to conduct him on the way to his new diocese. In Panama, Piedrahita continued his labours in the spirit

that had marked his career in Santa Marta. He died in
1688, and in that year the first part of his *Historia* was
published at Antwerp.

During these years social chaos reigned in New
Granada. The president ordered the archbishop into
exile, and the archbishop excommunicated the president.
There was not only a conflict between the civil and the
ecclesiastical authorities, but the ecclesiastics were divided
against themselves. The regular and secular clergy were
contending for the government of the convent of Santa
Clara, and this case was finally settled by an order of the
Pope and the Monarch, providing that the keys of the
convent should be given to the provincial of the Franciscans. But the internal social confusion was increased
and prolonged by the interjection of the intrigues of
the Inquisition.

X

Both the Church and the civil government had apparently fallen into a state of temporary demoralisation, and
but for the heroic efforts to carry Christian civilisation
to the inhabitants of the plains of the Casanare, the Meta,
and the Orinoco, the last half of the seventeenth century
in New Granada would present little of inspiring interest.
The work of the Jesuit missionaries in that vast interior
region relieves much of the littleness and meanness displayed elsewhere. The devotion with which they faced
their task cannot but excite admiration, although one
may now see that their ideal could not be attained within
the limits of any period which they had contemplated.

The first visits of the Jesuits to New Granada were
made for the purpose of exploring the country. In the
early years of the seventeenth century they established
the missions of Cagica, Duitama, Fontibon, and Topaga
near the city of Bogotá. With the authorisation of the
archbishop and the president, they crossed the eastern
cordillera and took possession of the towns which the
Spaniards had formed in that region. These were Mor-

cote, Chita, Támara, Pauto, and Guaseto. Their domination here, however, was brief, for the archbishop a little later distributed these towns among the secular clergy. The early opposition to the Jesuits, which provoked this action, was based on their participation in industrial affairs to the prejudice of secular traders. In 1659, in the presidency of the Marquis of Santiago, and while Piedrahita was vicar-general and governing the archbishopric, the Jesuits were permitted to return to the plains of Casanare, but they did not come into possession of all the towns which they had previously occupied. They established themselves in Guayana in 1664, but later the region of the Orinoco was included in the Llanos de Casanare, which in 1669 was left to the Jesuits ; and out of this concession, made without any adequate knowledge of the geography of this interior country, arose certain controversies concerning the pretensions of the different religious orders.

Under the organisation provided for the missions of the plains, several districts, or partidos, were recognised : the partido of Casanare, that of the Orinoco, and that of Rio Meta. The provincial elected at Rome to govern the ecclesiastical province of Santa Fé, appointed a procurador for the partido of Casanare, and similar officials for the other districts. The provincial of the province of Santa Fé was expected to visit the missions in his period of three years, or send a visitador with the title of vice-provincial, to inquire into the state of the missions, their funds, and the order in which their records were kept. In the last decades of the seventeenth century, a number of soldiers, paid by the Crown, were assigned to the padres to assist them in establishing these missions.[1]

[1] A list of the missions of Casanare, Rio Meta, and the Orinoco is given in Cuervo, *Colección de documentos inéditos*, iii. 120–8. Concerning the escort of soldiers, see *ibid.*, 140–4 ; Gilij, *Saggio di Storia americana*, iii. 42–9 ; *Relaciones de los vireyes del Nuevo Reino de Granada* (New York, 1869), 37.

One of the first efforts of the missionaries was to provide clothing for the Indians. This may have been necessary for the realisation of the missionary's idea of civilisation, but considering the heat and the abundance of rain in this region, this measure doubtless added greatly to the discomfort of the natives without improving their prospects of health.[1]

The labour of the Indians on the lands was rendered without wages, and the product of this labour was held by the missionaries, who controlled the use of the land. But the store of products thus created in the hands of the padres was designed to meet the needs of the Indians ; and if these needs were not always met, this misfortune arose, perhaps, from an imperfect administration rather than from any fundamental defect of the organisation. The system carried out here was not widely different from that established in Paraguay ; and no more reasonable or effective method of dealing with the Indians of South America has been practised than that applied by the Jesuits.[2]

[1] Here is a description of the clothing furnished, taken from one of the documents of Cuervo's collection : " A los varones los visten con un calzon y una que llaman camiseta de un tegido de algodon, que hacen en el Reyno de Santa Fé, de una vara de ancho y vara y media ó dos de largo, que abierto por el centro entra la cabeza como una casulla, y quedan honestamente cubiertos, los calzones son de cualquier lienzo, si bien por lo regular de otro que fabrican en los Llanos de Casanare, que llaman Palma, y de este hacen á las mugeres unas enaguas, las cuales en lugar de atarlas por la cintura quedan pendientes del cuello con los brazos desnudos, que salen por las dos divisiones de los costados, y les llegan á medio pierna cubriendo asi el pecho y los dos tercios del cuerpo." The Indians evidently had their own ideas with respect to this clothing, for it is said that " muchas veses es indispensable vestirlos por fuerza " (Cuervo, *Colección de documentos*, iii. 144, 145).

[2] Cuervo, *Colección de documentos*, iii. 146. An elaborate account of the missions of the plains of Casanare is found in Juan Rivero's *Historia de las misiones de los llanos de Casanare y los rios Orinoco y Meta*, which was first printed in Bogotá in 1883, after having remained one hundred and forty-seven years in manuscript. The author was born in Miraflores de la Sierra in Spain, August 15, 1681. He studied medicine and began the practice of his profession, but gave it up, entered

XI

Gil de Cabrera y Dávalos acceded to the presidency of New Granada in 1686, and in the beginning of the period of his government occurred the phenomenon which became known in the traditions of the country as *El Ruido*. Events of this time were later referred to as having happened in "the period of the noise." On March 9, 1687, the sky was clear and the air was still, and night came on without any apparent change. At ten o'clock in the evening a great noise was heard, which lasted for a quarter of an hour, but no one could tell whence it proceeded. All persons who were asleep were awakened; and they rushed out of their houses, persuaded that the Day of Judgment had come. In a moment all of the inhabitants were in the streets; some clothed, others naked, and all in the condition in which the supposed summons to judgment had surprised them. They ran up and down, not knowing whither, crying for mercy.

Those who sought other than a supernatural origin of the terrifying noise, fancied it proceeded from the discharging artillery of an advancing foreign host, or the rolling and crashing of the rocks of the overturning mountains. The odour of sulphur which pervaded the atmosphere convinced the common people that devils were traversing the air, and that the disturbance was their work. The frightened inhabitants would probably have

the Society of Jesus, and in 1704 was sent to Bogotá. In spite of an illness evidently produced by the hardships of the long journey, he entered at once upon his missionary work at Tunja, but as he grew worse under the low temperature of the highlands, he was transferred as an instructor to the college at Honda, and later to that of Mompox. He was, however, not contented in either of these positions, and consequently petitioned his superiors to send him to the missions of the Llanos. In 1720 he set out for Casanare. He was convinced that the Indians could be induced to adopt the faith of the Church, and that this act would transform them into civilised beings. This belief afforded him a mighty stimulus in his arduous missionary labours. He died in 1736. Vergara, *Historia de la literatura en Nueva Granada*, 206; Azuolo, Ramon Guerra, *Prólogo* to Rivero's *Historia*.

derived no enlightenment from the fact, even if they had
known, that this event coincided in time with the earthquake of 1687 which destroyed Callao.

The moral effect upon the residents of the town was
so great that they were easily persuaded that Providence
had warned them to be more zealous and attentive to
their religious duties; and after the noise had subsided
they rushed to the churches and demanded admission.
Their cries filled the cathedral, until one of the prebendaries ascended the pulpit, and commanded the multitude to be silent; then, taking advantage of the semi-
darkness and the terror of the excited throng, exhorted
them to repent and flee from the wrath to come. That
night is said to have been the beginning of a great change
in the inhabitants of Bogotá. They crowded to the confession, and were anxious to make their peace with God
before it might be too late. For many years, on March 9,
a number of the churches of the capital celebrated the
anniversary of this event.

XII

On April 12, 1697, the inhabitants of Cartagena became
aware that a number of vessels were approaching their
harbour. They were a French fleet under the command
of De Pointis, which had sailed from Brest on January 9.[1]

[1] The following is the list of ships with the numbers of guns and
men given in De Pointis' *Relation*, pp. 4–6:

	Guns.	Men.
1. Sceptre	90	650
2. Saint Louis	70	500
3. Fort	70	550
4. Vermandois	60	470
5. Apollon	56	400
6. Furieux	56	400
7. Mutine	46	280
8. Saint Michel	56	400
9. Avenant	40	260
10. Marin	36	250
11. Providence	10	60
12. Galiotte á Bombes	2	80
13. Diépoise	18	100
14. Ville de Amsterdam	6	80
Total	616	4480

On April 14, De Pointis began cannonading the defences of the harbour of Cartagena ; but, in spite of the limited and undisciplined garrison, the summons to surrender was rejected. The French then disembarked the bulk of their force, and a number of filibusters who had joined them, with eight cannon of forty-pound calibre, and continued their cannonading and bombarding the whole of the night of the fifteenth and during the sixteenth, until four o'clock in the afternoon, when they prepared to scale the walls. When this movement was observed by the besieged, some of them raised a cry demanding quarter, whereupon the French commander ordered the firing to cease, and required Sancho Jimeno, the chief of the garrison, to have the gate of the fort opened. Jimeno, however, replied that he was a Spaniard, and that he would neither surrender nor ask for quarter, as some of the cowards had done. He affirmed that there were still with him those who would defend their post with honour. But now the French commander's positive order to scale the walls made the garrison willing to ask for quarter, and even to comply with the request that they should throw out their arms. Having no alternative but that of being put to the sword, in case the attacking party was obliged to climb over the wall, the garrison opened the gate of the fortress within the fifteen minutes specified as the period within which they must act.

When the gate was finally opened, Sancho Jimeno, the commander of the fort, presented himself before De Pointis and threw his sword upon the ground ; but De Pointis, recognising the heroism which the commander had displayed, caused a sword to be given to him. This heroism became especially manifest when it was discovered that the garrison consisted of only about a hundred men.

From this first conquest the invaders advanced to Fort Santa Cruz, which was thought to be stronger than that of Bocachica. It could mount sixty guns, and, by reason of its advantageous position, was believed to be able, with a garrison of two hundred, to defend itself against a force of ten thousand men. The French had expected to take it only with great difficulty ; but were surprised, on approaching it, to find the white flag displayed as a sign of surrender ; and they entered, therefore, without firing a shot. In fact, they met with little or no further resistance.

The popular opinion in favour of an immediate surrender to the French prevailed over the opposition of the governor and certain companies of merchants ; and, although definite terms of capitulation were framed, designed to fix the conditions under which the city should be held, it was found that these terms were disregarded, and that the restrictions on plundering which they proposed to establish were wholly illusory.[1]

The articles of the treaty having been signed, May 7 was fixed as the day for the departure of the garrison. The French troops were arranged in two lines, one on each side of the street, extending from the gate of the Faux-Bourg d'Imaine to that of the city. The women began to go out at about ten o'clock in the morning, followed by their slaves and their children. The governor departed at about three o'clock, at the head of sixteen

[1] The following points in the terms of capitulation are given by De Pointis, 87 :

" Le premier fut, qu'on donneroit deux ou trois jours au Gouverneur pour se preparer à sortir ; que la Garnison, à la tête de laquelle il devoit marcher, sortiroit tambour battant, Méche allumée, Drapeaux deployez, et deux petites piéces de Canon. ⸱

" Le second, que tous les Marchands et Bourgeois de la Ville ne pourroient détourner ny argent ny pierreries, qu'ils ne pourroient emporter avec eux que ce qu'ils pourroient porter personellement ou faire porter par leurs Esclaves.

" Le troisiéme, que les Marchands, Bourgeois et Habitans de la Ville seroient les maîtres d'y rester sans qu'il leur fut fait aucun tort, ny qu'il fut permis d'entrer dans leur Maisons, à condition toutes fois qu'ils aporteroient leurs Pierreries, Or et Argent qu'ils auroient en leur pouvoir et dont ils auroient connoissance, que tous ceux qui découvriroient de l'Argent caché auroient pour récompense le tiers de al somme."

hundred men, all carrying arms, and taking with them two little cannon.[1]

De Pointis, on horseback and surrounded by a guard of thirty or forty marines, reviewed this retiring procession. Then, accompanied by his guard, he went to the cathedral; the *Te Deum* was sung, and prayers were offered for the King of Spain as well as for the King of France. " Vous jugez bien," De Pointis remarks, " que leur joye apparente étoit aussi feinte que la nôtre étoit naturelle."[2]

After the ceremony in the cathedral, De Pointis dismissed his guard, and went to the lodgings prepared for him in the Contaduria. This was the building in which the precious metals set apart for the king were ordinarily kept, awaiting the arrival of the galleons that were to take them to Spain. The paragraphs in De Pointis' *Relation* covering the following days indicate the subjects that especially occupied his attention: the gathering of the treasure that was to be found in the city, and the increasing mortality among his men.[3]

[1] De Pontis, *Relation de ce qui s'est fait a la prise de Cartagene* (Bruxelles, 1698), 89.

[2] *Ibid.*, 90; Vergara y Velasco, *Capitulos de una historia civil y militar de Colombia*, 48–50.

[3] " Le huitiéme l'on fut dans plusieurs endroits chercher de l'Argent, on en trouva beaucoup, le soin que les Espagnols avoient en de le cacher fut inutile, tout fut porté à la Consedorie. Le Sieur Valon, Enseigné de Vaisseau, mourut de ces blessûres.

" Les neuf, dix et onze, l'on ne fut occupé qu'à voiturer de l'argent dans de petits barils et dans des sacs, nous eumes 80. Soldats qui ne firent autre chose. Mr. de Monban, Capitaine de Vaisseau mourut le onze.

" Les douze, treize, quatorze et quinze, se passerent à recevoir de l'argent de particuliers: leur empressement faisoit plaisir a voir, et se faisoient une gloire d'en apporter le plus. Ils se déclaroient tous et crioient que l'on les expediast promptement, c'est-a-dire de les debarasser de notre presence.

" Il y en eut qui apporterent jusqu'e quatre cens mille écus, d'autres moins. Nous poussames l'honnêteté si loin que nous leur laissions quelque chose pour boire a nôtre santé, cette generosité nous attiroit milles remerciemens et souvent de presens. Vous voyez que par rapport à nôtre conduite ils avoient raison d'en agir ainsi" (*Relation*, 91–3).

According to testimony taken in Madrid, the French carried off 2800 marks of gold in bars and round ingots (*tejos*), and gold and silver and jewels in other forms amounting in value to seven million dollars.[1] But this was not obtained without sacrifice on the part of the captors ; for, during the six weeks which they spent in Cartagena, disease carried off half of their number, and, on account of this great loss, they determined, on May 25, to abandon the city. And after they had put to sea the ships presented a horrible spectacle. On the *Sceptre* there were one hundred and eighty sick ; on the *Vermandois*, one hundred ; on the *Fort*, one hundred and fifty ; and the *Avenant* had only eleven men fit for service. From each of the other ships ten or twelve bodies were thrown into the sea daily.[2]

The twelve hundred pirates who had been recognised by De Pointis as participants in the undertaking, at the time when the task seemed to him difficult, fancied themselves slighted in the distribution of the spoils. In order, therefore, to improve their fortunes, they turned back upon the city, prepared to glean the field from which the French forces had gathered the harvest. The determination of the pirates to sack the city was followed by a reign of terror. The nuns and many others who had remained after the previous emigration, now fled to the surrounding country. The clergy of all classes were imprisoned, and the women who had not taken flight, and all other persons who were supposed either to possess property or to be able to reveal the places where valuable articles had been concealed, were gathered into the cathedral ; but the

---

[1] Among the articles of value which they carried off, "fué una de ellas el sepulcro de plata, con ocho mil onzas de metal, usado en la ceremonia del entierro de Cristo el viernes santo, en su cofradía erigida en el convento de San Agustin ; pero esta prenda fué rescatada poco después con otras de la confradía." This restoration was made by Louis XIV, but in the siege of Cartagena in 1816 this *sepulcro* and various other articles were made into coins. Groot, i. 462 ; Martin, *Histoire de France*, xiv. 227.

[2] De Pointis, *Relation*, 109 ; Martin, H., *Histoire de France*, xiv. 227.

details of what happened there have not entered into the historical record ; still, forty years afterwards, the survivors from that period in Cartagena retained an oppressive memory of that phase of the piratical invasion of 1697.

CHAPTER VI

THE INDIAN QUESTION IN CHILE, 1600–1650

I. The Araucanian war. II. Report of the commission appointed by the Count of Monterey. III. The reaction against emancipation. IV. The Esquilachean regulations.

I

THE Indian question in Chile, as in all the provinces of the viceroyalty of South America, presented two distinct aspects. One related to the hostile and unsubdued Indians ; the other, to the Indians who had been conquered and made the slaves or vassals of the Spaniards. In the beginning of the seventeenth century, the Indian question in both of its aspects had reached a more critical stage in Chile than in any other part of the continent. This was due in part to the character of the independent Indians, and in part to the fact that the Spaniards and the Indians occupied different portions of the long and comparatively narrow valley which embraces the bulk of the lands of Chile that are most productive and most desirable for human habitation. An extension of Spanish territory was necessarily an encroachment on the territory of the Araucanians. This state of things made hostilities inevitable as long as the Indians retained their determination to maintain their independence.

The story of the relation of the hostile Indians to the Spaniards is a chapter in the history of the struggle between the two races, of which this half-century saw neither the beginning nor the end—a struggle which, at different periods, displayed different degrees of activity, but with no abatement of the warlike spirit. The seventeenth century opened with no hopeful prospects for the Spaniards. Many of the towns or military posts that had been established were swept away, often after periods of great suffering by the garrisons or inhabitants; and territory that was supposed to be permanently occupied by the Spaniards was lost and had to be fought for again. Governor succeeded governor, but each arrived to face the same unsolved problem. From time to time troops were sent from Peru or Spain, but still the Araucanian held his ground. The change of the conflict into a defensive war along an established line, in the third decade, only provided a period of rest for the two parties. No progress was made towards the attainment of permanent peace. The events of this war are recounted by Barros Arana in his *Historia jeneral de Chile,* but even his great power as a narrator is not able to relieve the course of events from a certain wearisome monotony.

II

With respect to the Indians who had been conquered, a definite settlement of their status was apparently as far off as ever. Two parties among the Spaniards were contending for the execution of their opposed policies. The encomenderos, the most influential owners of property, stood for the continuance of the system of personal service; while the Crown, supported by a minority of the Spaniards in Chile, including many ecclesiastics, wished to abolish the personal service of the Indians, and to dissolve their feudal obligations, or reduce them to the payment of annual fees or tribute. The Count of Monterey, when he was the viceroy of Peru in the first decade of the seventeenth century, appointed a commission, consisting of Juan de Villela, a member of the audiencia, Doctor Acuña, *alcalde de corte,* Governor García Ramon, and two

Jesuit priests, Luis de Valdivia and Francisca Coello. After certain inquiries, this commission reported the following recommendations :

" 1. That all personal service should be abolished ; 2. that the holders of repartimientos and Indians bound to personal service might avail themselves of the work of the Indians for two years, during which time they might be able to gather voluntary labourers ; 3. that during this period all work in the mines should be suspended, and there should be paid to the Indians elsewhere engaged a daily wage fixed beforehand for their labour ; 4. that a new rule respecting tribute should be published ; 5. that the Indian prisoners held as slaves should be liberated, but the three hundred held in Lima should remain until the end of the war ; 6. that negotiations should be had with the view of introducing negroes to replace the Indians." [1]

These recommendations received the enthusiastic support of the viceroy, and he ordered Governor García Ramon to carry them out. But it was found to be practically impossible to do this in Chile ; for the Mapuche Indians of the encomiendas were averse to all kinds of work, and the encomenderos resisted all attempts to give them liberty ; and at the end of the viceroy's reign the emancipation of the Indians of the encomiendas and peace with the Araucanians were still unattained.

The two Jesuits who had helped to frame these recommendations, and who gave them their unqualified support, found their position inconsistent with the practice of the Jesuit institutions that were receiving forced service from the Indians. The conduct of these institutions in this respect was, moreover, inconsistent with the principles of the order, and it seemed to those in authority advisable to set an example of emancipation before urging emancipation on others. In keeping with this view, Diego de Torres, provincial of the Jesuits in Chile, issued an order liberating the Indians who had continued to render per-

[1] Amunátegui Solar, *Las Encomiendas*, i. 317–8.

sonal service to the college of San Miguel. They were given land for cultivation, cattle, and sufficient free time for work on their own account. They were to receive compensation for their labour on the days when they were employed by the Jesuits. This order was to take effect in 1608. Its complicated details were not fully understood by the Indians, and it is affirmed that the liberty granted was only nominal, and that the order had no other force than that of a promise to treat the Indians paternally, and to remunerate them fairly for their services. Yet this action of the Jesuits produced, if not alarm, at least a very disagreeable impression on the encomenderos, whose ill-will for the time being was turned against the Jesuits.[1]

The antagonism of the encomenderos, however, did not prevent the spread of an opinion in favour of reform. When the audiencia was established in Chile in 1609, the judges were instructed to abolish the personal service of the Indians; and in the beginning the members of the audiencia devoted more attention to this subject than to any other. But the passionate advocacy of reforms encountered an equally passionate opposition. The Jesuits, the Bishop of Santiago, and a few of the encomenderos were ranged against the majority of the encomenderos, the cabildo of Santiago, and García Ramon, the governor of Chile. In order that the audiencia might be in a position to act wisely, a general meeting was called to enable it to consult with all parties interested. The discussion was long, but no agreement was reached. In

[1] The antagonism between the Jesuits and the encomenderos existed elsewhere : " The encomenderos of Mendoza, Salta, Tucuman, and Cordova broke completely with the Jesuits, who preached against the slavery of the Indians, denouncing the corruption and cruelty of their masters. From this time the encomenderos separated themselves from all relations with the priests ; with their families and servants, they deserted the churches where were proclaimed doctrines subversive of their interests, and suspended the contributions with which they had helped to support the Jesuit order."—Manuel R. García, in *Revista del Rio de la Plata*, i. 377.

the deliberations of the audiencia, after that body had learned the different views entertained concerning the question at issue, the opinion favouring the maintenance of personal service triumphed, the judges holding that they had not only to defend the Indians, but also to secure the well-being of the colony as a whole.[1]

III

The reaction against the movement for emancipation appeared to be complete when Philip III imposed slavery upon all Araucanians taken in war. The king's decree of slavery was opposed to the views of Governor García Ramon, and was not issued in Chile until after the governor's death, when it was published by his successor, Luis Merlo de la Fuente, on August 20, 1610.

This decree was naturally acceptable to the encomenderos, since it furnished them a prospect of increasing the number of their dependents. But a little later this prospect was obscured by the announcement of a new policy respecting the Araucanians. This policy, first suggested by Juan de Villela, of the audiencia of Lima, involved a strictly defensive war on a specified line of the southern frontier, which was the river Biobio ; and the defence of this line was to furnish protection to central Chile. It involved, moreover, the plan of a peaceful conquest of the Araucanians.

The decree establishing the new policy was issued in March 1612. Military operations were to be defensive, but the soldiers were to be maintained, armed, and equipped, and in such numbers as might be necessary. Christian doctrine should be carried to the Indians by

---

[1] "La guerra del Reino de Chile se ha continuado de 70 años á esta parte, y pienso que ha sido la causa el mal uso que hubo en el servicio de los Indios, y lo mismo hubiera sucedido en el Perú si tuvieran estos los ánimos tan inquietos y rebeldes como tienen los Chilenos."—*Memorias de los Vireyes*, i. 112.

Jesuit priests; and the Jesuit, Luis de Valdivia, as visitador-general of the province of Chile, was commissioned to act with the governor in securing a proper execution and observance of this order. The previously published royal decree respecting the slavery of Indians taken in war was suspended; and the penalty of death was decreed for soldiers or officers who should pass beyond the line of defence. This decree also announced the abolition of personal service, and the establishment of a system of pecuniary tribute.[1]

The publication of this decree produced a serious state of agitation and indignation throughout Chile. The soldiers and the encomenderos were especially affected. For the soldiers it substituted the stagnant life of garrisons for a life of adventure, plundering, the capture and sale of Indians, and all the license incident to warfare on a savage frontier. The encomenderos saw in the depletion and ultimate loss of their dependents, the destruction of their wealth, or their prospects of wealth, and the overthrow of the economic system, on which at this early period the society of Chile rested. The attempts made to execute the provisions of the decree abolishing personal service encountered an insurmountable obstacle in the impossibility of procuring voluntary labourers for the fields. In this connection appeared the perennial demand for the introduction of negroes; but neither the government nor individual persons were in a position to comply with this demand; and the plan for substituting a pecuniary tribute for personal service seemed still far from accomplishment in 1620.

IV

In spite of this and all previous regulations, the encomenderos were generally disposed to consider their interests as their guide of action. Luis de Valdivia was,

[1] Rosales, *Historia jeneral del Reino de Chile*, ii. 527–44.

however, persuaded that the new policy might be maintained by an effective law. Towards the end of the second decade he appeared in Lima, where, as he affirmed, the viceroy " heard him for more than four months.''
There was then formed a body of elaborate regulations which were signed on March 28, 1620, by the Prince of Esquilache, who was at that time the viceroy of Peru. A month later Valdivia left Callao for Spain. He went to report to Philip III on the state of affairs in Chile, and to secure the royal confirmation of the Esquilachean regulations. The following provisions reveal the general character of these regulations :

1. The obligatory personal service of the Indians should be abolished, and the Indians should be declared free, except those who were more than ten and a half years old, and who should be taken in offensive war two months after the publication of these regulations ; these should be held as slaves.

2. Neither the Indians living south of the garrisoned frontier nor those living in the Spanish camps of Biobio should be subject to encomenderos. All other Indians in Chile between the ages of eighteen and fifty should be subject to encomenderos and pay a tribute.

3. The amount of this tribute was different in different places. The amount generally stipulated was ten dollars, seven and a half for the encomendero, a dollar and a half for the priest, half a dollar for the corregidor, and half a dollar for the protector.

4. Work in the mines was prohibited, but the Indians might pay their tribute in agricultural labour, at a rate of wage fixed by ordinance.

5. Only a third of the Indians of an encomienda should be required to work in any given year. The other two-thirds might rest, or work for themselves, or work for others for hire. In case the encomendero did not wish to employ all of the third part of his Indians, he

---

[1] Amunátegui Solar, *Las Encomiendas*, i. 409.

might rent the balance to another person, or to other persons.

6. The Indians of the repartimientos were required to live in reductions, or pueblos. Each reduction, or Indian pueblo, should have a league of land for cultivation or for buildings, and the encomendero should not pasture the land within a specified distance of the reduction.

7. The Indians having trades, such as carpenters, tailors, and shoemakers, should be exempt from service in the *mita*, but mere apprentices should not enjoy this exemption. Such skilled workmen might pay their tribute in money.

8. The Indians residing on the estates in the country, called in Chile *inquilinos*, were required to work on the estate one hundred and sixty days in the year. The owner of the estate should furnish them a piece of land, on which they might raise maize, barley, wheat, and vegetables ; and he should lend them the oxen and implements necessary in their work of cultivation. The wage of these *inquilinos* should be a real a day, and this, after the deduction of the tribute, should be paid in clothing and the products of the estate.

9. The Indians working as domestic servants should be treated as free persons. The encomendero was obliged to furnish them food and quarters, and to provide for them when they were sick. After deducting the tribute, these persons should be paid an annual salary, ranging from twelve to sixteen dollars, which should be paid in clothing. But the Indians in domestic service might not be rented to other masters.

10. The corregidores should make an exact list of the Indians. For every two hundred Indians paying tribute, there should be established a curacy, and the Indians should be taught the catechism ; and the curate should be required to keep a record of baptisms. And the Indians of each parish should be required to build a church with

materials furnished by the owners of the neighbouring estates.

Although the encomenderos found the regulations of Esquilache more favourable to their interests than the rules established by Governor Gamboa, they nevertheless opposed their execution. They objected to the prohibition of slavery; to the suppression of forced labour in the mines; to the limitation of the number of days in the year on which the Indians would be required to work in the fields; to the privilege granted to the Indians to live in their reductions; and to the proposed domiciliary visits of the corregidores, who might liberate the Indians if they were ill-treated by their masters.

But no policy was continued long. Governor Osores de Ulloa, as indicated in an ordinance issued December 8, 1622, held views that were in general favourable to the encomenderos. He suspended the provisions under which the Indians were to be prohibited from working in the mines, and ordered that they might be employed in these undertakings with the permission of the governor. He revoked also the regulations respecting labourers skilled in the trades, and ordered that all the artisans of the encomiendas should serve in the *mita*. But these and other changes in the regulations of the viceroy were to have force only until the king should determine otherwise.

Several months before the date of this ordinance by Governor Osores de Ulloa, Philip IV had approved the regulations of Esquilache, but with extensive modifications. One of these changes was a reduction of two dollars in the amount of the tribute. Another was the re-establishment of slavery in certain specified cases. But neither the regulations of Esquilache nor the royal decree based on them received the obedience of those to whom they were directed. In fact, the regulations decreed by Philip IV were not known to the audiencia of Chile for three years after the date of their approval by the king; and, having no adequate support among the persons most influential in Chile, they were practically suspended.[1] Subsequently other regulations were formed and issued, but neither the earlier nor the later determined the actual relations that existed between the encomenderos and their dependents. The encomenderos constituted the most powerful class·in the colony, and their interests determined a practice which became customary, and thus too thoroughly grounded to be set aside even by a decree of the king, or, much less, by an ordinance of a viceroy or a governor.

It is noteworthy that in this controversy, lasting through many decades, the will of the king, even when expressed in the solemn form of a royal decree, had very little influence in shaping the course of events respecting the encomiendas of Chile. The king wished to have the Indians gathered into towns or villages, and to be under no obligation to render personal service to the encomenderos. In this he was supported by the most influential members of the Church in Chile. But the royal will could not prevail against the opposition of the encomenderos.[2]

[1] Gay, *Historia de Chile*, ii. 351–2.
[2] The governors of Chile during this half-century were :

Alonso García Ramon	1600–1601
Alonso de Ribera	1601–1605
Alonso García Ramon	1605–1610
Merlo de la Fuente (*interim*) and	
Juan Jara Quemada	1610–1612
Alonso de Ribera	1612–1617
Hernando Talaveráno (*interim*) and	
Lope de Ulloa y Lémos	1617–1620
Cristóbal de la Cerda (*interim*) and	
Pedro Osóres de Ulloa	1620–1624
Francisco de Alaba y Nurueña (*interim*) and	
Fernandez de Cordova (*interim*)	1624–1629
Francisco Laso de la Vega	1629–1639
Francisco Lopez de Zúñiga, the Marquis of Baides	1639–1646
Martin de Mujica	1646–1648
Alonso de Figueroa (*interim*) and	
Antonio de Acuña y Cabrera	1648–1656

CHAPTER VII

THE PROVINCES OF BUENOS AIRES, PARAGUAY, AND TUCUMAN

I. Hernando Arias de Saavedra. II. The division of the river province. III. The Mamelucos. IV. Buenos Aires. V. Pedro Bohorquez. VI. Internal affairs of the three provinces.

I

IN the beginning of the seventeenth century, and until the creation of the viceroyalty of New Granada, in the first half of the eighteenth century, the political authority of the viceroy of Peru extended to all parts of Spanish South America. The existence of governors and audiencias in the various provinces made it unnecessary for the viceroy often to intervene directly in the affairs of the remote provinces; for the officer known as governor, president, and captain-general, exercised almost absolute power within the limits of his jurisdiction. Ordinarily, during his incumbency, the audiencia, after this institution had been organised within the boundaries of his territory, confined itself to judicial affairs. As the population of any of these districts, such as Chile, Tucuman, or Rio de la Plata, increased, and the administrative system became more completely organised, the government of these districts gradually acquired a greater measure of independence, until the difference between one of these presidencies, or captaincies-general, and a viceroyalty was largely a matter of dignity and the importance of the district governed.

The movement towards Rio de la Plata's practical independence of the viceroy of Peru was facilitated by the great distance which separated that province from the viceroy's capital, and by the desire of the Peruvians and their government, on account of Portuguese smuggling, to maintain a commercial barrier against Buenos Aires. At the beginning of the century, however, the superiority of the viceroy was not questioned. In 1602, Hernando Arias de Saavedra became governor and captain-general of Paraguay a second time, appointed by the viceroy of Peru, and continued to hold this office until 1609. During this period he undertook to restore order in Asuncion, and made expeditions for discovery to the Strait of Magellan and to the region of the Chaco. In internal affairs he made provision for the preservation and security of the archives of the province,[1] and undertook to introduce means for public instruction. In spite of an earlier attempt to found a school at Buenos Aires, there were, in 1608, no adequate facilities for instructing the children of the settlement ; and, on the invitation of the municipal council, Felipe Arias de Mansilla undertook to meet this want, charging those who would learn to read a tuition fee of four dollars and a half a year, and those who would learn to write nine dollars. This venture appears not to have been successful, and, somewhat later, in 1610, a licence to open a school in the city was granted to Alexander Taurin, and on this occasion a subsidy of twelve dollars a year for each pupil was offered by the cabildo. The payment might be made quarterly in flour, hides, tallow, or cattle.[2]

At this time not only the ordinances regulating the

---

[1] As early as 1607 attention began to be directed to the necessity of preserving and properly caring for the archives of the colony. To this end the cabildo commissioned the alcalde, Cristoval Pérez de Aróstegui, to make an inventory of the papers and place them in a chest under three locks with different keys. The keys were then to be distributed among three important officers of the colony. One was given to the deputy governor, one to the first member of the council, and a third to the secretary of the cabildo.—Zinny, i. xxi.

[2] Zinny, i. xxiv.

movement of goods were violated at Buenos Aires, but also the ordinances established to control immigration. In view of this violation of the law, a royal decree was issued in 1610, imposing the penalty of death on those persons who might help to secrete, or in any way favour, passengers introduced without a licence from the king. And in the following year all persons were prohibited from giving lodging to anyone who might come to the town without being able to present a licence from the governor.[1]

Conflict between the views of the encomenderos and the designs of the Crown appeared here as well as in other parts of South America : the Crown wished to release the Indians from personal service, while the encomenderos found that only through this service were they able to make use of their lands, and acquire means for their support. In order that its plans might be carried out, the Crown appointed Francisco de Alfaro, a judge of the audiencia of Charcas, to consider, as visitador, the state of the Indians, and frame the necessary regulations for their relief. The result of this investigation was the ordinances of 1612, which provided that tribute should be substituted for personal service. The task of realising such features of the proposed reform as were possible under the existing circumstances fell to Hernando Arias de Saavedra, who, in 1615, was appointed for the third time to the governorship of this extensive province. This period of his administration was marked by two important events. One was the division of the territory that had hitherto been subject to a single governor, into two provinces. The other event was the call extended to the Italian Jesuits, Mazeta and Cataldino, who laid the foundations of the missions of Paraguay.[2]

[1] Zinny, i. xxiv., xxxiii.

[2] Prior to 1618 all the settlements of the valley of the Paraguay and La Plata were governed as one province. In this year, however, they were separated into two groups. The province of Buenos Aires, or Rio de la Plata, comprehended the cities of Buenos Aires, Santa Fé, Corrientes, and Concepcion ; while the northern province embraced Asuncion, Ciudad Real, Villa Rica, and Santiago de Jerez.—Zinny, i. xxvii.

II

After the division the southern province had Buenos Aires for its capital, and was sometimes known as the province of Buenos Aires. The northern province, in which Asuncion was the chief town, received the name of Guaira, but it continued to be known as Paraguay. As a separate province its first governor was Manuel de Frias, while the first governor of Buenos Aires was Diego de Góngora. The provinces of Buenos Aires and Tucuman, with certain additions, have become the territory of the Argentine Republic ; while Paraguay, isolated in the interior of the continent, has retained its individuality, and made but little progress beyond the semi-barbarism of its colonial days. After the close of Saavedra's rule, it became customary for the governor of Tucuman to be promoted to the governorship of Buenos Aires ; and after serving here he might be transferred to a post on the Pacific. The position of viceroy in Peru or Mexico was the highest object of political ambition in America. The governors of Buenos Aires during this period were usually military officers, and they were appointed for terms of five years, but the king might extend this service. Besides the gradual development of internal conditions, the attention of the governors was directed to the encroachments of the Portuguese from the side of Brazil.[1]

Tucuman was protected by its inland position from attacks by foreigners, yet the government of this province showed itself unwilling to profit selfishly from this advantage, and sent troops to assist Buenos Aires in its resistance to the proposed invasion of the English in the last decade of the sixteenth century. These troops were led by the commander, whom Funes calls the " immortal Tristan

[1] The geographical limitations of these provinces are discussed by Vicente G. Quesada in *Nueva Revista de Buenos Aires*, iv. 442–63, vii. 126–45, viii. 497–523. V. G. Quesada, *Vireinato del Rio de la Plata*, cap. vi., vii., viii.

de Tejeda." The province was fortunate not only in having the services of so able a military officer as Tejeda, but also in the turn of fortune which gave it Alonso de Ribera as governor. Ribera had won distinction in the campaigns of Italy and Flanders, and the king was persuaded that he had the talents required in a governor of Chile, where the Araucanians threatened to exterminate the Spaniards. After his appointment, he undertook the duties of his office with so much force and spirit as to arouse the discouraged minds of the Chileans, and to enable them to stay the progress of the enemy. But in marrying without the king's permission, he violated a rule which the Crown had imposed upon certain high officials in America ; and for this transgression he was deprived of his office and sent to be the governor of Tucuman.[1]

[1] Funes, *Ensayo*, lib. ii. cap. xvi. The following is a list of the governors of Tucuman down to the middle of the seventeenth century :

Juan Núñez de Prado	1550–1553
Francisco de Aguirre. . . .	1553–1554
Juan Gregorio Bazán ⎫	
Rodrigo de Aguirre ⎬ . . .	1554–1558
Miguel de Ardiles ⎭	
Juan Pérez de Zurita ⎫	
Gregorio Castañeda ⎭ . . .	1558–1563
Francisco de Aguirre (second term) .	1563–1570
Diego de Arana ⎫	
Nicolas Carrizo ⎭	1570–1572
Jerónimo Luis de Cabrera . .	1572–1574
Gonzalo Abreu	1574–1580
Hernando de Lerma . . .	1580–1584
Juan Ramírez de Velasco . .	1584–1593
Hernando de Zárate ⎫	
Pedro de Mercado Peñaloza ⎬ .	1593–1605
Francisco de Barraza y de Cardenas ⎭	
Francisco Martínez de Leiva ⎫	
Alonso de Ribera ⎭ .	1605–1611
Luis de Quiñones y Osorio . .	1611–1619
Juan Alonso de Vera y Zárate .	1619–1627
Felipe Albornoz	1627–1637
Francisco Abendaño . . .	1637–1640
Baltasar de Figueroa y Guevara .	1642–1644
Gutierre de Acosta y Padilla . .	1644–1650

In administering the affairs of Tucuman, Ribera put down with impressive vigour the hostile movements of the independent Indians, and at the same time supported Alfaro's attempt to remove the burden of personal service from the Indians who had been subdued. But this undertaking, even with the governor's support, was without important result. Under Ribera's successor, Luis de Quiñonos y Osorio, however, some of the grievances of the conquered Indians were redressed, and the hostile tribes were made to see the advantages of peace. The work in favour of peace and civilisation was, moreover, furthered, during the administration of Quiñones, by the founding of the University of Cordova.[1]

Paraguay, during the three or four decades after its division and the formation of the province of Buenos Aires, revealed conditions less favourable for the development of civilisation than either Buenos Aires or Tucuman. Unfriendly relations arose between Bishop Torres and Governor Manuel de Frias ; and their supporters formed themselves into two hostile parties. The bishop went to such extremes in his denunciation of the governor that the audiencia of Charcas was obliged to take account of the case.

While this internal quarrel agitated the community, the governor was obliged to proceed against the hostile Payaguaes and Guaicurúes. After a decisive victory over the Indians had been won, the surrender of a number of young men as hostages into the hands of the Spaniards, where they might be prepared to become missionaries to their tribesmen, seemed to promise a fortunate settlement between the members of the two races in this region. But the welfare of the province was checked by incursions of the Mamelucos from Brazil, and the embarrassment of the inhabitants was increased by the absence of the governor, who had been cited to appear before the audiencia, and who died at Salta, while returning to Paraguay in 1627.

[1] Garro, *Bosquejo histórico de la Universidad de Cordova ;* Funes, *Ensayo,* lib. ii. cap. xvi.   See also chap. ix. of this second volume.

III

The Mamelucos found in Luis de Céspedes, the successor of Governor Frias, a coadjutor in their enterprise of slave-hunting. The Indians of the Jesuit reductions by his consent, became the victims of the half-savage slave-traders, and the governor received a share of the profits. Eleven of the newly-created towns were destroyed, the cities of Villa Rica and Ciudad Real were depopulated, and the country over which the Mamelucos passed was laid waste. According to Estevan Dávila, the governor of Buenos Aires, sixty thousand captured Indians were sold as slaves in Rio de Janeiro between 1628 and 1630. The audiencia of Charcas heard complaints concerning the outrageous conduct of Céspedes, caused him to appear for trial, and imposed upon him a fine of twelve thousand pesos. But no means were at hand adequate to check the invasion of the enemy, who designed not only to enslave the population, but also to destroy the settlements of the province. They appeared not as little groups of slave-hunters, but as an organised military force. After Pedro de Lugo Navarra became governor in 1636, a troop of five hundred Mamelucos, and two thousand Tupíes prepared to descend upon the reductions which they had not previously destroyed. The Indians of the missions appealed to the governor for protection, which he prepared with surprising alacrity to render; but at the critical moment his courage failed, and the Indians were left to defend themselves. Fortunately they had been armed, and their victory was so complete that of the five hundred Mamelucos and the two thousand Indians only thirty returned to San Pablo. The pusillanimous governor was not disposed to applaud the bravery displayed by the reductions, but charged them with an offence, in that they defended their settlements while not under a legitimately commissioned leader.[1]

[1] Funes, *Ensayo*, lib. iii. cap. i.

Death overtook Governor Lugo on the journey to Spain, and thus withdrew him from the penalty which his cowardice and injustice merited. He was succeeded in the governorship of the province, in 1641, by Gregorio de Hinostrosa, who was born in Chile, where he had been engaged in the war against the Araucanians, and had been a captive among them for fourteen years. Under Hinostrosa and his successors, two important topics especially occupied the attention of the governors and the inhabitants of the province. One was the active hostility of Bishop Cárdenas to the civil authorities, and his determination to procure the expulsion of the Jesuits from Paraguay ; and the other was the continued raids of the Mamelucos.

IV

After its separation from the northern province of Paraguay, the province of Buenos Aires enjoyed the advantage of an extended territory which had been won from the wild tribes of the plains. Yet without mines and with very little direct trade with Spain, life in this province had few attractions. Everything which ministered to taste or comfortable living had to be imported, but on account of the commercial restrictions then existing, these articles, on account of their great cost, could be obtained by only a small part of the inhabitants. In contrast with the conditions of civilised life which the abundant wealth and the denser population of Peru made possible, the sparse and slowly increasing population of this region drifted towards a state of barbarism. As long as legal restrictions on commerce placed the colonists of Buenos Aires in a disadvantageous position as compared with the inhabitants of Peru, it was natural for them to be impatient of their subordination to the authorities of Lima. On the other hand, the Peruvians had grievances which provoked hostility towards the inhabitants of the

region of La Plata. The contraband trade of Buenos
Aires with the Portuguese and the enlargement of the
commercial privileges of that port appeared to be an
invasion of Peru's commercial monopoly and a menace to
her material prosperity.

After the permanent establishment of Buenos Aires in
1580, the position of this settlement was more favourable
for industrial and commercial growth than that of Asuncion, yet its advantages in the beginning were less than
those of Lima. Even before the division of the original
province, Buenos Aires had outgrown the northern city,
and become the commercial and political capital of the
whole territory. The legal restrictions under which the
port was placed discouraged the growth of the northern
not less than the southern settlement. Both were on the
extreme frontier of the region that looked to Lima as
a centre. Whatever European wares the inhabitants of
Buenos Aires consumed, at a certain period, came to
them from Peru. The cost of these wares was such that
persons living far from Lima were compelled to forego
their use, and order their living in a manner so simple
that little besides their own rude products would be demanded. The overland communication between Buenos
Aires and Lima gave, however, to certain settlements in
the interior of the continent an importance which they
would not otherwise have acquired. The conductors of
the caravans carried on a private trade with the inhabitants of these settlements. By means of the caravans
the settlers had facilities for communicating with both
Buenos Aires and Lima ; and the halting-places of the
caravans became markets for articles of food both for
man and beast, which were produced along the route.

In the beginning of the seventeenth century, it was
found that the tailors, shoemakers, and smiths of Buenos
Aires were charging prices which the people were hardly
able to pay, and as a measure of relief the cabildo, in
August 1610, fixed a list of prices that might be charged

for articles of clothing and for boots and shoes. At the
same time it was provided that one half of these prices
might be offered in the products of the country, and the
other half in silver. The products that might be offered
in exchange were such as flour, wheat, corn, suet, candles,
bread, wine, and pork, and these were to pass at the
current cash prices. The prices here established were
changed the following year, and other lists were fixed for
the services of carpenters and smiths.[1]

The commerce of Buenos Aires was in a measure re-
volutionised in the beginning of 1597. In that year the
inhabitants began to export the products of their country,
which had been prohibited during the eleven previous
years. A royal decree permitting this trade was issued
by Philip III on the 20th of August 1602 ; but for six
years this commerce had been carried on without formal
authorisation by the Crown of Spain.[2] The limited trade
allowed to the port of Buenos Aires by the decree of 1602
did not involve giving up the principle that " it was not
advisable for the provinces of Rio de la Plata that the port
should be opened to trade with Spain, nor with any other
country ; and the prohibition should be guarded inviolably, and no person should enter or go out without
the express permission of the king."[3]

The cost of transporting goods by land over the long
and difficult route from Lima to Buenos Aires stimulated
the Portuguese trade. By bringing their wares directly
from Europe, and smuggling them over the border to
the Spanish river settlements, they could sell them at a
small part of the necessary price of goods brought from
Peru ; and thus what the Peruvians feared would lessen
their prosperity, was to a certain extent the basis of
whatever prosperity the inhabitants of Buenos Aires
enjoyed.

But as long as the direct trade with Spain was limited

[1] Zinny, i. xxiv.   [2] *Ibid.*, i. xviii.
[3] Rubalcava, *Tratado*, cap. xiii.

to what could be carried on by means of two small
vessels arriving once a year, the economic progress of
Buenos Aires was necessarily very slow. The province
had great resources in its herds and its agriculture, and
for the development of these resources there was·required
only the market which they would have had but for the
rigid and unreasonable restrictions which were imposed
upon the port. Without the opportunity for industrial
or commercial activity, there was very little to relieve
the monotony of existence in the seventeenth century,
except the campaigns against the Indians and the more
or less active hostility between the governor and the
bishop. To these checks on the somnolent tendency of
the society, there was added another in the form of an
unpleasant anticipation of trouble suggested by the fact
that the Dutch had established themselves at Pernambuco, and were known to be planning to obtain more
favourable possessions. And about the middle of the
century it was known, moreover, that the French were
no longer indifferent to the treasures of America, and
that they were fitting out a little squadron of three
frigates under the command of Timoleon de Osmat, with
orders to take possession of Buenos Aires.

The town of Buenos Aires at this time, the middle of
the seventeenth century, contained about four hundred
houses, which were built of clay or adobes, and had
thatched roofs. They were generally low, of one story,
and were surrounded by gardens filled with orange, lemon,
fig, and other fruit trees. The inhabitants had already
begun to cultivate excellent vegetables, in addition to
their abundant fruit. The houses of the rich had their
walls hung with valuable draperies, and their table service was largely of silver. In these houses there were
many servants, negroes, mulatoes, mestizos, and Indians,
all of whom were slaves. The town had five hundred
men who could bear arms, and there were at least fifteen
hundred slaves ; but the slaves were not permitted to

carry weapons, and could not be counted as a part of the defensive force. The only fortification of the town was a little fort, which occupied the side of the plaza towards the river, the site on which the Government House (la Casa Rosada) was later built. The garrison consisted of about one hundred and fifty men, subject to the command of the governor, who resided at the fort.[1]

The three provinces of this region, Buenos Aires, Paraguay, and Tucuman, each under a governor and all within the jurisdiction of the audiencia of Charcas, had a troubled existence during the last decades of the century. Under Alonso Sarmiento, who became the governor of Paraguay in 1659, the Indians of Arecayá rose in rebellion, led by their cacique, Rodrigo Yaguari-guay. They were nominally Christians, but the change effected in their conversion was nothing more than the partial renunciation of one series of superstitions and the acceptance of others. For the sake of the influence it would give him over ignorant and stupid followers, the cacique caused himself to be worshipped as God the Father, and his wife and daughter as other persons of the Christian mythology. By appealing to the hatred entertained by his tribesmen towards the Spaniards, he incited them to unite and take up arms against their natural enemies. A thousand Indians, following the counsel of their leader, laid siege to Sarmiento and his comparatively small force in their extemporised fortress ; and for several days there was grave doubt as to what

[1] Zinny, i. xxix, note. In the beginning of the seventeenth century the population of Buenos Aires did not exceed five hundred, not counting the Indians and negro slaves (Mitre, *Belgrano*, i. 33). A royal decree, issued by Philip III on August 20, 1602, permitted the inhabitants to export their products, but this, according to Rubalcava, did not involve giving up the principle that " it was not advisable for the province of Rio de la Plata that the port should be opened to trade with Spain, or with any other country ; and the prohibition should be guarded inviolably, and no persons should enter or go out without the express permission of the king " (*Tratado*, cap. xiii.; Mitre, *Belgrano*, i. 35).

would be the result of the conflict. The Spaniards were finally victorious ; the town of Arecayá was depopulated and a hundred and seventy-eight families were removed to the capital, and were compelled to submit to enforced service. But before the migration several of the leaders were executed, and still others on the journey. The cacique Yaguariguay and nine of his associates were hanged near the river Itay ; and others were executed by the way before they reached Asuncion. These merciless punishments were designed in part, like other cruelties which the Spaniards had practised on the Indians on other occasions, to terrify them to such an extent that in the future |they would abstain from hostilities. But this policy seldom had the desired effect, and after these events Governor Sarmiento found himself compelled to continue his campaigns against the Indians until he was superseded in 1663.[1]

V

Tucuman was at this time not more fortunate than Paraguay. It was agitated by the pretensions of the impostor, Pedro Bohorquez. This remarkable man has been described as " at once simple and astute, timid and audacious, quick to form plans, but slow in their execution, without principles, but effective in persuasion, and particularly fortunate in making his wild talk pleasing to many persons of discretion." [2]

Bohorquez was born in Andalucia, and went to America in 1620. At Pisco he married the daughter of a sambo, and very soon began to show his real character as a noisy, lying charlatan. Shortly after the middle of the century, he appeared in Tucuman, cultivated the friendship of the Indians, and, when it seemed to him opportune, gravely informed them that he had been recognised as the legitimate successor of the Incas in

---

[1] Funes, *Ensayo*, lib. iii. cap. 4.   [2] *Ibid.*, i. 269.

Paititi, where he had left his son in peaceful possession of
that kingdom, and that he had come to claim his inheritance from the usurpers, and to liberate the Indians from
their oppressors. They received his words as the utter-
ance of an oracle, and rejoiced that at last they had found
a liberator. The caciques of the Calchaquíes became his
adherents, and under their protection he appeared among
their tribesmen, whom he aroused by vivid descriptions of
their condition under the Spaniards, where children were
torn from their parents, wives from their husbands, and
all doomed to perpetual labour without a prospect of
enjoying the fruit of their toil. At the same time he
exhorted them to unite for his support, in order that they
might re-establish their rights and the throne of the Incas.

The Indians were won by the demagogue's seductive
speech, and by various ceremonies acknowledged him as
their great chief. Bohorquez was fortunate in finding in
the office of governor a person who was " convinced that
he had reached a degree of penetration and sagacity
which gave him the right to demand that the most reliable and established judgments should be subordinated
to his conjectures," and gave way to his will.[1] The
governor was Alonso Mercado y Villacorta (1655–1660),
to whom his own whims and capricious judgments
appeared more worthy of recognition than even the
fundamental laws of the government. But his unwisdom
as an administrator culminated in his approval of the
usurpation of Bohorquez. He visited Poman, on the
frontier of Calchaqui, where he caused extensive preparations to be made for the reception of Bohorquez and the
one hundred and seventeen caciques, who, with the multitude of their servants, had been called to an assembly.
It is said that the governor did not remain for this reception because he had provided that Bohorquez should
make his public entry at London, where Mercado proposed
to wait for this ceremony. When the time had come for

[1] Funes, *Ensayo*, i. 271.

this event, and it was known that Bohorquez and his train were approaching the town, a great procession went out a league and a half to meet them. The procession was composed of a large number of " caballeros decentemente vestidos," a company of infantry, a company of cavalry, and a large number of the inhabitants of the district. At the place of meeting, the Calchaquíes offered their salute, and to this, response was made by the infantry. The governor then rode forward to the Inca, saluted him, and accompanied him into the town, amid the acclamation and enthusiastic applause of the multitude.[1]

The public entry was followed by elaborate ceremonies and festivities. Various honours were conferred upon Bohorquez, and to meet the expenditures of the occasion, the treasury of the government was exhausted. An assembly of notables was convened to discuss serious measures demanded by the extraordinary state of affairs, but the meeting was marked rather by adulation of the pretending Inca than by sober deliberation. A resolution was, however, adopted, which required that Bohorquez should return to Calchaqui, bearing the titles of justicia mayor and captain general, and there should be accorded to him the respect and consideration which belonged to him as Inca.[2]

The governor had succumbed to the fascination of the idea of an Inca renaissance. Bishop Maldanado, however, had not fallen under the spell of the illusion, and, through his statement of the case, the viceroy was enabled to see the danger into which Mercado was running. It was clear to him that decisive action must be taken, and in 1658 he sent orders to the governor, pointing out the criminal character of that official's conduct, and showing that it was injurious to the King of Spain and detrimental to the peace of the kingdom. At the same time, the viceroy commanded the governor to arrest Bohorquez and send him to Potosi. The pretender, on his part, in

[1] Funes, *Ensayo*, i. 273.   [2] *Ibid.*, i. 274.

136 THE SPANISH DEPENDENCIES

order not to be surprised in a defenceless state, constructed a fort, and moved the Calchaquíes to be prepared for war.

The viceroy's order placed the governor in great embarrassment, who recognised that his relation to Bohorquez had magnified the importance of the pretender's position among the Indians, and that to proceed openly to his arrest would plunge the province into a ruinous war. The governor, therefore, decided to write a friendly and flattering letter, asking Bohorquez to meet him for a personal conference. The intended victim was, however, wise enough to avoid this trap, and leave Mercado to try to devise some other means for executing the viceroy's repeated orders. The spies maintained by Bohorquez among the governor's domestics rendered the project for assassination ineffective, and seemed to compel a resort to force. But, anticipating war, Bohorquez appealed to the Indians to protect his " royal person " from the conspiracy of the Spaniards. At this point the superior of the Jesuit missions in that region intervened. In his interview with the " stage king," he found him by no means a brave man, in spite of his extravagant pretensions, and willing, at the first sign of real danger, under a pardon, to renounce his prospects of greatness, and abandon his subjects and their country.

When Mercado received this proposition from Padre Patricio, he refused to assent to it, and demanded an unconditional surrender. He undertook, moreover, to make the Indians see that they were following only a discredited Spaniard. But before this view became widely entertained or had produced any important effect, active hostilities were begun, which Bohorquez directed from safe quarters. The victory of the Spaniards helped to undeceive the Calchaquíes, and left Bohorquez only a limited choice of misfortunes. He appealed for mercy to the audiencia of Charcas, and threw the blame for the unfortunate events on Governor Mercado, " whose bloody vengeance had placed him under the sad necessity of arming the Indians for his defence." [1] He concluded his appeal with the offer, in case his life was spared, to give himself up into the hands of a royal minister, other than Mercado, and to leave the province in peace. This proposition was not attended by a cessation of hostilities, and even after a favourable reply had been received and Bohorquez had placed himself in the hands of the oidor Juan de Retuerta at Salta, the Calchaquíes were persuaded that the maintenance of their independence was worth fighting for, and that they would prefer their own leader, or Inca, whatever might be his character, to submission to the Spaniards.

After his surrender, Bohorquez was still not disposed to desist from conspiracies, and those which he formed while on the journey to Lima and while in prison were of such a character that they could not be overlooked. Through them he forfeited the pardon which he had received, and was later brought to the scaffold. It is affirmed by Funes that Bohorquez, instead of leaving the province in peace, as he had promised to do, left the Indians instructions for war. [2] Since Bohorquez received punishment which he deserved for other acts, it is not important that the doubts which exist regarding these instructions should be solved. It is sufficient for the present purpose to know that the war was continued, and that it engaged the attention of the governor and all the troops he could muster for a period of five months. The result of the conflict was a victory for the Spaniards, after which some of the Indians were carried off into service ; others were executed, and their country was depopulated and laid waste. Mercado returned to Salta from this campaign, November 15, 1659 ; and the following year Jerónimo Luis de Cabrera arrived from Lima to become his successor.

[1] Funes, *Ensayo*, i. 283.
[2] *Ibid.*, i. 285 ; Lorente, *Hist. del Perú*, 1598–1700, 162 ; Mendiburu, ii. 33, 52.

VI

The population of the three provinces of the southeast increased very slowly during the dreary decades of the seventeenth century. The restrictions on communication between Spain and Buenos Aires permitted only a limited number of persons to enter by that port ; and the majority of these were disposed to remain in Buenos Aires rather than to undertake the long journey to Asuncion. For this reason the southern town grew more rapidly than the northern. Another line of immigration lay through the mountainous region of Upper Peru, and the mines of this region intercepted the migration by this route. A few persons passed over the Andes from the west, but for the most part only such as failed to gain an advantageous footing in Chile. The inhabitants of these provinces, by reason of their slow increase in numbers, were not in a position to crush or crowd out the native tribes, but for many years they were obliged to wage undecisive wars with them. Even if it were possible to set forth at length the campaigns against the Indians of Paraguay and Tucuman, the necessarily monotonous account would not furnish great enlightenment. In Paraguay the story is relieved by the history of the Guarani Indians of the Jesuit reductions, large numbers of whom on many occasions appeared as an armed force in the service of the Spaniards against the hostile tribes, particularly against the Guaicurúes.

Governor Mercado was transferred from Tucuman to Buenos Aires in 1660, and one of his first acts illustrated his disposition to be guided by his individual judgment rather than by the provisions of existing laws. A Dutch ship appeared in the port of Buenos Aires, and offered to exchange its valuable cargo for twenty-one thousand hides, ten thousand pounds of Vicuña wool, thirty thousand dollars, and provisions for the crew for the voyage. In spite of the laws prohibiting foreigners from trading with Spanish-American ports, Mercado accepted the proposition of the Dutch, and undertook to secure the assent of the king, but acquired, instead, his reprobation ; for the king was less interested in a measure that might ameliorate the economic condition of the province than in the rigid enforcement of existing legal provisions. Mercado evidently took as his model for his administration the policy of Pedro de la Gasca, without having the full power of his sovereign, which had been conferred upon Gasca.[1]

The inhabitants of these provinces felt the inconvenience involved in the long journey which they were compelled to make in order to bring any cases that might arise among them to the attention of the audiencia of Charcas. To set aside this inconvenience an audiencia was created at Buenos Aires in 1663, with Governor José Martinez de Salazar as its first president. It was designed to obviate the necessity of recourse to the audiencia of Charcas, to provide a body of men, who through their local knowledge and their extensive administrative as well as judicial authority would be able to put an end to the contraband trade of the Portuguese from Brazil, to cause the laws to be respected, and the security and tranquillity of the society to be maintained. But after nine years, the Crown ordered that the institution should be abolished. The authorities of Spain recognised that they had been deceived with respect to the need of an audiencia at Buenos Aires, where the population was small and increasing very slowly, and where there were few important interests. The false step taken at this time apparently made the Crown reluctant for a long time to move at all ; and the province remained without an audiencia for more than a hundred years, or until it was finally established in 1782. The formal opening of the court was not celebrated, however, until 1785.

[1] Funes, *Ensayo*, i. 295.

In Upper Peru, towns were formed near the mines from which they derived their revenues ; but in the southeastern provinces they were established where they would derive advantage from commerce and agriculture. In the seventeenth century all of them had the character of dull provincial towns. None had acquired an overshadowing superiority, like that which Buenos Aires attained in the latter part of the nineteenth century. Exposed to raids by the Indians, it was desirable that the houses should have some of the qualities of a fort, and the form of the ordinary house of the ancient Romans, which had been carried over from Spain to America, was well adapted to this purpose. In the provincial towns they were generally large, with two or three *patios*, or courts, in one of which the horses and other working animals were kept. The labourers employed in their construction were for the greater part Indians. The walls were usually built of adobes, and the roofs were covered either with straw or palm leaves, the places of building determining which should be used. Although with the increase of population there was a certain improvement in the construction of the houses, yet the conservative spirit of the towns was opposed to variations in the architectural style, and in some cases it was provided by ordinance that the houses should be built in a single given form for the adornment of the town.

Since the precious metals were not to be found in Tucuman, it became evident to the settlers that most of their Indian dependents must be turned to agriculture. In this occupation their fate was essentially that of slaves. It was probably not much better nor much worse in Buenos Aires, Paraguay, and Tucuman than in other provinces. They were not only employed in agriculture, but were also required, under severe penalties, to gather the products of the forests, such as pitch, honey, and wax. In whatever kind of work they were employed, they were held to a strict account, and whoever failed to perform the task required of him " was whipped or put in the stocks for his neglect ; and in inflicting these punishments the majordomos and their assistants were horribly cruel." The Indians lived in the workshops under the control of their masters. Here they were " deprived of their liberty, and, in this position, they were unable to control their property, or even to take care of their own children and wives." Since the judges, the encomenderos and all persons having authority over the Indians were interested in the profits to be derived from their labour, there was no one to whom the poor wretches could turn for protection ; and thus they perished in great numbers, " worn out with labour merely to satisfy the avarice of the stranger." [1]

Although the Indians as a class derived little or no profit from their work, they furthered cultivation in the province and helped to build up certain primitive industries ; and it was largely through their efforts that the province was advanced from the barbarism of the early decades to a social state having many of the features of civilisation. The towns of Salta, Tucuman, and Cordova increased in population, and became the more important centres of provincial trade, while Santiago del Estero, the ancient capital, declined. With the establishment of the College of Monserrat and the University at Cordova, that town began to assume the character for which, as a centre of learning, it later became famous. The instruction here, as in all the higher educational institutions of South America, was almost entirely devoted to ecclesiastical subjects. In the University of Buenos Aires, even as late as '1871, two-thirds of all the professorships were foundations for teaching the *ciencias eclesiasticas*. The earthquake of 1692 also contributed to change the relative importance of the provincial towns. Santiago del

---

[1] *Memoria de la provincia de Tucuman*, 39 ; Lozano, i. 3.

Estero was destroyed, and it is reported that two-thirds of the inhabitants were buried beneath the ruins. The survivors, instead of attempting to reconstruct their dwellings and business houses, abandoned the wreck and joined the inhabitants of the more prosperous towns of the province.

CHAPTER VIII

THE BEGINNING OF THE JESUIT MISSIONS IN PARAGUAY

I. Foundation of the missions. II. The offices of the government. III. Appointment of cura and vice-cura. IV. Punishments. V. Agriculture and trades. VI. Civilisation by precept. VII. Statement of Florentin de Bourges. VIII. Estimate of the system.

I

THE foundation and conduct of the Jesuit missions in Paraguay constitute the most noteworthy episode in the colonial history of the provinces near the great rivers which unite to form the Rio de la Plata. The earliest missions of this region encountered the hostility of the Indians and the Portuguese slave-hunters, and were abandoned. A number of years later, in 1610, the Jesuits, Joseph Cataldino and Simon Mazeta, arrived in Paraguay and established themselves in the wilderness near the Paraná and the Uruguay rivers. Here, among the Guarani Indians, they were far from any European settlement and under conditions which seemed to favour the isolation they desired; for it was proposed that the Indians should be associated with the fewest possible persons, besides members of their own race, and under the direction of the missionaries advanced to civilisation. Cataldino and Mazeta received from the governor authority to assemble the Indians in towns, to govern them without dependence on any other Spanish establishment, to build churches, and to resist, in the king's name, all attempts of other persons to subject the converted Indians to personal service. Their first mission was the reduction, or

village, of Loreto. The rapid increase in the number of
proselytes led to the founding of a second mission which
was called San Ignacio. These and thirty or more other
missions, or reductions, that were founded later, constituted the field of the Jesuits' labours with the Indians for
more than a hundred and fifty years, or until their expulsion in 1767.

II

The Indians in each village, or pueblo, or reduction,
were subject to the authority of two resident Jesuits.
One of these was called a cura, but, in spite of his title,
his functions were those of an administrator rather than
those of a parish priest. He was the manager of all the
property belonging to the reduction. The spiritual affairs
were confided to the cura's associate, who was known as
the *vicario*, perhaps sometimes as *compañero*, or vice-cura.
In all of the reductions, or pueblos, the Jesuits were subject
to the supervision of an officer known as the superior.
In nominal subordination to the superior, the Jesuits
exercised over their pueblos an authority that was practically absolute, yet this authority was exercised through
a local government of Indians, consisting of a corregidor, a lieutenant, two alcaldes, and regidores, who were
" elected by the pueblo in the presence of the cura, and
were subject to him in both temporal and spiritual
matters." [1]

The elections were held annually, and the persons
elected were confirmed by the governor of the province.
Besides these elected officials, there were resident in each
pueblo a cacique, whose functions were those of a military
chief of the reduction.

[1] Funes, i. 210.

III

Each reduction was a little theocracy, in which certain precepts and the will of the cura took the place of formal laws. There was no need of civil laws, governing the relations of individual persons to property, since the right of property was not one of the possessions of the Indian. The cura and the vice-cura were appointed, under the royal authority, by the governor of the province, after they had been presented by the provincial of the Jesuits, and been recommended as having the qualifications necessary for the proper discharge of their duties ; but they were assigned to their respective churches by the bishop.

A decree of the Crown touching this subject declared, in 1654, " That the provincial of the Jesuits, or, in his absence, the superior of the missions, each in his respective department, should present, at the departure or death of any missionary, three Jesuits to the governor of the province, who, in quality of vice-patron, was to choose one of them ; and that, if the Jesuits should refuse to submit to this regulation, then the governor, in conjunction with the bishop of the diocese, might name to these cures other secular or regular priests." [1] But neither the governor nor the bishop was in a position which permitted him to have an independent judgment concerning the priests whose names were presented to him by the provincial, and in the course of time both the governor and the bishop ceased to perform their parts in this transaction, and left the provincial free to select the person most suitable for the post in question.[2]

[1] Charlevoix, *The History of Paraguay* (Dublin, 1769), i. 256.
[2] Juan and Ulloa, *A Voyage to South America*, ii. 179.

IV

In the practical affairs of the reductions, there was no appeal from the decisions of the Jesuits to any other Spanish authority. For a violation of the precepts or the regulations established by the curas, punishments were frequently imposed on the offender by causing him to wear in a public place the garb of a penitent ; and flogging in the plaza was resorted to for crimes of a more serious nature. But, in case it became necessary to impose capital punishment for some atrocious crime, " for which it would be difficult to produce precedents, the affair was carried to the tribunal of the governor of the province, in whom alone was vested the power of condemning an Indian to death." [1]

According to Muratori, if one were guilty of a fault that might produce a scandal, the guilty person was " brought in a penitential habit to the church, to beg pardon of God in a public manner for the offence, and a penance was enjoined on the offender. He was then brought out to the square, where he suffered in public a punishment suited to the nature of the offence." [2]   Since much of our information concerning the Jesuit missions is derived from the Jesuits themselves, allowance must be made for the roseate atmosphere through which their affairs are sometimes seen. We are told that after the punishment had been inflicted, the criminal " kissed the hand that had punished him," and thanked God that by this slight correction he had been helped to avoid eternal punishment ; and that " men, and even women, who had secretly committed the fault that they saw punished in another, ran of their own accord to the regidor and accused themselves, withal earnestly begging to suffer the same penance." However credible these statements may be, for some of the things reported the critical historian has need of further corroborative evidence.

[1] Muratori, *Missions of Paraguay*, 126.   [2] Muratori, 70.

The real object of the priest, in cases where punish-ment had become necessary, was to make the offender see that his act was criminal, and that the infliction of the punishment was just. In this manner he aimed to prevent the rise of a spirit of resentment and rebellion in the mind of the person punished, which might be communicated to the other Indians of the reduction.[1]

V

While the industrial organisation of the reductions rested on a strictly socialistic basis, at a certain period there was granted to each father of a family a piece of land which he might cultivate, but since all the Indians were in a state of tutelage, and could not dispose freely of the products of this land, this case hardly constitutes a departure from the socialistic plan that was otherwise carried out. The land belonging to the reduction was generally cultivated in common. In each reduction, moreover, some of the more useful trades were carried on, particularly those of the blacksmith, the silversmith, the gilder, the carpenter, the weaver, and the founder. In some cases, instruction was given to the Indians in the arts of music, painting, and sculpture, which were needed in the construction and decoration of the churches and in the conduct of the worship.

In addition to the revenues derived from the pueblos for ecclesiastical purposes, the royal treasury was ex-pected to make substantial contributions. These covered, among other things, three hundred piastres each for the evangelical workers sent from Europe to Paraguay by the king's authority ; the cost of their passage ; and ten thousand piastres annually for the support of the mis-sionaries in Paraguay. The king provided, moreover, the necessary sacred ornaments and a bell for each church ; also the wine used at the altar, and the oil

---

[1] Juan and Ulloa, *A Voyage to South America*, ii. 174.

which was burned day and night before the altar; and finally one hundred and forty piastres to purchase drugs for the use of each pueblo.

At first the public buildings of the pueblo were very simple. The most important of these was the church.

Besides the church and the missionary's house, which adjoined it, there were storehouses and public granaries, where all sorts of grain and other provisions were stored, to be distributed to the inhabitants when needed; also near them there were workshops for the different trades, and houses for the Indians. The houses occupied by the Indians were simple structures, consisting of one room, where all the members of a family were lodged. They were made of reeds plastered with mud or mortar, and had neither chimney nor windows. The single door served to let in the light and let out the smoke of the hearth-fire in the middle of the room.

VI

Usually when civilised and uncivilised peoples are brought into peaceful contact, the ruder people acquires knowledge of many of the arts of civilised life by observing their new neighbours. A fault in the organisation of the reductions as centres for the development of civilisation was that it kept the Indians in isolation; their only instructors in the arts of enlightened society were the missionaries, who, by reason of their peculiar training and an abnormal position in the world, could not be expected to be the most efficient guides. Instead of having an enlightened society as a model, they were directed by the precepts of the missionaries, and by the neophyte superintendents who were set over them to " observe whether they work, sow, and reap, in due time; whether measures are taken to make the provisions of grain hold out from one harvest to the next ; and to conclude whether the cattle be well looked after." [1]   But it is possible that by this isolation a greater evil was avoided ; since the existence of the reductions depended on their success in warding off not only their savage neighbours, but also the slave-hunters of other nationalities.

VII

The missionary, Florentin de Bourges, on his journey to Pondichéry, visited the missions of Paraguay in 1712, and left an interesting account of his visit, which is printed among *Lettres Edifiantes et Curieuses.* He wrote with admiration of the order and manner in which provision was made for the maintenance of all the inhabitants of the reduction. He found that those who gathered the harvest were obliged to transport all the grain to the public storehouses, where there were persons appointed to guard the stores and keep an account of what was received. At the beginning of each month, officers who had charge of the grain delivered it to the chiefs of the several quarters of the pueblo, who in turn distributed it to the families, allowing each family what was needed for its maintenance during the month. Essentially the same process of distribution was observed with respect to beef and mutton. On the basis of investigations made at the missions in the last half of the eighteenth century, Felix de Azara described the life of the reductions, and pointed out its socialistic character. But Azara did not begin his investigations until fourteen years after the expulsion of the Jesuits ; they belong to the years from 1781 to 1801, and at this time the organisation of the missions had lost some of its important original features. He found that all, without distinction of age or sex, were compelled to

[1] Muratori, 142.

work for the common interest of the mission, and that the cura undertook to provide food and clothing for all.[1]

The surplus of the products of the reduction was disposed of by the cura, and was sent to the Spanish settlements, Buenos Aires and Santa Fé, and exchanged for tools and such other articles as were needed for the support of the population of the pueblo, for use in the industries, or for the construction and decoration of the churches. It is sometimes affirmed that under this socialistic system the stimulus to the exercise of individual powers was removed, since the same provision of food and clothing, and other means of enjoyment was made for the lazy, stupid, and unambitious, as for the diligent, skilful, and virtuous.[2] But this view loses somewhat of its force, when it is remembered that the neophytes were savages assembled from their wandering life in the forest ; that they had not only no habit of regular work, and, furthermore, no idea of work as a part of their régime of life. For such a people, the system established by the Jesuits presented two important steps forward : it substituted a fixed abode for their wanderings in the forest ; it gave them a regular occupation in place of their spasmodic pursuit of means of subsistence. To fix the habit of a settled life and of regular work was about

---

[1] *Descripcion e Historia de Paraguay y del Rio de la Plata*, i. 276. Writing forty years after the expulsion of the Jesuits, Humboldt expressed an unfavourable opinion of the effects of the Jesuits' administration. " The effects of this insulated system have been such that the Indians have remained in a state little different from that in which they existed, while yet their scattered dwellings were not collected around the habitation of the missionary. Their number has considerably augmented, but the sphere of their ideas is not changed. They have progressively lost that vigour of character and that natural vivacity which in every state of society are the noble fruits of independence " (*Travels in the Equatorial Regions of America*, i. 201). Humboldt's opinion, in so far as it was based on what he saw, rested on observations of a generation of Indians that had grown up after the system had been overthrown, and the Indians had been subjected to the demoralising influence of corrupt political administrators.

[2] Azara, i. 279.

all that civilisation could do for the Guaranis in six or eight generations. At the end of the first century, the Jesuits had made a hopeful beginning.

VIII

When it was suggested after a century and a half that the Indians ought to be able to maintain themselves in an individualistic society, the Jesuits urged with justice that such an experiment should not be made then, because the Indian were still immature, and had taken only the first steps towards the position where they would be able to maintain themselves in a civilised state. It was proposed, however, to give them a safe opportunity to practise self-reliance by assigning them certain pieces of land and liberty during two days in the week for its cultivation, and by this means to accustom them gradually to self-control in freedom and the possession of property. It is possible that the unwillingness of the priests to be deprived of power and position made them desire to have the status of the Indians remain unchanged.[1]

De Doblas has rendered concerning the Indians a more

[1] In the statement of Azara, setting forth the position of the priests in the missions, is the following : " The priests and companion or vicar had houses which they did not enter in the ordinary way, but through the great enclosed garden from the school ; they never went out of them to walk in the streets of the town, nor to enter the house of an Indian ; they did not allow themselves to be seen by the women, nor by others except those to whom it was necessary to give their orders. If an invalid needed spiritual aid, he was taken from his miserable house to a clean room near the school, set apart for this purpose, and the vicar, carried in a sedan, with great pomp, administered to him there the holy sacrament. When they appeared in the church, although it was only to say mass, it was with the greatest possible ostentation, clothed with the greatest richness, surrounded and assisted by clerks, acolytes, and musicians, whose number, I believe, did not fall below a hundred. All their churches were the largest and most magnificent in that part of the world, full of splendid altars, pictures, and gilding ; the ornaments could not be better or more precious in Madrid or Toledo."—*Descripcion e Historia de Paraguay y del Rio de la Plata*, i. 283.

favourable judgment than that expressed by Humboldt. In his view the bulk of this population manifested fair ability in whatever it undertook ; but the power of the Indians in imitation exceeded their capacity of original creation. They were humble and obedient, and submitted readily to the commands of those whom they recognised as superiors. This was said of them after some generations of life in the missions. Like all uncivilised peoples, they appeared lazy when judged by the standard of civilisation. They were ambitious to learn, but in their isolation, with no object-lessons of the higher forms of society, and without a knowledge of the language of their superiors, the most direct avenues to enlightenment were not open to them. Though submitting formally to the practices of the Church, they yet regarded with indifference certain lines of conduct which civilised men consider as grossly immoral. If they were seldom overcome in drunkenness, it was not from lack of inclination, but from lack of opportunity. They delighted in music or rhythmical noise, and were pleased to have it as an accompaniment of all their tasks. They were patient and uncomplaining under their severest work ; and sickness and suffering they bore with calmness and almost stoical severity. In their houses, or huts, they were careless of the conventionalities of clothing, and in all matters of domestic life and labour they cast the heaviest burdens on the women. Yet even under the cruel treatment which the women often received, they seldom complained ; perhaps they were aware that complaints would only bring additional grievances.[1] No people has been brought from the practices of savage life to assign women their proper place in society in one hundred or two hundred years. Under the system of the community of goods, which was maintained in the several missions, the Indian was not careful about the education of his children, but he had never

[1] De Doblas, *Memoria histórica, geográfica, política y económica sobre la Provincia de Misiones*, 19.

been careful. Here at least, the neophytes had a certain object-lesson in the government's solicitude for the training and general welfare of the children of the reduction.

Many attempts made to control and to improve the status of the undeveloped peoples have underestimated the conservative force in the traditions of savage life, and consequently overestimated the capability of the savage for immediate improvement or progress towards civilisation. Persons making this mistake are disposed to condemn the plan of the Jesuits, because its ideal for the condition of the Indians was not sufficiently high ; whereas a large number of the projects of civilised society for improving the condition of the lower races have produced unsatisfactory results largely because they have required too great immediate changes in the status of the uncivilised man. The Indian in the territory of the United States was doomed by the fact that the European invaders provided no way for a slow rise from savagism. Practically his only alternatives were either to accept the Englishman's standard of civilisation or to move on and disappear with the wilderness. He was not able to avail himself of the first of these alternatives, and the second, under the circumstances, was his inevitable fate.

The great merit of the Jesuits' plan in Paraguay was that it made no considerable change in the Indian's condition ; it aimed simply to give him a settled life and regular activity, a sufficiently long first step upward. In a thousand years of this slow process was apparently the only prospect of counteracting the Indian's inheritance of barbarism, and bringing him to the status of civilised man. The expulsion of the Jesuits brought to naught this experiment of a superior race entering, in isolation, upon the systematic tutelage of an inferior race. In time of continuance the experiment fell far short of the necessary thousand years, and for this reason all opinions concerning what might have been its result are more or less speculative.

CHAPTER IX

THE UNIVERSITY OF CORDOVA

I. Bishop Trejo, founder of the University. II. The organisation of the University. III. The studies. IV. Degrees and graduation. V. The University after the expulsion of the Jesuits.

I

ANOTHER important event in the history of the south-eastern provinces in the seventeenth century was the founding of the University of Cordova. It was founded by Fernando de Trejo i Sanabria, Bishop of Tucuman. In point of age it holds the third place among the universities of America. It was preceded by the University of San Marcos, in Lima, and by the University of Mexico. Bishop Trejo was one of the few creoles who, under the Spanish régime, attained to the episcopal dignity. He was born in Asuncion in 1554, sixteen years after the foundation of the city. He studied in Lima, and here became a member of the Franciscan order. He had been provincial of the Franciscan province of the Twelve Apostles, of Peru, and was guardian of the principal monastery of Lima, when Philip II appointed him Bishop of Tucuman.[1] He was consecrated in Quito by Bishop Luis de Solis, and assumed the duties of his diocese in 1595.

Trejo held the office of Bishop of Tucuman for nineteen years, and during this period he made his influence felt as the protector of the generally despised Indians and negroes. He caused them to be organised in brotherhoods

[1] Tucuman in the seventeenth century embraced the present districts of Cordova, Tucuman, Salta, Jujuy, La Rioja, Catamarca, Santiago del Estero, and a part of Chaco.

in connection with the churches in all the reductions and towns within his jurisdiction. But his supreme claim to the grateful memory of his countrymen rests on his zeal in behalf of the education of youth, at a time when it was difficult to penetrate the dense ignorance that over-shadowed them. In the heart of the continent, with long stretches of the wilderness on all sides, with no schools, no books, and no associations except such as made for barbarism, it required more than ordinary hope and courage to undertake the task of educating that depraved generation. In Santiago del Estero, Bishop Trejo estab-lished, in 1609, a school under the name of *Colegio de Santa Catalina ;* and a few years later he carried out his desire to found a University, in which " Latin, the arts, and theology " would be taught. By a formal document, dated June 19, 1613, he agreed to give within three years to the proposed university forty thousand dollars. In the meantime he would give fifteen hundred dollars a year for the support of the instructors and the building. And as there might be needed more than the two thousand dollars which it was supposed the forty thousand dollars would yield, he agreed to make to the university a dona-tion " pure, perfect, and irrevocable, which the law calls *inter vivos*, of all my property, real and personal, which I have or may have, money, wrought silver, books, slaves, and inheritances, and in particular that which I have called Quimillpa, within the jurisdiction of the city of San Miguel, with all the lands, mills, goats, asses," and all the other property.

The bishop did not live long after making this gift. Finding his health failing while in Cordova in 1614, he acted on the advice of his physician and set out to return to Santiago del Estero. The Jesuits, to whom this donation was made and with whom he was living in Cordova, opposed his going ; but he persisted, and on the second day of the journey he was obliged to halt. Knowing his end was near, he sent Padre Vasquez

Trujillo on to Santiago to take possession of his property, which he had donated for the establishment of the university. He died on the 24th of December 1614, and his body, in accordance with his request, was taken back to Cordova and buried in the church of the Jesuits. Before his death, however, he issued a second document confirming the gift of 1613.[1]

In February 1614, the institution founded by Trejo, under the title of *Colegio Maximo*, opened at Cordova with fifty students, but it was not until eight years later, 1622, that it was formally authorised by Pope Gregory XV.[2] At this time it assumed the name and character of a university as then conceived. Like all other documents issued by the pope relating to American affairs, this bull of authorisation was submitted to the Council of the Indies. After it had been approved by that body, the king ordered his officers and subjects in the Indies to comply with its terms and assist in its execution.

The death of Bishop Trejo before his foundation had been approved left the institution without a certain important force it would have had in case his life had been prolonged. In fact, the forty thousand dollars which he had agreed to convey was never actually turned over to the Jesuits. At his death, however, the university inherited all, or the greater part, of the articles of property which formed his patrimony ; yet these did not amount to the sum specified in the instrument of his gift.[3]

By the approval of the pope, confirmed by the king, the Colegio Maximo assumed the rank and dignity of a university in 1622, and in the following year it awarded its first degrees under its new title. In the early period of the university the degrees were conferred by the bishop of the diocese, whose seat was not Cordova, but Santiago del Estero. The students who were prepared to receive

[1] Garro, *Bosquejo histórico de la Universidad de Cordova*, 29.
[2] This document is printed in Garro, 42–4.   [3] Garro, 32.

their degrees were, therefore, either obliged to wait until the bishop might come to Cordova, or to make a journey to the place where he might then be. Both courses involved inconvenience and expense. This system, moreover, provided ample opportunity for fraud. It was sometimes easy for a person wishing a degree, although he had not made the requisite studies at the university, to deceive the bishop. There were serious abuses growing out of the power of the bishop to confer the degrees of the university wherever he might happen to be when the applicant presented himself; and knowledge of these abuses came to the king, as may be seen from the decree issued by Philip IV in 1664. In the introduction to this decree the king affirmed that the bishop had given the degrees "sometimes to those who had not studied at the university, nor attended the examinations." [1] As a remedy he ordered that whenever the bishop was absent from Cordova the *maestre-escuela* might give the degrees. Somewhat later other steps were taken to set aside this difficulty. In 1680, the king authorised the rector of the university to confer degrees in the absence of the bishop and the "*maestre-escuela.*" Then, in 1700, Cordova became the seat of the bishop.

II

In the fifty years immediately subsequent to its foundation the university passed through a preliminary stage of imperfect and unstable organisation. But in 1664 it adopted a fundamental law that determined its form and usages for about one hundred and fifty years, or until its reorganisation in the beginning of the nineteenth century. This law is an important source of information respecting the character of the university during the colonial period. It recognised Ignatius Loyola as the patron saint of the university, and required

[1] This decree is printed in Garro, 49, 50.

that his statue or picture should be assigned a conspicuous place, and that the anniversary of the saint's day
should be solemnly celebrated, and the celebration be
attended by all the doctors and masters.

The university should keep as its archives all papers,
such as papal bulls, royal decrees, and other provisions,
relating to it, as well as all books of record.   It should
have a chest in which to keep all of its funds and all
funds entrusted to it, such as the *propinas*, or fees to be
distributed on behalf of the candidates for degrees.   The
chest should have two keys, one held by the rector, and
the other by the dean of the doctors residing in the city,
or by the treasurer ; and it should not be opened except
in the presence of the holders of both keys and of the
secretary.   The secretary was required to make a record
of the amounts put into the chest, and the amounts
taken out, as well as the purpose for which they were
withdrawn ; and the book containing this record should
be kept in the chest.

The two most important officers of the university
were the rector and the treasurer.   They administered
the affairs of the institution.   The subordinate officers
were the beadles and the secretary, who were appointed
by the rector.   The functions of the beadle were a com-
bination of those of a chief janitor and master of ceremonies.   On the secretary devolved the duty of keeping
all the ordinary records of the university, and of acting
as secretary of the meeting known as the *claustro*.   This
was a meeting called by the rector, and was composed
of all the doctors and masters who were in the city or
who might wish to attend though residing elsewhere,
together with the professors and the treasurer ; or, in
the terms of a modern university, a meeting of the
members of the faculties and all the alumni residing in
the neighbourhood of the institution, or who might wish
to attend wherever residing, together with the principal
officer of the financial administration.   The *claustro* dis-

cussed general questions of university policy, and took action on them, which became effective as amendments to the fundamental law. It guarded attentively the observance of this law, insisted on the maintenance of discipline, and kept the government consistent with its traditions. It constituted a broad basis of university government, under circumstances where both the church and civil affairs were subject to a system of absolute rule. The first *claustro* was held in December 1664, and afterwards it was called annually.

The students were required to matriculate annually, and for this they were allowed forty days from the beginning of the instruction. Applicants, after this period, could not enter upon the courses without the permission of the rector, and all were required to take an oath of obedience to him.[1]

The annual courses of instruction lasted six months and a day at first, but later they were made to continue seven months ; and, except in the case of the students of Latin, no examination was required in passing from one course to another. Certain evidence of attendance had, however, to be presented. In some courses the student had to show, as a minimum, that he had heard two lectures, but in other courses a more extensive attendance was required.

III

Like most medieval universities, the university of Cordova was primarily a school of theology. It embraced two faculties, a faculty of arts and a faculty of theology ;

[1] " Ego N. juro per Sancta Dei Evangelia corporaliter per me gratis tacta, quod vobis Domino Rectoi i meo, et pro tempore futuro rectoriam exercentibus, et omnibus, et singulis mandatis vestris in licitis, et honestis obedientiam, et in negotiis Universitatis, et factis consilium, auxilium et favorem fideliter præstabo ; nec prædicta contra ipsam Universitatem, seu ejus bonum altcri dabo ; et ad vocationem vestram veniam, toties, quoties fucre requisitus, sic me Deus adjuvet, et hæc Sancta Dei Evangelia ; neque ero in consilio acversus constitutiones, et statuta prædictæ Universitatis."—See Garro, 443.

but the studies of the first—logic, physics, and Aristotelian metaphysics—constituted a preparation for those of the second. A knowledge of Latin was prerequisite for the study of philosophy. Of the study of Latin, here, Dean Funes, later rector of the university, said it was carried on " without that accumulation of trifles which makes the memory groan." It was conducted with great efficiency and profit by excellent instructors. The students acquired familiarity with the best Latin authors, whose writings became their models for compositions both in prose and verse. Having shown their proficiency in this subject by a public examination, they were admitted to the study of philosophy with the faculty of arts. The studies with this faculty were continued for three years. The first year was devoted to the study of logic, the second to physics, and the third to metaphysics. There were two lectures daily of one hour each. The lecturer devoted a quarter of an hour after each lecture to answering questions and solving the difficulties that had arisen in the minds of the students. In the course of time the discipline became more strict, and the attendance of the students was rigidly required. The course of instruction was then concluded with an examination before " five incorruptible judges," and still later, examinations of greater length were held.[1]

After three years of philosophy, the student passed to the study of theology, which was continued at first four years, and later five years and a half. Of this longer period, the student was required to be in residence only three and a half years. At the conclusion of two and a half years of theology, he might receive the degree of master of arts ; and at the end of the whole course, the degrees of licentiate and doctor.

Writing of the quality of this instruction, Dr. Funes said that these studies were corrupted with all the vices

[1] Funes, *Ensayo*, lib. ii. chap. xvi. ; *Primeras Constituciones de la Universidad ;* see Garro, Appendix III.

THE UNIVERSITY OF CORDOVA 161

of their century. Logic suffered notable defects. The ideas of Aristotle obscured by the barbarous comments of the Arabs could not enlighten the reason. Dialectics was a science of vague notions and insignificant terms, better adapted to forming sophisms than to discoursing with effect. Metaphysics presented phantasms which passed for true entities. Physics, full of formalities, quiddities, forms, and secret qualities, explained by these means the most mysterious phenomena of nature.

" Theology was in no better state. Like philosophy it was also corrupted. The philosophy of Aristotle, applied to theology, formed a mixture of things sacred and profane. Theology had abandoned the study of the Fathers to devote itself to frivolous and irrelevant questions. Purely human reasoning, subtleties, deceptive sophism, this was what had come to form the dominant taste of these schools."

IV

In each of the faculties there were three degrees. Those of the faculty of arts were bachelor, licentiate, and master. Those of the faculty of theology were bachelor, licentiate, and doctor, the doctorate of theology being the highest degree conferred by the university. In order to attain it it was necessary, among other things, to pass five " rigorous " examinations. The first of these covered the first part of the *Summa* of Thomas Aquinas, and dealt with the subjects, God, predestination, the trinity, and angels; the second, beatitude, good and evil, laws, sin, and grace ; the third, faith, hope, and charity, contracts and restitution ; the fourth, incarnation, sacraments, penitence, and the eucharist, the third part of the *Summa ;* the fifth was called the *ignaciana,* in recognition of the

¹ Funes, i., lib. ii. chap. xvi. ; *Revista del Rio de la Plata*, ii. 420.

VOL. II.

patron saint, and lasted five hours, divided between the morning and afternoon.

The student having completed the courses of study required for the degree which he sought, there remained only the ceremony of his promotion. If he was to be a doctor, this ceremony began with a public procession, in which all the doctors, masters, and invited guests appeared mounted, with all the insignia pertaining to their rank. In the afternoon of the day preceding the final ceremony, the procession passed to the house of the candidate, in whose doorway was placed, under a canopy, the standard of the university, showing not only the arms of the university but also the arms of the student to be promoted. A shield also bearing his arms was placed near the standard. At the hour designated the procession moved. It was led by musicians and the beadle carrying the burnished mace, followed by the standard-bearers and the masters, among whom was the secretary ; then the doctors in their gowns and hoods, the city council, the principal citizens of the city ; and, at the end of the procession, the candidate in a white gown, but without a cap, between the eldest doctor and the *padrino*. Formed in this order, the procession passed through the principal streets of the city, following an itinerary determined beforehand, and returned to the starting-point, leaving the candidate at his house, " where," the record says, " he awaited with infinite anxieties the emotions of the following day."

On this day the candidate was conducted by the same procession to the place where he was to receive his degree, usually the church of the Jesuits adjoining the university, where a tribune had been erected for the doctors, masters, and other graduates. In front of this tribune, under a canopy, were placed the royal arms ; at the right of them the arms of the bishop or of the person who might confer the degree in his name ; on the left the arms of the university, and, a little lower, those of the candidate. On a table also in front of the tribune were placed the insignia of the doctor, the Bible, and the *propinas*, which were required in case of granting the degree in question. " Considering the rich hangings, the luxurious carpets, the splendid chairs, the flowers, and the perfumes, one will have an approximate idea of the improvised temple of Minerva."

When the members of the company had taken their seats in the order of their ages, the *padrino* went up to the speaker's stand and proposed a question for the candidate to discuss. At the conclusion of the candidate's discourse the beadles accompanied the *padrino* to his seat. The master or doctor who had to reply took the speaker's place and made his criticism, which lasted about half an hour. This address was not an extemporaneous criticism, but it had been prepared beforehand by the rector or by some person appointed by him, and committed to memory by the speaker. At the close of this reply, the beadles conducted the *padrino* from his seat to the table, where he presented the candidate to the bishop or the person who was to confer the degree, who now made a brief address, to which the candidate or one of the doctors replied. The candidate then knelt before the bishop and took the oath that was required as a part of the ceremony of granting the doctor's degree. He afterwards made the confession of faith, the form of which was a part of the fundamental law of the university. The degree was conferred by placing on the candidate's head the cap with the tassel, and the bishop or the person conferring the degree made use of the appropriate formula established by law.[1]

The *padrino* performed the rest of the ceremony. He first bestowed the kiss of peace on the candidate's cheek, with the formula, *accipe osculum pacis in signum fraternitatis et amicitiæ.* Then he placed a ring on his finger saying : *accipe annulum aureum in signum conjugii inter te et sapientiam tamquam sponsam clarissimam.* Finally

[1] See Garro, 438.

he handed to him the *Maestro de las Sentencias*, saying : *accipe librum sapientiæ, ut possis libere et publice alios docere.*

The final scene of this ceremony may be presented in the language of the law :

" The degree having been conferred, the *padrino* shall come with the new doctor, who will be embraced by the rector, or the person who confers the degree ; then by the doctors and masters in their order ; first those on the right, then those on the left, and finally by the *padrino*. Afterwards they shall take their seats, the *padrino* on the left of the rector, and the new doctor on the right, while the *propinas* and the gloves are distributed. This last act concluded, the procession will return and leave the new doctor at his house." [1]

The *propinas*, it may be said in explanation of the use of the term here, are the fees paid to certain persons who participate in the procession and other parts of the ceremony. The payment of these fees is imposed as an obligation on the candidate for graduation. They were established under the supposed necessity of furnishing compensation for the loss of time and the expenses incurred by the graduates and officers of the university who took part in the ceremony. They varied with the degrees conferred. For the doctor of theology they were more than for the lower degrees. The new doctor was, moreover, required to pay most of the expenses of his graduation, even the cost of arranging and decorating the places of meeting.

There were other expenses that fell to the graduate, particularly for clerical work for which the secretary received payment. But a reference to the fees required is sufficient to indicate that graduation involved an expenditure which many students would find it difficult, if

[1] *Primeras Constituciones de la Universidad, Constitucion* 52 ; see Garro, 421.

not impossible, to meet. This fact was recognised, and an effort was made to establish such provisions as would secure to every student, however poor, an opportunity to acquire a degree. This was found to be difficult without making the student's poverty the object of public attention.

In the university community, on the occasion of any public exercise, great care was taken to have a definite and well-established order of precedence observed. The licentiates and doctors in theology preceded the masters in arts, who in their turn preceded the bachelors in arts. The minor distinctions in dress made observable any departure from this rule of precedence. After beginning the studies in arts or philosophy all students were required to wear the clerical dress, and without complying with this requirement no one would be approved for any degree in theology. Anyone who would have a doctor's degree from the university, whether intending to be a priest or not, was obliged to wear the clerical dress, and this was, in fact, since the instructors were Jesuits, the only dress that was worn in the university.

At first when there were no strictly enforced requirements concerning attendance and examinations, the results of the instruction were unsatisfactory. The students gave little or no attention to any subjects except those on which they were to be examined for their degrees. They passed from one course to another with a very imperfect knowledge of the subjects supposed to constitute a necessary introduction to the course before them. When they found themselves near the final examination, a few undertook to repair their deficiencies by assiduous effort, but the majority found that the career of a scholar had not the attractions they fancied, and turned away to other pursuits. The evil of this state of things clearly demanded correction, and this was attempted, in 1680, by lengthening the course to ten months, and insisting on attendance. Annual examinations were established

three years later, and it became necessary to pass them
with approval in order to be advanced to the succeeding
courses.   This tightening of the lines of discipline led to
acts of insubordination on the part of the students.
That in an institution of learning they should be required
to listen to lectures and pass examinations seemed to
them an interference with their rights as students, and
they instituted a rebellion.   The *claustro*, however, firmly
supported the other authorities, and the two leaders of
the rebellion were expelled, and order restored.

In the course of the eighteenth century, the number
of students was greatly increased.   They came not only
from Tucuman, but also from Rio de la Plata, Paraguay,
and even from Chile and Peru.   When in the course of
time they had acquired their degrees, and in considerable
numbers attended the ceremonies of graduation, the
propinas, or fees, which the candidates had to pay,
became a greatly increased burden.   In order to avoid
the payment of these fees many students took their
certificates of record and applied for degrees at other
universities, in Chile, Chuquisaca, and Cuzco.   But others,
who wished neither to bear the expense nor to undertake
the long and difficult journey over the mountains, retired from the university without taking a degree.   To
set aside the inconvenience of the burdensome fees, it
was provided that they should be reduced by one-third
of their several amounts.   Even this reduction left them
so great as to make the degree quite beyond the reach
of the majority of the students ; and more and more of
them took advantage of the special provisions that had
been made for the poor.   This was regarded as an abuse
of a privilege, and steps were taken to limit the number
to three annually in each course who might be graduated
under these provisions.   Somewhat later greater liberality
was shown to candidates coming from Buenos Aires and
Paraguay.

The primary purpose of the university in the mind of

the founder, a Franciscan friar, was instruction in theology to prepare young men for service in the Church. In keeping with this design, the fundamental law of 1664 provided that the taking of holy orders was a prerequisite for receiving the degree of doctor. One hundred years later, in 1764, seven candidates were absolved from this requirement, and were given their degrees, but under certain other restrictions. This was the beginning of a liberal policy with respect to graduates, and it was made more liberal after the Franciscans came into control of the university on the expulsion of the Jesuits. By the end of the eighteenth century all restrictions of this kind with respect to graduation had been swept away. In the meantime another restriction had come into force. The early law did not raise the question of the legitimacy or illegitimacy of the candidate. When, therefore, in 1710 a person of illegitimate birth applied for a degree, it was conferred upon him, since there was no special prohibition touching the subject. It was, however, later definitely provided by the *claustro* that no degree should be given by the university to any person who was not of legitimate birth and whose legitimacy had not been established.

V

The expulsion of the Jesuits effected important changes in the affairs of the university. The *Instructions* of March 1, 1767, framed by the Count of Aranda, required that, in the towns which might have houses or seminaries of education, secular priests should be substituted for the Jesuit directors and masters, that the schools and seminaries should be continued by these substitutes, and that the instructors who were not priests should remain and continue their instruction. The provisions of Aranda's instructions were, however, not carried out, and the places of the Jesuits were filled by Franciscans, apparently in direct violation of the royal will. After the departure of the Jesuits, the independence which the university had enjoyed under their administration was in a large measure lost. The superior authority in its affairs became vested in the governor of Buenos Aires, and afterwards in the viceroy. By virtue of his powers as vice-patron, he appointed the rector and the professors, and almost immediately the institution began to experience the baneful effects of its political dependence. The first evidence of political scheming was the project to have the university transferred from Cordova to Buenos Aires. Aranda opposed this project, and begged the king to allow the university to remain in Cordova ; and when the arguments for and against removal had been considered by the Council of the Indies, the conclusion was that it should remain in Cordova, as being there in the most central position. At the same time the king and his council decided that the peculiar doctrines of Jesuits and their books should be excluded from the institution. In another respect, the university suffered from its political connection. The viceroy interfered in the internal affairs, and sought to set aside in certain cases the established prerequisites for graduation. In the presence of these attempts at political aggression, the *claustro* stood stoutly for the rights of the university, although the rector affirmed that he was compelled to act in accordance with the will of his superior. As a political appointee the ancient virtue of independence had gone out of him.[1]

The question as to the fees to be paid by the graduate continued to engage the attention of the university community. In spite of all previous reforms, they still remained, in 1780, sufficiently burdensome to prevent many persons from receiving degrees. Finally it was decreed that there should be certain fixed sums for the several

[1] For a discussion of the removal of the Jesuits and the project to transfer the university to Buenos Aires, see article by Garro in *Nueva Revista de Buenos Aires*, iii. 410–26.

degrees, and the sum pertaining to any given degree had to be paid into the treasury of the university before the degree sought would be granted. The parts due individual persons under the regulations were then distributed, and the balance remained in the treasury. The amount to be paid by the doctor was two hundred and fifty dollars.[1] These regulations continued in force with unimportant modifications until the final abolition of the system of fees.

For nearly two hundred years, through all the petty discussions as to forms and fees, the intellectual horizon of the university remained unchanged. Latin, Philosophy, Theology, these constituted the whole world of thought which the student was invited to survey ; not the philosophy or theology of an enlightened age, but the semi-barbarous discussions that went under the name of Aristotle, and theology as set forth by Thomas Aquinas. There was no library to which the students might be directed to pursue free inquiries ; on the contrary, they were practically confined to their notes written as dictated by the lecturer.

The first important step out of the depths of mediævalism was the introduction of the study of jurisprudence in 1791. A practical beginning was made by establishing a professorship of the *Institutes*. With this the university ceased to be purely theological ; yet it was the last of the universities in Spanish America to depart from its primary plan. Gradually other chairs in law were established and the university acquired the right to confer the degrees of bachelor, licentiate, and doctor of civil law. The first degree of doctor of civil law was conferred in 1797.

A contest between the Franciscans and the secular clergy for the control of the university marked the last forty years of its history under the old régime. As already indicated, the *Instructions* of the Count of Aranda

[1] See Garro, 153–6.

of March 1, 1767, ordered that the Jesuits should be replaced by members of the secular clergy. In spite of this expression of the royal will, Bucareli, the governor of Rio de la Plata, handed over the government of the university and of the affiliated college of Montserrat to the Franciscans. By this the expectations and aspirations of the secular clergy were defeated. They, therefore, began a struggle to acquire the authority which their rivals had usurped. This little war brought into the dull and monotonous life of Cordova a subject that interested everybody; but, in spite of the arguments and appeals to the law, the Franciscans held their position. The governor favoured them, and his support was more immediately effective than the will of the king in opposition. In 1800 the subject was finally before the Council of the Indies, and that body rendered a decision justifying the claims of the secular clergy. The decree was issued on the first of December of that year. It had the form of a new act of foundation. The sovereign resolved that there should be founded and erected anew in the city of Cordova, in the edifice which belonged to the *Colegio Maximo* of the Jesuits, " a greater university with the privileges and prerogatives which are enjoyed by institutions of this class in Spain and the Indies with the title of Royal University of San Carlos and of Our Lady of Montserrat." The decree also provided that " the Franciscans should be separated from the government and direction of the new university, as had been established by the royal resolution of 1778." The rector, vice-rector, and treasurer, and the other officials were to be appointed by the *claustro*. This action appeared to involve the immediate overthrow of the friars, but the political authorities of Buenos Aires again came to their rescue, and succeeded in burying the decree in the archives of the viceroyalty. Its resurrection was, however, effected seven years later by Liniers, who, on November 29, 1807, ordered that it should be carried into effect immediately.

The reorganisation introduced by the decree of 1800 made the beginning of a new period in the history of the university.   Henceforth the university of Cordova was to be regarded as having the same standing as the renowned universities of Salamanca and Alcalá de Henares, in Spain, and the universities of Mexico and Lima in America.   But before it had fully entered upon this later period of its career, Spain's domination had ceased, and the inhabitants of Rio de la Plata had undertaken to form an independent republic.

CHAPTER X

PERUVIAN AFFAIRS, 1650–1680

I. Earthquakes and Spanish faith. II. The mines of Laicacota.
III. Indians and the *obrages*. IV. The Maynas missions. V.
Henry Morgan. VI. Castellar and the viceroy-archbishop.

I

On the 13th of May, 1647, Chile was shaken by a severe
earthquake. Others had occurred in 1570 and in 1575,
which were felt with special force in Concepcion and the
region about Valdivia.[1] The shock of 1647 affected particularly Central Chile. It occurred at half-past ten
o'clock in the evening, when, without any sound of
warning, all of the buildings of Santiago were destroyed,
and thousands of persons were buried in the ruins.
Great rocks were torn from the hill of Santa Lucia and
thrown into the streets, and at the same time immense
fragments were loosened from the neighbouring mountain-
sides and hurled into the valley. The agitation lasted for
several minutes, and the walls that withstood the first movement were finally overthrown by the repeated thrusts.[2]

The western coast of South America suffered other
physical disturbances about the middle of the century.
The earhquake of November 13, 1655, caused great
destruction in Lima, and on the 15th of March 1657,
Chile was again severely shaken. Three years later,
October 12, 1660, the inhabitants about Pichincha experienced the effects of a violent eruption of the volcano.[3]

[1] Barros Arana, *Historia jeneral de Chile*, ii. 415, 442.
[2] *Ibid.*, iv. 426–42.
[3] Writing of this mountain about eighty years later, Juan and
Ulloa affirm that " at present no fire is ejected nor does there any

172

A noteworthy characteristic of the mental attitude of the Spanish inhabitants of South America in the seventeenth century was their conviction that the earthquake was a divine punishment imposed on the people for their wickedness. Under this conviction, the appalling calamity of a ruined city, with its long list of dead and maimed, naturally made them anxious to propitiate a god who was willing to let the just and the unjust alike feel his terrible wrath. They crowded to the confession, that their angry god might know of their penitence, and might pardon their sins. The bishop stationed forty or fifty confessors in the plaza of Santiago after the destruction of the city in 1647, and made provision for others in the streets. With the aid of the oidores he erected an altar in the plaza, and carried thither the consecrated host taken from the ruins of one of the churches. An image of the virgin was carried in procession, and from all sides came the religious punishing their sinful bodies with cruel flagellation. In Lima, after the earthquake of 1655, Pedro Castillo mounted a table in a public place, and exhorted the inhabitants to repentance ; although no lives had been lost in this case, it was clearly a divine threat, and if it did not serve to effect a reform, God would not fail to punish the community with a more terrible earthquake. These words of the venerable priest fell on the ears of the frightened inhabitants like the trumpet-call for the Day of Judgment. Men gave up such wealth as they had acquired unjustly, and hastened to make confession of their sins ; they listened to sermons, and performed all manner of exercises of devotion and penitence. The 21st of November, eight days after the shock, was a day of general

smoke issue from it. But sometimes the inhabitants are alarmed by dreadful noises, caused by winds confined in its bowels, which cannot fail of recalling to their minds the terrible destruction formerly caused by its eructations, when the whole city, and neighbouring country, were often, as it were, buried under a deluge of ashes, and the light of the sun totally intercepted, for three or four days successively, by impenetrable clouds of dust."—*A Voyage to South America*, i. 267.

fasting ; in the morning the sacrament was administered to more than ten thousand persons ; and in the afternoon there was a procession with an astonishing display of crowns of thorns, hair-cloth garments, shackles, chains, heavy crosses ; women of rank and beauty, clothed in sackcloth, burdened with heavy shackles, and with ashes on their heads ; men carrying the crucifix, with their backs bared to the lash, while those who inflicted the punishment cried : " Divine justice demands that this sinner be punished for the enormity of his sins." " The awful procession moved slowly amid distressing groans, sobs, and sighs, the clamour of bells, the clanking of chains, and the hissing of the lashes." [1] Many of the persons who took part in this act of community penance fell desperately ill, and a considerable number died of exhaustion or of the frightful wounds which they caused to be inflicted on their backs.

II

In 1655, a few months before the earthquake of that year, Luis Henriquez de Guzman, Count of Alba de Aliste, entered Lima as the Viceroy of Peru. He had been the Viceroy of Mexico, and was appointed to his new office as early as 1651, but on account of the delay in the arrival of his successor, he was not able to leave Mexico until near the end of 1654. In the six years of his administration in Peru, he improved the fortifications of Callao, and determined to recoin the money of the kingdom, in order to eliminate the large number of counterfeit coins that had been brought into circulation. In this period, moreover, the university of Lima celebrated with great magnificence the decree of Philip IV, according to which no one might receive one of the higher degrees in theology without first taking oath to

[1] Lorente, *Historia del Perú*, 1598–1700, 157–9 ; Barros Arana, *Historia jeneral de Chile*, iv. 426–32.

believe and to teach by speech and writing that the Virgin Mary was conceived without original sin. In case the candidate refused to take this oath, he would not be graduated. Of about equal importance with the matter of this decree were the numerous questions of etiquette, which arose with respect to the relation that should be maintained between the viceroy and other dignitaries of the State and the Church.

At this time the resources of the Crown of Spain were in such a low state that more than usual stress was laid on the sale of offices, and by this a new impulse was given to political corruption not only in the Peninsula but also in America. In addition to the revenues to be received from this source, voluntary contributions were called for from the American dependencies. The flow of silver from the New World was diminished by the decline in the production of some of the richest mines. Potosi was far past its most fruitful years, and the discovery of the mines of Laicacota was, therefore, hailed with great interest, when it was announced that it promised to be especially productive.

The decline in the amount of silver produced at Potosi, whether by reason of the exhaustion of the mines or because it was impossible to obtain the needed labourers, was not without a certain compensation. When the product diminished, Potosi ceased to attract adventurers, and its social affairs assumed a more nearly normal state. The conflicts of factions became less violent; there were fewer brawls and murders; and if much of the conspicuous extravagance continued to be maintained, this was made possible only by the practice of economies where they would not be observed. After the middle of the century, the mines of Laicacota became the centre of social disturbance. These were discovered in 1657, in the ancient province of Paucarcolla, and became the property of José Salcedo. Some notion of their richness may be inferred from the fact that Gaspar

Salcedo extracted in a single night metal valued at one hundred thousand dollars, and on another occasion a mass of pure solid silver, which weighed one hundred and seventy-five pounds.[1]

The marvellous reports concerning the mines of Laicacota that were spread abroad, soon attracted seekers after fortune from all quarters, and the hundred years of Potosi's history appeared destined to be repeated in the province of Paucarcolla. The avaricious, the envious, the covetous, and unruly adventurers of every sort gathered at the mines and became a prominent element in a rapidly increasing population. The owners of the principal mine, the brothers José and Gaspar Salcedo, became immensely rich, and, although they disposed of a large part of their wealth for purposes of charity, they were soon the objects of the envy and hatred of the less fortunate. The horrible scenes of Potosi were repeated. On the 24th of June 1665 there was a bloodly encounter between the supporters and dependents of the Salcedo, on the one hand, and the men of the less important mines on the other, in which both lives and property were destroyed. The viceroy sent Angel Peredo as governor to allay the passions and re-establish peace, but, through his attitude as a partisan and his opposition to the brothers Salcedo, he only succeeded in making the condition of affairs worse than it was before his arrival ; he drove a large party into a state of open rebellion.

In the active hostilities which followed Peredo's visit, some were killed, but more were robbed, and among the killed was Peredo. Finding that the agents of the government at Lima only tended to excite and exasperate the people and increase the confusion, and render life and property unsafe, Gaspar Salcedo constructed a fort and prepared to defend himself and his possessions. In 1668, when the affairs of the mine had reached this crisis, the

[1] The story of the manner in which Salcedo became the owner of this mine is given by Ricardo Palma, *Tradiciones peruanas*, i. 247.

viceroy arrived at Paucarcolla, and by measures of unnecessary severity put an end to the conflict. Many
persons were imprisoned, forty were executed, and more
than two thousand fled. Among the victims of execution
were José Salcedo, his dependents, and his principal
friends. Gaspar Salcedo was condemned to pay the costs
of the processes, amounting to twelve thousand dollars,
and was sent into exile for six years. The viceroy, as a
further manifestation of his folly, ordered the town of
Laicacota, consisting of three thousand houses, to be
razed, and designated the town of Puno as the capital
of the province, which was to be called San Carlos of
Austria, in honour of Charles II. The rich mines became
inundated and closed ; and after this exploit the viceroy
visited the province of Chucuito, encouraging Christian
worship ; spent some time in the sanctuary of Copaca-
bana, and returned to Lima by way of Cuzco in 1669.[1]

III

Before these events, and, indeed, long after them, the
miserable state of the Indians employed in the manufactories engaged the attention of many persons, who wished
to make the fate of these labourers more tolerable. In
the manufacturing establishments the conditions of service were not less oppressive than in the mines. The
Indians were drawn into them under the system of the
mita, or as a punishment, by deception or violence, or
under some other scandalous pretext. The owner of the
establishment usually had in his service a wretch called
Guataco, whose business it was to hunt for labourers. In
pursuit of the Indians he showed no respect for their
rights, but kidnapped those whom he thought might be
serviceable wherever they could be found, even taking
them from their houses ; and when they had been delivered

[1] Mendiburu, iii. 224-7 ; Lorente, *Historia del Perú*, 1598-1700,
183-5 ; Ricardo Palma, *Tradiciones peruanas*, i. 245-51.

to the overseers of the establishment, they were subject to a régime so severe that some died of hunger, some perished of fatigue at their work, and some who survived bore the marks of cruel punishment during the rest of their lives. The viceroy, the archbishop, the judges of the audiencia, and the alcalde del crimen deliberated with respect to means for setting aside these abuses, and adopted an ordinance relating to the *obrages*, or manufactories, which was proclaimed July 14, 1664.

This ordinance embraced a large number of prohibitions: no one should establish a manufactory without the express permission of the government; the *guataco* should not be tolerated; there should be no prison or stocks in the *obrage*, and corporal punishment should not be inflicted; the hours of work should extend from seven o'clock in the morning until six in the evening in summer, but only until five in the winter; and the labourers should have half an hour for breakfast and the two hours from noon until two o'clock for rest. Other provisions related to the allotment of tasks, the wages to be paid, and the abuses hitherto practised, and indicated a sincere desire on the part of the officers of the government to ameliorate the condition of the Indians. But the state of the labourers in the following century furnishes sufficient evidence that this ordinance, like much other legislation relating to the affairs of Spanish America, was entirely ineffective, in so far that it traversed the economic interests of proprietors or encomenderos.[1]

IV

While the Count of Santisteban was viceroy of Peru (1661–1666), much attention was drawn to the country of the Maynas by the extension of the Jesuit missions in

[1] Lorente, *Historia del Perú*, 1598–1700, 167–71; Juan and Ulloa, *Noticias secretas*, 276–8.

that region. The rapid increase in the number of reductions and the hospitable reception given to the missionaries seemed to justify the expectation that the mysterious region on the upper tributaries of the Amazon would soon be brought under the influences of the Spanish conquest. But in the course of time it became evident that it would be impossible to give to these reductions the degree of stability which characterised the reductions of Paraguay. The Maynas lacked both the docility and the reasonableness of the Guaranis. "Sometimes a fit of anger, as violent as it was sudden, provoked by a mild reprimand or by a command not wholly agreeable, would lead them to kill the missionary, whom shortly before they had reverenced as a divine being ; and then, possessed by fury or fear, they would scatter into the impenetrable wilderness." [1]

The Indians of the reductions were subject to equally violent passions in their relations among themselves. Having been brought together into a village, they remembered their ancient traditional hatred and hostilities, and were unwilling to renounce their hereditary feuds. Their puerile fears and superstitions, added to their family and tribal antagonisms, rendered it practically impossible to reduce them to the reasonable mood required for a settled life in social contact with their fellows. The tranquillity and prosperity of the reductions were, furthermore, disturbed by the Indians, who had not been subdued, and by the Portuguese of the Amazon territory, who sought to play with reference to the reductions the rôle of the Mamelucos in Paraguay. To their other afflictions was added the plague of small-pox, which appeared among the neophytes in its most contagious and most destructive form. On one occasion, when this disease was epidemic, there were twenty-eight thousand victims, and terrified by this dreadful pestilence, the survivors fled to the forest.

[1] Lorente, *Historia del Perú*, 1598–1700, 174.

V

Philip IV died September 17, 1665. This was in the last year of Benavides' rule as viceroy of Peru. Nine months after the death of the king and the accession of his son as Charles II, the news of these events reached Lima, and in the meantime the viceroy had died, leaving the supreme power in Peru in the hands of the audiencia. In Spain the queen-mother was the regent during the minority of the king, and during this period the government was dominated, in succession, by the Jesuit Nitard, the favourite Valenzuela, and Don Juan of Austria. After the king had attained his majority, the country was ruled by an incompetent king advised by incompetent ministers, and by a larger circle of other incompetents, including the queen, the queen-mother, covetous chamberlains, and at last by a friar, who made the king believe that he was under the influence of witches or demons, or possessed of the devil.

The Spanish government at this time, with no statesman to give it rational guidance, and with the other powers planning, even during the life of the king, to divide up his possessions among themselves, was not in a position to give any effective assistance in the task of governing Spanish America ; in fact, the communications sent to the viceroy of Peru contained chiefly requests for funds to enable the government of Spain to put off the day of its complete bankruptcy. With the announcement of the accession of the new king, there was received in Lima a request from the queen-mother for a donation to meet the expenses of inaugurating the new government. The audiencia was not disposed to comply with this demand, since all available funds were needed to provide means of defence. Jamaica had fallen into the hands of the English (1655), and had become the threatening headquarters of filibusters and pirates, and this fact impressed upon the Peruvian government the need of extending the defences of the coast. The audiencia was opposed to complying with the demand also on the ground that the presence of a viceroy was necessary to secure a proper donation. Means were, however, found for an elaborate ceremony in commemoration of the death of the king, and for a brilliant celebration of the accession of Charles II. There was apparently no lack of funds in Peru, for the mines were especially productive, and not the least important of these were the mines of Laicacota, which, in 1667, had been worked for ten years. The resources of the government of Peru enabled it, moreover, to send assistance to Chile and Buenos Aires ; to aid the province of Tucuman in its war with the Indians of the Chaco ; and to furnish the governor of the Isthmus means to resist the attacks of the filibusters.

The preparations for resisting the attacks proved, however, to be entirely inadequate, and in 1670, during the reign of the Count of Lemos (1667–72), the famous Henry Morgan appeared on the northern coast of the Isthmus, assaulted and took Porto Bello, led his forces across the Isthmus, overthrew the Spanish forces sent out against him, and sacked and burned the city of Panama. This event is notorious among the exploits of the filibusters, not merely on account of the vast amount of booty obtained by the victors, but also for the outrageous cruelty which they manifested towards the inhabitants of the ruined city. The year before this display of British barbarity, in Panama, the city of Lima celebrated the beatification of Santa Rosa, and two years later her canonisation. The magnificence of the latter celebration made a powerful impression on those persons who witnessed it, and descriptions of it have survived in the literature of that day.[1]

[1] " Comparsas á caballo, numerosos procesiones, carros y arcos triunfales ; suntuosos altares enriquecidos de piedras preciosas, adornos

VI

A few months after this celebration, the Count of Lemos, the viceroy, died, leaving a reputation for piety, cruelty, and injustice ; and during the next two years (1672–74) the general affairs of the viceroyalty were controlled by the audiencia. Its administration was characterised by its ordinary weakness as an executive, and when Baltazar de la Cueva, Count of Castellar (1674–78), arrived in Lima and assumed the duties of the viceregal office, he found the capital in commotion over information received from Chile that the English were colonising the coast of the Strait of Magellan and the southern coast of the Pacific. Under the stimulus of this supposed danger, there was manifest great zeal in collecting funds and preparing means for driving out the invaders. Since there was doubt concerning the truth of the information received, resting as it did largely on the testimony of Indians, the viceroy was anxious to avoid burdening the treasury with the expenses of an

y entapizados de las calles, habiendose empedrado algunas de barras de plata y colgado otras de costosas alhajas ; fiestas de toros con juegos de cañas y torneo de cuadrillas de caballeros ricamente adornados, entre quienes se halló el mismo Virey Conde de Lemos, todo esto coronado de los octavarios que se solemnizaron en los templos de Santo Domingo y de la Compañia de Jesús, ilustrados de la mayor riqueza á que se añadió el ingenioso aplauso de un certámon poético con singulares premios ; excedió á cuanto supiera ostentar la devocion y la grandeza y pudieran espresar la historia y la elocuencia" (José Manuel Bermudez, in his *Vida de Santa Rosa*, see Mendiburu, vii. 216). Pedro de Peralta Barnuevo made reference to this celebration in *Lima Fundada*, canto vi. stanza 51 :

> " Argénteas barras todo el pavimento,
> Todos, áureos tapices, los balcones,
> Cada altar diamantino firmamento,
> Cada arco todo ya constelaciones :
> Cada carro un triunfo, á quien atento
> Ate el asombro las admiraciones,
> Todo tal lustre hará, que de su pompa
> El tiempo será fama, el orbe trompa."

expedition designed merely for investigation. He therefore made an appeal for voluntary contributions, and 87,793 pesos were collected, of which he gave 12,000 pesos from his private funds. The vessels sent to reconnoitre the coast made careful observations as far as the fifty-second degree of latitude, but neither on the mainland nor on the adjacent islands were there any indications of foreign settlements.[1]

Many of the persons engaged in this expedition were enlisted in the capital, and when it was discovered that the reported danger did not exist, they returned to their ordinary occupations. The danger from filibusters, however, remained, and various means were instituted for defending the towns of the coast against them. New fortifications were constructed at Valdivia, and plans were formed for garrisoning Valparaiso, Arica, and Guayaquil. Assistance was sent to Panama, which, as the northern gateway to the Pacific, was especially exposed to hostile attacks. The walls of Callao were repaired, and a rigid discipline established for the garrison. The viceroy caused a number of cannon to be made, a great quantity of balls to be cast, and requested twelve thousand firearms from Seville.

On arriving in Peru, Viceroy Castellar found the affairs of the royal treasury in great confusion ; many persons were indebted to it, and some of the accounts were so old that it was no longer possible to collect the sums due. A number of the debts were for the purchase of offices, which indicates that offices, such, for instance, as that of regidor, were sometimes purchased on credit, with the intention, perhaps, on the part of the purchaser, of paying for them out of the profits of the posts. In spite of the large amounts received from the mines, the viceroy found that the treasury at Lima had an annual

---

[1] The cost of the expedition was 84,152 pesos and 4 reales ; instead, therefore, of causing a draft on the treasury, there remained of the 87,793 pesos collected a surplus of 3640 pesos and 4 reales.

deficit of more than two hundred thousand pesos. In seeking a remedy for this state of things, he ordered that he should be informed daily of all of the receipts, and that no payments should be made until the account had been examined and approved by him. Through this rigid system, a very considerable saving was effected, so that during the four years of his incumbency he sent to Spain 4,462,597 pesos ; and during the same period he spent 7,000,000 pesos in salaries and supplies for the different parts of the kingdom, and at the end of this period he left 2,391,562 pesos in the treasury and only 383,727 pesos of debts contracted while he was viceroy ; while of the old debts he collected 535,503 pesos, not counting those of Lima and Pasco, and of this sum 353,788 were collected in Potosi.[1]

In reforming the fiscal affairs of the kingdom, the viceroy sent agents to inspect the different offices of the royal treasury,[2] in some of which great abuses were found to exist. The officials of the treasury at Arica were taken to the presidio at Valdivia ; and the treasurer at La Paz, who had embezzled 400,000 pesos, was hanged. In these and other cases, much was done to improve the condition of the treasury, but, through the process, the viceroy acquired powerful enemies, who were ready to seize any opportunity to bring charges against him. The sending of a ship with a cargo of quicksilver to Mexico, which returned laden with articles from China, was made the occasion for forwarding complaints to the king. The merchants and the consulado affirmed that this was a serious interference with the trade of Porto Bello, and that by it the commerce of Peru had been

[1] Mendiburu, ii. 476 ; Lorente, *Historia del Perú*, 1598–1700, 211–29.

[2] Offices of the royal treasury in Peru then existed in Lima, Huancavelica, Potosi, La Paz, Chucuito, Cailloma, Oruro, Carangas, Caravaya, Cuzco, Arequipa, Arica, Trujillo, Piura, and Otoca (Mendiburu, ii. 474).

brought into a lamentable condition. In spite, therefore, of the viceroy's great service in improving the affairs of the treasury and the advantageous exportation of quicksilver to Mexico, accusations against him were presented to the Crown, which led to his summary recall. Without waiting to hear his side of the case, the king issued a definite order removing him from office and transferring the viceregal power to Archbishop Melchor Liñan y Cisneros.

Archbishop Liñan was born in Madrid in 1629, and was therefore forty-nine years old when he assumed the duties of viceroy in addition to the duties of his ecclesiastical office. His career in America to the end of his term as viceroy extended over a period of seventeen years. He was appointed Bishop of Santa Marta in 1664 ; became Bishop of Popayan in 1666 ; was for a number of years Visitador-General of New Granada, exercising the powers of president, governor, and captain-general ; and in 1672 was appointed Archbishop of Charcas, but he did not arrive in Chuquisaca until August 1675. He was appointed Archbishop of Lima, December 14, 1676, and entered that city in February 1678. In July of the same year, he was charged *ad interim* with the government of the viceroyalty.

In the three years, 1678 to 1681, during which he administered the affairs of the viceregal office, he gave much attention to the hospitals and ecclesiastical institutions. The monasteries were a source of social disorder. The conflicts of the parties in them often reached such a degree of violence that persons were seriously wounded, and on one occasion at least a friar was killed. These conflicts arose in connection with the election of priors, or as manifestations against an unpopular official. They were not always kept within the walls of the monastery, but were sometimes carried into the streets, and were there taken up with such violence by two groups of partizans that the secular authorities were obliged to intervene for the purpose of restoring order.

The tranquillity of the kingdom was also disturbed by the attacks of filibusters on the coasts. They crossed the Isthmus, and records of their depredations are found at Barbacoas, Tumaco, Coquimbo, Serena, and Arica. At Arica they expected to obtain a rich booty of the silver sent down from Potosi, but they encountered a vigorous resistance, and in a fight in the town, which lasted for seven hours, they lost twenty men killed and a large number of prisoners. These events raised doubts in the minds of the inhabitants of the capital concerning the adequacy of Callao's defences; for they recognised that their security depended on the ability of these defences to prevent invasion; and from these doubts arose the suggestion that it would be desirable to build a wall around Lima, but, during the next three or four years, the suggestion did not pass beyond the stage of discussion.

The clergy, moreover, failed to fulfil the expectations of the king and the council with respect to the conversion of the Indians; and the fact that only insignificant results were attained was attributed to the inferior quality of the workers. In view of this state of things and the practical failure of the missions of the Amazon territory, the viceroy-archbishop petitioned the king for authority to form a junta, or commission, to meet in the palace at least once a month to consider ways and means for making the missions more efficient. But progress in this task was hindered by the selfish aspirations of the persons involved in the undertaking, and by quarrels among the ecclesiastics in different parts of the country. The canons of Cuzco were in conflict with their bishop about questions of discipline; and the nuns of Santa Catalina of Quito repudiated all interference with their elections, and indignantly left the convent, creating a great scandal, and dividing the city into two excited and hostile factions. In spite of the archbishop's desire for ecclesiastical peace, he was unable to secure it, even when clothed with the powers of a viceroy.[1]

[1] *Relacion de Don Melchor de Liñan y Cisneros, dada al Señor Duque de la Palata, del tiempo de tres años y cuatro meses que gobernó, desde 1678 hasta 1681,* in *Memorias de lo Vireyes,* i. 261–79 ; Lorente, *Historia del Perú,* 1578–1700, 230–48 ; Mendiburu, v. 1–25.

CHAPTER XI

THE REIGN OF THE DUKE OF PALATA

I. The distress of the Indians and efforts for their relief. II. The
hostility of the archbishop. III. The earthquake of 1687.
IV. The walls of Lima. V. Peru under the Count of Monclova.

I

ARCHBISHOP LIÑAN surrendered his viceregal authority to
Melchor de Navarra y Rocaful, Duke of Palata, on the
arrival of that officer in Lima, in 1681. The Duke of
Palata, a descendant of the kings of Navarre and a member of the Council of the Regency during the minority of
Charles II, is characterised by Ricardo Palma as *el virrey
mas virrey* of all of those who have ruled in Peru.[1] The
formal entry of the new viceroy into the capital was
made on the 20th of November. " Installed in the
palace, he displayed the luxury of a minor monarch,
introduced the etiquette and refinements of a court, and
was seldom seen in the street except in a carriage with
six horses and a brilliant escort." [2]

The viceroy was not, however, absorbed in the forms
and ceremonies of his little court ; in the business of
governing he was sagacious, energetic, laborious, and
just ; and it is said that no one could have uttered with
more reason the phrase : " God is in heaven, the king is
far away, and I rule here." [3]

The grave abuses in the treatment of the Indians early

---

[1] Palma, *Tradiciones peruanas*, i. 272.
[2] *Ibid.*   [3] *Ibid.*

attracted the attention of Palata, and moved him to seek a remedy. On the 20th of February, 1684, he issued an ordinance, which was designed to prevent the spoliation of the Indians by the clergy. Among the provisions of this ordinance were the following : When an Indian dies, the curate, or parish priest, shall not appropriate his property, but it shall be inherited by his children, his relatives, or other persons legally entitled to receive it. No will shall be valid if made by an Indian at the instance of a curate, particularly if the property is left, under the pretext of providing masses or of other acts of charity, to the church or to a brotherhood of his repartimiento or pueblo. The Indians shall not be required to pay for marriages, baptisms, burials, nuptial benedictions, or other ceremonies ; but only such fees as are approved by the government. The curates shall instruct the Indians in the Christian doctrines on Sundays and other holidays, and the boys every day. Obligatory offerings shall not be demanded of any one ; and no one under any pretext of service to the Church shall employ the Indians without paying them.[1]

In spite òf these and other provisions, the Indians remained the victims of their curates, or parish priests, who, instead of protecting them from the extortions of the corregidores, united with these officials to wrest from the Indians the fruit of their toil. Even the next four or five decades brought no relief. Juan and Ulloa, when they wrote their *Noticias secretas de America*, in the first half of the eighteenth century, found the Indians in a most miserable state, struggling to preserve their existence in the face of robbery and oppression by the priests. The character and scientific attainments of these writers, their loyalty to the Crown and their devotion to the interests of the Church are a sufficient guarantee of the truth of their report. They affirm that " as soon as the parish priests are promoted to their cures, they usually bend all

[1] Lorente, *Historia del Perú*, 1598-1700, 258-60.

their efforts to amassing wealth ; and for this purpose they have devised various measures, by which they appropriate to themselves the pittance which may have remained to the Indian, and which has escaped the rapacity of the corregidor."[1]

There were fees on the occasion of a saint's festival, four dollars and a half for high mass, " and an equal amount for the sermon, which consists in merely repeating a few words in praise of the saint "; " to this is to be added the customary offering which the overseers are compelled to make to the curate on every saint's festival, which consists of two or three dozen hens, as many chickens, guinea-pigs, eggs, sheep, and a hog if they happen to have any ; so that when the saint's day arrives, the curate sweeps off all that the Indian has been able to collect in money during the whole year, and also all the fowls and animals which his wife and children have reared in their huts, so that his family are left wholly destitute of food, or have no other aliment than wild plants, and the grain which they cultivate in their small gardens. The Indian who has not been able to rear a sufficient number of animals for the customary offering is bound of necessity to purchase them, and should he not have the money, as is usually the case, he is to take it upon pledge, or hire it for the time required, in order to obtain it and pay it without delay. As soon as the sermon of the day is concluded, the curate reads a paper on which he has inscribed the names of those who are to be masters of ceremonies for the festival of the following year, and if any one does not accept it of his free will, he is forced to give his consent by dint of blows ; and when his day comes, there is no apology that can exonerate him from having the money ready ; for, until it is all collected and delivered to the curate, mass is not said, the sermon is not preached, and the whole service is deferred until three or four in the afternoon, if necessary, to allow time to

[1] Juan and Ulloa, *Noticias secretas*, 335.

collect the amount, as we have had occasion to observe repeatedly.

" In order to be more thoroughly acquainted with the excess to which this is carried, and the enormous gains made by the curates at these festivals, it seems proper to mention here what a curate of the province of Quito told us as we were passing through his curacy, which was that, including the festivals and the commemoration of departed souls, he collected every year more than two hundred sheep, six thousand hens and chickens, four thousand guinea-pigs, and fifty thousand eggs ; and it should be remarked that this curacy was not one of the most lucrative.

" We are then forced to the conclusion that such contributions could be sustained in no way but by tasking to the uttermost not only men and women, but the whole family, in order to exact the payment of the sum total of their earnings during the whole year." [1]

When the Indian boys and girls came every afternoon to be taught the Christian doctrine, they were required to bring bundles of sticks or hay, and by this means fuel was provided, as well as feed for the cattle and horses that belonged to the priests.

" By having recourse to such methods, they have no occasion to spend money for anything ; and while they are maintained by the Indians, they become rich at their expense, for all the offerings they can accumulate are sent to market in the neighbouring cities, hamlets, and mining towns, and are converted into money. By this means, they augment the revenue of a curacy to such a degree, that although the customary fees might not exceed seven or eight hundred dollars, it gives them an income of five or six thousand dollars annually." [2]

But the oppression appears to have been carried to

---

[1] Juan and Ulloa, *Noticias secretas*, 336, 337.   [2] *Ibid.*, 338.

its utmost bounds by the monks who held curacies, and not only by the monk but also by his concubine.

" This woman, who is known as such, and without exciting surprise, because it is everywhere so common, takes under her charge all the Indian women and children, and converting the whole village into a manufactory, she assigns to some tasks in spinning wool or cotton, and to others pieces for weaving ; and to the aged, and to those who are incapable of performing this service, she gives hens, and imposes on them the obligation of delivering to her, within a definite time, ten or twelve chickens for each one ; it being their duty to feed them at their own expense and, if the fowls should die, to replace them with others ; and by these means no one is exempted from contributing something to the revenue of the curate." [1]

Moreover, the curate's farm was cultivated by the Indians on Sunday.

" The wretched state of the Indian is to be attributed to the vices of the priests, the extortions of the corregidors, and the bad treatment which they generally receive from all Spaniards. Unable to endure the hardships, and longing to escape from bondage, many of them have risen in rebellion, and found their way to unconquered districts, there to continue in the barbarous practices of their idolatrous neighbours ; and in view of the foregoing, what conclusions are they to form from the scandalous lives of their parish priests ? especially when we reflect that the Indian is but partially civilised, and taught rather by example than by precept." [2]

The Indian town of Pimampiro furnished a case in point. It contained more than five thousand inhabitants.

" The behaviour of the parish priest drove them to desperation. Uniting in one body, they rose in rebellion, and proceeded by night to the cordilleras, where they

---

[1] Juan and Ulloa, *Noticias secretas*, 340.   [2] *Ibid.*, 343.

merged themselves with the Gentile Indians, with whom they have continued until the present time." [1]

Similar instances were found in the disappearance of the towns of Lograno and Guariboya.

The Laws of the Indies lay much stress on the religious education of the Indians. A glimpse of the system employed and of the results obtained is presented by this report on the ceremony of instructing the Indians in Christian doctrine on Sundays :

" All the Indians, male and female, great and small, are to present themselves, and, gathering in the cemetery or square in front of the church, they sit upon the ground, arranged according to age and sex, and the catechising or doctrine commences in the following manner : Each curate employs a blind Indian, whose duty is to repeat the *doctrine* to the rest. The blind Indian is stationed in the centre of them all and, with a kind of recitative, which is neither singing nor praying, he repeats the collects or offices word for word, and the audience responds in the form of a dialogue. The doctrine is sometimes rehearsed in the language of the Inca (which is that of the Indians), and sometimes in Spanish, which is not intelligible to any of them. This saying of prayers lasts somewhat more than half an hour, and it comprises all the religious instruction which is given to the Indians— a method from which they derive so little benefit that old men of seventy know no more than the little Indian boys of the age of six, and neither these nor those have any further instruction than parrots would obtain if they were so taught, for they are neither questioned personally, nor are the mysteries of faith explained to them with the needful simplicity, nor are they examined to see if they understand what they say, nor do they endeavour to make it more intelligible to those who are dull of comprehension. As the whole instruction is confined rather to the tone of the recitative than to the sense of the

---

[1] Juan and Ulloa, *Noticias secretas*, 343.

words, it is only by singing that they are able to re-
hearse detached portions ; for, when they are questioned upon any distinct point, they cannot join two
words together." [1]

" The curate has no other object in view than to make
everyone bring the little presents required ; and when he
has collected these, which consist of what they may
happen to have, and has taken a note of those who have
failed to bring any, in order afterwards to call them to
account, he thinks he is discharged from any further
obligation." [2]

At the church festivals, which were followed by orgies
of intoxication, the priests did not interfere to preserve
order, but were apparently interested only in the gain
that was derived from them.

To the authors of the *Noticias secretas*, the religion of
the Indians who were said to be converted or christianised
did not resemble the Christian religion any more than it
resembled " that which they had while they were in a
state of paganism ; for, if we examine the subject with
care, it will be found that, notwithstanding the nominal
conversion of these tribes, the progress they have made
in knowledge is so inconsiderable that it will be difficult
to discover any difference between the condition in which
they now live and that in which they were found at the
time of the conquest." [3]

II

The archbishop resented the intervention of the viceroy
in the affairs of the Church. He resented, in fact, the
action of the Crown, which deprived him of his civil
functions ; and he expressed his resentment in an unreasonable and abusive opposition to Palata's administration. He introduced into his sermons bitter denunciation

[1] Juan and Ulloa, *Noticias secretas*, 351.
[2] *Ibid.*, 352.　　　[3] *Ibid.*, 353.

of the viceroy's conduct, describing it as anti-catholic, and attributing to it the misfortunes and reverses of the kingdom. He affirmed, moreover, that it had provoked the anger of God, which was shown in the disasters that had afflicted Peru : the earthquakes, the incursions of the pirates, and the destruction of the warship *Capitana* by fire. In his jealous hostility, the archbishop declared that the Church and even the pulpit had been scandalously profaned by the family of the viceroy.

While the archbishop remained pertinacious, the viceroy requested the ministers of the audiencia not to visit him, and ordered the judges of the other tribunals not to go to the cathedral on the occasion of certain ceremonies. The ecclesiastical cabildo went to the palace and made excuses for the archbishop ; but while the viceroy expressed his appreciation of the spirit of these ecclesiastics and of their willingness to mediate, he preferred that the archbishop, who had delivered the obnoxious sermons, should make his excuses in person. He, moreover, ordered the archbishop not to interfere in the government, although he might not approve of it ; for it was not his function or the function of the pulpit to censure the civil government. The controversy which followed revealed various phases of the archbishop's puerile vanity, and his desire not to have it forgotten that he had been the viceroy of Peru. He wished to drive with a carriage and six horses, in order that his former state might not appear to have suffered any diminution, and that the viceroy might not seem to exceed him in dignity. On one occasion, when the viceroy was returning from Callao, the archbishop went out to meet him, and the two officials returned to the city in the same carriage ; but this was only an apparent reconciliation, and a little later the hostility of the archbishop reappeared in unabated force.

The archbishop entered the more willingly, and with the more zeal, into the conflict with the viceroy, because he regarded himself as defending a sacred cause, and in his quality as a priest enjoyed a support in the sentiments of the inhabitants which no secular officer possessed. He derived, moreover, no little confidence from the fact that the Church received an enormous income, which, to a very great extent, was subject to his control. In the enjoyment of these advantages, and persuaded that his power was derived from a superhuman source, it was easy for him to assume that he ruled without responsibility to any temporal authority. A consequence of this pretension of the archbishop was the claim of the lower members of the ecclesiastical organisation to be independent of the local civil government. In the reductions of the Indians, therefore, the expressed will of the missionary became the law, and the power of each priest in his district, or parish, was absolute.[1]

An instance of the unwillingness of the archbishop to co-operate with the viceroy appears in connection with the rebuilding of the churches destroyed by the earthquake of 1687. In this undertaking neither the archbishop not the ecclesiastical cabildo would render any assistance, and they held that all the cost of reconstruction should be borne by the royal treasury, and that they were under no obligation to assist in the work.[2]

III

The earthquake of 1687 occurred on the 20th of October; but there had been frequent shocks during the previous months of that year. The first shock on this occasion was felt at four o'clock in the morning. Many persons rushed to the churches, and two hours later a more violent shock occurred, which threw down the walls of the buildings, already more or less shattered by previous shocks. The tower of the Dominican church fell,

[1] Lorente, *Historia del Perú*, 1598–1700, 263.
[2] *Memorias de los Vireyes*, ii. 4.

crushing the edifice, and burying many persons in the ruins. The surviving inhabitants fled to the open spaces, and made temporary camps in the squares and in the suburbs. The viceroy and the principal families took refuge in the central plaza ; but here the continuance of earthquakes kept everybody in a state of terror, which was intensified by the panic that prevailed throughout the city, and by the exhortations of priests calling the people to repent of their sins, which had brought this disaster upon the country.

On the night of December 2, it was reported that the sea was rising and overwhelming the land ; and this report, believed by everybody, spread terror and consternation throughout the city, and there was a mad rush for the hills, in which each person was unmindful and careless of the fate of others, even though these might be persons for whom ordinarily he felt the greatest solicitude and affection. The viceroy, however, remained at his post, in order to prevent the city from being pillaged by the unterrified bandits. He sent a captain of his guard to ascertain the truth concerning the reported advance of the sea, and during the hour and a half of the captain's absence the bulk of the city's inhabitants believed themselves in the presence of inevitable destruction.

As a consequence of this earthquake, many persons became ill from excitement and fear, from privation and exposure, and from the impossibility of obtaining proper treatment, on account of the lack of physicians and the destruction of the shops of the apothecaries. Through the earthquake, moreover, an important change was effected in the coast lands of Peru. Much of their productiveness was destroyed, and the inhabitants became dependent on Chile for their required supply of wheat. These lands remained unproductive for three or four decades, after which the cultivation of wheat was resumed. Juan and Ulloa, in their *Voyage to South America*, affirm that before the earthquake " the harvests of wheat and barley were sufficient to supply the wants of the country without any importation, especially of wheat; but by this convulsion of nature, the soil was so vitiated, that the wheat rotted soon after it was sown, occasioned, probably, by the vast clouds of sulphureous particles then exhaled, and the prodigious quantities of nitrous effluvia diffused through it. This obliged the owners of the lands to apply them to other uses, and accordingly many of them were turned into meadows of clover, plantations of sugar-cane, and other vegetables, which they found not subject to the same misfortune." [1]

IV

For more than a hundred years after the arrival of Francis Drake in 1578, Lima had been subject to the attacks of filibusters, and in the reign of Palata, they extended their depredations along the coast, sacking the towns of Guayaquil, Paita, Saña, Pisco, Arica, and others of less importance. With the growth of the towns, and the accumulation of jewels and other articles of great value that might be easily carried away, there was manifest an increasing desire on the part of the inhabitants to have some means provided to protect them against piratical incursions. The report of the sacking of Vera Cruz, in 1683, offered a concluding argument in favour of fortifying the capital. Previously there had been much fruitless discussion of various projects; but this event impressed upon all classes the need of practical action. In October of this year, the viceroy wrote to the ayuntamiento of Lima, and asked it to consider the question of building the proposed wall about the city, and to decide what means for carrying on the work would be the least burdensome. He wrote also to the consulado, the university, the religious orders, and to various other organisations. After somewhat elaborate negotiations,

[1] *A Voyage to South America*, ii. 94.

it was finally determined how much each association should pay, or what part of the wall it should build, and what taxes should be levied in order to obtain the funds needed for the undertaking.[1]

The building of the walls was not a measure interesting merely one class, party, or faction ; it concerned everybody ; and every social group exerted its influence to support it. For many weeks the preachers based their sermons on biblical texts that referred to walls, towers, and battlements. The general interest in the undertaking caused important voluntary contributions to be made to the fund created to meet the expenses of the structure. The merchants agreed to construct three thousand varas of the main wall, and the Jesuits undertook to build one of the bastions. The university gave ten thousand pesos, and an equal amount was contributed by each of several organisations : the ecclesiastical cabildo ; the order of the Dominicans ; and the order of La Merced. The enterprise was carried on so successfully that in less than three years, fourteen thousand varas of the main wall, fourteen bastions, and five gates had been constructed. When completed the wall had seven gates, and it was flanked by thirty-four bastions. It was built of brick, and was between eighteen and twenty-five feet high, but was not surrounded by a moat.[2]

The three achievements that have been mentioned as constituting the most lasting monuments of Palata's government, were the construction of the walls of Lima, the establishment of the mint in the capital, and the writing of the memorial which Palata left to his successor. The shipment of silver from Lima to Panama for transportation to Spain, sometimes took away from the city

---

[1] For Palata's account of the voluntary contributions and the various taxes imposed to furnish funds for the construction of the wall, see *Memorias de los Vireyes*, ii. 365–96.

[2] *Memorias de los Vireyes*, ii. 384 ; Lorente, *Historia del Perú*, 1598–1700, 291–3 ; Juan and Ulloa, *A Voyage to South America*, ii. 33 : *A True and Particular Relation of the dreadful Earthquake*.

so much of the coined money that there was not enough remaining in circulation to enable the government to make its payments or to mediate the commercial exchanges, since the coin received from Potosi was all demanded for other purposes. A mint was, therefore, required at Lima to furnish coin to take the place of that which was withdrawn from circulation from time to time for exportation or to be sent to distant garrisons. Both Potosi and Seville were opposed to the creation of a mint at Lima, lest it might diminish the work at the mints of those cities, from which they derived a considerable advantage. And the viceroy in turn, and more successfully, opposed the erection of a mint at Cuzco, notwithstanding the fact that a concession had been obtained from the Crown, permitting the creation of such an establishment in that city.

The Duke of Palata held the post of viceroy of Peru for eight years. He ruled with dignity, and displayed many of the qualities of a clear-sighted statesman. He did not, however, solve all the problems which the kingdom presented in his time. The questions relating to the status of the Indians remained unanswered when he surrendered his authority, and for the greater part they have remained unanswered ever since. The honours to which he might legitimately have aspired on retiring to Spain after successful service were never attained. He was obliged to wait at Porto Bello some days for a vessel, and died there a victim of yellow fever.

V

Melchor Portocarrero, Count of Monclova, succeeded the Duke of Palata as viceroy in 1689, and governed the viceroyalty for sixteen years, or until 1705. The reputation which he had acquired in Mexico contributed to his favourable reception in Peru, where his many virtues, his conciliatory conduct, and his interest in his subjects, made him respected and admired by all classes. His long reign covered the last years of the government of Charles II, which was too feeble to exert any beneficent influence in the affairs of the viceroyalty. With the Crown incompetent to contribute any force for the improvement of Peruvian society, and with the viceroy disposed to compromise all factional differences, there existed the con ditions of peace, but no prospects of progress. The uncertainty concerning the fate of the Spanish Crown, in view of the anticipated death of Charles II, tended, moreover, to paralyse the colonial administration. The officials of all classes felt that their tenure of office was insecure, and in this position they were not disposed to put forth any positive energy in carrying out new measures of administration ; and Monclova's lack of creative power fitted him to rule in a period of social stagnation.

Only four years had passed since the earthquake of 1687, and the first business of the viceroy was to encourage the inhabitants to complete the reconstruction of Lima. By a liberal expenditure of the wealth that had been gathered from the mines, the new buildings became superior to those that had been thrown down ; and thus the new Lima was more worthy than the old to be the seat of the viceregal court. It had at this time seventy thousand inhabitants, comprising thirty thousand Indians, ten thousand whites, ten thousand mestizos, and twenty thousand slaves. The houses, built around extensive courts, or patios, occupied large lots, but for the most part were only one story high. On all sides there were evidences of wealth and of a desire on the part of the citizens for luxurious display. There were paintings from Rome and Seville, fine cloths from Flanders, velvets from Toledo, taffetas from Granada, and various articles of ornament from China ; and there were gold, diamonds, pearls, and precious stones in abundance.

The convents and monasteries occupied much space in the city : the Jesuits had four houses ; the Dominicans

202 THE SPANISH DEPENDENCIES

and Franciscans each three ; the Augustinians and the order of La Merced each two ; and one each belonged to San Juan de Dios and the Beletmitas. The university had twenty-four professorships and fifteen hundred students. The city was the seat of a number of tribunals : the audiencia ; the Inquisition ; the principal tribunal of accounts ; the consulado ; the ecclesiastical tribunal ; the tribunal of the cruzada ; and the probate court. The nobles of Lima eclipsed with their luxury the grandees of Spain. The favourite drive, called the *Alameda de los Descalzos*, at the fashionable hour was crowded with carriages and calesas. There were guilds and associations of various kinds, and public and private charity made the lot of the beggars of Lima such that it might be envied by the artisans of Madrid.[1]

Callao was not merely the port of Lima ; but was a town of four thousand or five thousand inhabitants, with five monasteries, a hospital, and a house where the viceroy resided during his visits to the port. The cities of Cuzco, Arequipa, Guamanga, and Trujillo derived a certain social importance from the fact that they were residencies of bishops. Cuzco, moreover, a city of forty thousand inhabitants, enjoyed the prestige that came to it as the capital of the ancient Inca kingdom. It was the seat of a flourishing university, and was regarded as the advanced post of civilisation towards the unconquered tribes beyond the Andes. Arequipa, occupying a fertile oasis in the desert, had only a small population, but its delicious climate and its opportunities for cultivation by irrigation gave it hopeful prospects of permanent prosperity. Many of the other towns founded by the early explorers had not realised their expectations. Potosi still continued to be a populous and influential city, although the product of its mines had suffered a material diminution. In the later decades of the seventeenth century the towns grew, in relation to the whole population, less

[1] Lorente, *Historia del Perú*, 1598–1700, 328.

rapidly than earlier ; for as the Indians no longer made
life in the country dangerous, and as the profits of mining
had declined, many persons turned to the cultivation of
sugar-cane and such other products as were adapted to
the soil and climate.

Groups of persons, men, women, and children, were
gathered on the various plantations, where they lived
under the proprietor of the estate in a condition of dependence not greatly unlike that of the feudal vassals
under the medieval baron. This form of life received
recruits from the towns and from some of the reductions
established by the missionaries. But an examination of
the native population shows that there was not merely a
redistribution of the Indians ; it indicates that large
numbers of them had disappeared. Some had undoubtedly fled to the tribes that were still unconquered ;
yet this will not account for the diminution in the number
of those who rendered service under the system of the
mita, and for the lessening amount of the tribute received.
The Indians shared what appears to be the inevitable
fate of an undeveloped people when conquered by a
civilised race. The severe and regular labour, under
which the civilised man will thrive, leads to the destruction of the undisciplined race. The civilised man has,
moreover, means for defending himself more or less
successfully against certain diseases, before which the
Indian was entirely helpless. In this period and at
various other times, the Indians, in their ignorance and
fatalistic prejudices, were destroyed in great numbers by
the smallpox. But, in the larger cities, they disappeared
less rapidly than in the country, for they participated to
a certain extent in the provisions against diseases enjoyed
by the community under a civilised administration.

The lot of the Indians in Peru, where the negro slaves
were numerous, indicates that the introduction of the
negroes did not produce the results anticipated. The
oppression of the native race was not set aside, and

wherever the negroes appeared in great numbers, they brought into the commonwealth an element of corruption and demoralisation. The European part of the population, by reason of the restrictions which were placed on emigration from Spain, did not grow with sufficient rapidity to enable it to preserve itself from the contamination of mixture with the less developed race. Moreover, the great importance that was attached to luxurious living by the creoles often accentuated the discouragement of those persons whose economic affairs were not prosperous ; and their inability to satisfy a worldly ambition often led to the renunciation of a career that promised only labour and disappointment in favour of the security and repose of the conventual life. Under this state of things, moreover, young men found a new attractiveness in the priestly calling, where it was not difficult to conform to the established standard. Monasteries and convents were multiplied, and many persons became social parasites, who, in another capacity, might have made important contributions to the creation and organisation of that material basis which is essential to the permanence and development of civilisation.

In the last decades of the century, the country had only imperfect facilities for transportation, and on this account its agricultural products had a very narrow market. This tended to set a limit to the cultivation of the soil. The inhabitants of the towns that had grown up about the mines were the most liberal purchasers, on account of the generally larger incomes which they received. The finer manufactured articles demanded by a comparatively small number of persons, were imported from Spain, while those made in the country for the use of the bulk of the population were usually much cheaper and of rude construction. Some of those produced by the silversmiths were, however, of excellent design and careful workmanship. The Chinese wares which had already become conspicuous in Lima, were derived from

China through Mexico, and constituted the principal item in the Peruvian-Mexican trade. The three principal commodities of the internal trade were coca, maté from Paraguay, and mules from Tucuman. But whatever profits were derived from agriculture, industry, and commerce accrued to a small minority of the inhabitants. The negro slaves, the Indians, and the greater part of the persons of mixed blood had little or no share in the general material improvement which resulted from the better social organisation and the development of the country's abundant resources.

CHAPTER XII

THE CHURCH IN RELATION TO THE CIVIL GOVERNMENT

I. The royal patronage.   II. The beginnings of the ecclesiastical organisation in America.   III. The great power of the king in ecclesiastical affairs.   IV. The general organisation of the Church.

I

THE peculiar relation which the Church in Spanish America held to the King of Spain and to the Spanish colonial government in America was due, in a great measure, to the fact that independently the pope was unable to occupy the great missionary field that was opened to the Church by the discovery of America. He "could do nothing by himself in this immense territory; he had not the means of establishing in it the institutions necessary for the propagation of religion, nor was it even possible for an order by him to reach that region unless carried by a costly expedition." [1]   Whatever ecclesiastics or other persons went thither were obliged to follow the direction of the Spanish Crown, or the captain to whom they were subordinated.   It was not possible for the Holy See to proceed in christianising the inhabitants of the New World, except by abiding by the rules, and soliciting the aid, of the civil power.   The pope had subjects who were not Spaniards, whom he might wish to employ in the work of converting the Indians, but the execution of such a plan was in a large measure prevented by the king's order limiting the emigration to the colonies to Spanish subjects; but in

[1] Velez Sarsfield, Dalmacio, *Relaciones del Estado con la Iglesia en la antigua America Española* (Buenos Aires, 1889), 18.

spite of this order there were members of other nationalities in the various religious organisations who served as
missionaries in America. Whatever power over America
the pope may have claimed, with or without valid ground,
had been transferred to the Crown of Spain by the bull
of Alexander VI in 1493. This transfer with respect to
the territories in question was absolute and entire : " We
give, concede, and assign them in perpetuity to you and
the Kings of Castile and of Leon, your heirs and successors ;
and we make, constitute, and depute you and your heirs
and successors, the aforesaid, lords of these lands, with
free, full, and absolute power, authority, and jurisdiction." [1]

The king, by reason of his position as monarch, was
the supreme patron of the Church in Spanish America.
In a royal decree of 1574, it was declared that " the right
of patronage of the Indies is, alone and undivided, forever
reserved to us and our royal crown, and may not be
alienated therefrom either wholly or in part." [2]

In keeping with this power, the bull of Julius II, concerning the patronage, conceded primarily that in the
regions discovered, or which in the future might be discovered, no churches, monasteries, or pious places might
be established without the consent of the king. It
conceded also the power to present suitable persons for
the metropolitan churches and the other cathedrals

[1] The bull of Alexander VI, May 4, 1493 ; Peschel, *Die Theilung
der Erde unter Papst Alexander VI and Julius II*, 13–15. In the appendix are printed the first and second bulls of Alexander VI and the
treaty of Tordesillas. The gift of Alexander VI was modified by the
treaty of Tordesillas, which was confirmed by Julius II in 1506, and
which partitioned the world between Portugal and Spain by a line
through the ocean from the north to the south pole, three hundred and
seventy leagues west of the Cape Verde Islands. Inasmuch as these
islands lie scattered over two and a half leagues of longitude, the real
position of this line of demarcation was still not precisely determined.
See *Doc. inéd.*, xvi. 356.

[2] Parras, in *Gobierno de los Regulares de la America*, i. 3, affirms :
" No puede darse real patronato mas completo, mas singular y priva-
tivo, que el que gozan los Reyes Católicos en Estado de las Indias."

already erected or which in the future might be erected, and for all other ecclesiastical livings whatsoever.

In the decree of 1574, Philip II based the claim of the Spanish Crown to the right of patronage in the Indies not merely on the fact that it had been granted by the popes, but also on the fact that the New World had been discovered and acquired by the king and that churches had been built and endowed in it at his expense and at the expense of his predecessors, the Catholic kings.[1]

The papal bull conceded to the Catholic kings " all the tithes of the state of the Indies, under the provision that they should endow the churches and provide the priests with proper support." [2]   The king, however, transferred his right to receive the tithes to the bishops, the churches, the hospitals, and other institutions destined to receive them.   To this end the mass of the tithes was divided into four parts.   Two of these parts were assigned, in equal shares, to the prelate and the chapter ; and the sum of the other two parts was subdivided into nine divisions and further distributed.   In this distribution, two of these secondary parts were reserved for the king ; [3]   three

[1] Restrepo, *La Iglesia y el Estado en Colombia* (London, 1885), cap. i. See Castel-Fuerte on the patronage in *Memorias de los Vireyes,* iii. 103–19.

Zamora, moved by his ecclesiastical prejudices, holds a view somewhat narrower than that entertained by Philip II concerning the basis of the royal patronage : " El Real Patronato de Indias descansa todo entero en los siguientos documentos pontificios : I. Bula de Alejandro VI, 1493, 4 de Mayo, concediendo á los Reyes Católicos el dominio de Indias. 2. Idem íd., 16 de Noviembre de 1501, concediendo á los Reyes de Castilla los diezmos y primicias en Indias. 3. Idem de Julio II, 28 de Julio de 1508, que concedió á los Reyes de Castilla, taxativamente, el derecho de Patronato universal, cabal y completo."— Zamora, Matías Gómez, *Regio Patronato español é indiano* (Madrid, 1897), 292.

[2] Parras, i. 6 ; Bula en que se concedió á los Reyes Cathólicos, los Diezmos e primicias de las Indias (December 16, 1501), *Doc. inéd.,* xxxiv. 22–5 ; Bull of Pope Julius II on the creation of cathedrals and the presentation of bishops (July 28, 1508), *Doc. inéd.,* xxxiv. 25–9 ; Zamora, *Regio Patronato,* 299–301.

[3] On the disposition of these parts, see *Leyes de Indias,* lib. i. tit. xvi. ley 24.

were divided between the hospital and the fund for building churches; and from the remaining four was drawn the support of the curates, whiie the rest was given to the prebendaries. In ca⁻·: of a vacancy in the position of a prelate, the tithes reverted to the king; but he relinquished them in favour of the church, one half going to maintain the worship during the vacancy, the other half to the succeeding prelate.

The position assumed by the Crown set aside the grounds of the medieval debate between the Church and the State. With respect to Spain's American dominions, papal action was subject to criticism and veto by royal authority. That this power was not used to hinder the work of the Church may be inferred from the fact that, as new settlements were made, the field of practical activity of the Church was expanded. The work of attempting to convert the Indians everywhere attended the conquests of the civil power; the Church even encountered no opposition in erecting its peculiar tribunals of the Inquisition. The king was dominant, but he was in sympathy with the purposes and methods of the Church; and it was this sympathy which made peaceful co-operation possible where the relations of the Church with the sovereign had " no precedents either in law or in ecclesiastical usages or customs."[1] In this phase of American history we have to do not with the ecclesiastical law of Europe transplanted, but with laws and pontifical briefs and bulls framed for America and a new body of civil legislation which comprehends the administration and government of the Church of the New World.[2]

At the beginning of the conquest the plan for converting the Indians was only partially formed. Any ecclesiastics available were employed, and these served as priests for the Spaniards and Indians without obtaining or even asking a licence from the bishop; in fact, there were at the time no bishops whose jurisdiction embraced

[1] Velez Sarsfield, 22. [2] Ibid., 23.

any part of America. " The whole region was governed by the king, and was subject to his direction, administration, or nomination, or to those who acted in his stead in virtue of the commission and delegation which they held for this purpose from the Apostolic See." [1]

II

The first bishopric organised in America was that founded by Leo X in 1518. The seat of the bishop was to be at Baracoa, Cuba, which at that time possessed the only church on the island. But before the decree creating the bishopric had been carried out, other towns had been established, and Santiago had become the residence of the governor and of the principal men of the colony. In 1522 the town of Santiago was made the capital of the bishopric. The position of bishop was first offered to Bernardino Mesa, and then to Julian Garcés, but it is not known that either of these ever actually performed any of the functions of the office. The first person consecrated Bishop of Cuba was John De Witt, who was born in the Netherlands. He, however, never went to Cuba, but undertook some of the duties of his office while at Valladolid. From that city, on March 8, 1523, he issued instructions for the organisation of the chapter of the cathedral of Santiago. In 1525 he retired from the bishopric, and the see remained vacant till 1536. In the meantime the ecclesiastical affairs of the island fell into disorder.

In the beginning, the island of Jamaica fell within the jurisdiction of the Bishop of Cuba, but it was soon separated from the Cuban diocese, and erected into an abbacy. Subsequently an effort was made by Bishop De Witt to have it reincorporated in his bishopric, but in this he was unsuccessful.[2]

[1] Solórzano, *Política Indiana*, ii. 122.
[2] Pezuela, *Historia de la Isla de Cuba*, i. 123–5.

Under decrees of the Church authorising the various religious orders to undertake work for the conversion of the natives in the Indies, a rapidly increasing number of ecclesiastics found their way to the New World. As early as July 1524, we find Martin de Valencia in Mexico assembling the friars who had come with him from Spain and those already in the country for the purpose of assigning to them their several fields of labour. The region about the City of Mexico was divided into four districts, and to each four friars were assigned, while Valencia himself devoted his efforts to the capital. In these districts convents were established, the religious life organised, and plans matured for bringing the natives into submission to ecclesiastical authority.

The Franciscan and Dominican friars had extended their missionary efforts over a large part of New Spain before these regions were formally brought under the jurisdiction of the organised Church. In 1519 Julian Garcés was made Bishop of Cozumel, an island off the coast of Yucatan. There were found to be very few settlers within the limits of this bishopric, even after it had been extended to the neighbouring peninsula, and in 1526 it was made to embrace the districts of Tabasco, Vera Cruz, and Tlascala. The official seat of the bishop was in Tlascala. About the time that Garcés appeared in Tlascala to assume the duties of his charge, another bishopric was created with the City of Mexico as its capital ; and in December 1527 it was bestowed upon Juan de Zumárraga. The new bishop was also charged with the power of Protector of the Indians ; but in attempting to perform the duties implied in this title, he found himself opposed not only by the Spanish settlers but also by the audiencia.

The fact that the spiritual teachings of the bishop and his followers were not heeded by men of his own nationality, that organised authority was employed to further measures of injustice, and that great wrongs were inflicted on the natives by the Spanish settlers, helped to weaken the moral influence of those who pretended to preach a gospel of peace and goodwill to all men. The authorities in Spain, however, appeared to have confidence in Zumárraga, and sought his advice concerning the government of the Indians, and the means of improving their condition. For this purpose he was recalled to Spain in 1532. On this occasion his plans and previous labours were approved, his title of Protector of the Indians was confirmed, and the audiencia was instructed to co-operate with him in carrying out his designs. On this occasion, also, he was solemnly consecrated as the first Bishop of Mexico. This ceremony was performed at Valladolid on April 27, 1533 ; and before he returned to Mexico he issued from Toledo a letter appointing the members of the chapter of the cathedral, and establishing rules for the government of his diocese. The chapter as organised consisted of a dean, archdeacon, precentor, chancellor, treasurer, ten canons, and other officials, whose salaries ranged from thirty-five to one hundred and fifty dollars a month.

In 1534, the year of Zumárraga's return to America, New Spain was divided into four political divisions, which were designated as the provinces of Mexico, Michoacan, Goazacoalco, Miztecapan. In addition to the two bishoprics which had already been created, two others were now formed, and the four were known as Mexico, Michoacan, Tlascala, and Oajaca. These were made to correspond to four political provinces ; but their boundaries were only imperfectly determined. It was ordered that each bishopric should embrace all points within a radius of fifteen leagues from its cathedral town taken as a centre ; that the intervening territory should be divided equally between the adjoining sees ; and that if any principal town lay near a boundary, its district should belong to the diocese in which the town lay. Of the new bishoprics, that of Oajaca was conferred upon Juan Lopez de Zárate, while that of Michoacan was given to Vasco de Quiroga, who had been a member of the audiencia, and who took priestly orders after his appointment.

In the course of time other bishoprics were created, and that of Mexico was made an archdiocese. The papal bull confirming this change was issued July 8, 1547. The jurisdiction of the Archbishop of Mexico was extended over the Bishops of Tlascala, Michoacan, Oajaca, Nueva Galicia, Yucatan, Guatemala, Chiapas, Honduras, and Nicaragua. The position of archbishop was offered to Zumárraga, but he declined it on account of his great age. A few days after the arrival of the documents conveying to him the appointment, he died in his eightieth year, on June 3, 1548.[1]

Attempts were made to avoid conflicts of interests between the regular and secular clergy. The bishops and archbishops were instructed neither to establish parish priests in Indian towns and reductions where there existed monasteries and monks holding curacies, nor to found a monastery of any order whatsoever, where parish priests had already been established ; and if " monks should preach in the towns where there were parish priests, the archbishop or the bishop should request them to go elsewhere or return to their monasteries," and to confine their missionary labours to places where it might be necessary or possible, in accordance with the law, and under the proper authority, to found a monastery or monasteries.[2]

No monk could become a curate or parish priest, except through a special nomination by the vice-patron, and in case of such nominations it was required that there should always be due recognition of the authority of the king as the supreme patron. The person thus promoted was required to know the language of the natives he was expected to teach. His fitness in this and other respects

[1] In searching out Aztec manuscripts and causing them to be destroyed, Zumárraga acted under laws and instructions issued by the authorities in Spain.

[2] *Leyes de Indias*, lib. i. tit. xiii. ley 2.

was determined by an examination held by the prelate of the diocese or by persons of his appointment. In appointing the priest, the name was sent to the viceroy, president, or governor, who exercised the functions of royal patron in the name of the king.[1]

Not only the archbishops and bishops, but also the viceroys and governors were instructed " by all possible means to seek continually to know the monks who were in their districts " ; and they should inquire if more were needed, keeping an account of the number admitted, and of the special religious work they were called to perform. The provincials of all the orders were required to reside in the Indies ; and each was expected to keep a list of all the monasteries in his district, and of all the persons belonging to them. Any commissioner taking monks to America had to report to the Council of the Indies their names, ages, places of birth, and the provinces or monasteries in Europe from which they came. After they had been approved by the council, their names were also recorded in the casa de contratacion at Seville. The expenses of supporting and transporting them were met by the royal treasury through the casa de contratacion. Great care was taken that all the monks who had been approved by the council should be embarked for America ; and if at the time of embarking any were wanting, they should be brought in and embarked with the rest. Nor should they be allowed to remain in the Canaries, if for any reason the vessels halted there on the outward passage; but from those islands no monk might go to America without the royal licence. Generally, foreigners, even when they held licences from their superiors, were not permitted by the casa de contratacion to go to the Indies. Also, monks not in obedience to their prelates were not passed, nor were those belonging to orders having no convents in the Indies. If any such should find their way to America, the governors of the ports of their landing

[1] *Leyes de Indias*, lib. i. tit. xv. leyes 1–14.

were instructed to return them to Spain, unless they carried a special licence from the king. A licence to go to America served only for the first voyage. Having returned to Spain, one was not permitted to go a second time without a new licence. If monks were sent to the Indies at the expense of the royal treasury, they were obliged to go to the places to which they had been assigned. And they were held to this order, even though they returned to the royal treasury the amount that had been advanced in their behalf. Those, however, who wished to go to the Philippine Islands were allowed to do so without hindrance ; and by a law of 1572, the civil authorities were commanded to allow Jesuits bearing licences from their superiors to pass unhindered from province to province, and they were to be aided in accordance with their needs.[1]

Regarding the monasteries to be founded in the Indian towns, the law provided that they must be at least six leagues distant from one another, and that the buildings should be plain and of moderate size. In case the encomiendas had been incorporated in the Crown, the cost of construction should be borne by the king ; but in case the encomiendas were held by private persons, they should be built at the expense of the king and the encomenderos, aided by the Indians of the towns as they might be able. Each monastery founded in the Indies with the royal licence and in new towns should be provided out of the royal treasury with an ornament, a chalice with its cover, and a bell.

Every three years the viceroys, presidents, and governors were required to make a detailed report concerning the monks in their respective districts, and on the basis of these reports, the king determined whether it was advisable or not to send inspectors to the Indies. If sent, they were to observe the state of the monks, on what points reform was needed ; they were also required to

---

[1] *Leyes de Indias*, lib. i. tit. xiv. leyes 1–26.

avoid unnecessary disturbance, and always aim at the perfection of the religious life.[1]

The close union of civil and ecclesiastical affairs is seen in the fact that the laws regulating both are brought together in a single code. The *Recopilacion de Leyes de las Indias* contains not only the purely political laws, but also those regulating the conduct of the officers of the cathedral. The latter provided that the prebendaries should reside in the churches to which they belonged ; that they should not absent themselves from the services in which they had been assigned parts ; and that they should not go out for visits or for any other purpose, except under permission granted by superior authority. The penalty for violation of these regulations was a loss of office. Permission, in cases of great necessity, might be granted by the prelate and the chapter ; but if the prelate and the chapter could not agree, the viceroy, the president, or the governor should unite with them to effect a decision. The archbishops and bishops were required to take such measures as would enforce, on the part of the prebendaries, a complete fulfilment of their obligations, and to collect a fine in case of failure in this respect. The prelates, the viceroys, the presidents, and the governors were expected to make detailed reports to the king concerning the prebendaries ; those actually in service, those who had died, and the existing vacancies and the causes of them. These civil officers were prohibited from granting licences to go to Spain to the archbishops, bishops, or the holders of any other ecclesiastical office or benefice, the granting of such licences being strictly reserved to the king.[2]

In relation to the conduct of affairs the clergy were subject to important limitations. No member of the clergy might be an alcalde, an advocate, or a notary, nor an agent of the encomenderos, or of any other person ; neither were

---

[1] *Leyes de Indias*, lib. i. tit. xiv. leyes 42-4.
[2] *Ibid.*, lib. i. tit. xi.

the clergy permitted to engage in any kind of business. They might not work mines, inasmuch as this, besides being unbecoming their positions, might result in a scandal or an evil example.[1]

According to a law of March 17, 1619, the parish priests were required to know the language of the Indians to whom they were appointed to carry the Christian doctrine ; by a later law, however, they were ordered, in 1634, to take such measures " that all the Indians should be taught Spanish, and, in this language, the doctrines of Christianity, in order that they might the better comprehend the mysteries of the holy Catholic faith." [2]

If we were to judge from the language of the laws of the Indies, we might conclude that the king, in dealing with the Indians, regarded no object as of more importance than their conversion to the Christian faith. His obligation to seek this end he considered greater than that of any other prince, as his dominions were greater. In this view, he commanded the officers of the Crown in the several provinces to make the Indians lay aside their savage vices, and to instruct them in the holy Catholic faith. He charged the archbishops and bishops and other ecclesiastical officers to preach, teach, and persuade the natives to accept the articles of this faith. Through the law he commanded the viceroys, the audiencias, and the governors " to take very especial care to convert and christianise the Indians," and provided that they should instruct them in the things of the holy Catholic Church and the evangelical law. They should, moreover, attempt to root out idolatry among the Indians, destroying or carrying off their idols, and preventing the natives under severe penalties from worshipping them. Those among the Indians who taught idolatry should be taken and distributed among the convents, where they might be instructed in the doctrines of the Church. In each of the

[1] *Leyes de Indias*, lib. i. tit. xii.
[2] *Ibid.*, lib. i. tit. xiii. leyes 4 and 5.

Christian towns there should be indicated definite hours each day, in which all the Indians, negroes, and mulattoes, the slaves as well as those who were free, should be brought together to listen to Christian doctrine ; and the law required, furthermore, that these persons should not be hindered or occupied with anything else at the appointed hour.   The negroes, mulattoes, and Indians who lived outside of the towns should be called together for the same purpose when they came into the towns on holidays. All persons who had slaves, either negroes or mulattoes, should send them to the church or monastery, at the hour which the prelate might indicate, and they should there be instructed in the principles of the Christian faith ; the archbishops and bishops should have specially in mind their conversion and instruction.   On Sundays and feast days no one might be hindered from going to the church or the monastery to hear mass and receive Christian instruction, not even the slave by his master.   The penalty for such interference was fixed at two hundred thousand maravedis, one half of which would go to the general treasury, and the other half to the building of churches. Whoever had unconverted Indians in his service, whether by the day or by the year, should send them to church every morning ; and in case one should not comply with this requirement, he should be deprived of the service of the Indian or Indians concerned, who would never be permitted to serve him again, and he should, moreover, pay a fine of four dollars for each day of his failure to comply with the law, one half of which should go to the *Confradia* of the Indians, and the other half to the judge. On Sundays and other days when they were obliged to hear mass, the Indians, negroes, and mulattoes might not be compelled to work.[1]

In order that the natives of the Indies might have due reverence and respect for the churches, for the ecclesiastics, and for the holy sacraments and doctrines, the law

[1] *Leyes de Indias*, lib. i. tit. i.

imposed numerous restrictions on conduct in the churches, and provided that those should not be admitted who ought not to take advantage of the immunity which the sacred places afforded. The immunity of the Church should not extend to soldiers and sailors who had passed to the Indies in the armadas or fleets, and had remained without licence. Because their remaining was opposed to the public good, they might be taken from the churches, convents, or sacred places, and handed over to commanders of their vessels.

III

Thus, as sovereign and as supreme patron of the Church, the king controlled with practically absolute power the organisation and conduct of ecclesiastical affairs in America. He claimed and exercised this power before any formal cession of it was made by the pope ; and the formal granting of it by the bull of July 28, 1508, made little change in the real relation between the civil and ecclesiastical departments of the State. The position which the king assumed was announced by a decree, dated July 10, 1574, which was in the following form :

" The king, to our viceroy of the provinces of Peru, or to any other person or persons who for the time may be in charge of the government of that country. As you know, the right of ecclesiastical patronage, throughout the whole dominion of the Indies, belongs to us, not only because it was at our expense and that of the Catholic sovereigns, our predecessors, that that part of the world was discovered and acquired, and that churches and monasteries were built and endowed therein, but also because that right was granted to us by bulls issued by the supreme pontiffs, of their own accord ; and in order to preserve it, and maintain our just title thereto, we order and command that said right of patronage, one and undivided throughout the whole dominion of the Indies, may always remain preserved to us and to our royal Crown, without any possibility of our losing it, either wholly or in part, and that we may never be understood as conceding the right of patronage by favour or disfavour, by statute or by any other action that we ourselves, or the sovereigns our successors, may take.

" And, moreover, that neither by custom, nor by prescription, nor by any other title, shall any person or persons, or ecclesiastical or secular communities, churches, or monasteries, be able to use the right of patronage, except the person who in our name and with our authority and power shall exercise it ; and that no person, be he a layman or an ecclesiastic, no order, convent, religion, community, of whatever state, condition, quality, and rank it may be, may dare to intermeddle on any occasion or by any reason whatever, either judicially or extrajudicially, in any affair that may concern our royal patronage, neither to prejudice us respecting it, nor to appoint to any church or benefice, or ecclesiastical office, nor to accept such appointment when made in any part of the dominion of the Indies, without our nomination or the nomination of the person whom we by law or by patent shall have authorised ; and whoever shall act contrary to this, shall, in case of being a layman, incur a loss of the privileges which he shall hold from us in the whole dominion of the Indies, and he shall be incompetent to hold others, and shall be for ever banished from all our kingdoms and dominions, and in case of being an ecclesiastic, he shall be regarded as a stranger and an alien in all our kingdoms and dominions, and shall not be able to hold any benefice or ecclesiastical office therein, and shall, moreover, incur the other penalties established against such acts by the laws of these kingdoms ; and our viceroys, audiencias, and royal justices shall proceed with all rigour against those who shall so stand or act in opposition to our right of patronage, proceeding on the charge or demand of our fiscals, or of any party whatso-

ever who may ask for such prosecution ; and great dili-
gence shall be observed in the conduct of the case.   We
wish and command that there shall not be erected, instituted, founded, or constituted any cathedral or parochial
church, monastery, hospital, votive church, or any other
pious or religious place without our express consent, or
that of the person who shall have our authority and commission for this purpose.   And again, that there shall not
be instituted or established any archbishopric, dignity,
canonry, prebend, benefice, either simple or parochial, or any
other benefice, or ecclesiastical or religious office, without our
express permission, or that of the person on whom we shall
have conferred full power and authority for the purpose."

Under the order of things thus established, any persons
appointed to an ecclesiastical position in the Indies was required to give notice to the viceroy, president, audiencia, or
to whatever person might be at the head of the government
of the province in question, and show him his certificate of appointment in order that he might receive whatever favour or assistance might be necessary to enable him
to perform the functions of his office.   The right of patronage held by the king excluded the existence of a similar
right in any other person.   Every ecclesiastical office in
America was, therefore, filled by the king's nomination.
By law, however, as in the Ordinance of Intendants, in
Buenos Aires, the right of patronage might be vested in
a vice-patron.   In this case the right of patronage in the
viceroyalty of Buenos Aires was made to reside in vice-
patrons, and these were the viceroy in the metropolis and
the governor-intendants in the provinces.

In maintaining practically the right of patronage,
the courts of the civil government and not the ecclesiastical authorities considered all cases of violation of the rules
involved.   They considered all questions involving the
limits of bishoprics, the rights and prerogatives of the
holders of benefices, controversies between ecclesiastical
councils and their bishops or archbishops concerning the

administration of the Church, all disputes between parish priests and their parishes—in a word, all cases that in any manner touched the royal patronage. Even matters spiritual and cases between persons of a privileged tribunal were not excepted from the civil jurisdiction ; but certain cases might be brought before the viceroy, and, if desired, an appeal might be taken from the viceroy's decision to the audiencia.[1]

There was, however, in each bishopric an ecclesiastical court. Although the bishop, the fiscal proctor, and the provisor were the members of the court, all ordinary cases were tried by the provisor, and the decisions were rendered by him. The more important cases were decided by the bishop. An appeal from any of the decisions might be taken to the archbishop. In case the appellant won, the defeated party might make a final appeal to the nearest bishop, and the decision on this appeal was executed. In case the appellant lost, no further appeal was permitted. Cases that might be brought before the ecclesiastical courts were such as concerned benefices, patronages, tithes, marriages, legitimation, funerals, donations to churches and to other pious uses, legacies to churches by will or contract, and all those matters which fall within the scope of pious works. If a civil, or temporal, case arose between priests, or a case arose in which a layman brought action against a priest, these were tried before an ecclesiastical court ; but if a priest brought action against a layman in a civil, or temporal, suit, the case was tried before a secular tribunal. In the ecclesiastical courts essentially the same form of procedure prevailed as in the secular tribunals.

IV

Although the general council was a council of the Church as a whole, it is noteworthy that the individuality of nations was recognised in it, as when on certain occa-

[1] Velez Sarsfield, 51, 52.

sions the vote was taken by nations. In the general administration of ecclesiastical affairs, the individuality of the nations was furthermore recognised by the Church in holding national councils—that is to say, councils of the Church, all the members of which were drawn from within the limits of the nation. Such a council was composed of all the bishops and archbishops of the Church whose jurisdictions were embraced within the national boundaries. Such a council was held under the presidency of the patriarch,[1] or primate. In Spain, a national council was held under the presidency of the Archbishop of Toledo, the Primate of Spain. The title of primate, although sometimes applied to the Archbishop of Santo Domingo, and to the Archbishop of Lima, never existed by authority in America.

An ecclesiastical province consists of a union of several dioceses, at the head of which stands an archbishop, who presides at a meeting of the bishops of the province, called a provincial council. It appears to have been the design of the Church to have the ecclesiastical divisions correspond with the civil divisions of the territory of the State, thus making the political capitals the seats of the archbishops. The organisation in Spanish America has not always followed this plan. After the bishopric of La Plata, or Chuquisaca, was made an archbishopric, the province under the archbishop embraced the bishoprics of Upper Peru, Salta, Cordova, Paraguay, and Buenos Aires. This pro-

[1] The title of Patriarch of the Indies which we encounter in accounts of Spanish affairs was merely a title of honour held by the first chaplain of the king, " to whom was given the general vicariate of the Spanish army and navy ; but this vicariate was not extended to the troops and armies of America " (Sarsfield, 60). In 1524 Clement VII appointed Jaén D. Esteban Gabriel Merino Patriarch of the West Indies. Concerning the patriarch, it is affirmed in the bull: " qui ecclesia, sede, capitulo, choro, clero, et populo, omnique cura, regimine et jurisdictione, tam spirituali quam temporali caret, sed solum in dignitate patrichalis tituli et honore consistit ; " and, moreover, that no fixed income is attached to the office, but that the patriarch depends upon the munificence and patronage of the King of Spain (Zamora, *Regio Patronato Español é Indiano*, 563).

vince, although there was in it a subordinate court or audiencia, was nevertheless subject to the viceroy of Peru. The viceroyalty of Rio de la Plata was created in 1776, and Buenos Aires became the capital, but the Archbishop of Chuquisaca continued to be the metropolitan and the Bishop of Buenos Aires a suffragan. The captaincy-general of Chile became independent of the viceroyalty of Peru, except in matters of war, yet the Bishop of Santiago, the capital of Chile, remained a suffragan of the Archbishop of Lima. In the beginning it was not permitted to hold a provincial council in the Indies without first notifying the king and receiving his consent. Later the holding of such a council might be authorised by a viceroy or a captain-general. These councils might be held regularly every twelve years. If it was desirable that there should be a meeting in the intervening period, it might be had, if specially ordered by the pope and approved by the proper civil authority. The call for a provincial council proceeds from the metropolitan; but if the metropolitan see is vacant, the call may be issued by the senior bishop of the ecclesiastical province. Not only the bishops but also the canons and other officials are invited, and the viceroy is present representing the king; but the bishops alone have an authoritative vote, which is taken by the bishops present voting individually. The conclusions of the provincial councils of America under the rule of Spain were remitted to the Council of the Indies, and if the Council of the Indies approved them for publication, it sent them to the pope. These conclusions of the provincial councils, when properly confirmed, were authoritative only within the limits of the ecclesiastical province where the council was held.

The Church in America recognised the provision of the Council of Trent which required the bishop to hold every year a synod of the members of the clergy of his diocese. The bishop, who was in the full exercise of his episcopal powers, issued the call for such a meeting. The resolutions of the synod, having been approved by the bishop, were sent to the viceroy and the governor of the district, who finding nothing in them controverting the rights of the sovereign, or likely to produce any inconvenience, ordered their execution, and the bishop then caused them to be published. But if they did not meet the viceroy's approval, they were overruled, and sent to the Council of the Indies, for such action as that body might see fit to take concerning them. Thus at every step in the administration of ecclesiastical affairs in America the presence and dominance of the civil power were recognised.

This general control of ecclesiastical affairs by the king and his Council of the Indies is made evident and emphasized by the law which required all bulls, briefs, rescripts, and despatches of the Roman Curia, which contained laws, rules, or general statements, to be presented to the Council of the Indies before their publication, in order that their execution might be sanctioned in so far as they were not in opposition to the regalias, concordats, customs, laws, or decrees of the nation ; or did not stand in the way of the nation's achieving its proper purposes.[1]

In case the king refused to allow a bull to pass and be published in America, he made no report to the pope of the grounds of his objection, nor did he suggest any course of papal action that would be acceptable to him. The attorney who had examined the bull for the king simply begged his Holiness to retain the document. But in practice this formal petition of the attorney never reached the pope ; and the government conveyed the information it contained at such time and under such circumstances as appeared to it opportune ; usually by an oral statement to a diplomatic officer.[2]

The monks who came to America required the consent

[1] Velez Sarsfield, 77, 78 ; when these documents were brought before the Council, they were copied in the record books of the secretaries and the originals were placed in the archives of the Council or in the archives of Simancas, authorised copies being made for convenient use.　　　　　　　　　　　　　　[2] Velez Sarsfield, 86.

of the viceroy or governor, together with that of the prelate of the diocese, before they were able to construct a monastery; in fact, these officers determined the towns in which the monasteries should be established. The several orders distributed their members into different provinces, but the permission of the governor of the state was needed to form these provinces. From time to time the padres of a province assembled to elect their provincials, guardians, and priors of the monasteries; and these early applications of political methods were sometimes attended by serious conflicts. They furnished an instance of democratic procedure without the laws democracy has found it necessary to establish to preserve order at the polls. In view of this state of things, the law finally provided that the viceroy should be present at these meetings to preserve the peace and cause the constitutions of the order to be respected; but if the viceroy was absent from the place of holding the meeting and unable to attend, he was required to write to the monks admonishing them and charging them to abide by and preserve their institutions. In case of disturbance, he might even cause them to be arrested, and taken out of the province; and when the election had been held, the bishop or archbishop might exercise the power of veto, if, in his opinion, the person elected was not fitted to fill the office for which he had been selected.[1]

The consent of the civil authority was also required for the erection of cathedral or parochial churches, temples, monasteries, and other places for religious exercises.[2]

"And if in fact or by dissimulation any person shall make or begin to make any of these edifices, without this prerequisite, the viceroys, audiencias, or governors shall cause them to be demolished, and everything reduced to its previous state, without excuse or delay."[3]

---

[1] *Leyes de Indias*, lib. i. tit. 13, ley 2; lib. i. tit. 14, leyes 60, 61.
[2] *Ibid.*, tit. 6, ley 1.   [3] *Ibid.*, tit. 3, ley 1.

And the substance of this injunction was always contained in the general instructions given to the viceroys of Mexico and Peru.[1]

The expenses of erecting the cathedral churches were in three parts : the first part was contributed by the royal treasury ; the second part by the Indians of the bishopric or archbishopric; and the third part by the encomenderos of the diocese. These three parties were, moreover, the contributors to the funds by which the parochial churches were built, but it was understood that the contribution from the royal treasury was simply for the first construction of the church, not for later enlargements or modifications. The archbishops, bishops, and abbots were required to report to the king the number of churches that had been erected ; and when the building of churches had been undertaken, the viceroys and prelates were to take care to have them completed as soon as possible.

The licence for building a church or monastery having been issued to one of the regular orders, the viceroy, president, or governor, each in his district, was required to prohibit more space being taken for the building than was necessary for the convenient accommodation of the occupants. A term, moreover, was set for the completion of the establishment, and if it was not completed within this term, the viceroy might transfer it to another order.

The pope sometimes created archbishops, under whom there were no bishops ; archbishops who were given their titles not because there was work for them to do as archbishops, but because it was desired to accord honourable distinction to certain persons. In America this form of ecclesiastical favouritism did not appear. There were various reasons for its absence. In the first place, almost all the bishops and archbishops were Europeans ; in the second place, there were not many towns in South America, in the early period, which a European would select because of the opportunities it afforded for luxurious living ; and

---

[1] Solórzano, lib. iv. cap. 23.

in the third place, the king was anxious that no more of his revenues than was necessary should go for salaries of archbishops. If, therefore, one was to be an archbishop without a province, he would doubtless find it more agreeable to be archbishop of Lucca or Ferrara, than archbishop of Oruro or Riobamba, and he would not have the objections of the king to overcome.

Besides the bishops and the chapters, the curates were especially inportant in determining the character of the religious work in the colonies. In some of the parishes Spaniards constituted a predominant part of the population. The curates who officiated in these parishes were called rectoral curates. There were other parishes composed almost entirely of Indian villages, and the religious teachers who officiated in them were known as doctrinal curates. The differences of function between these two classes were chiefly only such as were made inevitable by the differences of the communities concerned. There was a third class of religious teachers who were appointed to instruct the Indians in the catechism and in the manners and customs of civilised life. These were the missionaries who led the advance against paganism and savage customs. When the Indians had adopted the essential features of civilisation, they were transferred to the parish of a doctrinal curate, and the missionaries moved their posts farther into the wilderness, and renewed their crusade against ignorance and unbelief. Enlistment in the ranks of the missionaries was without any compulsion whatsoever ; those who entered upon the great undertaking, in the early decades, appear to have been moved by a desire to propagate the faith, and thereby to redeem the race. Later, enthusiasm gave way to indifference and members of the religious orders, leaving Spain full of zeal for the spiritual conquest of the Indians, found " the lives of their brethren rather fashioned according to the spirit of man than the spirit of God," and under the influence of those already in the field, they came to regard a life of indolence more attractive than a death of glory.[1] In the later years of Spanish rule, the missionaries on the frontier made few conversions, and did little to advance a knowledge of civilisation among the Indians ; and on the basis of the facts observed, Depons concluded that neither the cause of religion nor national sovereignty derived any material advantage from their labours.[2]

The curate of a parish inhabited chiefly by Spaniards was not entirely dependent for his support on his salary. There were numerous fees and perquisites to supplement the compensation which he received from the king. The missionaries, on the other hand, who ministered solely to the Indians, were generally obliged to maintain themselves with the royal stipend, since the services of the Church in these cases were gratuitous. Sometimes, however, they violated the spirit while they observed the letter of the law. They sold the Indians various articles, such as rosaries and little images of the Virgin, at a thousand per cent. profit ; and persuaded them to work without compensation.

In America the monks were given a somewhat unusual position. According to the canon law they were not able to hold beneficed curacies, but the extent of the American field, and the limited number of the clergy available to occupy it, induced Leo X, Adrian VI, Paul III, Clement VIII, and Pius V to permit them to become parish priests. Under this order a very large number of the parishes in America in the sixteenth century were occupied by friars. But in the middle of the eighteenth century, this privilege was withdrawn, leaving them only two parishes in a conventual province.

Wherever the Spaniards established themselves in America, with their Indian serfs and their negro slaves, labour soon came to be regarded as the proper occupation

[1] Depons, *Voyage à Terre-Ferme* (Paris, 1806), ii. 136.
[2] *Ibid.*, 137.

of the inferior races. Through this fact it very naturally became despised by the Spaniard and the creole, and yet other openings for their profitable employment were not numerous. The door of the monastery was, however, always open. There one might lead a tranquil life. If he had sufficient intellectual cultivation to enable him to engage in some narrow field of inquiry, there was his opportunity. If he found delight in vague contemplation and mystical day-dreaming, the atmosphere of the monastery favoured his desires. There his support was assured; there behind the walls that enclosed him and his brethren he might have a hand in directing the other social classes ; and, in his theoretical poverty, he might enjoy more of the things of this world than fell to the ordinary lot of man.

Yet at the end of the eighteenth century there was observed a diminution in the number of ecclesiastics. This was true both of the monks and of the secular priests. Several causes have been pointed out as contributing to this result. One has been found in the greater prominence given to the organised militia, in which there was an opportunity for honourable maintenance without a form of labour humiliating to Spanish pride. Another was found in the multiplication of posts in the civil service, which furnished attractive livings to persons who might otherwise have accepted places in the Church. In the beginning, turning from the wars against the Moors, the Spaniards were strongly moved by a desire for ecclesiastical conquest ; but in the course of time the spread of stories of the fabulous wealth of Peru and the possible spoils of other chiefs naturally attracted to the colonies a large number of persons who were more interested in the attainment of wealth than in the conversion of the Indians. There was observed, however, no diminution of zeal on the part of the ecclesiastical organisations to accumulate property ; and men of wealth recognised that donations to churches and monasteries furnished the surest means of securing for their names a fragrant memory. Facing the end of life, many persons did not hesitate to purchase the favour and service of the Church in their own behalf, even to depriving their families of their expected inheritances. The government recognised this evil and sought to offer a remedy by issuing a law forbidding any notary to pass an act or an instrument of donation by which a sick person, or a person on a bed of death, proposed to convey his property to his confessor or to an ecclesiastical organisation for pious uses. This law, however, found no adequate support in public opinion, yet on the initiative of the Spanish government it was revived in Caracas in 1802.

The monotonous routine of the monastery in Spain must have been irksome to many of the more active and venturesome members of the orders. It was inevitable that some men should find themselves in the religious houses who were better fitted by nature for the practical work of pioneers than for contemplation and a continuous round of religious exercises. To such men the opportunities for a more adventurous life in America appeared attractive, and made them willing to respond to the call for missionaries Fretting under a rigid discipline, they looked to the colonies for a larger measure of freedom. This expectation of freedom was usually realised when charged in America with the duties of a parish priest. While performing the functions of this office they were removed from the immediate supervision of their monastic superiors, and the results of this independence with respect to their conduct were such as to indicate that their training had not been of a character to enable them to withstand their inevitable temptations and meet properly their responsibilities. The scandalous lives of some of the regular clergy while in charge of parishes called forth strong protests from many of the most zealous members of the Church. The secular clergy regarded the assignment of monks to parishes as an encroachment on their peculiar functions. This view became widely accepted, and in 1757 King Ferdinand VI issued an edict, prohibiting monks from taking charge of parishes, and providing that, as regulars holding these positions died, only members of the secular clergy would be appointed to the vacancies thus created. This edict made complete the change that had been initiated earlier.

CHAPTER XIII

THE CLERGY AND THE SCHOOLS IN CHILE
IN THE SEVENTEENTH CENTURY

I. Chilean affairs civil and ecclesiastical in the beginning of the century. II. The Franciscans and the Mercedarios. III. The Dominicans and the Jesuits. IV. The Augustinians. V. Schools in other towns than Santiago. VI. Instruction in the universities.

I

THE Indian wars of Chile in the seventeenth century were even more serious than those of the south-eastern provinces; and in the beginning of the century the king provided for the creation of a permanent army paid by the Crown. Under the supposition that by this means the war would be soon ended, this provision was at first designed to be temporary; but as the Araucanians persisted in their hostilities, the force supported by the Crown became a permanent institution. The amount required for the support of this body of soldiers was paid out of the funds which Peru was accustomed to set aside annually for the royal treasury.

This arrangement was advantageous for the colony, in that it brought into circulation a certain amount of coined money, which prior to this time was almost unknown in Chile, and this gave new incentives to traders and facilitated exchanges. The existence of a regular military establishment relieved the colonists from the necessity of abandoning their lands when their presence was needed to prepare for the year's harvest, and thus contributed to increase the production and the commerce of the province. While military service was required of the bulk of the colonists, the population of Chile increased very slowly; immigrants coming to America hesitated to settle where their military duties would be an effective obstacle to their prosperity. But after the establishment of a standing military force, the population increased more rapidly, and instead of continuing to live in towns as heretofore throughout northern and central Chile, it became gradually more and more the custom for the inhabitants to live on their lands. The numerous restrictions, however, that were placed on emigration from Spain to America, operated as a general check on the growth of the population in Chile, as well as in other parts of America.[1]

In spite of the fact that foreigners were prohibited from either living in, or trading with, the Spanish colonies, except under conditions with which few would or could comply,[2] a number of them had found their way to different parts of these possessions; and in his financial need Philip IV proposed to help himself out of his state of want by compounding with such foreigners as had taken up their residence in the colonies without the necessary royal licence. They were required to pay sums varying according to their wealth, and, although they had violated the law, they were to be left in peace and quiet in consideration of these payments.[3]

[1] *Leyes de Indias*, lib. ix. tit. 27, leyes 1, 3–7; Amunátegui, *Precursores de la independencia de Chile*, i. cap. 7; Barros Arana, *Historia jeneral de Chile*, iv. 225–32.

[2] In order that a foreigner might obtain a certificate of nationalisation, which would enable him to trade in the Indies, it was necessary : (1) that he should have lived in Spain or America continuously for twenty years; (2) that he should have owned for ten years a house and land worth at least four thousand ducats; (3) that he should have married a Spanish woman or the daughter of a foreigner born in Spain or America; (4) that the Council of the Indies, after a careful inquiry, should have declared him entitled to enjoy this privilege. *Leyes de Indias*, lib. ix. tit. 27, leyes, 31–4. See vol. i. 260.

[3] " . . . i les obligueis á que contribuya cada uno segun o conforme á la hacienda que tuviere, . . . dándoles á entender el beneficio que se les hace i cuán grande es para ellos dejarlos en sosiego i quietud." Cédula of June 14, 1621. See Barros Arana, iv. 231.

The Spanish system of colonial government, which provided that the audiencia under certain conditions might exercise the powers ordinarily exercised by the governor, made conflicts between these two authorities almost inevitable. During the governor's long absences on his campaigns against the Araucanians, he entrusted the government of the capital and the civil administration of the colony to the corregidor of Santiago. This gave rise to a controversy, since the audiencia held that a corregidor was not to be maintained in cities where there was an audiencia, and that in this case the audiencia was properly the governor's deputy. To remove this difficulty two of the governors, Lope de Ulloa y Lémos (1617–1620) and Luis Fernandez de Cordova (1624–1629), proposed to the king that the audiencia should be transferred to Concepcion; another governor, Pedro Osóres de Ulloa (1620–1624), made the more radical proposition to abolish the audiencia. The king, however, refused to adopt either of these recommendations, and held to the original design of the system, which regarded the audiencia as furnishing a counterpoise to the governor. The dissension between these principal offices tended to diminish the authority and prestige of both.[1]

The presence of the bishop as a third independent authority in the State, setting forth the extravagant pretensions of his divine mission, added a new source of confusion and scandal. In contrast with the fate of the secular officers, the bishop's participation in quarrels with the governor and the audiencia did not lessen the respect in which he was held by the community. The Spaniards of Chile in the seventeenth century maintained their reverence for the clergy, whatever might be the conduct of individual priests ; and with respect to the controversies between the secular and ecclesiastical officials, many of the inhabitants were always and unreservedly on the side of the Church. Chile, moreover, shared in the revival of

[1] Barros Arana, *Historia jeneral de Chile*, iv. 232–4.

devotion, which manifested itself at the court of Spain in the beginning of the seventeenth century; and this popular sentiment was intensified by the early work of the Jesuits, who organised various fraternities, not only of Spaniards, but also of Indians and negroes, and gave to the functions of the Church, the processions and *fiestas*, a brilliancy and impressiveness which had not been known previously in Chile.[1]

The effect of this theatrical display, which impressed upon the spectators the idea of miracles, doubtless led many minds to a more constant contemplation of the supernatural, but public morals were not thereby greatly improved. The Indians, the mestizos, and the ignorant of every sort stared with wonder and delight at the gorgeously dressed images, the brilliant and abundant lights, and the richly robed priests, but they were not brought by what they saw either to Christianity or to civilisation. Referring to the statements of the ecclesiastical writers and their claim to have christianised and civilised thousands of Indians, Barros Arana affirms that " the mature study of the documents shows that these statements are nothing more than inventions destitute of all truth. The Indians readily allowed themselves to be baptized either to recover their liberty or to obtain a gift ; but they remained as thoroughly pagans as they were before ; they fled to their districts at the first opportunity, and returned to the life of savages without remembering anything of their pretended conversion." [2]

This fact is not in itself a charge against the sincerity and zeal of many of the ecclesiastics ; it only suggests their ignorance and their failure to perceive, according to Barros Arana, that the Indians, " by their moral and intellectual inferiority were not prepared to appreciate the

---

[1] Ovalle, Alonso de, *An Historical Relation of the Kingdom of Chile*, (London, 1703), book v. chap. vi., vii., and viii; Barros Arana, *Historia jeneral de Chile*, iv. 245–52.

[2] *Historia jeneral de Chile*, iv. 252.

benefits of a superior civilisation, and much less to receive religious ideas that could not enter the mind of a savage."[1] A savage race could not be transformed into a civilised race by presenting to the savages a catechism of a new religion. The Spanish ecclesiastics expected results from the acceptance of their doctrines, which could not be reasonably looked for, except from the operation of all the forces that make for civilised life, extended over many centuries. This mistake appears less conspicuous in the Jesuit reductions of Paraguay than anywhere else in South America.

II

But the clergy founded schools, and made important contributions to the means of instruction. By their efforts in this field they promoted the cause of civilisation. Friars of the order of Merced established a school in connection with their monastery in Santiago. This school embraced courses in Theology and Philosophy, which were open to persons not belonging to the order. In this isolated colonial society, zeal in learning did not always follow the creation of facilities for instruction ; it was, in fact, difficult to maintain either among the pupils or the teachers an interest in the affairs of education. The indifference of both parties with reference to the work of the school may be inferred from the great amount of time given up to vacations, and from the frequent absences of the instructors at the hours appointed for their lectures. The higher authorities of the order continued to manifest their interest in instruction, and moved by this interest they made frequent attempts to correct these abuses.[2]

The Franciscans paid not less attention to education than the Mercedarios. It is affirmed by their chronicler that studies in Arts and Philosophy flourished in their

[1] *Historia jeneral de Chile*, iv. 255.
[2] Barros Arana, *Historia jeneral de Chile*, iii. 180–2 ; for the schools of the Jesuits and Dominicans, see *Ibid.*, iv. 278–84.

monastery at Santiago in the middle of the seventeenth century. There were professors of Latin, Philosophy, and Theology, and not only members of the monastery but also other persons were admitted to the instruction given by them.

In the middle of the seventeenth century there were three hundred and seven persons in the schools of all grades in Santiago, and the town had at this time about five thousand inhabitants. The numbers of the Spaniards in the other districts, or corregimientos, ranged from one hundred, in the district of Melipilla, to seven hundred in that of Serena. These were chiefly soldiers and adventurers, and many of them were illiterate. Such a population had naturally little interest in education, and spent little of its force in establishing schools. In the absence of means of instruction in Chile, some of the richest and most enterprising of the inhabitants sent their sons to Lima ; and this practice was continued into the eighteenth century.

There were, moreover, in the colony few books for any use. There were not enough for the services of the cathedral ; the number of missals and breviaries was insufficient for the needs of the friars of the monasteries ; and the royal audiencias found it for a time impossible either in Lima or elsewhere to obtain the books containing the royal decrees that constituted the basis of the administration. The work of the few schools already established was greatly embarrassed, as were also all other efforts contributing to colonial progress, by the large number of recognised holidays, which numbered one hundred and fifty-nine out of the three hundred and sixty-five days of the year.

In the last half of the seventeenth century Mariana de Cordova left to the Franciscans an important legacy for the foundation of a college, and Maria de Viera gave a valuable tract of land at Santiago, a part of which was sold for an endowment, while the rest was retained as a site for the institution. The president of Chile and the bishop petitioned the king to concede to the Franciscans a licence to found a college near the great monastery, for studies in Arts and Theology, where persons might be trained to be confessors and preachers of the holy gospel. In reply, the queen regent, in the minority of Charles II, asked for further information and the opinion of the president and the audiencia as to the desirability of the proposed college. On the basis of the information and the opinions received affirming the utility of the institution which the Franciscans desired to establish, the king granted the required licence. The correspondence on this subject lasted fifteen years, from the date of the donation, in 1664, to the concession of the royal licence, in 1679. The organic law of the college, which was adopted in 1680, remained in force until 1732, when it was amended in a manner to promote a better administration and more rapid progress in the studies. The college was finally opened with five professors and five students.

Besides this institution, the Franciscans maintained two other schools in their monasteries. The examinations were held every four months. The answers were written and the results were certified as good, medium, or bad. Those who had achieved only the third grade were required to be re-examined after four months, and by a second failure they were prohibited from continuing their studies. The library of the college was collected and supported by funds contributed by several provinces of the order, each province contributing annually two hundred dollars. The books were expected to be accessible and the librarian present one hour in the morning, from eight to nine o'clock, and one hour in the afternoon, from three to four. The members of the order could take out books on leaving a receipt for them, and could keep them one month.

III

The Dominicans arrived in Chile somewhat later than the Mercedarios and the Franciscans. Towards the end of the sixteenth century Friar Cristobal Nuñez, on behalf of the order, petitioned the king for licence to establish in the monastery of the Dominicans a university, whose graduates might enjoy all the rights and distinctions that had been granted to the graduates of the university that had been founded in Lima. In replying to this petition, March 1, 1589, the king asked to be informed as to what advantage would accrue from the establishment of the proposed university, or if any inconveniences would result from its foundation. This inquiry meant that if the request set forth in the petition were ever granted, it would be only after years of delay. In the meantime, provision was made for teaching Latin in the monastery. The salary of the teacher who was appointed for this purpose appears to have been expected from subscriptions at first, but later by royal decree it was ordered that it should be paid for a period of four years from the royal treasury in Lima. But here new difficulties arose in the inability of the monastery to secure the execution of this decree. The instruction was, however, continued, and later an effort was made to have the order revived, which had imposed upon the royal officials the obligation to pay the salary. It was proposed that they should pay the salary of the instructor not only for the future but also for the four years past when it had been expected from the royal treasury. Yet in spite of these difficulties the services of the teacher were continued, and in 1595, to the teaching of Latin in the monastery there was added instruction in the Arts, Philosophy, and Theology.[1]

[1] The first instructor in these subjects was Friar Cristobal Valdespino, who was born in Jerez de la Frontera in 1570. He began his studies in the Colegio de la Asumpcion which the Jesuits maintained in Cordova in Spain. He went to Chile in 1596, in company with other members of the order, and was appointed by royal decree

A few years later it was determined to send one of the friars, Hernando Maxía, to Spain, commissioned to solicit assistance from the king, to recruit friars, and to obtain a licence for founding a university in the monastery of Rosario in Santiago. At this time action by Spanish authorities or by the authorities of the Church concerning the Spanish colonies was taken only after long delay and after opportunity, at least, for mature deliberation. The privilege sought by Maxía and those who followed him on behalf of the Dominicans of Chile was finally granted in 1619.[1] The university authorised by this grant was destined to be in a large measure eclipsed in a short time by the more efficient instruction of the Jesuits. This superior efficiency was recognised by the Pope ; for while in 1627 he ordered that degrees granted by the Dominicans and the Jesuits should be valid only in America, he annulled this decree in 1634 with respect to the Jesuits, ordering at the same time that the degrees granted by the Jesuit colleges in America should be recognised everywhere. This was clearly an exercise of papal influence in favour of the Jesuits, and was not merely an important hindrance to the progress of the Dominican university, but also made it more than ever difficult for that institution to maintain the standing which it had in the beginning.

The Jesuits arrived in Santiago, April 12, 1593. Within six weeks after this date they had purchased a house, and taken up the work of their mission. Devoted, according to Olivares, " to youth and the education of children, they appointed one day in the week when the children of the schools might come to their *colegio ;* they came with their crosses decorated, and repeating their prayers. Here the Christian doctrine was taught and

---

missionary to the Indians. He was elected prior of the monastery, and soon after, in 1598, became provincial, but resigned this office at the end of the year, continuing, however, his work as instructor.

[1] Medina, *Instrucción pública*, Documentos, No. 1.

explained to them by the questions and answers of the catechism. They were also taught to sing certain songs in praise of the divine, in order to drive out of their mouths other profane songs which corrupted their innocent manners. This exercise having been concluded, they returned as they had come, delighted when they had received a prize for having responded well." [1] This course was continued until the Jesuits had established a school for reading and writing where all might come and receive instruction. This instruction was later extended by introducing a course in Latin. The first teacher of this course was Juan de Olivares, who began his instruction in 1595. This was followed by the addition of a course in the Arts, which was attended not only by citizens of Santiago, but also by members of the other orders. A few years later, in 1608, a professorship of Theology was established. During the following years, instruction by the Jesuits in Santiago suffered embarrassing changes, particularly after the founding of the University of Cordova, in 1613, to which students were transferred from Santiago. Finally, in 1623, the bull of Gregory XV was received in Chile. This permitted the Jesuits to found public universities in the Philippines, in New Granada, in Tucuman, in Rio de la Plata, and in Santiago de Chile, and in the other provinces and cities of the Indies, where there was no provision for general studies, and where the sites of the proposed universities were two hundred miles from universities already established. The licence from the king provided, moreover, that the students of the college, or university, organised under it, having complied with the customary conditions, should receive the degree of bachelor, licentiate, or doctor from the hands of the bishop or the ecclesiastical cabildo. [2] With the advantages enjoyed under the royal concession, and by means of the large donations made to the order from time to

---

[1] *Historia de la Compañia*, 24.
[2] Medina, *Instrucción pública*, Documents, 63–66, 67.

time, the Jesuits were not only able to carry on the work of the university, but also to maintain seminaries for the special training of persons for their missionary and educational enterprises.

With the arrival of the bull of Gregory XV in Santiago a new question arose. The rector of the university, Rodrigo Vasquez, presented the bull to the audiencia in order that the university might have the formal approval of that body. It was found, however, that the document lacked certain necessary signatures of certification, and on this ground the audiencia agreed that the university might continue its instruction, but that it must abstain from giving degrees until the bull should be presented with the requisite signatures.

This delay led the Dominicans to petition to have it proclaimed that they had a university already founded. They expected that by obtaining such a declaration first the pretensions of the other party would be defeated. The result of the petition was a decree authorising the *padres* of Santo Domingo to maintain a university. At length the bull in favour of the Jesuits was returned from Lima with the proper certificates; this did not bring about peace between the two orders, but on the contrary intensified the conflict. Each party sought to prevent the other from exercising the right to confer degrees. Nevertheless instruction was continued at both universities, but that given by the Jesuits was generally preferred and was attended by the larger number of students. In the meantime arguments and a judicial controversy engaged the attention of both orders. " The case of the Jesuits against the Dominicans concerning studies was a mere reproduction of other similar cases that arose in Manila and Quito." [1]

[1] Medina, *Instrucción pública*, ccxxxix.

IV

The Augustinians established themselves in Chile somewhat later than the other orders. Their monastery was founded in 1595, but it is not clear at what time their first school was opened. Much apparently reliable testimony, however, indicates that the Augustinians " from the date of their foundation had studies in Latin, the Arts, and Theology, as well for members of their order as for all those who wished to go to their monasteries." [1]

It is easy to understand, when we know that the other religious orders had opened their schools, that there could not be many students who would take the courses of the Augustinians, particularly when it is added that the place itself which was occupied by the order was the lower part of the houses of Riberos that had not yet been made habitable after they had been burned. [2] But at this stage Andrés de Elosu appeared, and through his capacity for organisation reduced the studies of the monastery, by 1615, to a certain systematic order. The Jesuit historian Olivares, calls Elosu " one of the most learned, serious, and zealous priests this province of Chile has had, and it was he who gave form to literary studies in his monastery." [3] The organisation given to instruction in the school of the Augustinian monastery was further developed by the friar, Baltisar Pérez de Espinosa. Still the Augustinians continued to suffer the disadvantages of not having the power to confer degrees ; and this disadvantage appeared especially conspicuous when their prospects were compared with those of the Dominicans and the Jesuits. All students were quite naturally disposed to go where at the expiration of a certain term of study they might legitimately present themselves as candidates for

---

[1] *Carta de la Real Audiencia al Rey*, Feb. 10, 1634, quoted by Medina.

[2] Medina, *Instrucción pública*, ccxlix.

[3] *Ibid.;* Gaspar Jorro, *Estudios conventuales en Chile* (1553–1625), in *Revista chilena*, xiii, 42–68.

one or another academic degree. The early educational institutions of Santiago that were able to confer academic degrees derived this power from the king, who usually made this concession on the basis of information derived from the audiencia, and with the advice of the Council of the Indies.

In view of their want of power to confer degrees, the Augustinians petitioned for authority to create a university in their monastery. The king sent this petition to the audiencia of Chile, and asked that body to inform him as to what advantages or inconveniences would accrue from the foundation of the proposed institution. When finally the king made his reply to the petitioners, it was unfavourable to the project of the friars, who were thus compelled to confine their efforts to a less ambitious task. In spite of the subsequent foundation of a college with the title of San Ildefonso de los Reyes, the educational branch of the monastery fell into a serious decline, attended by lamentable consequences for the preaching and ceremonies of the Church. A large factor in the demoralisation of the instruction, as well as of all of the affairs of the community, was the earthquake of 1647, which laid the city in ruins and cut off the revenues of the monastery.

A certain revival, or a reorganisation, of studies was effected somewhat later by Friar Augustine Carrillo de Ojeda ; and the funds required to carry out Ojeda's ideas were obtained through a donation made by Doña Mariana de Cordova y Aguilera, in 1659. The donation of Doña Mariana consisted of several blocks of land in Santiago with a large house, a vineyard, ten slaves, and a large quantity of jewelry, and was designed for the establishment of a college under the title of Santo Tomás de Villanueva. For this proposed institution a charter was sought that would convey " all the privileges of any other university," and would provide that those students who might take the courses in the proposed college would have an opportunity to receive by royal authority any academic degree up to that of Doctor of Theology. The king refused to grant this petition ; whereupon Ojeda, speaking for the Augustinians, requested that there might be granted to the principal monastery of his order the privileges of a university and of general studies, so that those persons who were there instructed might be graduated in the faculties of Arts and Theology.

Having received this request, the king, as on other occasions, avoided the necessity of making a decision immediately by asking the audiencia of Chile for information.[1] When finally a decision was rendered, it appears, as in many other cases, to have been a denial of the request of the Augustinians. As the validity of the donation depended on the establishment of the college within six years, the friars feared that, in view of the difficulties they encountered in attempting to carry out their plans, the property would revert to the donor. In order, therefore, to avoid this loss, a rector of the contemplated college was appointed, who would assume active duties in case the college should be established. But at the expiration of six years the proposed college had not been established. Nevertheless the studies of the principal monastery were transferred to the edifice on the land embraced in Doña Mariana's donation ; and the college of San Miguel Arcángel was substituted for the proposed college of Santo Tomás de Villanueva. Towards the end of the eighteenth century this college became the college of Nuestra Señora del Carmen.

V

An early attempt to organise instruction in Chile outside of Santiago was made in the city of Imperial. It was here proposed to establish a seminary for ecclesiastical

[1] The memorial of Ojeda on this subject and the king's reply, addressed to the audiencia, are printed in Medina, *Instrucción pública*, cclxx., cclxxi.

studies, as well as a university, and the king's reply to
the request for authority was dated January 26, 1568.
This reply was in the usual form of a demand for information, addressed to the audiencia. It was found that
the conditions did not warrant the establishment of a
university, but in the course of time a seminary was organised. Somewhat later this seminary was transformed
into " a school that was attended by all the youth of the
bishopric of Concepcion to study Philosophy and Theology." [1] By a royal order of 1697, provision was made
for a professorship of the Araucanian language ; and a
similar professorship was established at the same time in
Santiago. These foundations were designed for the instruction of missionaries to the Araucanian Indians, who,
from time to time, were sent from Spain. Even before
the foundation of this school, the monasteries had given
a little elementary instruction in their houses. The
earliest positive notice we have of such instruction in
Concepcion refers to the teaching of the Jesuits. A noteworthy practice of the *colegio*, or school, that grew out
of the seminary, was that once every week, when the
weather permitted, the pupils " went out under the direction of the master of the school or some other priest,
singing the *doctrina* through the streets, which they repeated in the form of a dialogue, concluding the walk with
an explanation of some point of Christian doctrine, or
with a moral exhortation." [2]

When the Jesuits were expelled in 1767, the school
which they had established and the seminary were united
and became the college of San Carlos. The new institution practically monopolised the instruction given in
Concepcion, since that offered in the monasteries was
unimportant.

Among the other towns of Chile, Serena, Valparaiso,
and Copiapó were the only ones in which, in the colonial
period, provision was made for teaching even reading and

writing. The Franciscans opened the first primary school in Serena, as they were the first of the orders to establish themselves in that town. The Jesuits came a little later, after the cabildo of Serena had petitioned the king to permit them to establish a school there. The beginnings of this school belong to the decade between 1670 and 1680. Serena had then about seventy houses, three-fourths of which were miserable straw huts, and less than ten thousand inhabitants. The town had already been ruined by an earthquake, and plundered by pirates.

The first school in Valparaiso was founded by an Italian Jesuit, Antonio María Fanelli. In Copiapó each of the three orders, the Franciscans, the Mercedarios, and the Jesuits, made certain provisions for primary instruction.

The provision made, through the professorships established in Concepcion and Santiago, for teaching the Araucanian language, was without effect, since no one came to be taught, and for this reason it was found desirable to abandon the project of giving such instruction in the schools as would fit missionaries to preach in the Araucanian language. It was found, moreover, that the Indians learned Spanish readily, and that this language was better adapted to convey the doctrines of the Church than a language that had come into existence among semi-savages, who had always been ignorant of many of the conceptions which the Church wished to give them. To render the Araucanian language fit to convey ecclesiastical doctrines many new words would be necessary, and the Indians would have had quite as much difficulty in understanding these as the words already in use in Spanish. It was, therefore, determined to establish schools for teaching the Indians Spanish, instead of pursuing the hopeless task of trying to prepare missionaries to preach in Araucanian. Experience in other parts of America led the Spaniards to a similar resolution with respect to their missionary work among the Indians

They came gradually to the opinion, which is no longer debatable, that in order to civilise the savage, it is necessary to give him a language of civilisation. In keeping with this view, a royal decree of May 30, 1691, provided that in the Indian towns there should be schools, one for boys and one for girls, where the Indians might be taught Spanish. But when the small number of the inhabitants did not permit the maintenance of two schools, both sexes should be taught together. Although this decree was issued with special reference to Peru and New Granada, it was found desirable to apply it to Chile. " The condition of the Indians was such that it was not only necessary to teach the Spanish language to those who had recently been brought into subjection, and to assign salaries to teachers, but also to provide means of support for the boys who attended the schools " [1] Just before the close of the seventeenth century, Charles II sent ten Franciscans and forty Jesuits to Chile to carry on the educational and religious work among the Indians. They arrived in Santiago in May 1699. About the same time, by a decree directed to the audiencia, the king provided for the creation of a council of missions. This body, when organised, was composed of the oldest member of the cabildo of Santiago, the bishop and dean of the cathedral, the royal officials, and two ecclesiastics who were familiar with the work that had been done among the Indians. This decree provided, moreover, that " there should be founded a *colegio seminario* for the education of the sons of the Indian caciques," and that instruction in this school should be in the hands of the Jesuits, who should teach reading, writing, arithmetic, Latin, and morals. The government of the school was committed to the council of missions, which was required to frame for the institution a constitution and the necessary regulations. This decree was brought to Chile in 1698, and after some

[1] Don Tomás Marin de Poveda, President of Chile, to the King of Spain, June 2, 1696 ; printed in Medina, *Instrucción pública*, cccxxx.

discussion it was determined to establish the *colegio seminario* at Chillan. When the three Jesuits, who were to have charge of the instruction, arrived at Chillan, they found that only mean and inadequate quarters had been provided for their accommodation and for the school.

The most serious problem was not that involved in the foundation of the school, but that of getting the pupils for whom provision had been made. Don Pedro Riquelme, who as a child had been a captive among the Indians, was commissioned to go into their territory and ask the chiefs to send their sons to be educated by the Spaniards. Some of the chiefs received this proposition with great disfavour ; and the suggestion that their sons might be taught to read and write and even to become priests awakened no enthusiasm in the minds of any of them. The pride and conservatism of the Indians led them to oppose the project of having their sons taught to read and write if thereby the younger generation were to be caused to forget the traditions of their people, or to regard their ancestors with less respect. Without learning to read or write, the caciques affirmed, they had known how to defend themselves, their liberties and the customs of their people. It was only with the greatest difficulty that any of the sons of the caciques were persuaded to go to the school. When the authorities of the *colegio seminario* found it to be practically impossible to assemble from the families of the Araucanian chiefs the sixteen pupils for whom provision had been made, President Ibañez sent a captain to the region east of the Andes to recruit pupils. The captain succeeded, and brought back seven entrants, but, as the Jesuit historian Olivares observed, " God knows by what means." The impossibility of attracting the sons of the chiefs, for whom the school had been established, was only one of the difficulties encountered. The income designated by the king did not continue to be available, and the institution fell into financial embarrassment. Then came a revival of Araucanian hostility towards the Spaniards ; and in 1723 it became clear that the school had failed ; not, however, without leaving in the mind of the Spaniard the hope that by some similar process these vigorous barbarians would some time be civilised and brought into the Church.

The schools of Chile in the early decades usually occupied quarters in or near the centre of the town, the schoolrooms opening directly on the street. Pedro de Padilla's school in Santiago was on the street at present called Ahumada, only half a block from the principal plaza, while the rooms of the Jesuits' school in Concepcion opened on the plaza itself. The furniture was of the rudest kind. Sometimes there were wooden benches, but " in certain instances seats for the children were entirely wanting, and for this reason they had to remain standing or squatting." [1] There were no maps or blackboards on the walls, but sometimes two or three prints of saints. No general regulations governing teaching and discipline appear to have been issued with exclusive reference to the schools of Chile, but it may be supposed that the rules issued by Benito Juárez de Gil, in 1598, for the teachers of reading, writing, and arithmetic in Lima, also represented the ideas entertained in Chile concerning the conduct of schools. This document shows how much more attention was given to practices and ceremonies imposed by the Church than to acquiring knowledge of subjects on which secular instruction lays stress.

It is hardly possible to classify the schools below the university as primary and secondary, for in all of them much of the work was elementary, the teaching of pupils to read and write. In those cases where the pupils lived in a building or in buildings belonging to the school, they were kept under the strict supervision of one of the members of a religious order or brotherhood, whose principal function was to supervise their conduct, and to teach them the practices and doctrines of the Church.

[1] Medina, *Instrucción pública*, cccxl.

VI

The universities conferred three degrees : that of bachelor of arts ; that of licentiate of arts ; and that of doctor. The degree of bachelor was given after the candidate had studied Logic and Metaphysics two years, and passed an examination before five members of the university. The degree of licentiate was given after a successful examination held at the end of the third year of study. For the degree of doctor a longer residence was necessary, and the candidate was required to give evidence of extensive reading in scholastic philosophy and medieval theology. The curriculum of the university of the Jesuits in Santiago was simliar to that of the universities maintained by this order in Córdova, Bogotá, and Manila.[1]

In the Jesuit and Dominican universities, the rector's power was limited to establishing and arranging the courses of instruction, and conferring degrees ; " but he was without any jurisdiction whatever over the graduates."[2] Although the universities did not differ from one another greatly with respect to organisation, they stood for somewhat different doctrines. The Dominicans followed Thomas Aquinas, while the Jesuits were Molinists, taking the *Concordia liberi arbitrii* of Luis de Molina as their guide.[3]

Although the Dominicans and the Jesuits had established schools empowered to confer degrees, there were some persons who thought the need of instruction was not fully satisfied. The character and scope of the teaching in each of these institutions were in a large measure determined by the special purposes of the controlling order. There arose, therefore, the idea of a university with less exclusive claims. The Bishop of Imperial, Antonio de San Miguel, gave early expression to this idea, and Juan

[1] Medina, *Instrucción pública*, ccclvi–ccclxiii. See Garro.
[2] Medina, ccclxiii.   [3] *Ibid.*, ccclxiv.

Pérez de Espinosa, Bishop of Santiago, wrote to the king advocating the founding in Chile of a royal university. He affirmed that such an institution would be important, as it would attract students from the provinces of Tucuman and Rio de la Plata, and make it unnecessary for young men to go from Chile to Lima for instruction.[1] But in view of the poverty of the colony, the small number of inhabitants, and the constant war with the Araucanians, it was difficult to make the projected university appear as an immediate necessity. The authorities of Spain, having granted charters to two universities in Chile, were persuaded that through them ample provision might be made for the education of the Chileans.

In view of the fact that the higher instruction was directed by the clergy almost exclusively to subjects that were supposed to prepare young men for the priestly office or the work of the missionary, it was evident that the little group of educated persons in Chile at the close of the seventeenth century possessed a cultivation that was strictly medieval in character, such a cultivation as could be derived, in an isolated colony, from the study of Latin Grammar, Medieval Philosophy, and Theology. In spite of circumstances apparently unfavourable for the cultivation of letters, a number of writers with sufficient talent to make themselves remembered belong to this middle age of Chile's colonial history. Their works indicate that the period was by no means barren. Some of the more noteworthy were : Fernando Álvarez de Toledo, Gonzalez de Nájera, Sotelo de Romai, Melchor Jufré del Águila, Alonso de Ovalle, Diego de Rosales, Jerónimo de Quiroga, José Basilio de Rojas y Fuentes, Santiago de Tesillo, Francisco Nuñez de Pineda y Bascuñan, Pedro de Oña, and Bishop Villarroel.

[1] Letter to the king, March 20, 1692 ; see Medina, ccclxxviii.

CHAPTER XIV

THE BEGINNING OF THE EIGHTEENTH CENTURY

I. The accession of Philip V. II. The hostility of the Portuguese.
III. French trade with the Indies. IV. Exploits of Charles Wager.
V. The theft of the ciborium in Lima. VI. The Asiento de
Negros of 1713. VII. The Prince of Santo Bono. VIII. Changes
in New Granada. IX. Hostility of civilians and ecclesiastics.

I

WITH the reign of Charles II (1665–1700), the line of
the Spanish Hapsburgs came to an inglorious end. The
nation that had played a great rôle in the drama of
European politics had lost its power and prestige, and
ambitious neighbours prepared to fight for the spoils of a
bankrupt state. The armies of Spain that had won
victories in many lands were now defeated and de-
moralised ; the navy that was thought to be invincible
was annihilated ; and reliance on the wealth of the Indies
had caused the industries of the country to fall into decay.
Unworthy favourites, corrupt officials, and the armies in
foreign wars had consumed the public revenues ; and the
fair prospects of a high-spirited people had been destroyed
by ecclesiastical fanaticism and the despotism of an un-
enlightened government.

The Count of Monclova, who had been viceroy of Peru
for ten years, was still the incumbent of this office when
the royal power of Spain passed from the Austrian to the
Bourbon dynasty. The Dutch, the English, and the
Portuguese, who were feared and detested in the colonies,
were among the enemies of the new king, and this fact
tended to bring the bulk of the colonists into sympathy

with him ; although the higher clergy were disposed to favour the Austrian pretender. The Spaniards and the descendants of the Spaniards in South America were still in large part loyal to the crown of Spain, and the knowledge that Charles II had designated Philip as his successor was sufficient to make them partisans of the Bourbon. They were, moreover, maintained in this attitude by the expectation that France, in supporting Philip, would protect the dependencies of Spain from the aggressions of their enemies.

II

Of these enemies, the Portuguese were in conflict with the Spanish colonists concerning the affairs of Paraguay, the region about the Rio de la Plata, and the undefined eastern frontier of Peru, on the Upper Amazon and its tributaries. The contest in the valley of the Rio de la Plata culminated in the struggle for the possession of Colonia. On the Peruvian frontier, the hostility of the Portuguese showed itself in excursions into the territory occupied by missionaries who had proceeded from Spain or the Spanish colonies. One of the most noteworthy of these missionaries was the Jesuit, Samuel Fritz, who entered the missions of Maynas in 1686. In addition to his work of establishing a large number of reductions of the Omaguas, he compiled various vocabularies and grammars of the languages used in the region of the missions, and constructed a map of the principal tributaries of the Amazon. Exhausted and in ill-health after the labour of three years, he descended the Amazon to Pará in 1689. His presence and a report of his work among the Omaguas aroused the suspicions of the Portugese governor, Arturo Sá de Meneses, who retained him at Pará, under the assumption that his purpose was to explore and claim for Spain territory which was already claimed by the Portuguese. In 1691 he was permitted to return to the Omaguas, but he was accompanied by a Portuguese official and a number of soldiers. The next year he was in Lima, where he endeavoured to persuade the viceroy to resist the encroachments of the Portuguese. Monclova, however, oppressed by the burden of advanced years, and unwilling to carry out a vigorous policy, replied that, since the Portuguese were Catholics and a warlike people, he had no means of bringing them into subjection, and he was excused from undertaking the task by the fact that the vast forests of the Amazon region produced nothing desired by the King of Spain ; moreover, that the great extent of the Indies offered all the land that would be needed by both crowns. Padre Fritz returned to the missions in 1693, but their prospects were ruined by the invasions of the Brazilians, and in the beginning of the eighteenth century they were entirely swept away. His permanent achievements were in the field of exploration and geography.[1] For losses on the Brazilian frontier the Spaniards received a certain compensation in the possession of Colonia.

With respect to encroachments from the sea, the viceroy displayed less indifference than he had shown concerning the Portuguese advances on the east. When he learned of the capture of Cartagena by Baron de Pointis, he ordered troops to be taken from Quito to the Isthmus, and at Callao prepared a squadron, with soldiers and whatever seemed to be necessary to repel the invaders, and at the same time ships, with infantry and the munitions of war, were sent from Spain for the purpose of rehabilitating the dismantled city. The ships of war available at this time in the Pacific were for the most part constructed at Guayaquil. They were constructed without great expense, and their quality was in keeping with their low cost. Monclova, like his predecessors and some

---

[1] Besides making the map already mentioned, Fritz wrote a work called *Del gran rio Marañon o Amazonas en las misiones de la compañia de Jesus geograficamente delineado* (Mendiburu, iii. 355).

of the viceroys who came after him, caused a number of warships to be built in the dockyards of Guayaquil. These were the *Concepcion*, the *Sacramento*, and the *San Lorenzo*. This work was forced upon the Peruvian government by the fact that, while other nations found the route around Cape Horn practicable for their ships, the Spaniards, either for lack of ships or because they did not dare to entrust them to these stormy seas, did not send vessels for the defence of the western coast until many years later.[1]

The American dependencies, in fact, received very little assistance from Spain during the early years of the eighteenth century. In these years Philip V was not in a position to look beyond the affairs of Europe. His attention and the revenues of the nation were absorbed by the war of the succession; and he was, moreover, ignorant of the state and needs of the colonists. And the viceroy, by reason of the inactivity of age and habits of mind induced by his long arbitrary rule, found himself out of touch with the movements of the society of his kingdom. A certain evidence of this is seen in a decree issued by him in 1701, which was designed to prevent the admission of mestizos, sambos, mulattoes, and quadroons to the higher courses of instruction in medicine, on the ground that they were excluded by the constitution and ordinances of the university. The king and the Council of the Indies, however, disapproved of this measure as contrary to the interests of the colonial society and as limiting the opportunities of persons who might be of service to their communities.

---

[1] " De manera que mièntras el paso del Cabo de Hornos era practicable para los buques enemigos que causaban frecuentes conflictos en las costas peruanas, los españoles ó porque no se atrevian ó porque no contaban en la península con buques suficientes, no los enviaban para custodiar estos mares ni lo hicieron hasta muchos años despues " (Mendiburu, vi. 542).

III

Shortly after his succession, Philip V appointed Manuel Oms de Semanat, Marquis of Casteldosrius, (1707–1710), to succeed Monclova as viceroy of Peru. The marquis at the time of his appointment was the Spanish Ambassador at the court of France. His departure for America was delayed for several years, and in the meantime Monclova continued to act as viceroy until his death on September 22, 1705. An important consequence of the connection formed between Spain and France by the accession of a Bourbon prince to the throne was the violation of Spain's restrictive policy by French ships loaded with European wares. By a royal decree, dated at Madrid January 11, 1701, it was provided that in consequence of this alliance and the close relations which existed between the two nations, French ships might enter the ports of the Indies, and for payment in money might receive the necessary supplies of provisions and material for such repairs of the ships as might be necessary to enable them to defend themselves against their enemies. This regulation did not authorise the introduction of French wares into the Spanish colonies ; but, as Governor Ibañez wrote to the king on the 2nd of May, 1702, it was impossible to prevent ships enjoying this privilege from introducing a certain amount of merchandise ; for they were authorised to receive supplies, and the persons who furnished these supplies were obliged to take goods in payment, since the ships were not provided with sufficient money for this purpose.[1]

The trade established by the French through these vessels with all the principal ports of the western coast of South America filled the towns with an abundance of articles of commerce, which the inhabitants either had not been able to obtain before, or had been able to obtain

---

[1] Barros Arana, *Historia jeneral de Chile*, v. 480.

only at much higher prices than were now demanded for them. Through the competition of many foreign buyers, moreover, the colonists reaped an advantage in the higher prices which they received for whatever they had to offer in exchange ; and the knowledge derived from this experience rendered them more dissatisfied than ever before with restrictions involved in Spain's commercial policy. The disclosure of Spain's inability to defend her ports against a foreign commercial invasion stimulated the British not only to extend their trade with South America, but also to obtain territorial possessions in that part of the world.

While the contraband trade carried on by the French was profitable to many persons, it added to the confusion that prevailed in the kingdom during the later years of Monclova's reign. This confusion was a consequence of Spain's neglect of her colonies in this troubled period, and of the inefficiency of the viceroy's government. On the death of Monclova, the audiencia assumed the supreme authority in Peru, and conducted the government until the arrival of the Marquis of Casteldosrius. Little improvement was expected from the new administration, for the audiencia in an interregnum had always the weakness of an interim government.

On the 7th of July 1707, the Marquis of Casteldosrius entered Lima, and began his long-postponed labours as viceroy. He had been ambassador in Paris and Lisbon, and in Paris he had presented the will of Charles II to Louis XIV. Devoted to the Bourbon cause, and knowing the impoverished state of the Spanish treasury, he sent 1,203,937 pesos to the king soon after his arrival in Lima. This sum was made up from funds accumulated by the audiencia, from loans from the treasury of *Obras Pias*, and from other sources. Although this sum was not sufficient to furnish any effective relief to the Spanish government, its withdrawal from Peru helped to increase the stagnation of the colony, where it might have contributed to make progressive action possible. Proceedings like this, repeated, as they were repeated, whenever funds could be appropriated by arbitrary power, help to explain the stagnation of the Spanish colonies.

IV

The continuous sending of funds to Spain deprived the colonial government of means that might have been advantageously used to provide for defence, which was especially needed in the period of the war of succession. At this time the enemies of Spain bore heavily upon Spanish and colonial interests. The exploits of Wager, Colb, and Rogers furnish a sufficiently accurate idea of what the colonists had to endure. The British vice-admiral, Charles Wager, sailed with a squadron from Jamaica on the 8th of June 1708. Off Cartagena he attacked the galleons returning to Spain, under the command of the Marquis of Casa Alegre. A number of the Spanish ships were lost, and with the *San José* five hundred and seventy-eight men perished. The *Gobierno*, commanded by the Count of Vega Florida, carrying 5,000,000 pesos, was surrendered to the British commander. About a month before this event, Thomas Colb, an English pirate, sailed from Darien, entered the Chagres river, and captured a number of small vessels loaded with wares that were reported to be worth five hundred thousand dollars. To this year belongs also the expedition fitted out by the merchants of Bristol. It consisted of two vessels, the *Duke* and the *Duchess*, under the chief command of Woodes Rogers, with William Dampier in the second position. Rogers passed around Cape Horn, and visited the island of Juan Fernandez. On the island he found Alexander Selkirk, who had been abandoned there somewhat more than four years before. From Juan Fernandez Captain Rogers sailed northward, and in February 1709 took and sacked Guayaquil. After this he compelled the inhabitants to pay a large sum as a ransom for their city. He captured a number of vessels, and, off the coast of California, he took a galleon from Manila. The report of these exploits stimulated the viceroy to extraordinary efforts for defence. He made a general enrolment of the men of the ages in which they are usually held to be subject to military duty, not excepting the members of the clergy and the students of the university and of the colleges of Lima. He manned and equipped five vessels at an expenditure of 146,656 pesos, which necessitated the resort to funds that had been set aside for other purpoess. This squadron sailed from Callao on the 16th of July 1709, proceeded along the coast of Peru, Central America, and Mexico, but, in a cruise that lasted more than a year, failed to encounter the enemy, who was already returning to England by way of the Cape of Good Hope.

The disappearance of the enemy and the birth of the Prince of Asturias, later Ferdinand VI, were celebrated in Lima with great display. As a part of the celebration, the viceroy caused a drama to be represented, which he had written, and which was called *Perseo*. At this time the viceroy's palace was the meeting-place of an academy of writers, who came together every Monday to present their writings, and discuss subjects relating to literature. Among these was Dr. Pedro Peralta Barnuevo, the encyclopedic author of *Lima Fundada*.[1]

These reunions of well-known men of letters had more

---

[1] This remarkable writer was born in Lima, and, like Lord Bacon and Georg Stjernhjelm, seems to have taken " all knowledge to be his province." He was rector of the University of San Marcos during the years 1715, 1716, and 1717, and served as cosmographer from 1708 until 1743. He was a lawyer, directed an academy which he had founded, served many years as engineer-in-chief of Peru, and in this capacity planned and directed important works at the port of Callao. According to Mendiburu, Peralta was " a master of six languages, and in the most of them he wrote poetry correctly and in good taste ; he was well versed in sacred and profane history, was a profound mathematician, chemist, botanist, and student in medicine ; and his studies

or less influence on the society of Lima, in that they emphasized the fact that a number of persons of recognised ability and position thought it worth the while to devote a part of their time to literature. Some persons, however, expressed their regrets that the palace of the viceroys had been, as they said, turned into a theatre, and the viceroy, in violation of ancient customs and the dignity of his office, had permitted himself to become the head of a literary club.

On the death of Casteldosrius, April 22, 1710, the audiencia referred to the papers containing the provisions made for the succession, in case the viceroy died before his successor had been appointed by the king ; and it was found that Juan Gonzalez de Santiago, Bishop of Cuzco, was named to assume the viceregal authority ; but that, in default of this person, this authority should pass to Antonio de Leon, Bishop of Arequipa ; and, in default of both of these, to Diego Ladron de Guevara, Bishop of Quito. As the first and second persons named had died before the viceroy, the Bishop of Quito was recognised as the head of the viceroyalty. He arrived in Lima on the 30th of August 1710.

Shortly after the accession of the Bishop of Quito,

in jurisprudence and canonical and theological matters he carried as far as the first professors of his time " (vi. 265). A view of the wide range of his work may be derived from the following imperfect list of his writings : *Desvíos de la naturaleza, ú origen de los mónstruos ; Tratado fisico-médico-teológico ; Lima triunfante ; Imágen política, ó Gobierno del virey-obispo de Quito ; Causa académica ; Júpiter Olímpico ; Certámen para el recibimiento del Virey Arzobispo de Charcas ; Observaciones astronómicas* (in Latin) ; *Elógio del Cardenal Alberoni* (in Italian) ; *Templo de la Fama ; Diálogo de la Justicia y de la Verdad ; Historia de España ; Alegaciones jurídicas ; La gloria de Luis el Grande* and *El Truunfo de Astrea* (in French) ; *Lima Fundada, ó conquista del Peru ; Gobierno del Conde de la Monclova ; Tratado fisico-matemático ; Defensa política y militar de Lima ; Gobierno de Virey Castellfuerte ; Tratado músico-matemático ; Nuevo sistema astrológico demostrativo ; Geometría especulativa, y aritmética ; Pasion y triunfo de Cristo ; Obras poéticas, líricas y cómicas* (in two volumes).

On the academy of Viceroy Casteldosrius, see *Mercurio Peruano*, Nos. 16 and 17, February 1791.

(1710–1716), the inhabitants of Lima prepared a brilliant celebration of the victory of Villaviciosa, in which the French under Vendome defeated the Austrians under Starhemberg, and thus destroyed the hopes of Philip's rivals. One feature of this celebration was the production in the palace of Peralta's comedy called *Triunfos de Amor y Poder*.

V

In this period of increasing religious devotion among the common people, the community of Lima was shocked to learn that at the end of January 1711 the ciborium had been stolen from the sagrario. This became known on the morning of the 31st, and the report of it spread rapidly throughout the city. The high altar and the towers of the cathedral were draped in black ; the bells of all the churches were tolled ; and everywhere there was an oppressive sentiment that a great act of sacrilege had been committed. When the property was finally found, there was as much excitement in the city as would have been caused by the discovery of a new Potosi. The populace crowded about the place where it had been buried, shouted their " vivas " for the viceroy, the faith, and the holy sacrament, and the bells of the churches changed their tone and filled the city with the clamour of rejoicing. Viewing the frequent earthquakes as divine punishment for their transgressions, the people had a very natural fear that awful consequences might attend this desecration of their holy temple. The place where the sacred object was discovered became the goal of numberless pilgrimages, and over it was erected the church of Santa Liberata.[1]

Among the other causes of the continued popular agitation were the reports of new British expeditions

---

[1] Palma, Ricardo, *La Fundación de Santa Liberata*, in *Tradiciones Peruanas*, i. 291–5.

that were preparing to make war on Chile and Peru, and the threatening attitude of runaway slaves, who were assaulting the carriers of goods and passengers, and plundering estates in the country.

VI

Towards the end of the bishop's administration, the war of succession was closed by the Treaty of Utrecht. The features of this treaty that specially interested the Spanish colonies were the confirmation of Philip V as King of Spain, and the concession to a British company of the right to introduce slaves into Spanish America, together with a limited quantity of British wares in a " privileged ship."

The *asiento*, or contract, of 1713 was not the beginning of a new policy with respect to the slave trade, but was merely a grant of privileges to a British company. The Spaniards had been dealing in black slaves for two hundred and sixty years, and had carried them to America as early as 1510. They were taken on the private account of King Ferdinand. But in 1516 the exclusive privilege to transport negroes to America was granted to a person named Chevris, who ceded his right to a company of Genoese merchants for the sum of 23,000 ducats. The first negroes despatched under this privilege were one thousand sent to Santo Domingo in 1517.[1] After the recommendation of Las Casas concerning the importation of negro slaves had been adopted, it was thought that four thousand would be adequate to meet the immediate demands. By the *asiento* of 1517, Charles V extended the privilege of this trade to De Dresa, a Fleming, under the assurance of a monopoly for eight years, which had the effect of increasing the price of negroes. In the last years of the sixteenth century, Philip II had great need of money, and he sought to procure it by granting for a

[1] *Present State of Peru*, 89.

consideration the exclusive privilege of the slave trade with America. Gomez Reinel held this privilege from 1595 to 1600, when it was granted to a Portuguese named Juan Rodriguez Contineo, who agreed to furnish to the Indies annually 4250 slaves, and to pay to the Crown 160,000 ducats. On the death of Rodriguez Contineo his privilege and obligations under this contract fell to his brother, and at the time of the transfer the annual payment to the Crown was reduced 22,000 ducats. A few years later, in 1615, the *asiento* was granted to Antonio Fernandez Delvas for the period of eight years. Delvas was a Portuguese, and under his contract he was obliged to introduce into America each year 3500 slaves, and to pay 115,000 ducats to the Crown. At the expiration of the period of this grant, the *asiento* was assigned for another eight years to another Portuguese, Manuel Rodriguez Lamego, who agreed to introduce the same number of slaves, 3500, but to increase by 5000 ducats the annual payment. During the eight years following 1631, the contract called for a payment to the Crown of 95,000 ducats, and the introduction of 2500 slaves. After this period there was an interruption of this form of the slave trade till 1662. In this year the *asiento* was granted to Domingo Grillo and Ambrosio Lomelin, for a term of seven years, during which they were required to introduce 24,500 negroes, and pay the king 2,100,000 dollars. In 1674 the privilege of this trade passed to Antonio Garcia and Sebastian de Siliceo, who were required to import annually 4000 slaves, and pay 450,000 dollars. Owing to a failure on the part of this company to comply with the terms of the grant, it was recalled in 1676, and conferred on a company in Seville. In 1682 the privilege of this trade was granted for five years to Juan Barroso del Pozo and Nicolas Porcio, residents at Cadiz. They had agreed to pay 1,125,000 dollars, but, as they failed in this, the contract was transferred to a Hollander, Baltasar Coimans. Prior to this time the holders of this privilege had been Europeans, but in 1692 it was assigned to Bernardo Francisco Martin de Guzman, of Venezuela, for five years, on the payment of 2,125,000 dollars. He was followed in 1696 by the Portuguese company of Guinea, who held the *asiento* for six years, after which it passed to the French Guinea Company, and finally, by the treaty of 1713, the monopoly of the slave trade with Spanish America fell into the hands of the British.[1]

Under the *asiento* of 1713, an English company was obliged to introduce 144,000 negroes into Spanish America within thirty years, beginning May 1, 1713, at the rate of 4800 each year. For each negro the company was required to pay thirty-three dollars and a third, which would cover all duties that existed then or that might be imposed later. The company was required, moreover, to advance to the Spanish king 200,000 dollars in two equal payments, the first to be made two months after the signing of the contract, and the second two months after the first. This amount was not to be returned to it until after twenty years; then for the last ten years of the specified term it might withhold 20,000 dollars a year from the duties otherwise payable. In consideration of the advance payment of 200,000 dollars, the risks, and the interest, the company was required to pay duty on only 4000 negroes annually, the remaining 800 being admitted without payment. The importation in any given year was, however, not limited to the prescribed 4800. There was, in fact, an inducement offered to have it exceed that number; for each negro imported over that number in the first twenty-five years of the term, there was required a duty of only sixteen dollars and two-thirds.

For carrying on this trade, the company might employ

---

[1] Calvo, *Colección Completa de los Tratados de la America Latina*, ii. 53–5; for the *Asiento* of 1696, see pp. 5–42; for that of 1701, see pp. 61–77; for that of 1713, see pp. 78–101; also *The Asiento; or Contract for Allowing to the Subjects of Great Britain the Liberty of Importing Negroes into the Spanish America*, printed by John Baskett (London, 1713).

either British or Spanish ships. In case Spanish ships were used, it must be with the consent of their owners, freight being paid them. The ships, moreover, might be manned with either English or Spanish sailors. In view of the fact that those provinces which had not had landing-places for slaves hitherto, had been considered as enduring great hardships, it was by this contract provided that negroes might be sold in all ports of the Atlantic where there were royal officers to certify to the number imported. At the same time three hundred dollars was fixed as the maximum price for which negroes might be sold in the ports of Santa Marta, Cumaná, and Maracaybo, but in the ports of Mexico and Central America, the company might sell them for whatever it might be able to get for them. Of the annual importation of 4800 negroes, 1200 might be taken to the Rio de la Plata, 800 for Buenos Aires, and 400 for neighbouring provinces, and there sold without restriction as to price. On the Pacific coast of South America, only the ports of Peru were open to the company. To these it was permitted to ship negroes from Panama, and to enter at Panama without duty the gold and silver brought back as the produce of their sales. This trade enjoyed other exemptions from the established duties. Whatever cables, sails, iron, or other stores and provisions were necessary for the ships engaged in the trade between Panama and Peru might be entered at Porto Bello without duty, but the articles so entered might not be sold. For the management of the trade in negroes, the company was permitted to employ either English or Spanish,

" his Catholic majesty dispensing for that end, with the laws which forbid strangers entering into or inhabiting that country ; declaring and commanding that the English, during the whole time of this *asiento*, shall be regarded and treated as if they were subjects of the Crown of Spain, with this restriction, that there shall not reside in any one of the said ports of the Indies more than four or six Englishmen." [1]

For the administration of its affairs, the company was empowered to appoint " in all the ports and chief places of America, Judges Conservators of this *asiento* whom it may remove and displace, and appoint others at pleasure." For their removal, however, it was necessary to show cause that would be approved by the president, governor, or audiencia of the district. These judges were to have exclusive jurisdiction in all cases relating to the *asiento*, and the authorities of the country, even the viceroys, were forbidden to interfere. But from the decisions of these judges appeals might be taken to the Council of the Indies.

The royal officers might not lay an embargo on the ships of the company, or detain them for any cause whatsoever ; but they were " obliged to afford them all favour, assistance, and succour " ; nor could they under any pretence seize their stock, goods, or effects, or search their warehouses, except after proved fraudulent importation, and then only with the assistance of a judge conservator. In shipping their goods to Europe the company was permitted to make use of Spanish vessels, by " agreeing for the freight with the captains and owners of the ships " ; or it might employ its own vessels under the free convoy of the Spanish ships of war. And all goods thus imported into Spain would be admitted free of duty, the stock of the company being regarded as having " the same privilege as if it belonged to his Catholic majesty."

The formation of this contract made it unlawful " for the French Guinea Company or for any other person whatsoever to introduce any negro slave into India," under the penalty of confiscation of ships and negroes.

[1] *The Asiento ; or Contract for Allowing to the Subjects of Great Britain the Liberty of Importing Negroes into the Spanish America*, printed by John Baskett (London, 1713), art. xi.

The ships engaged in the trade in negroes under this contract might not be used for taking to Spain either Spanish passengers or goods belonging to Spanish subjects ; and on arriving at American ports they should be " searched to the bottom, even to the ballast," and any goods found on board should be seized and the guilty parties punished. But provisions put on shore to maintain the negroes should be exempt from duty. In case, however, more were landed than could be consumed, the surplus might be sold after paying the duties established at the port in question. The duties on negroes imported were due as soon as the arrangements preparatory to landing had been made by the royal officers. If any of the negroes should die before they were sold, this fact would not exempt them from duty, except in cases where they were found to be ill, and were landed not for sale but for the sake of improving their health, and should die within fifteen days after landing. If they were alive at the expiration of fifteen days, they would be subject to duty. Having paid duty at one port, negroes might be transported to another port, and entered without payment, on the presentation of the proper certificate from the officers of the first port.

This contract was not formed without regard to the revenues of the kings of England and Spain.

" It is agreed and stipulated that both their majesties shall be concerned for one half of this trade, each of them a quarter part which shall belong to him, pursuant to this agreement. And whereas it is necessary that his Catholic Majesty, in order to have and enjoy the benefit and gain that may be obtained by this trade, should advance to the said company one million dollars, or a quarter of the sum which shall be judged necessary for the putting of this commerce into a good order and method, it is agreed and settled that if his Catholic majesty shall not think it convenient to advance the said sum, the aforementioned *asientists* do offer to do it out of their own money, upon condition that his Catholic majesty shall make good the interest out of what they shall be accountable for to him, at the rate of eight per cent. yearly."

At the end of the first five years, the company was required to render to the King of Spain a sworn account

" of the charge of the purchase, subsistence, and sale of the negroes, and all other expenses upon their account ; and also certificates in due form, of the produce of their sale in all ports and parts of America belonging to his Catholic majesty, whither they shall have been imported and sold ; which accounts, as well of the charge as of the produce, are first to be examined and settled by her Britannic majesty's ministers employed in this service, in regard to the share she is to have in this *asiento*, and then to be examined in like manner by this court ; and his Catholic majesty's share of the profits may be adjusted and recovered from the *asientists*, who are to be obliged to pay the same most regularly and punctually, in pursuance of this article."

Out of the profits of the first five years the company might reimburse itself for the advance of the Spanish king's quarter part and for the interest. A similar account was required every five years successively. For three years after the expiration of the thirty years specified in the contract, the company should enjoy the same privileges and immunities as were guaranteed to it for the term of the contract, in order to give it opportunity " to adjust its accounts, and gather in all its effects in the Indies, and to make up a balance of the whole." A special provision was made for collecting debts due the company, by placing them on the same footing as debts due the king.

The participation of Spain in the affairs covered by

this contract was through a committee of three appointed by the king from the Council of the Indies. In case of war between Spain and England, the company should have a year and a half to withdraw its effects from Spain and the Indies ; but in case of war between either of these kingdoms and another nation, the ships belonging to the company should be neutral and carry passes and special colours. For the thirty years of the contract and three additional years, all Spanish laws in conflict with the terms of this agreement were set aside in favour of the contract. And whatever liberties, favours, privileges, and exemptions had been granted to any former company were turned to the advantage of the company under this contract, in so far as they were not in conflict with any of its specific provisions. In addition to the trade in negroes, the company was permitted to participate in the general trade with the Indies to the extent of the capacity of one ship of five hundred tons a year during the specified thirty years. In this trade the King of Spain was to have one-fourth interest, and to receive five per cent. of the net gain of the other three-fourths. The goods imported into America under this provision were to be exempt from duty, and could be sold only at the fair of Porto Bello. If the vessel carrying them should arrive before the Spanish fleet, they were to be stored in warehouses locked with two keys, one of which should be held by the royal officers of the port, and the other by the agents of the company.

The articles of the treaty of 1713, which referred to the participation of the English in the annual fair at Porto Bello, were explained and modified by a subsequent treaty made in 1716. The English had complained that, on account of irregularity as to time and place of holding the fair and of the difficulty of preserving their wares, particularly at Porto Bello, the trade was likely to be attended with loss rather than gain. In this treaty the King of Spain agreed " to inform the English court of the exact time of the sailing of the Spanish vessels for the Indies, so that the company might cause its ship to sail at the same time." In case the Spanish vessels should not leave Cadiz in the month of June, the English company might send its vessel, having informed the Spanish government of the time of its departure. If it arrived at the port where it had been determined to hold the fair, at Cartagena, Porto Bello, or Vera Cruz, before the arrival of the Spanish vessels, it should wait for them four months, after which its wares might be sold without restriction.

This treaty contained another concession to the English company. It was found that sometimes more wares were taken to Africa for the purchase of slaves than could be used. In such cases, as there were no warehouses in Africa, the company wished the privilege of transporting the surplus to the Indies. The King of Spain acceded to this wish with respect to Buenos Aires, because " between Africa and the port of Buenos Aires there was no island or landing-place under the British king where the vessels of the *asiento de negros* could halt." This was not true of the ports of Caracas, Cartagena, Porto Bello, Vera Cruz, Havana, Porto Rico, and San Domingo ; for Jamaica and other islands of the West Indies were already under British authority, and furnished as accessible harbours as those under the control of the Spaniards. It was, moreover, determined to make the term of the *asiento* begin on May 1, 1714, instead of one year earlier, as had been provided in the treaty of 1713, and to have the terms of the payments arranged accordingly.[1]

Under this treaty the English had been granted the privilege of participating in the trade of the Indies to the extent of the wares that might be carried in one ship

[1] Tractado declaratorio de algunos articulos del asiento de negros que se pactó el 26 de marzo de 1716 con la Inglaterra, concluido en Madrid el 26 de mayo de 1716. This treaty is printed in Calvo's *Colección*, ii. 181–6.

of five hundred tons sailing annually. In order to derive from this concession the maximum advantage, the representatives of this thrifty nation took with their privileged ship sometimes five or six smaller vessels loaded with goods. When they arrived near Porto Bello, the provisions and furniture were removed from the privileged vessel, and she was filled to the rigging with wares taken from the little ships in attendance. By this simple artifice the privileged ship was made to carry more than five or six of the largest ships of Spain. The English being able to sell cheaper than the Spaniards, that indulgence, according to the Spanish view, " was of infinite detriment to the commerce of Spain." [1] After this first invasion of Spain's exclusive control, that country appeared unable to furnish the goods that were demanded by her transatlantic possessions, and their wants had to be supplied from other countries. Holland followed England, and in the course of time every manufacturing nation of Europe had part in the trade with Spanish America.

To surround the violation of commercial regulations with all the terrors of the law, it was provided that in case foreigners should succeed in entering Spanish-American ports, the inhabitants should not trade with them, on pain of death and confiscation of property. But these laws were not effective. The number of foreigners in the seaport towns and the amount of foreign trade increased, and in certain quarters, particularly at Buenos Aires, the contraband trade very early exceeded the legal trade with Spain. In fact, the city of Buenos Aires outran in its growth other towns because of the great advantages of the contraband trade over the legitimate trade.

VII

Ladron de Guevara was deprived of the viceregal office on March 2, 1716, on account of charges that were made

[1] Juan and Ulloa, *A Voyage to South America*, i. 103.

against him. Some of these charges were unjust, some were made in ignorance and malice ; but some were sufficiently important and well founded to persuade the king to supersede him. The chief authority in the government was assumed by the audiencia, and was passed by that body to Diego Morcillo, the Archbishop of Chuquisaca, who, after fifty days, was relieved of his temporary post by the arrival of Carmine Nicolás Caraccioli, Prince of Santo Bono (1716–20). Ladron de Guevara remained in Lima until the conclusion of his residencia, and embarked at Callao for Acapulco, March 18, 1717, and died in Mexico the same year, on November 9.

Caraccioli was born in Naples. Before he went to Peru, he had been the Spanish ambassador in Rome and in Venice, and had acquired the distinction that attached to a grandee of Spain. He entered Lima as viceroy on October 5, 1716. Among the orders which the Crown sent to the viceroy during the administration of Ladron de Guevara was one requiring him to prohibit all trade with foreign nations ; and this policy was especially emphasized in the royal instructions to Caraccioli. During the early years of Philip's reign, while the court of France dominated the government of Spain, Spain's protective policy suffered serious damage ; but the assertion of national independence from French domination was followed by attempts to repair the breaches in the ancient commercial system. It was decreed that vessels contravening the established rules should be taken and burned, and the goods should be confiscated. The viceroy, moreover, organised at the ports a system of guards for the purpose of patrolling the coast ; and he re-enacted the regulations of his predecessors prohibiting the exportation of gold that had not paid the king's fifth, and sought to keep the management of the mines subject to strict rules.

VIII

An important change in the organisation of the north-western part of South America in the reign of Caraccioli was the establishment of the viceroyalty of New Granada. The order effecting this modification of the government was issued in 1717.[1] The desirability of this or some other change in the government of New Granada became evident in the disgraceful conflicts between the audiencia and the president, and between the ecclesiastical and civil officials. President Meneces was deposed by the audiencia in 1715, and sent to Spain, but it was there shown that the action of the oidores was without justification. During the next three years the government was at first directed by the audiencia, then by Nicolas Infante de Venegas, afterwards by Francisco del Rincon, of the order of San Francisco de Paula, who was promoted from the position of Arch-bishop of Santo Domingo to be the Archbishop of Santa Fé de Bogotá, and who assumed the office of president in 1718. The same year Antonio de la Pediosa y Guerrero, of the Council of the Indies, was appointed by the king to organise the viceroyalty of New Granada, and to become the first viceroy. In 1719 he was succeeded by Jorge Villalonga.[2]

As a part of this reform, the audiencias of Quito and Panama were suppressed ; the province of Panama, however, remained subordinated to the viceroy of Peru. This reform was effected not only to put an end to the confusion existing in the government, but also to avoid the expenses involved in the salaries of a number of officials. But a brief experience under the new order showed the great inconvenience to which the inhabitants

[1] Real cédula de erección del vireinato, dated Segovia, May 27, 1717 (*Documentos sobre límites de los Estados-Unidos de Colombia*, por Ricardo S. Pereira (Bogota, 1883), 5–8).

[2] It has been frequently stated that Villalonga instead of Pedrosa was the first viceroy. See Groot, *Historia de Nueva Granada*, ii. 20.

of Quito and the Isthmus were subjected in being compelled to resort to Lima to obtain a judicial settlement of their controversies ; for, although Quito was embraced in the new viceroyalty, it was, in judicial matters, subject to the audiencia of Lima, in such form that cases decided in the presidency might be carried to that tribunal as a court of appeal.[1] It was found, moreover, that the sum made available by the suppression of offices was insufficient to support the viceregal government. The authorities had, therefore, to face the alternatives, either to make a considerable addition to this sum from the royal treasury or to abolish the viceregal organisation, and to re-establish the offices that had been suppressed. The latter alternative was adopted, and a decree was issued, terminating the reign of Viceroy Villalonga and re-establishing the audiencias. But the embarrassment of the too extended jurisdiction of the viceroy increased from year to year, and, in 1739, it was ordered by royal decree that the viceroyalty of New Granada should be reorganised and its jurisdiction extended over the territory subject to the audiencias of Quito, Bogotá, and Caracas.[2]

The first viceroy of New Granada under the new order was Lieutenant-General Sebastian Eslaba, who was occupied during the whole of his administration, from 1740 to 1749, in defending the coast of the country against foreign aggression, particularly against the attacks of the British under Admiral Vernon, on Cartagena ; and during this period he did not visit Bogotá, the capital of the kingdom.[3]

IX

In the year of the reform of the government of New Granada, the ordinarily latent hostility of the civil and

---

[1] Cevallos, Pedro Fermin, *Historia del Ecuador*, ii. 9.

[2] Real cédula de reerección del vireinato, dated San Ildefonso, August 20, 1739 (Pereira, *Documentos sobre límites*, 11–14).

[3] *Relaciones de los Vireyes del Nuevo Reino de Granada*, Prologo, xviii.

ecclesiastical authorities came into open conflict over the assassination of Alonso Esquivel, the major-domo of Diego Morcillo, the Archbishop of Charcas. The assassin was Juan Manuel Ballesteros. After the commission of the crime, Ballesteros took refuge in the church of the bare-footed friars, but the alcaldes went to the church with an armed force and arrested him. On the 21st the vicar-general sent a demand to the alcaldes requiring them to return the criminal to the church within an hour. He informed them, moreover, that, in case of their refusal, they would be placed under an ecclesiastical interdict. But the alcaldes retained Ballesteros, and an anathema was promulgated against them " in a nocturnal procession with great noise and the clangor of bells," and they were declared excommunicated. In the meantime the criminal had died under torture, and the ecclesiastics found them-selves in a somewhat embarrassing position ; they had not carried their point, and the alcaldes were disposed to go about their business, although they were under the ban. It was seen by the Church that this would be in effect flouting the decree of excommunication before the people. To avoid a loss of prestige, and to escape from this unpleasant situation, Archbishop Zuloaga summoned a council of ecclesiastics, and it was agreed that the alcaldes should be absolved. This absolution, however, only enabled the officials of the Church to get out of the cul-de-sac into which they had run. It was of no importance to the alcaldes ; for, although absolved, the king took up the case and decreed that they should be perpetually prohibited from holding any administrative or judicial office, and each was condemned to pay a fine of one thousand pesos.

Two months later the inhabitants of Lima were moved by finding the body of a Chilean, named Juan Portales, hanging from the high window of his shop, and near him on a table his will, written a few days before his death. In this document he bequeathed his soul to the devil on condition that the devil would assist him in executing his plan to kill his wife and the man who had become her paramour.   Five days later, in a room in a neighbouring street, the bodies of the wife and a monk were found, and no one doubted that they had been murdered by Portales.[1]

In these years the inhabitants of Peru suffered from the lack of certain important articles of food, particularly such as they had been accustomed to derive from wheat, the production of which had almost entirely ceased on some of the lands that had formerly been fruitful. Although wheat was imported from Chile, the supply was not sufficient to prevent the price from rising to fifty pesos the fanega.

At the same time a pest, or an infectious disease, appeared in Upper Peru, which carried off its victims by the thousand.   There is no reliable statement of the number of those who perished, but it is affirmed that in many cases mines and agricultural estates were deprived of their labourers ;   the herds were abandoned, and crops were not harvested.   The dead often remained unburied for days, and even at last were only imperfectly interred.   Ignorance of sanitary precautions and the carelessness displayed in the disposition of the dead and their effects contributed to spread the disease ; and among the victims were counted some who died of terror.[2]

It is reported that Archbishop Morcillo predicted his return to the office of viceroy when, after his brief reign of fifty days, he surrendered the staff of command to the Prince of Santo Bono.   That such a prophecy was ever uttered is not perfectly clear, but it is known that Morcello entered Lima as viceroy (1720–1724) on January 26, 1720.

[1] Mendiburu, vi. 523.

[2] Regarding the nature of the disease, a Peruvian writer makes the following statement : " Los síntomas más comunes fueron fiebre intensa, fuertes dolores de cabeza y vientre, delirio, sangre negra por la nariz, y vómitos mortales de sangre " (Lorente, *Historia del Perú bajo los Borbones*, 32).

One of his early acts, after his accession, was to despatch a number of armed vessels in pursuit of the English pirate, John Clipperton, who had entered the Pacific by way of Cape Horn with a frigate carrying forty guns. Near Guayaquil, Clipperton captured a vessel which was conveying the Marquis of Villa Rocha to Callao from Panama, where he had been president of the audiencia.[1]

At Nicoya Clipperton landed the marchioness and her baggage, but held the marquis for a ransom. He returned to the Chilean coast, and later crossed the Pacific. At the Marianna Islands Villa Rocha escaped, and thus put an end to the pirate's expectation of a ransom. The vessels sent by the viceroy to search for the pirate returned to Callao without accomplishing the object of their mission. Clipperton, in the meantime, having lost a vessel which he had captured off the coast of Mexico, proceeded to the Philippine Islands, where he was taken and imprisoned.

In internal affairs, the quicksilver mines of Huancavelica continued to be the source of controversy and social disturbance. These mines were the property of the State, and the labourers employed in them were obtained under the system of the mita. At this time it was proposed that the mita should be abolished, and volunteer labour substituted for forced labour. This and other regulations ordered by the Crown were opposed by the authorities in immediate control of the mines ; and in the controversy which followed the supreme government

---

[1] The Marquis of Villa Rocha was born in Quito, June 20, 1661. In 1699 he was appointed president of the audiencia of Panama. After he had held this office for six months he was replaced by Pedro Luis Henriquez de Guzman. Later he held the same office for about a year, when he was removed on certain accusations that were brought against him. He was tried and acquitted ; and was then appointed to the presidency of the audiencia for the third time. Under this appointment he was to hold the office until the arrival in Panama of José Hurtado de Amézaga. This proved to be a period of six hours.

appeared, as in many other cases, issuing decrees respecting economic affairs without adequate knowledge for its guidance.

Near the close of the reign of the viceroy-archbishop, Paraguay, in the antagonism that existed between Asuncion and the Jesuit missions, seemed to be on the eve of civil war.

CHAPTER XV

ANTEQUERA AND THE REVOLUTION IN PARAGUAY

I. The reign of Castel-Fuerte. II. Industrial domination of the Jesuit reductions. III. Reyes governor of Paraguay. IV. Antequera's usurpation and rebellion. V. The battle of Tebicuary and Antequera's advance towards the reductions. VI. Zebala appointed to put down the rebellion. VII. Antequera's departure from Paraguay. VIII. His imprisonment and execution.

I

In 1724 José Armendáriz, the Marquis of Castel-Fuerte, succeeded Morcillo in the office of viceroy (1724–36). He sailed from Cadiz, December 31, 1723, and arrived at Cartagena in February 1724. On the voyage from Cartagena westward, he captured, near Porto Bello, four ships engaged in contraband trade. He caused the fortifications of Chagres and Panama to be strengthened, and, proceeding to Peru, arrived at Lima on May 14, 1724. At this time Spain's commercial regulations were violated at many points, sometimes under the cloak of the limited concession granted to Great Britain in connection with the slave trade. British wares were introduced into the Spanish colonies, not only by the "privileged ships," but also by each vessel that carried negro slaves. Each vessel that carried slaves to Buenos Aires carried also fifty tons of baize, and this importation disturbed seriously the direct trade between that port and Spain.[1]

[1] " Por Buenos Aires introducia la bandera britanica con cada cargamento de africanos, cincuenta toneladas de bayetas, cuya concesion daba márgen á muchas desmanes " (Mendiburu, i. 347).

The British, moreover, found it advantageous to limit the number of negroes carried in each ship, in order that more ships might be required to deliver annually the four thousand and eight hundred slaves which the contract required them to introduce. By this means it was expected that the incidental trade under the concession would be increased. In some years the number of negroes carried to America exceeded the number specified.

II

The most notable event in the reign of Castel-Fuerte was the revolution in Paraguay, in which Dr. José de Antequera y Castro played a principal part. During the fifty years preceding 1720, Paraguay and Tucuman were almost constantly engaged in wars with native tribes, suffering often severe losses through invasions by the savages of the Chaco. Only in the Jesuit missions had the Indians been brought into peaceful and friendly relations with the Europeans. Here the Guaranis had been led by the Jesuits to abandon the wild life of the forests, and turn their faces towards civilisation. On the lands about the missions they had raised great herds of cattle ; they had monopolised trade in the products of the country ; and maintained factories for making wares designed for their consumption and exportation. By working as communities and producing on a large scale, they were able to prevent individual persons from carrying on a profitable competition with them. The inhabitants of Asuncion considered the industrial success of the missions as a hindrance to their material progress, and, as a consequence of this view, they assumed a hostile attitude towards the Jesuits. They asserted that the Jesuits were priests and merchants at the same time ; that they were subjects in name and absolute sovereigns in fact ; that they united in themselves the characters of the soldier and the monk, substituting a worldly policy for the inspiration of the Gospel, and sacrificing by their calumny and powerful influence all bishops and governors who dared to resist their increasing power.[1]

The report of Matías de Anglés, in the case of Antequera, deals extensively with the production and commerce of the Jesuit missions : " The Fathers of the Society have, on the banks of the rivers Paraná and Uruguay, twenty-six pueblos, or *doctrinas*, embracing a multitude of Indians, and four other pueblos, lying between the Paraná and the Tebicuary, and near the latter river, and it is commonly reported that they have four or six other pueblos besides those already mentioned, which are withheld from the knowledge and records of the Spaniards. But the thirty mentioned are known. . . .

" Each of these thirty pueblos, or *doctrinas*, which are called Missions of Paraguay, has such an abundance of wealth that it might maintain with what is necessary six other pueblos, since it has at least thirty or forty thousand cows, and the usual proportion of bulls, abundant and fruitful fields of all kinds of grain, and especially of cotton, from which they gather very large crops, and which the Indians spin and weave. They also cultivate cane and tobacco, which are esteemed, and which are consumed in great quantities. Each pueblo has also numerous colts, horses, and mules, and large flocks of sheep. On account of the great industry of the Fathers, and the multitude of Indians whom they hold in service and continually at work, and the fertile lands and fields which they occupy, they are able to produce and sell as much as they will." [2]

[1] Lorente, *Historia del Perú bajo los Borbones*, 39.

[2] *Informe que hizo el General D. Matías de Anglés y Gortari, corregidor de Potosí, sobre los puntos que fueron causa de las discordias sucedidas en la provincia del Paraguay.* See Mendiburu, i. 258.

The succeeding pages of this report deal with the various industries and commerce of the missions ; the gathering of the *yerba del Paraguay ;* the production of tobacco, sugar, and cotton ; the importations and exportations, and the disposition made of the revenues.

III

Paraguay at this time, the beginning of the eighteenth century, was under the general jurisdiction of the viceroy of Peru, and immediately subject to the judicial authority of the audiencia of Charcas. In 1717 Diego de los Reyes was appointed to be the governor of Paraguay, and from the beginning of his administration he pursued a course of conduct that aroused hostility on the part of those who were more directly subject to his authority. He was presumptuous, overbearing, and disagreeably ostentatious of his power. He was the creature and partisan of the Jesuits, an advocate of their views, and a supporter of their industrial and commercial operations. He was thus regarded by the inhabitants of Asuncion as unfriendly to their interests. In their view, " careless of, justice and equity, he was not a ruler jealous of the public good, but an instrument of the most insatiable avarice." [1]

The opposition to Governor Reyes finally found expression in charges presented to the audiencia of Charcas by Tomas de Cárdenas. Moved by these charges, the audiencia appointed José de Antequera as a magistrate to examine the case. Antequera, born in Panama, was the son of an official who was for forty years in the royal service, much of this time as a member of the audiencia of Charcas. In his early studies he had given evidence of distinguished talents, and the reputation which he acquired in America was sustained by his knowledge of jurisprudence which he obtained in Spain, where he was given the degree of Doctor of Laws. His spirit and learning were recognised at the court of Madrid, and he was there decorated with the military order of Alcántara. Having returned

---

[1] " El gobernador Reyes hechura de los jesuitas, parcial de ellos, agente de sus miras y operaciones absorventes, carecia por tanto de independencia ; y en sus procedimientos, agenos de la justicia y equidad, no era un gobernante celoso del bien público, sino instrumento de la mas insaciable codicia " (Mendiburu, i. 289).

to America, he was made fiscal of the audiencia of Charcas, and appointed to the indefinite office of protector of the Indians. In a community where there were many persons skilled in intrigue and misrepresentation, he would have found a sober judgment and political shrewdness more useful qualities, if he had possessed them, than his profound knowledge of the law. By the terms of his appointment (January 15, 1721), he was authorised to succeed Governor Reyes on the expiration of the period for which that officer had been appointed, or on his removal as a result of the proposed examination.

IV

Five months before the expiration of Reyes' five years' term, Antequera declared himself governor of Paraguay. He then convoked the cabildo, and persuaded the members to recognise him as governor and captain-general, and at the same time he retained the office of examining magistrate (*juez pesquisidor*). He caused to be published the order of his appointment, which had been issued by the viceroy, but by fraud withheld from publication that part of it which referred to the expiration of Reyes' term of office.[1] This action very naturally outraged all persons who believed in fair play, and Miguel de Torres, the first alcalde, was bold enough to call attention to the law that was here violated; but for this display of independence he was imprisoned, and kept in close confinement for two years, until, by the assistance of a friend, he escaped. Antequera's next step was to summon Reyes to surrender his office, and give himself up as a prisoner. The deposed governor was then confined in his own house under a guard of soldiers, and subjected to a trial from which the element of justice was excluded. Witnesses who wished to appear for Reyes were threatened, terrorised, and im-

[1] Lozano, Pedro, *Historia de las Revoluciones de la Provincia del Paraguay* (1721–35), i. 23.

prisoned, and in the presence of these proceedings the victim was helpless.

Antequera's attention was now devoted to increasing his private income rather than to advancing the public interests of the community. He took into his service the artisans of the city, of the suburbs, and even of the district, and employed them in making beds, desks, boxes, carts, doors, and windows, from which, by reason of the demand for these articles in the district, he was able to derive a large profit. Finding that mate, the *yerba del Paraguay*, was universally used in the province, he employed agents, who purchased all of it that was gathered and offered in the market, and sold it at exorbitant prices. Traders were obliged to sell their wares to Antequera, since, by his control over the Indian carriers, he was able to prevent them from transporting it from the province. In these and in other ways he curtailed the opportunities of the inhabitants, generated a spirit of dissatisfaction among them, and created hostility to his tyrannical administration and the nefarious agents who served him.

After an imprisonment of eight months, Reyes escaped disguised as a domestic. He succeeded in reaching the Jesuit missions, in spite of the vigorous search for him that was instituted. His escape, and, particularly, his flight to the missions, excited in Antequera and his followers violent indignation against the Jesuits and the Indians subject to their control.[1]

From the missions Reyes descended the Uruguay to Buenos Aires, intending to embark for Spain in order to lay his case before the king. But on February 26, 1722, he received a despatch from the viceroy authorising him to continue his administration in Paraguay until the end of the term for which he was appointed. The viceroy, moreover, disapproved of Antequera's assumption of power, and ordered him to leave Asuncion and Paraguay within a specified period. Acting on advice received in

[1] Lozano, *Revoluciones*, i. 34.

Buenos Aires, Reyes abandoned his proposed voyage to Spain, and returned to the missions by the Uruguay. He sent a message to Antequera and the cabildo, demanding his reinstatement in the government of Paraguay, and he supposed that no resistance would be offered to this request, since it was supported by the viceroy's order. He then proceeded towards Asuncion, with no other following than his son, an ecclesiastic, his servants, and the Indians who conducted his three carts. He was, however, undeceived, when about thirty miles from the city, by learning that Antequera had despatched a force to arrest him, consisting of two hundred men under the command of Ramón de las Llanas. The unexpected arrival of Llanas left Reyes barely time to escape by flight ; and Llanas and his men, failing to find their expected prey, showed their indignation by abusing Agustin de los Reyes, the servants, and the miserable Indian drivers, at the same time imprisoning the cura, José Caballero Bazán, who had assisted them. The friendly relations which existed between Reyes and the Jesuits of the missions made Antequera especially hostile to the clergy everywhere ; in fact, any person rendering assistance to the deposed governor was liable to severe persecution, as is illustrated by the treatment received by Doña Juana Gamarra, who was placed under a guard and despoiled of her property when it became known that she had given him a cup of mate during a halt which he made at her house in the country on his way back to the missions.

When the decree of the viceroy had become known to Antequera, he convoked the members of the cabildo for the purpose of finding some way of continuing his rule without direct disobedience ; and after the order had been read he expressed his willingness to surrender his authority to Reyes, in case the community would not thereby suffer inconvenience. In a skilfully framed address he exhorted the members to express their opinions on this point. His partisans, who evidently knew the wishes of their leader, opposed as with a single voice the return of Reyes, and suggested that they should petition the viceroy to appoint a new governor, and that in the meantime Antequera should continue to conduct the affairs of the government. To this plan he pretended to see himself forced to submit, and expressed his willingness to carry out their will and not to abandon his beloved city and province, for the amelioration of which he had been designated by Providence.

It had been found advisable to organise and arm some thousands of the neophytes of the reductions, in order that they might defend their villages and their property against the hostile Indians, and also assist the Spaniards in their conflict with the Portuguese about the possession of Colonia. In 1722, moved by his hostility to the Jesuits and all persons in sympathy with their undertaking, Antequera prepared to make war on the reductions. He assumed, forgetting that he would have to do with men trained to use firearms, that a few hundred or a thousand men would enable him to subdue them, although the Jesuits could put an armed force of eight or ten thousand into the field. In view of a state of things that seemed to portend civil war, the priests of the four reductions near the Tebicuary addressed a communication to Antequera, and pointed out the evils that would result from the contemplated active hostilities. The herds that provided animals for the cultivation of the fields and for the support of the people would be destroyed. An irreparable breach of hatred and rancour would be opened between the Indians and the Spaniards. The villages would be ruined, and fields would be laid waste, and thousands of peaceful and loyal vassals would be scattered and driven back to the ways of barbarism. There would be no more Guarani soldiers to be relied on to defend the port of Buenos Aires against the encroaching Portuguese.

---

[1] This document was dated at the pueblo of Santa Maria, October 18, 1722. Lozano, *Revoluciones*, i. 55–9.

In his reply, Antequera expressed his appreciation of the work of the Jesuits and of the debt of gratitude due them.[1] He also gave his reasons for his warlike preparations, and offered to desist from proceeding against them, but affirmed that he would return and punish them, if in the future they did not show themselves disposed to submit to his orders.

It was doubtless an act of discretion, considered from a military point of view, for Antequera to withdraw from his campaign against the Missions before the two forces came into collision. But when he returned to Asuncion his partisans received him with applause, acclaiming him as victor and as the father and defender of his country. To the audiencia of Charcas he sent elaborate documents, presenting an exaggerated account of his achievements, which he had reason to believe would be approved by that body, since it had shown a positive inclination to his side of the controversy.

By means of a public sermon in the cathedral, the glory of Antequera and his deeds was magnified and made known throughout the province. The sermon was delivered by an ecclesiastic whom Antequera had brought from Peru as his confessor, and, based on statements communicated by the interested party, proved to be a high-flown panegyric of the usurping governor. The sanctity then attributed to the utterances of a priest prevented the eulogy from appearing to the people in its true character as bombast.

In the meantime Antequera's reports had reached the audiencia, where his partisans prepared for them a favourable reception ; and the audiencia sent copies of them to the viceroy for his consideration. In reply the viceroy ordered the contending parties in Paraguay to

[1] According to Lozano, i. 59, this "era artificio para desbocarse con mas libertad contra los jesuitas, que esa es el arte diabólica muy propia de los malignos, acariciar al mismo tiempo que más cruelmente hieren."

maintain in peace their respective positions; and on February 26, 1723, he wrote to the audiencia of La Plata (Charcas) announcing that he had issued a decree, in which he had ordered that Antequera should immediately cease to perform the functions of governor, which he had assumed, as well as those of his commission, and appear within five months in the city of Lima ; and that Reyes should be restored to his office, and be placed in possession of his property and his salary. At the same time he informed the audiencia that it had been disposed to over-estimate its authority ; that sovereignty was vested solely in the royal person of his Majesty, and not in any other tribunal or judge, however exalted such tribunal or judge might be.[1]

Relying on the known sympathy of the audiencia with his cause, Antequera refused to obey the order of the viceroy, and interpreted it as applicable to the period prior to the expiration of Reyes' lustrum of service. In a subsequent letter, May 26, 1723, the viceroy gave more direct evidence of the strained relations that existed between him and the audiencia.[2]

The futility of his previous orders induced the viceroy to send a second communication. This was dated June 7, 1723, and in it he repeated his command that Diego de los Reyes should be restored to his post as governor of Paraguay ; that to Governor Reyes, to his Lieutenant-General Delgado, and to all other persons interested,

---

[1] This letter is printed in Lozano, *Revoluciones*, i. 76–8.

[2] " Y finalmente, debo decir á V. S. que aunque esa Real Audiencia ha sido muy arreglada en todos tiempos, sólo en el de mi gobierno se experimenta que en ella se quitan y proveen fácilmente gobernadores, se suspenden corregidores y oficiales reales, que se hace empeño de autoridad proceder á todo esto sin darme cuenta, aunque yo ordene lo contrario con motivos justos del servicio de Su Majestad y bien publico, y se retienen mis despachos y se retiene pertinazmente el cumplimiento de ellos, creyendo que hubiera cesado en los cargos que ejerzo, como si aunque faltara la persona no hubiera de haber sucesor que cuide igualmente de respecto que se debe á esta representación" (Lozano, i. 84).

all their confiscated property should be restored, although it might have been sold and passed into the hands of third parties. Antequera was, moreover, required to leave Paraguay, and to proceed to Lima without entering La Plata ; and it was ordered that his property should be confiscated, wherever it might be found, and all his acts against the Jesuits should be annulled. In order that there might be no delay in carrying out these orders, Colonel Baltasar García Ros, of Buenos Aires, was charged with their execution. In case the members of the cabildo or the military officers should refuse to obey the decree of the viceroy, they might be fined, deposed from their offices, and exiled from the province. The viceroy also appointed Baltasar García Ros interim governor of Paraguay, with all the powers and duties that had been devolved upon previous governors, and anyone resisting his authority would be subject to a fine of six thousand pesos and banishment.

In Corrientes, Reyes, having had the orders of the viceroy properly attested, took the necessary legal steps to seize the property which Antequera had sent to his principal agents at that port and at Santa Fé. This consisted of six hundred loaves of sugar, six thousand and five hundred seroons of *yerba del Paraguay*, two thousand seroons of which, together with certain jewels and a number of slaves, were assigned to Reyes as a part of his property that had been confiscated. Other articles seized were carts, oxen, bulls, mules, horses, doors, windows, beds, desks, and boxes. This act enraged the usurper, and induced him to commit excesses more desperate than any that had marked his previous career. He determined in retaliation to imprison Reyes ; and in executing this design he sent a number of soldiers, between thirty and forty, down the river from Asuncion in two boats. They landed at Corrientes in the night, captured Reyes, plundered his house, and carried him off in his *paños menores*.[1]

[1] Lozano, *Revoluciones*, i. 94–107.

This exploit was followed by mutual recriminations, and each party wrote to the king abusive accounts of the other. There is no doubt that the prejudice against the Jesuits and their work, created at court by some of these communications, was instrumental in inducing the Crown, forty years later, to expel the members of the society from America. This hostility on the part of Antequera and the inhabitants of Asuncion was not without its basis of thrift. Seeing the large number of contented and industrious Indians devoted to the peaceful occupations of the reductions, they could not avoid contemplating the advantage they would enjoy if some part of these Indians, at least, were distributed among them under the system of repartimientos. The cabildo of Asuncion wrote to the king on November 10, 1723, urging that the Jesuits should be banished, and the reductions placed in charge of the secular clergy. In the same letter they petitioned the king to give seven of the thirty reductions *en encomienda* to the inhabitants of Asuncion, and to grant to the city the personal service of six hundred of the mission Indians.[1]

From Corrientes Reyes was taken to Asuncion, and imprisoned under conditions that gave evidence of the inhumanity of his captors ; and with this event Antequera had finally reached the determination to disobey and defy his superiors. He advised Colonel García Ros, who had left Buenos Aires for Paraguay, to remain in Corrientes, and send to Asuncion by messenger any communications he might wish to make. Ros, however, continued on his journey, and when he had reached the Tebicuary the cabildo sent him a second letter, dated January 3, 1724, asking him not to enter the city, on account of the evil consequences that would result from his presence there. In view of the fact that no adequate preparations had been made to maintain his authority by force, and that Antequera had sent a company to Santa Rosa to arrest

[1] Lozano, *Revoluciones*, i. 105.

him, Colonel García Ros found it advisable to return to Buenos Aires.

After the withdrawal of Ros, some of the adherents of Antequera thought that the government would make no further attempt to restore the legitimate order of affairs, and in their fancied security they sought by false reports to intensify the prevailing popular antagonism to the Jesuits and their neophytes. But in the summer of 1724 Ros determined to return to Paraguay; and on arriving at the town of Nuestra Señora de los Reyes del Yapeyú, he sent a message to Padre Tomás Rosa, the superior of the Missions, exhorting him to provide two thousand Indians, with arms, munitions, and the rations necessary for a campaign of two months. He requested him also to have these Indian soldiers assembled at a place designated near the Tebicuary, on August 1.[1]

This message reached Padre Rosa on June 30 in the reduction of Nuestra Señora de la Candelaria, and he complied immediately with the request which it contained. Some persons considered two thousand soldiers inadequate for the undertaking, and suggested that a larger number should be taken, calling attention to the fact that four thousand had been called into service in each of the campaigns against the Portuguese in Colonia. The leader was, however, persuaded that the force requested was sufficiently large, particularly as he expected many of the Paraguayans to join his party, and, perhaps, to deliver Antequera into his hands.

On August 4 Colonel Ros was at the reduction of Nuestra Señora de Fé, a pueblo near the river Tebicuary. Here he discovered that a body of soldiers was advancing to meet him. This consisted of two hundred men led by Ramon de las Llanas, the second alcalde of Asuncion, who had assumed the rôle of commander, and proposed to prevent Ros and his little army from crossing the river; but when Llanas learned the number of soldiers he would

---

[1] This message is printed in Lozano, *Revoluciones*, i. 137.

be obliged to encounter, he chose the better part and fled,
leaving Ros free to cross the river and fix his camp on the
northern bank. From the estate where he had taken
refuge, Llanas, assuming the tone of a despotic ruler,
ordered Ros to withdraw his forces from that region.
He at the same time sent a messenger to Asuncion with
the information that the enemy was advancing on the
capital.

On receiving this report, Antequera caused a shot to
be fired, which was a prearranged signal for the people
to appear with their arms. Only a few persons, however,
responded to the first signal or to its repetition ; whereupon Antequera sent abroad among the inhabitants the
false announcement that Ros had written to him, stating
that if the people of Paraguay did not receive him peace-
fully, he would enter Asuncion with fire and sword, would
massacre the men, and would compel the women to
marry his Guarani soldiers. Antequera also asserted
that Colonel Ros had issued a proclamation, that was
distributed in the reductions, offering to the Guaranis
the wives and daughters of the Spaniards of Paraguay.

A further indication of the complete breach between
the two parties was the expulsion of the Jesuits from their
college in Asuncion. In order to have the formal approval
by the cabildo of a measure on which he was already determined, Antequera convoked that body and laid before the
members a draft of a decree which they signed, some
willingly and others under compulsion of fear. This
document was a decree of banishment from the province ;
and the Jesuit fathers of the college to whom it was
directed were required to leave the city within three hours.
The rector protested against this action on the ground
of the ecclesiastical immunity which the Jesuits and the
college 'enjoyed : as the college was founded by royal
licence, they could not abandon it or be expelled, except
by the express mandate of the king. To the protest
was added a petition for such a delay as would permit a

consultation with the provincial. But neither the protest nor the petition were effective. The banished priests passed by a frequently interrupted journey to the Missions, and the college was left in charge of the vicar-general of the bishopric. They arrived at the reduction of Nuestra Señora de Fé on September 14, 1724.

The reluctance of the inhabitants of Paraguay to join Antequera's proposed military campaign was counteracted by threatened confiscation of property and banishment in case of refusal, and, on the part of the common people, by the penalty of flogging. So effective were these inducements to enlist that, when he was ready to set out, he had a miscellaneous force of three thousand men, representing all classes and conditions of Paraguayan society as it then existed. They were undisciplined and disorderly, and in his address to them Antequera announced that the undertaking in which he was engaged was not in his interest, but for their profit. He could not hope for any other advantage than to see them liberated from the tyranny of the sworn enemies of their country. He assured them that Baltasar García Ros was determined, if victorious, to hand over their daughters and wives to the barbarous Guaranis. Besides the opportunity that would be furnished them to avenge themselves for this intended indignity, he offered to enrich them with the booty of the four reductions that had led the opposition to him, and with the property of the deserted college, its lands, its herds, and its slaves. He swore by his *santo hábito* that he would distribute all this among them, without reserving anything for himself; for he wished only the glory of having delivered the illustrious province from Don Baltasar, who aimed to subject it to his tyrannical rule. And he closed his remarkable address by exhorting his followers to conquer or die in defence of their country and religion.[1]

[1] For the text of this address, see Lozano, *Revoluciones*, i. 181.

V

On August 10, Antequera and his troops came in sight
of the camp of the enemy on the bank of the Tebicuary.
By displaying the white flag he led Ros to believe that
an agreement might be reached without a battle. But
the exchange of cannon shots by the two parties dispelled
this belief ; and after this harmless demonstration,
Antequera withdrew his forces about a league to the estate
of Philip Cavañas. The correspondence which followed
impressed upon Ros a mistaken 'sense of security ; and
while his soldiers, unmindful of any approaching danger,
were celebrating a holiday, the army of Antequera fell
upon them with a disastrous result. Ros fled across the
river, and reached San Ignacio at midnight. His soldiers,
disorganised, and many of them without arms, maintained
a brief defence, but they were soon run down by the
cavalry, or overwhelmed by the superior numbers of the
unmounted men. Some were drowned in an attempted
flight across the river, many were killed, and more were
wounded.[1]

Near the end of August Antequera returned to Asuncion and celebrated his triumph. He had in his train
two captured Jesuit priests and a hundred Indian prisoners,
who were fastened together by their necks, and treated
with great cruelty. The Jesuits were conducted through
the town in a cart attended by mounted soldiers, and
placed in charge of the vicar-general. The Indian prisoners
remained three days in the public plaza, subject to the
inclement conditions of the weather, and without proper
provision for their support. Later they were distributed
among the Spaniards of Paraguay, and were employed

[1] In his report to his successor, Castel-Fuerte affirmed that six
hundred Indians were killed in the fight or were drowned, while the
loss of Antequera's forces was five killed and twenty wounded
(*Memorias de los Vireyes*, iii. 302).

as labourers on the lands. Each Spaniard received two, three, or four, according to the service which he had rendered in the rebellion. The contrast between the condition of these Indians under the beneficent administration of the reductions and their second state as bondsmen under merciless masters is a sufficient commentary on the purposes and characters of the two parties in the conflict.[1]

When the battle at the Tebicuary had been decided, Antequera and his soldiers proceeded to take possession of the spoils of the camp. The leader reserved for himself whatever had been the property of Colonel Ros, and the rest was turned over to the rank and file. The character of the victors made inevitable a certain amount of cruelty in the process of plundering. Some of the vanquished Indians were killed for their miserable clothing, and the wounded were in many cases treated with great brutality. Among the papers which Ros abandoned at his headquarters was the original despatch in which the viceroy ordered that Antequera should be arrested and sent to Lima. Although Antequera did not wish this fact to be generally divulged, he nevertheless confided it to a few of his intimate associates, and through them it became known to all the members of his party ; and this knowledge helped to undeceive them with respect to Antequera's position, and to cool their devotion to him. He was, however, determined to pursue still further his aggressive policy, to subdue the four reductions that had opposed him, and to take away their right to carry firearms, which they held by royal authority ; and when this resolution had become known, there was a reign of terror in the reductions.

Antequera began his advance towards the reduction of Nuestra Señora de Fé on August 27, but, in his approach,

[1] Lozano, *Revoluciones*, i. 218–42, cites letters from the Bishops of Buenos Aires and Paraguay, and from Governor Zabala to illustrate the character of Jesuit rule in the Missions.

the Indian inhabitants fled to the forests, and the soldiers were disappointed in not finding the expected booty. Proceeding to the reduction of Santa Rosa, he sought to make an agreement with the Missions, by which they would undertake to pay the expenses of his expedition ; but Padre Robles, with whom the negotiations were conducted, excused himself for not consenting to the proposed agreement on the ground that as only the vice-superior he was not competent to conclude a treaty of such grave importance. The plans of the invader were suddenly changed on September 2, when he heard of the approach of an armed force of five thousand Indians. He broke camp at noon, and directed his march again towards Nuestra Señora de Fé, recognising his temerity in entering this region with only seven hundred men, many of whom had received at the outset only two charges of powder, and who, although in large part mounted, were already exhausted by the journey. The troops, whose advance caused the change in Antequera's plans, were responding to a call issued by Colonel Ros. They were from the towns near the Uruguay, and were for the most part mounted and were skilful horsemen. Among them there were between forty and fifty Spaniards who had fled from the tyranny of Antequera. Before this formidable force Antequera retreated towards Asuncion, his soldiers expressing their great dissatisfaction that they had not had an opportunity to plunder any of the reductions, but, according to Lozano, " it was wiser to retreat with them disgusted than to leave them there dead." [1]

VI

To discredit the Jesuits of the Missions and prepare the way for their removal was one of the aims of the Antequerists. But the ambition of this party was destined

[1] *Revoluciones*, i. 260.

to suffer a check after the arrival of the new viceroy. The Marquis of Castel-Fuerte announced on July 18, 1724, that he had determined " to appoint a person of great experience and zeal in the royal service to proceed to the province of Paraguay and put an end to the disorder and scandals that had appeared there in disobedience to the orders of the supreme government." For this purpose he chose Bruno de Zabala, the governor of Buenos Aires, and ordered him to go to Paraguay and to take with him as many soldiers as might seem to him necessary for the pacification and good government of the province. All the officials of Paraguay were commanded to place no obstacles in his way, but rather " to give him all the support and assistance which he may need, obeying without offering any objections or causing any delay, the orders which he may give them either orally or in writing ; for, upon anyone who shall fail in any respect to obey this injunction, I shall inflict exemplary punishment." [1]

Under this commission Zabala wrote in a discreet and friendly spirit to Antequera, the secular cabildo, and Sebastian Fernández Montiel, the *maestre de campo*, informing them of the despatches of the viceroy, and of his determination to execute the orders which they contained. At the same time he wrote to the Bishop of Paraguay, enclosing a copy of the viceregal order, and solicited his co-operation in effecting the results desired by the superior government. These letters were sent to Asuncion by Captain Pedro Gribeo, of the presidio of Buenos Aires. After consulting with a number of influential persons in the province, the bishop determined to assist in carrying out the viceroy's plans. Antequera was, however, of a different mind ; he hoped still to make an effective resistance. He turned in every direction for support, but found little encouragement; for many of the principal

[1] For the text of this announcement, see Lozano, *Revoluciones*, i. 281.

men of the province had been undeceived, and he failed to find the following he desired.[1]

The bishop sought from the *de facto* governor information concerning the action of the cabildo, and this inquiry was followed by an interview between Antequera and the bishop at the latter's house, on May 25, 1725, which began with the usual polite exchange of compliments, but became very serious as it proceeded, and in the course of the conversation the bishop sought to make Antequera see clearly his position and the course of action which it would be advisable for him to adopt.[2]

Moved by the bishop's advice, Antequera was for the moment disposed to renounce his rebellious plans, and obey the orders of the viceroy. But this was only a temporary purpose ; for, in view of his many acts of disobedience and rebellion, he was unable to see any way by which he might escape the punishment his conduct merited. If there was no hope in submission, in resistance, provided he could obtain the support desired, there was at least a possibility of success. In the meantime Zabala left Buenos Aires with one hundred and fifty men from the garrison of that post. Near the end of December he reached Santa Fé, where he secured four boats and advanced northward by the Paranà, in January 1725. During this voyage he received various reports of the attitude of the existing authorities of the province towards him. The majority of the cabildo were in favour of receiving him, while Antequera and a minority were disposed to prevent him from entering their territory. Those who favoured his coming wished to persuade him to come

---

[1] " Se revolvía hacía todas partes y echaba mano de todos los arbitrios que le sugería su loca ambición, por ver si hallaba camino de proseguir sus errados designios ; mas halló poco fomento, porque la luz del desengaño habia ya hecho abrir felizmente los ojos á muchos, y como éstos eran de los principales, le faltaba el séquito que deseaba." Lozano, *Revoluciones*, i. 287.

[2] The bishop's account of this interview is printed in Lozano, *Revoluciones*, i. 288.

without arms, in order that the submission of the province might seem to be voluntary and not forced.[1]

Zabala did not find it advisable to accede to this request, but in his reply he said that he would not enter the province with a numerous body of soldiers, and would not have among them any of the Indians of the Tebicuary ; yet it was befitting his position that the detachment from the presidio of Buenos Aires should accompany him. These troops would not impose the least expense on the people of Paraguay, or cause any disturbance, since they were supported by his Majesty, and were subject to strict discipline ; and, as soon as the circumstances permitted it, they would be returned to Buenos Aires.[2]

VII

It is not necessary to follow Antequera in his varied efforts to avert his impending fate. Even the most daring of his ventures, the circulation of false viceregal despatches pretending to revoke the orders for his arrest and commanding him to remain as governor of Paraguay, had no permanent influence in his favour. The soldiers from whom he expected support either proved indifferent or went over to the opposition. But when the end must have been clearly in view, he commanded the officials and inhabitants of·Asuncion not to receive Zabala, and accompanied his injunction with severe threats ; for Zabala, he affirmed, belonged to the Jesuit faction, while he himself was the legitimate governor and alone competent to prevent the ruin of the province. Not long after the promulgation of this order, Antequera left the province of Paraguay, which had suffered under his misrule for nearly four years. He appointed Roman de las Llanas

[1] See Captain Miguel de Garay's address to the cabildo concerning this subject (Lozano, *Revoluciones*, i. 299).
[2] Lozano, *Revoluciones*, i. 303.

to be his deputy, and, according to Lozano, charged him
with " diabolical instructions." Llanas had been Antequera's chief agent, and appears to have been admirably
endowed by nature for carrying out instructions of this
character. Antequera embarked with about forty men
besides the rowers, on the 5th of March 1725, and, passing
down the river, was soon out of sight ; and there was
much rejoicing in Asuncion among those who regarded
him as the destroyer of the province. In appointing a
deputy-governor to conduct the administration until his
return, he appeared not to consider his rule as ended, but
many of his other arrangements suggest that he thought
of his departure as final.

While Antequera might not have prevented Zabala
from entering Paraguay or even Asuncion, his presence
would have offered a source of embarrassment that was
removed by his flight. There was, nevertheless, some
doubt as to the attitude of Antequera's adherents with
respect to the organiser of the proposed new régime.
Llanas was known to have six hundred men under his
command, but all uncertainty as to the use he would
make of them was removed when he surrendered publicly
his staff of office to Zabala. As Zabala approached Asuncion, the members of the cabildo and a large concourse
of the inhabitants went out to receive him. At the head
of the procession entering the city were the drummers
and the trumpeters ; and after them marched the militia
of Paraguay, followed by the soldiers from the presidio
of Buenos Aires. The bishop, surrounded by a large
body of the ecclesiastics of the province, received the
procession at the door of the cathedral. After the military salute and a religious service including the singing
of the *Te Deum*, Zabala was escorted to the house that
had been assigned for his residence.

Under the authority conferred upon him by the viceroy, Zabala appointed as governor of the province Martin
de Barúa, who had been attached to the expedition at

Santa Fé for this purpose. He then released Reyes from the prison, where Antequera had confined him, and directed him to go to Santa Fé. He also made provision for the return of those persons who had fled from the tyranny of Antequera, and the restoration of the confiscated property to the owners ; but the last part of this programme could not be executed without great difficulties, for much of this property had passed into other hands by more than one transfer. He also approved the project of the bishop permitting the Jesuits to return to their college in Asuncion. In the pacification of Paraguay, Bishop José de Palos rendered Zabala important assistance, and this was recognised by the viceroy Castel-Fuerte in a letter to the bishop, dated September 29, 1725.[1]

In his flight from Asuncion, Antequera descended the river to Santa Fé, and passed thence by unfrequented ways to Cordova, in order to avoid those who sought to arrest him. In Cordova he found an asylum in the Franciscan monastery, where he arrived at three o'clock in the morning ; and on the following day, when his presence in the city became known, he was visited by the principal residents of Cordova, "flattering himself with this favour as if he were already master of everything."[2] This agreeable illusion was, however, soon dispelled by the arrival of a requisition for his arrest, addressed to the lieutenant-governor, Ignacio de Ledesma Zeballos. During his sojourn in the monastery, he passed through various moods, now weeping over his misfortunes, now boasting of his importance, now seeking in great humility for assistance in his negotiations, now showing the qualities of a mystic, and now the threatening attitude of a man of unrestrained courage. In all his moods, there appeared the persistent mania of hostility to the Jesuits. His conduct was so extravagant that one of his more

[1] Quoted by Lozano, *Revoluciones*, i. 329.
[2] *Ibid.*, i. 342.

intimate friends was moved to write to him, urging him to lay aside his absurd pretensions.

Finally the safe-conduct which he desired appeared in an order issued from Salta by the Marquis de Haro, the governor of Tucuman.   It provided that he might pass freely to the audiencia, and that no one, under severe penalties, should hinder him or molest his person or his property.   But, not satisfied with this privilege, he endeavoured to make it appear that the viceroy was supporting him ; and he caused it to be announced that Castel-Fuerte had ordered Zabala to enter Paraguay quietly, and not to interfere with Antequera, but to allow him to leave freely, whereas the contrary was the fact, since Zabala " had strict orders to arrest and prosecute without hesitation Don José de Antequera as the head of the past lawlessness."   But any false conceptions which the pretensions of Antequera had given to the inhabitants of Cordova were swept away when the voice of the public crier proclaimed in the plaza and throughout the city that Castel-Fuerte, the viceroy, mindful of the crimes of Don José de Antequera, declared him proscribed, and that, therefore, any one might take his life, offering to the person who should deliver him up to justice a reward of four thousand pesos, and to him who should indicate where he might be found, so that he might be imprisoned, half of that amount.[1]

While the king and his council in Madrid were discussing the proper disposition to be made of Antequera, there arrived in Cordova an order from the viceroy, addressed to the lieutenant-governor, requiring the ecclesiastical authorities to surrender Antequera on pain of being deprived of their revenues and expelled from the country.   Antequera, having received knowledge of this order, escaped from the monastery, either by deceiving the guards or by their connivance.   He proceeded northward through the sparsely populated territory of Rioja,

[1] Lozano, *Revoluciones*, i. 352.

and presented himself before the audiencia of Chuquisaca, where he hoped for a favourable reception ; but the personnel of that court had changed since it supported his appointment as *juez pesquisidor* for Paraguay ; and from it as he found it constituted he could not reasonably expect favours. To the charges against him, which were stated by the president, he was able to make no effective answer ; and it was ordered that he and his four companions should be taken and delivered as prisoners to the corregidor of Potosi. In Potosi he continued to give expression to his hatred of the Jesuits, and even caused false and damaging reports about them to be spread abroad. At length, on the 8th of February 1726, he and his companions were taken from the prison of Potosi and transferred to Lima, where they arrived on the 16th of April. In the prison of Lima he was assigned quarters separate from those of his four associates. He remained imprisoned here for five years. At first it was the intention of the Crown to have him taken to Spain for his trial, but later the king determined that he should be tried and sentenced in Lima, and he gave the viceroy orders to this effect, in a decree issued from Buen Retiro, April 11, 1726.[1]

But the removal of Antequera did not bring peace to Paraguay. The Antequerists did not cease their opposition to the Jesuits, and, as they were the dominant faction at Asuncion, the governor, Martin de Barúa, accepted their views. The project to re-establish the Jesuits in possession of their college in the capital had met with vigorous

---

[1] " He resuelto, que no obstante de lo que está mandado por el citado real despacho de Iº' de Julio del año próximo antecedente, sobre que remitieseis á España al expresado Antequera, suspendáis esta providencia y en consecuencia de la que consta, que tomasteis, para que á este sujeto se le remitiese preso á esa ciudad, procedáis en esos, autos, con acuerdo de esa Audiencia ; pues aunque se ha considerado ser tantos y tan graves los delitos, sin oir á dicho Antequera y demas reos, no se puede pasar á sentenciarlos, y más teniendo este sujeto hechos autos."—From the royal decree of April 11, 1726, printed in Lozano, *Revoluciones*, i. 361 ; also in *Memorias de los Vireyes*, iii. 309 ; Mendiburu, i. 301.

opposition, and it continued to be a subject of partisan discussion. Considering the apparent impossibility of reaching an agreement that would ensure peace, the Jesuits wished to present to the king their view of the controversy. After various fruitless attempts to obtain a passage and permission to embark, Padres Jerónimo Herrán and Juan de Alzola were finally able to depart in a British slave-ship. They reached London after a voyage of somewhat more than three months, where they were detained two months by persistent rain, and when they crossed France, it was, as Padre Lozano says, " with great risks, since many of the provinces were full of Huguenots and Jansenists." [1]

At the time of their arrival in Madrid, October 1725, the council was discussing a project to reform the government of Paraguay. The plan with which they began the discussion was set aside, and it was then proposed that the province should be placed under the governor of Buenos Aires, and that its affairs should be controlled immediately by a lieutenant-governor, as were other cities or provinces of Rio de la Plata. But this plan was in turn dropped, and the council determined to maintain Paraguay as a separate district or territory. But the Jesuits, Herrán and Alzola, were chiefly interested in directing the attention of the king to the persecution, the false testimony, the calumny, and the banishments they had suffered and were still suffering. In seeking a remedy for these evils, they thought it would be found in releasing the reductions from the government of Paraguay, and in subordinating them to the government of Buenos Aires. Under the latter government, they believed they would be free from the vexations which they had hitherto endured. They petitioned his Majesty, moreover, for the restoration of the Jesuits to their college in Asuncion, since the orders neither of the audiencia nor of Governor Zabala had been effective.

[1] *Revoluciones*, i. 380.

About a year later, on the 6th of November 1726, the king issued a decree relating to the measure advocated by the Jesuits. " I have," he declared, " resolved that, for the present, and until I shall order otherwise, the thirty reductions of Indians who are in charge of the Jesuit Fathers in the district of Paraguay may be wholly under the authority and jurisdiction of the governor of Buenos Aires, with full and absolute inhibition of the governor and justices of Paraguay itself ; and the Fathers shall be immediately and without delay placed in possession of the college of the city of Asuncion, from which they were expelled, in order that they may continue the work of their apostolic mission. Therefore, I order the viceroy of Peru, and the audiencia of Charcas, as well as the governor and justices of the already-mentioned province of Paraguay, that the aforesaid Fathers, without the least delay, be placed in possession of the college of the city of Asuncion." [1]

This decree did not reach Paraguay until 1729, for Jerónimo Herrán, to whom it was entrusted, was not able to sail from Spain until near the end of 1728. After his arrival, its provisions with respect to the reductions were carried out ; but the viceroy had already ordered that the Jesuits should be put in possession of their college in Asuncion, and the royal decree had, therefore, no effect, except, perhaps, to serve as a confirmation of the viceroy's action. [2]

VIII

After his arrival in Lima in 1726, and during the events connected with the removal of the reductions from the jurisdiction of Paraguay, and their subordination to

[1] This decree is printed in Lozano, *Revoluciones*, i. 381-2.
[2] For the history of the process of restoration, together with much of the correspondence between Lima and Asuncion, see Lozano, *Revoluciones*, i. 383-422.

the governor of Buenos Aires, Antequera was held in prison while the government collected the evidence needed for his trial. The task was difficult, since it was necessary to answer the case presented in behalf of the prisoner, which involved a vast mass of information and misinformation contained in twelve thousand folios. It was performed under elaborate instructions[1] by Matías Anglés, the chief justice in the city of Cordova. Although the city of Asuncion contained many influential and unreformed Antequerists, Anglés succeeded in completing his investigations in about a year without causing any important social disturbance. But after his departure for Potosi to accept the office of corregidor of that city, Asuncion appeared to be dominated by the rebellious faction. Ramon de las Llanas and Sebastian Fernandez Montiel, whom Anglés had left in prison, escaped and went about the city as if they had been acquitted or had returned from a journey, and the governor made no effort to recommit them. This indifference or cowardice of Governor Barúa induced the viceroy to supersede him. Antequera seized this occasion to write two letters for the purpose of exciting his partisans against the new governor. These letters fell into the hands of the viceroy, and formed a substantial addition to the evidence in favour of the prosecution.

As a result of the trial, Antequera was condemned to be taken from his prison to a scaffold in the public plaza, and there to be beheaded. When the audiencia reported to Castel-Fuerte their conclusion that the sentence should be death, the viceroy responded, " Then let him die with all honour possible." One of Antequera's companions, Juan de Mena,[2] was sentenced to be garrotted, and the others were condemned to suffer banishment for a number of years. After the announcement of the sentence, the provincial of the Jesuits petitioned the viceroy, in the

[1] For a copy of these instructions, see Lozano, *Revoluciones*, i. 424–6.   [2] Lozano, *Revoluciones*, i. 429.

name of the Jesuits, against whom many of Antequera's crimes had been committed, either to pardon him or to suspend his sentence and send him to Spain. The viceroy, however, refused to accede to this request, on the ground that the decree of the king did not permit delay and that the offence of the criminal did not warrant the exercise of clemency.[1]

In obedience to the common sentiment of the age, and perhaps, in appreciation of the action of the Jesuits in asking the viceroy to pardon him, Antequera requested an interview with Padre Tomás Cavero, rector of the Jesuit *Colegio Maximo de San Pablo*, of Lima, in order that he might demand pardon for his offences against the Society and its members. Not long after the interview between the condemned man and the priest, the voice of the public crier was heard proclaiming the crimes for which Antequera was going to his execution. While he was advancing to the scaffold, July 5, 1731, a repeated demand for his pardon was heard in the plaza, and this was supposed to be a signal for a movement on the part of the populace to rescue the criminal. In fact, the repetition of the cry in various quarters and the increasing agitation of the crowd induced the officers to give the order to fire on the prisoner, who immediately fell dead from the mule on which they were conducting him to the place of execution. At the same time two ecclesiastics and a soldier were killed and a number of persons were wounded. The body of Antequera was then carried to the scaffold and there beheaded. The head was shown to the crowd from the platform, and then placed at the feet of the headless body. The sentence of Juan de Mena was afterwards carried out ; and during these events, the confusion and turbulence of the populace was so great that the viceroy, mounting the first horse that he found available, rode into the plaza, in order to make his supreme authority

[1] *Memorias de los Vireyes*, iii. 309-13.

and the public respect for his person effective in quelling the disturbance. But before the uproar had ceased, many persons fell victims of shots, sabre strokes, and the trampling of the horses.[1]

But Antequera's removal did not end the troubles of Paraguay. The persons who held his views constituted an influential party, not only in Paraguay but also in Peru. In Asuncion, under the designation of *Comuneros*, they rose in rebellion against the government, and continued the war on the Jesuits. They refused to receive a governor appointed by the viceroy, expelled the Jesuits from their college, and directed their campaign against the reductions. As the missions, or reductions, had been placed under the protection of the governor of Buenos Aires, Governor Zabala conducted the loyalist cause, and, after two years of social confusion, was able to enter Asuncion and re-establish civil order.[2]

Much of the persistent opposition to the Jesuits, which manifested itself at this time as well as earlier and later, was due to the Society's great and increasing prosperity.[3] And after the expulsion, when the Jesuits had lost completely all royal favour, it became customary to assign to them reprehensible conduct of which they were guiltless, and at the same time to overlook the disobedience and rebellion begun by Antequera. In condoning these acts, the partisans of Antequera naturally represented Castel-Fuerte as unjust and unwarrantably severe ;

[1] See the viceroy's account in *Memorias de los Vireyes*, iii. 312–4.

[2] The details of this rebellion are given in the second volume of Lozano's *Revoluciones*. See also Funes, *Ensayo*, lib. iv. cap. v, vi; Letter of Padre Herrán to Castel-Fuerte, in *Lettres édifiantes et curieuses* (Paris, 1839), ii. 192.

[3] In 1726 Matías Anglés wrote : " The Fathers of the Society are the only competitors of the province of Paraguay, and consequently are opposed and antagonistic to all the inhabitants of it, who with just Spanish zeal have succeeded, through the government of the province, in preserving it in its primitive condition." See Mendiburu, 258.

and these views were impressed with such force on the Crown, that Charles III declared Antequera an honoured and loyal minister, and conferred upon certain members of his family pensions to be paid out of the revenues derived from the confiscated property of the Jesuits in Lima.

CHAPTER XVI

THE VICEROYALTY UNDER CASTEL-FUERTE AND VILLAGARCÍA, 1724-45

I. The conduct of the clergy. II. Decline of the University of San Marcos. III. Mines. IV. Fate of the Indians. V. Popular ignorance and increase of monasteries and convents. VI. Confusion in affairs of commerce. VII. Manifest inefficiency of the viceregal government. VIII. British hostility ; Anson's voyage ; Vernon's attack.

I

THE rebellion in Paraguay was not the only subject on which the inhabitants of the viceroyalty were divided into parties. They were divided in their views respecting the attitude that ought to be assumed towards the scandalous conduct of many ecclesiastics. One party held that the vices of the clergy should not be exposed to the people, on account of the effect of the evil example that would thus be presented to them ; and, moreover, that the authorities should lend their influence to conceal these vices. Accepting the statement of Juan and Ulloa, contained in their *Noticias Secretas de America*, there would seem to have been no possibility of concealment in the fourth decade of the eighteenth century.

" The persons who compose the two orders of the clergy," they wrote, " are guilty of such licentiousness, that, making due allowance for the frailties to which human nature is liable, and the weaknesses to which men of every class are subject, it would appear that those ecclesiastics regard it as their peculiar privilege to go before all others in the career of vice ; for while they are under the most sacred obligations not only to practise virtue, but to correct the errors incident to frail nature, it is they who, by their pernicious example, sanction the practice of iniquity, and in a measure divest it of its heinous nature.

" The parish priests are extremely vicious in their habits ; but, whether it happen that an error or crime in them attracts less notice, or whether they are more careful to conceal it, or for both reasons, which is the more probable, disgraceful as the consequences are known to be, they never reach such a degree of scandal as do those of the monks ; for the latter, from the first step they take, and even without leaving the monasteries, pursue a course of conduct so notorious and shameful that it becomes offensive in the extreme, and fills the mind with horror.

" Concubinage is so general that the practice of it is esteemed a point of honour ; and when a stranger arrives and continues his residence there for some time without having adopted the customs of the country, his continence is attributed not to a principle of virtue, but to the passion of avarice, as it is generally supposed that he lives so in order to save money.

" In large cities, the greater part of the monks live in private houses, for the convents furnish an asylum to those only who cannot keep house, or to the choristers, novitiates, and such like, who live there from choice. The same is true of the small cities, villages, and hamlets. The doors of the monasteries are kept open, and the monks live in their cells, accompanied by their women, and lead in every respect the life of married persons." [1]

" The fandangoes or balls are usually devised by the members of the religious orders, or more properly by those who call themselves religious, although, in fact, they are far from being so ; for it is they who pay the expense, who attend in company with their concubines, and who

[1] *Noticias Secretas*, 490, 491, 492.

314 THE SPANISH DEPENDENCIES

get up the fray in their own houses.

314 THE SPANISH DEPENDENCIES

get up the fray in their own houses. Simultaneously with
the dance, the immoderate use of ardent spirits begins,
and the entertainment is gradually converted into acts
of impropriety so unseemly and lewd, that it would be pre-
sumption even to speak of them, and a want of delicacy
to stain the narrative with such a record of obscenities ;
and, letting them lie hid in the region of silènce, we shall
only remark, that whatever the spirit of malice could
invent in respect to this subject, great as it might be, it
could never fathom that abyss into which those corrupt
minds are plunged, nor give any adequate idea of the
degree of excess to which debauchery and crime are
carried." [1]

Another source of social disturbance and party hostility appeared in the ecclesiastical elections, in the monasteries and convents. The conflicts were not confined to
the members of the religious houses, but each party in
the convent had its sympathisers and supporters among
the other inhabitants of the town. The convent of En-
carnacion was one of the centres of disorder. The
majority of the nuns voted to re-elect as their head
Madre Doña Maria de las Nieves, who was then their
abbess. The other party voted for Madre Doña Rosa de la
Cueva. The archbishop, who was at that time also the
viceroy, refused to approve the re-election of the abbess
on the ground that it was in violation of the special law
of the convent. He, moreover, ordered the nuns to obey
Madre de la Cueva, the candidate of the minority. This
action of the archbishop very naturally caused a schism
in the convent ; not merely a clash of opinions, but also
an actual division of the members into two parties.
Troops were sent to surround the convent, in order to
prevent the conflict among the nuns from being taken
up by the partisans of each faction in the streets. By
order of the archbishop, Madre Nieves, the candidate for
re-election, was removed secretly to another convent, and

[1] *Noticias Secretas*, 497. See also the rest of parte ii. cap. viii.

her removal caused the field of the conflict to be extended.[1]

In the absence of any general law providing for a division of powers, establishing the precedence of officials and corporations, and defining their jurisdiction, questions relating to these subjects frequently arose and were referred to the superior officers, and often to the king, for settlement. The Church was never entirely disposed to accept without question the limitations that were involved in its position as a branch of the governmental organisation ; and the assertion by ecclesiastics of superiority in their rivalry with civil officials culminated in the pretensions of the Inquisition. The pretensions of the members of the Holy Office and of the ecclesiastics generally were in some measure supported by the assumption, which was often acknowledged, that the preaching of the Gospel was " the beginning and the end of the conquest " ; and that " temporal provisions are of an order inferior to those that point the way to the eternal." [2]

II

From questions of official precedence and jurisdiction the viceroy was called to consider other subjects which concerned more vitally the interests of the kingdom. The University of San Marcos, which was founded in 1553, and placed on a more independent basis by Philip II in 1572, had contributed elements of distinction to the society of Lima, during the one hundred and eighty years of its existence. But it had declined in its influence and in its

[1] Viceroy Castel-Fuerte, in *Memorias de los Vireyes*, iii. 74.

[2] The utterances of so severe and practical a ruler as Viceroy Castel-Fuerte indicate that this view of the Spanish government of its early conquests still survived in the first half of the eighteenth century : " Es la predicacion del Evangelio en estas partes un alto fin en que la eternidad del objeto es símbolo de la razon de su dominio, siendo ella, con un circulo de Religion é Imperio, el principio y el fin de su conquista " (*Memorias de los Vireyes*, iii. 119, 122).

power to attract the youth of Peru ; and in his memorial to his successor, Castel-Fuerte wrote : " It has thirty-three different professorships in all faculties, endowed by royal munificence with an income of fourteen thousand pesos, to which other sums have been added from different foundations. But to-day, unfortunately, the number of students has diminished to such an extent that there are more instructors than pupils, more masters than disciples." [1] The university had become " an institution for purely literary exhibitions, without serious study in any department." [2] Academic degrees were given to uneducated persons, who sought them that they might appear in the doctor's cap and gown. By this the prestige of the university was destroyed. But the Marquis of Villagarcia, in his memorial, addressed to his successor, affirmed that the decline of the university was due not only to the reckless granting of degrees to men without instruction, but also to the appointment of unqualified persons to the professorships. The Jesuit colleges, however, continued to demand of their students serious attention to their studies, and they furnished in some measure the means of instruction that were wanting at the university ; and Peru at this period produced men of intellectual distinction, whose instruction and discipline had been acquired without resorting to the schools of Europe. Conspicuous in this respect were Dr. Pedro Peralta, the author of *Lima Fundada*, and Dr. Antonio José Olavide.[3]

III

Mining became more profitable by the reduction of the contribution to the royal treasury from one-fifth to one-tenth of silver, and to five per cent. on the gold. The wealth of the kingdom was apparently maintained, for

[1] *Memorias de los Vireyes*, iii. 126.
[2] Lorente, *Historia del Perú bajo los Borbones*, 69.
[3] *Memorias de los Vireyes*, iii. 383.

the new veins that were discovered from day to day in the Cerro de Pasco supplied the defect resulting from the declining product of Potosi. In spite of this decline the town and the mines of Potosi continued to attract public attention ; but the government was more immediately interested in the quicksilver mines of Huancavelica. This mine was discovered in 1564, and for a few years it was worked by the owner, Amador de Cabrera, who then sold it to the king for two hundred and fifty thousand pesos. Thus, under Viceroy Francisco de Toledo, in 1573, it became the property of the Crown.[1] The practical operations of the mine were conducted by persons to whom it was rented on condition of delivering the product at a predetermined price. The difference between this price and the price at which the government might sell the quicksilver in the market represented the proprietary interest of the Crown. The labour was performed by Indians under the system of the *mita*, but in 1720 the king ordered that forced labour should cease, and that only voluntary labourers should be employed. It was found, however, that, paying the wages demanded by voluntary labourers and maintaining the fixed price of the product, the miners were unable to make a profit ; and this decree had to be set aside or ignored, suffering the fate of many other decrees that had been framed in Spain without a knowledge of the conditions existing where it was designed that they should be applied.[2] On account of the destructive character of the work, it had become more difficult from year to year to obtain the desired number of labourers. The supply furnished by the region immediately about the mines had been exhausted, and ruinous drafts had been made on more remote districts.

[1] See vol. i. chap. xviii. sec. 5.
[2] Castel-Fuerte's report on the mines of Huancavelica and Potosi is found in *Memorias de los Vireyes*, iii. 144–83.

IV

The decline and ruin of the Indian population did not escape the viceroy's observation. He reported that in many places in America the primitive inhabitants had so completely disappeared that hardly more than the memory of them remained. He referred to the valleys of Runahuana, Huarco, Chilca, each of which had had as many as thirteen thousand inhabitants; and to the province of Santa, that had had the population of a kingdom; but in the time of his writing, there were scarcely any inhabitants in these regions, and some of the towns were entirely deserted. Castel-Fuerte emphasized two causes of this ruin : one was the forced labour in the mines and the *obrages*, or manufacturing establishments; the other was the drinking of alcoholic liquor.[1] The viceroy's conclusion was abundantly confirmed by the remarkable investigations of Jorje Juan and Antonio de Ulloa, the results of which were published in the *Noticias Secretas de America*. These investigations refer to the condition of the Indians of the viceroyalty during the reign of Viceroy Castel-Fuerte (1724-36), and that of his successor, Juan Antonio Mendoza, the Marquis of Villagarcía (1736-45.)[2]

The system which required the corregidores to collect the tribute, and gave them the exclusive right to trade with the Indians within their several districts, furnished these officers an opportunity to make burdensome exactions. The chiefs as well as the Indian governors were exempt from the tribute, as were also those Indians under a certain age, and those over a certain other age ;· but these limits were not respected, and what was collected from persons legally exempt from the tribute the corre-

[1] *Memorias de los Vireyes*, iii. 132.
[2] An elaborate discussion of the various questions relating to the mines, by Castel-Fuerte, is found in *Memorias de los Vireyes*, iii. 144-83.

gidor might hold without being detected, since it was over and above what was required of him under the law. The *mita* Indians, those subjected to forced labour, did not pay in person directly to the corregidor, but the tribute required of them was paid by the masters, who collected it from the Indians in their service ; and those living in small villages paid their cacique, who turned over the whole amount collected to the corregidor. Besides the exemptions intended by the law, it was further provided that Indians who had been absent from their district for short periods, one or two years, on returning should pay only one-third of the regular contribution for the time of their absence. This provision of the law was, however, not observed, and the returning Indians were made to pay the full amount that would have been due if they had not been absent ; and two-thirds of this amount might be held by the corregidor as not legally required from him for the public treasury. When it is remembered that the corregidores collected tribute from Indians temporarily in their districts, it will be seen that, under this practice, such as were temporarily absent from their homes were obliged to pay double tribute for the years of their absence.

The monopoly of trade held by the corregidor in his district enabled him to prevent the Indians from continuing in their accustomed occupation. He took them into his service, with barely sufficient payment for their support, and thus received the profits which the Indians themselves had received before this interference. Where the Indians were weavers, the corregidor gave them the materials and very reduced wages, and received the profits of their labour as if they were slaves. But while keeping them constantly employed under conditions where gains on their part were practically out of the question, he still exacted from them the tribute money ; and as long as this was not paid they might not leave his service. Inasmuch as the corregidor exercised almost absolute power in his district, the Indians had no redress. If they appealed to the courts, they were ruined. To meet the costs of the suit, they were obliged to give up a mule or a cow, which furnished their principal means of support. " These acts of extortion, which have no limit, have reduced them to a condition so deplorable that the state of the most poor and miserable beings that can be imagined is not to be compared with that of the Indians.[1]

The Indians were also under the oppressive system of repartimientos, which made the office of corregidor a district commissariat. In organising this system it was thought that an intelligent European would be able to supply the Indians with those things which they might need, but which they would not be likely to have on hand when needed, on account of their lack of foresight ; therefore,

" It was ordered that the corregidores might introduce a quantity of such articles as were suited to each district and distribute them among the Indians at moderate prices, in order that, having implements for labour, they might shake off the apathy which is innate in their constitution, and make the exertion requisite for paying their tribute and supporting themselves."[2]

The principal error of the system was that it required for successful execution corregidores content with moderate profits. It presumed, moreover, that they would be sufficiently intelligent to discern the real needs of the Indians.

The tyrannical application of this system is described in the report :

" The articles of distribution are chiefly mules, foreign and domestic goods, and produce. The corregidores who are attached to the viceroyalty of Lima must necessarily go to that city to take out a licence, and to receive their despatch from the viceroy, in order to be inducted into

[1] Juan and Ulloa, *Noticias Secretas*, 239.   [2] *Ibid.*, 239.

office ; and as Lima is the principal depot of the trade of
Peru, it is in that city that an assortment of articles for
distribution is to be made, and for this purpose they take
the goods required from the shop of some merchant or
trader on credit, at an exorbitant price ; for, as the traders
are aware of the enormous profits the corregidores make
in the sale, they raise the prices of the goods in order to
have a share in the speculation. The corregidores have
no money before they come into office, and, being unable
to purchase for cash, they are obliged to submit to any
terms which the creditor may prescribe, since they are
under great obligations, on account of the money which
the merchant is to lend them for the purchase of the mules
required for transportation.

" As soon as the corregidor comes within his jurisdiction, the first act of his administration is to take a
census of the Indians according to their towns and villages.
Proceeding to this duty in person, and taking with him
the articles of merchandise to be distributed, he goes on,
apportioning the quantity and kind he selects for every
Indian, and affixing to each article its price, just as suits
his caprice, the poor Indians being wholly ignorant of
what is to fall to their lot, or how much it is to cost them.
As soon as he has finished distributing in one village, he
transfers the whole assortment to the cacique, with an
exact inventory of the articles belonging to each individual, from the cacique himself to the most humble of all
those who are to pay tribute ; and the corregidor proceeds
to another village, in order to continue the distribution.
It is a time of anguish, both to the cacique and the Indians, when they look at the quantity, quality, and prices
of these goods. In vain does the cacique remonstrate,
and to no purpose do the Indians raise their clamours ;
on the one hand, they maintain that their means are not
adequate to such a quantity of merchandise as is assigned
to them, being absolutely unable to pay for it ; again,
they urge that goods of such a description are utterly

useless to them, and that the prices are so exorbitant as to exceed anything they had ever paid before. The corregidor remains inexorable, and the Indians are obliged to take whatever has been allotted them, however repugnant it may be to their wishes, and however straitened they are for want of means to make the payments ; for these payments become due simultaneously with the tribute money, and the same penalty is imposed for failure to meet one as the other. All the payments of the first distribution must be made within two years and a half, to make way then for the second, which usually does not contain as many wares as the first." [1]

Whenever the corregidor goes to collect debts he takes with him other goods, and those Indians who have made their payments most promptly are now required to receive another allotment. The least useful wares are given out in the first distribution, in order that the Indians may be more ready to receive those of the second, and in the second distribution they are permitted to select the articles they will take, but the prices are fixed. The Indians are not allowed to get the desired articles elsewhere, and no shop is permitted in the village but that of the corregidor.

A large item in the corregidor's trade is the distribution of mules. They are allotted to the Indians, not in accordance with their need of them, but in accordance with their ability to pay for them. They are bought, five or six hundred at a time, at from fourteen to sixteen dollars, and the Indians are obliged to receive them at from forty to forty-four dollars a head. The gains made by the corregidor in purchasing and distributing goods often amount to more than four hundred per cent. of the cost. If the Indian would hire out the mules, he must first obtain the consent of the corregidor, which means that the corregidor must be permitted to have part of

[1] Juan and Ulloa, *Noticias secretas*, 240, 241.

the earnings. When hired out for transporting goods " the corregidor himself collects the amount of the freight charges, keeps back one half on account of the debt, delivers a quarter part to the owner of the mules to pay what may be needed for the purchase of hay to feed the animals on the road, and with the remaining fourth part he pays the peons, whose office is to drive and lade the mules ; so that, in consequence of this arbitrary distribution, the owner is left not only without any profit, but even without the means of making his expenses on the journey." [1]

Of the quarter part held for the peons, one half is deducted as part payment of what the peon owes the corregidor. Even if there were no recorded proof of the avarice and injustice of the corregidores, they " might be inferred from the consideration that all of them go from Spain to the Indies so destitute that, instead of carrying anything thither, they are in debt on account of obligations contracted from the time they leave Spain until they reach the district allotted to them; and that during their brief term of office, which is limited to five years, they make a gain of at least sixty thousand dollars, and many accumulate even more than two hundred thousand. This is to be understood as the net profits, after having paid their previous debts and fees of settlement, and after having spent and squandered beyond all bounds during the whole term of their administration; for the salary and emoluments of their office are so scanty as to be almost inadequate for their current expenses." [2]

Protests made by the Indians did not bring them relief from these abuses, but sometimes resulted in their punishment as seditious persons. Yet in being compelled to purchase goods which they could not use, they had abundant reasons for protesting, and as the courts furnished no way of escape, the Indians' only hope lay in

[1] Juan and Ulloa, *Noticias secretas*, 243.   [2] *Ibid.*, 253.

armed revolt, and such revolts in the eighteenth century begun or threatened kept the government in a state of anxiety and alarm.

The residencia, or official investigation, of the corregidor, at the close of his administration, failed to attain the end designed, by reason of collusion among the officers concerned.

" When the judge appointed to make the investigation arrives at the principal town of the corregidor's district, he gives public notice of his business, goes through the usual forms, receiving testimony from the friends and domestics of the corregidor that he has ruled well, that he has injured no man, that he has treated the Indians kindly, and in this way he collects all the evidence which may redound to the interest of the corregidor. But lest such a degree of rectitude and benevolence might excite surprise, three or four persons are employed to present trivial charges against him, which are substantiated by summoning witnesses to testify to their truth, and the accused, being brought in guilty, is fined in an amount proportioned to the offence. In the course of these proceedings, an immense mass of writs and documents is collected, and the time prescribed for auditing the accounts gradually slips away, when they are closed and presented to the audiencia for approval, and the corregidor is as legally innocent of the charges as he was at the time his administration began, and the judge who conducted the residencia is a gainer to the amount of what the settlement has been worth to him." [1]

In some cases the new officer investigated his predecessor, and reported a clean record in consideration of a certain amount of money paid. If Indians who had suffered at the hands of the corregidores presented charges, they were made to withdraw them by such means as might be employed by the accused or the judge.

[1] Juan and Ulloa, *Noticias secretas*, 255.

" If charges are made by Spaniards relative to other matters, the judge acts as umpire, and urges them to settle their differences amicably, and forget injuries that are past ; but if this method fails, the suit goes on, and, as the judge is biassed in favour of the corregidor, he always labours to acquit him ; and if he cannot do it by himself, he appeals to the audiencia ; and as all his investigations are so arranged as to present the best evidence in his favour, a little exertion on his part is quite sufficient to have the corregidor acquitted, and his accounts settled agreeably to his wishes." [1]

The wealth yielded by the American colonies, from the mines, the plantations, or the cattle ranges, came through the labour of the Indians, yet their state was not improved nor their enjoyment increased by the production. On the estates their work was required for three hundred days in the year, for which they were paid as a maximum annual salary eighteen dollars. The tribute of eight dollars, paid by the owner of the estate, was deducted from this amount, leaving ten dollars as the effective annual income.

" From this sum, two dollars and two reals are to be deducted, to buy three yards of cloth, at six reals a yard, that he may make a shirt for himself, as decency requires, and he will have the remaining seven dollars six reals, to maintain himself and his wife and children, if he have any, besides clothing them and paying such contributions as the curate may levy upon him. Nor is this all, for the piece of ground allowed him is so confined that it becomes impossible for him to raise all the corn required for the scanty support of his family, and he is obliged to receive from the owner of the estate half a bushel of corn monthly, which is charged to him at six reals (more than double the usual price), because the Indian cannot purchase of anyone else ; thus twelve times six reals make nine dollars, which is one dollar and two reals more than the

[1] Juan and Ulloa, *Noticias secretas*, 257.

Indian can earn ; so that the wretched serf, after toiling three hundred days in the year, besides cultivating a garden of vegetables in the remaining sixty-five, having received only a shirt of coarse cloth and six bushels of corn, becomes indebted to his master one dollar and two reals, on account of the labour he has to perform the following year. Were it no more than this, the patient Indian would endure it all ; but his sufferings are yet greater. It frequently happens (as we have witnessed) that an animal dies in the *paramo*, or heath ; the master has it brought to the farm, and, in order not to lose its value, has it cut to pieces, and distributes it to the Indians at so much a pound—a price which, however reasonable, an Indian cannot pay, and hence his debt is augmented by being forced to receive meat which is unfit to be eaten, owing to its bad condition, and which he is consequently obliged to throw to the dogs.

" If, as the climax of misfortune, the unfortunate mitayo should lose his wife or one of his children, the cup of his anguish is full when he reflects how he shall pay the inexorable fee of interment, and he is driven to enter into a new contract with the owner of the estate, to furnish him the money extorted by the Church. If he escapes the anguish of losing any of his family, the curate orders him to celebrate a church festival in honour of the Virgin, or one of the saints, and he is obliged on this account to contract a new debt ; so that, at the close of the year, his debts exceed his earnings, while he has neither handled money nor got in his possession any articles of value whatever. His master claims the right of his person, obliges him to continue in his service until the debt is paid, and as payment can never be made by the poor Indian, he becomes a slave for life ; and, in defiance of all natural and national law, children are required to pay, by their personal services, the unavoidable debts of their parents." [1]

---

[1] Juan and Ulloa, *Noticias secretas*, 268–70.

When the price of corn rose in an unfruitful season, and the prices of all other products rose also, the wages of the mitayo remained unchanged. The high price induced the master to sell where he had a prospect of immediate payment, and thus the Indians were left without even the usual opportunities of procuring food. But whatever hardships the Indians endured on the plantations, the cattle ranges, and the wool-growing estates, it was in the factories that their lot was hardest. In the factories cloths and woollen stuffs were woven by hand.

" In former years, the woollen manufactury was confined to the province of Quito ; but it has been recently introduced into other districts, although the articles manufactured in the provinces south of Quito are nothing but coarse cloths of very ordinary texture. In Cajamarca there are looms for the manufacture of cotton goods." [1]

" The labour of the *obraje*, or manufactory, begins before the day dawns, at which time every Indian takes his place at the piece which is in process of weaving and the tasks of the day are distributed as may be expedient ; and when this process is concluded, the owner of the house closes the door, and leaves them immured as in a prison. At midday the door is opened for the women to go in with their scanty allowance of food, which is soon partaken, and they are again locked in. When the darkness of the night no longer permits them to work, the owner goes round to gather up the stints ; those who have not been able to finish, in spite of apologies or reasonings, are punished with indescribable cruelty : and those unfeeling men, as if transformed into merciless savages, inflict upon the wretched Indians lashes by hundreds, for they use no other method of counting ; and to complete the punishment, they remand them again to the workshop, and although the whole building is a prison-house, a

[1] Juan and Ulloa, *Noticias secretas*, 275.

portion of it is reserved for fetters and instruments of torture, where they are punished with greater indignity than could be practised towards the most delinquent slaves."[1]

Those found delinquent during the day by the overseer were chastised with a whip at once, and also reserved for punishment later. All the delinquencies were noted and charged to the account of the labourer. From year to year they became more deeply in debt, " until, finding it impossible to make up their arrears, the master acquired a right, however unfounded, to reduce to slavery not only the mita Indian, but all his sons."[2] Those sentenced to the factories by the corregidores for failing to pay the tribute underwent even greater cruelties. The food they were able to get, partly rotten corn and barley and the meat of cattle that died, was inadequate for their support. Consequently, " their constitution being exhausted partly for want of nourishment, partly by repeated punishment, as well as by diseases contracted from the bad quality of their food, they die before they have been able to pay the tribute with the avails of their labour. Such is the spectacle exhibited, when they are taken out dead, that it would excite compassion in the most unfeeling heart. Only a skeleton remains of them to publish the cause which doomed them to perish ; and the greater part of these die in the very factories with their tasks in their hands."[3]

The practice of condemning the Indians to the workshop, for slight offences, became very general.

" We frequently meet Indians on the highway, tied by the hair to the tail of a horse, on which a mestizo is mounted, who is conveying them to the workshops, and perhaps for the trivial offence of having evaded the tyranny of the overseer, from fear of punishment. Let

[1] Juan and Ulloa, *Noticias secretas*, 276.
[2] *Ibid.*, 277.   [3] *Ibid.*, 277, 278.

what will be said of the cruelty practised by the patrons (encomenderos) towards the Indians at the commencement of the conquest, we cannot persuade ourselves, after what we have witnessed, that it could ever have been carried to the extent it now is by the Spaniards and mestizos." [1]

The statement that, without the forced labour of the mita, the Indians would have remained idle and the plantations have fallen into ruin, is sufficiently answered by the flourishing condition of those estates where the mita was not observed, and where a slight advance of wages over those paid under the mita gave to such plantations all the labour desired. If the Indians were reluctant to labour, this was no doubt in part due to the treatment which they received at the hands of their employers. Of what they accomplished by their work under other conditions sufficient remains to excite our admiration, and to furnish evidence of extraordinary activity. Moreover, " all the free Indians cultivate the lands belonging to them with so much care, that they leave no portion of them fallow. It is true that their arable lands are circumscribed ; but it is because they are not allowed to possess more, and not for want of care and toil to render them productive. The caciques, who have a larger portion assigned them, lay out extensive planting-grounds, rear cattle according to their means and opportunities, and husband all they can, without being compelled by force, and without using compulsion towards those who labour for them." [2]

On the plantations, as well as in the manufacturing establishments, there were three taskmasters who had constant supervision over the workers. These were the overseer, his assistant, and foreman. The last was always an Indian, and while, like the rest, he carried a whip, he was not accustomed to strike those under him.

---

[1] Juan and Ulloa, *Noticias secretas*, 279.　　　[2] *Ibid.*, 288.

"Each taskmaster holds his own scourge without letting it fall from his hand the whole day long : this instrument of torture resembles a rope's end, about a yard long, and a little less than a finger in thickness, and is made of cow's hide, twisted like a cord. In case the Indian has been guilty of any wrong or neglect, he is required to lie flat on his face, when his thin drawers, which make up his whole dress, are taken off, and he is scourged with the rod, being himself obliged to count the lashes that are inflicted upon him, until the number prescribed in the sentence has been completed. He then gets up, and is required to kneel in presence of the man with the whip, and, kissing his hand, to say to him, ' May God bless you ! ' the trembling lips of the wretched Indian thus giving thanks in the name of God for the stripes inflicted upon him, almost always unjustly. Nor are men alone subject to punishment, but their wives and children, and even the caciques, whose rank and dignity entitle them to consideration.

"The practice of scourging the Indians so unmercifully is not confined to the labourers in the manufactories or on the plantations, and to mita Indians, but the priests chastise their parishioners, and exact any service from them whatever by dint of blows ; for if the Indian should not do promptly what is required of him, it is deemed sufficient motive to make him lie down, and to inflict stripes upon him with a whip, or with the reins of the horse, until his strength is exhausted." [1]

But the punishment of the Indians was not confined to floggings of this kind. "The most insatiable spirit of revenge has never been able to invent any species of punishment which the Indian does not receive at the hand of the Spaniards." [2]

---

[1] Juan and Ulloa, *Noticias secretas*, 289, 290.　　[2] *Ibid.*, 291.

V

This period, moreover, showed few signs of progress in the Spanish part of the population. The neglect of the university was attended by an increase of popular ignorance, and by a tendency to give undue prominence to monastic life. The ignorance of the multitude found expression in attacks on La Condamine and his associates during their operations in measuring a degree of the meridian near Quito. Their observation of the stars and their tracing lines on the earth were regarded as signs of witchcraft. In the opinion of the populace, nobody but persons bewitched would consent to camp for days and weeks on the frozen tops of the lofty mountains, and endure the untold hardships that were there experienced. And the governor of Quito informed them that they might observe the heavens at pleasure, but that they must not explore the earth. In Lima, which Castel-Fuerte affirmed was " *todo el Perú en compendio*," the tendency to excessive emphasis on the religious life was observed in the increase in the number of monasteries and convents beyond any recognised limit of their proper relation to the population of the city. There were nineteen monasteries for monks and fifteen convents for nuns ; and the large number of persons who were disposed to accept this form of life was due to lack of evident opportunity for practical effort, and to the survival of the Spanish sentiment opposed to participation in agricultural and industrial work.[1]

VI

The twenty years during which Castel-Fuerte and Villagarcía conducted the viceregal government appeared as a period of change and confusion in the affairs

[1] *Memorias de los Vireyes*, iii. 137 ; La Condamine, *Relation abrégée d'un Voyage fait dans l'Intérieur de Amérique méridional* (1778).

of commerce. Vessels from Europe made frequent voyages around Cape Horn; the hostility of Spain's enemies on the sea caused the fair of Porto Bello to be suspended, and European wares to be landed at Cartagena and taken by the long overland route to Peru. These changes exercised a disastrous influence on the merchants of Lima, who had a practical monopoly of the trade between Peru and the Isthmus. Their position was further menaced by concessions made to the port of Buenos Aires, and by the privileges extended to ships of register between that port and Spain. Formerly they had complained that the contraband goods of the Portuguese were imported into Peru, and, sold at a low price, interfered with the legitimate trade by way of Panama. Now silver from the Peruvian mines was transported to Buenos Aires, and shipped from that port by the longer but safer route to Spain. At that port, moreover, European wares were entered, not merely for the province of Buenos Aires, but also for Chile. And while the ships of register which brought goods from Spain directly to Peru induced the monopolists of Lima to bewail the ruin of the State, the bulk of the inhabitants found a certain amelioration in the abundance of European wares thus made available. The supply of European goods was further increased by the cargoes brought in foreign ships and sold at various ports of the Pacific, in spite of the efforts of the government to prohibit this illegitimate trade.

VII

It was becoming more evident every year that the viceregal government was incompetent to maintain peace and order and to secure justice to the people throughout the vast territories of the kingdom. The unjust exactions which corregidores and other agents of the viceroy had made with impunity in the provinces remote from Lima, had weakened the confidence of the inhabitants in the government, and prepared them for rebellion. The manifest inefficiency of the central authority also provoked the unsubdued Indians to invade the established settlements. In Cochabamba the viceroy had ordered a new scrutiny of the list of tribute-payers, and that no one might avoid the payment of tribute on the ground that he was a mestizo, all persons who wished release on this ground were required to establish their quality as mestizos by proper evidence. This left it in the power of the officials to accept or reject the proofs offered, and consequently opened the way. to extraordinary abuses. The mestizos saw that in case the official in question demanded a payment before making a favourable decision, as they had reason to suppose he would do, they would be obliged either to make the payment demanded or consent to be ranked as an Indian and be compelled to pay the tribute. In the presence of this unattractive prospect, the mestizos of Cochabamba, under the leadership of a silversmith named Alejo Calatayud, rose in rebellion. A company of forty Spaniards proposed to put down the revolt, but they were overpowered by superior numbers ; nearly half of them were killed, and a large part of the survivors were severely wounded. Later an agreement was formed, the terms of which indicate that the creole's hatred of the Spaniards as officials was already an effective force ; for it was decided that no European should be a corregidor, and that the alcaldes of Spanish stock should always be creoles. After the summary and treacherous execution of Calatayud, the rebellion broke out anew, but it was suppressed with great severity ; and the viceroy fancied that the merciless execution of twenty-eight victims would bring perpetual peace to Cochabamba. The revision of the tribute list was carried out, and it was increased by the addition of a large number of Indians who thus became subject to this personal tax.[1]

[1] *Memorias de los Vireyes*, iii. 280–7 ; Lorente, *Historia del Perú bajo los Borbones*, 58–60.

The vast interior province of Tucuman lay open to the incursions of the Indians on all sides, particularly on the east. The expeditions that had penetrated the Chaco had made no progress towards civilising or subduing the inhabitants of that region. These Indians invaded the settlements not to conquer, but to rob, and the persons in the province who lost their lives were not the sacrifices of war, but the victims of the cruelty of thieves. The forts that had been constructed for the defence of the province had been only inefficiently maintained, and their feeble garrisons offered no adequate protection. Recognising his inability to direct the affairs of the province from Lima, the viceroy conferred upon the president and audiencia of La Plata the authority that might be needed to issue all the orders and decrees required to avert the attacks and punish the atrocities of the barbarians. At the same time he gave them power to remove the governor, and to appoint in his place a person whom they might consider competent to conduct the affairs of the province. Under this authority, Matías Anglés was appointed to be the governor of Tucuman, and there was placed at his disposal a quantity of arms and twenty thousand pesos from the royal treasury at Potosi, to provide for the work of pacification and defence.[1]

The viceroyalty was harassed not only by internal disturbances, but also by acts of hostility from without. Two of the most notable of the attacks were the depredations of George Anson on the western coast and the assault of Admiral Vernon on Porto Bello and Cartagena.

By the treaty of Seville, 1729, it was proposed to define more accurately the privileges which the British enjoyed respecting trade with the Spanish colonies. But the merchants who took advantage of these privileges were not disposed to abide strictly by any regulations, and

---

[1] *Memorias de los Vireyes*, iii. 352

considered themselves aggrieved whenever the Spanish
government undertook to make the prescribed limitations
effective. Mr. Keene, the British minister in Madrid,
wrote, " that the commanders of our vessels always think
that they are unjustly taken if they are not taken in
actual illicit commerce . . . and the Spaniards, on the
other hand, presume that they have a right of seizing,
not only the ships that are continually trading in their
ports, but likewise of examining and visiting them on
the high seas, in order to search for proofs of fraud which
they may have committed." [1]

VIII

The efforts to excite in the British people a spirit of
hostility to Spain were so far successful, that the Madrid
Convention of 1739 was rejected, and a declaration of war
was issued in October of that year. The public joy
which greeted this declaration was produced less by the
hope of redressing grievances than by the expectation
that treasure like that which had made Potosi famous
would be appropriated. It was proposed to attack Spain
in her colonies, and it was fancied that they would be an
easy prey.

This plan having been adopted, Captain George Anson,
of the *Centurion*, was summoned to appear before the
Board of Admiralty. He was there informed that two
secret expeditions would be despatched : one, under
Captain Anson, would proceed to Manila, halting only
at Java Head ; the other would pass around Cape Horn,
attack the settlements on the coast of South America,
and join Captain Anson's expedition at Manila. This
plan was finally modified ; the proposed expedition to
Manila was abandoned, and Captain Anson was placed

[1] Letter to the Duke of Newcastle, December 13, 1737, quoted by
Lord Mahon, *History of England*, cap. xx.

in command of an expedition to the western coast of
South America. The land force of this expedition was
designed to consist of five hundred pensioners from the
Chelsea Hospital, but nearly half of these deserted before
they reached the ship, leaving only two hundred and
fifty-nine to go on board, reported by the historian of the
expedition as the least fit for service of all the two thousand pensioners of the Hospital, " most of them being
sixty years of age, and some of them upwards of seventy." [1]
Two hundred and ten raw and undisciplined recruits were
sent to fill the place of the deserters. It was then determined, in opposition to the commander's wishes, to send
with the expedition two " agent victuallers," with merchandise of the value of fifteen thousand pounds sterling,
under the supposition that these persons would be able
to obtain food supplies for goods when money would be
less effective. It was also supposed that by this means
centres of trade would be established on the coast. The
squadron finally departed from England on the 18th of
September 1740. [2]

On the 10th of June the *Centurion* arrived at the
island of Juan Fernandez, after a passage around Cape
Horn that had cost the lives of half the crew, and left
the majority of the survivors suffering from scurvy, and
unfit for service. Even during the first ten or twelve
days after landing, the loss by death was rarely less than
six each day. The *Gloucester* came in sight of the island
on the 21st of June, but it was not until the 23rd of July
that she was able to reach the harbour. Her crew was
in even a more deplorable condition than that of the
Centurion, and but for the water and the food sent to

[1] *Anson's Voyage round the World*, by Richard Walter, 9.
[2] The squadron consisted of: the *Centurion*, sixty guns, four
hundred men ; the *Gloucester*, fifty guns, three hundred men ; the
Severn, fifty guns, three hundred men ; the *Pearl*, forty guns, two
hundred and fifty men ; the *Wager*, twenty-eight guns, one hundred
and sixty men ; and the *Tryal*, eight guns, one hundred men ; and two
small supply ships.

her from the island, while the few enfeebled sailors still competent for some measure of service were trying to bring her to the anchorage, all must have perished during the month of their almost hopeless struggle. The sloop *Tryal* appeared later, but the *Wager* was lost, and the *Severn* and the *Pearl* turned back. One of the little supply ships was the only other vessel that reached Juan Fernandez.

In the beginning of the summer the viceroy sent out four men-of-war to cruise off the coast of Chile and attack Commodore Anson; but when the summer was passed, and the British squadron had not been discovered, the Spanish commander concluded it would not be possible for it to round Cape Horn in the winter. There were, however, good reasons for his supposing that, on its arrival in the Pacific, it would halt at the island of Juan Fernandez. He failed to visit the island, where, if he had appeared in the last half of June, he would probably have been able to take Anson and all the survivors of the British expedition. But Lorente has suggested that he was " more solicitous to become rich through illicit trade than to run the risks of war." [1]

After the capture of a merchantman called *Nuestra Señora del Monte Carmelo*, Anson finally left Juan Fernandez on the 22nd of September, but his greatly depleted force made it imprudent for him to assume the risks of a conflict where a vigorous opposition might be expected. Prior to the departure from the island, the *Centurion* had lost from her crew two hundred and ninety-two men, leaving two hundred and fourteen, and of the land force of fifty invalids and seventy-nine marines, there remained only four invalids and eleven marines. The *Gloucester* had suffered even a greater loss; only eighty-two of the crew remained alive; all of the invalids had perished, and only two out of the forty-eight marines had survived.

[1] *Historia del Peru bajo los Borbones*, 75. See also Juan and Ulloa, *A Voyage to South America*, ii. 190.

The *Tryal* was more fortunate ; she lost only a few more than half of her crew. The three vessels had left England with nine hundred and sixty-one men, but six hundred and twenty-six had perished, leaving three hundred and thirty-five to be distributed among the three vessels, barely enough for the work of navigation, and any considerable further loss would place the rest at the mercy of the enemy. The *Tryal* having become unseaworthy, her stores and her crew were transferred to the prize ship *Carmelo*. On the voyage to Paita several small vessels were captured, but they were not important as prizes, since no profitable use could be made of their cargoes.

When the vessels had arrived off Paita, the commander sent a detachment, under Lieutenant Brett, to the shore, who took Paita in the night of the 12th of November, carried away the treasure discovered, and burnt the town. The Spaniards estimated their loss on this occasion at a million and a half of dollars, but the greater part of this loss consisted in goods destroyed by fire. No complete and accurate statement could be made of the total amount carried away by the invaders, since much of the property taken was the private plunder of those persons who discovered it. The chaplain of the *Centurion* reported that, over and above the private plunder, " the wrought plate, dollars, and other coin which fell into our hands amounted to upwards of thirty thousand pounds sterling, besides several rings, bracelets, and jewels, whose intrinsic value we could not then determine." [1] Of the vessels of the Spaniards in the harbour, the largest was added to the squadron ; the others were taken out to sea, scuttled, and sunk. But before his departure, Anson caused all the prisoners who had been taken with the several prizes to be put on shore and liberated.

From Paita Anson directed his ships northward, hoping at Panama to acquire information of the exploits

[1] *Anson's Voyage, 276.*

of Admiral Vernon. He expected, in case the plans formed in England had been carried out, to receive reinforcements from British garrisons in Porto Bello and Panama ; and, with these conquests made, he saw his countrymen " in effect masters of all the treasures of Peru," and having in their hands an equivalent for any demands, however extraordinary, which they might make " on either of the branches of the House of Bourbon." [1]

Another attack on the viceroyalty was that made by the expedition to the West Indies, under Admiral Vernon, which was designed to take Porto Bello and Cartagena as the key to Spain's possessions in South America. The squadron, on proceeding to Porto Bello, consisted of six ships, carrying two hundred West Indian soldiers and two thousand four hundred and ninety-five seamen. The greater part of the men were without military or naval training, and many of them were quite unaccustomed to the use of arms.

The town of Porto Bello at this time consisted of about five hundred houses, two churches, a building occupied by the royal treasury, a custom-house, and an exchange. It lay at the south-eastern corner of the bay. It was defended by Gloria Castle on the shore immediately west of it, the fort of St. Jerome in front of it, and the Iron Castle on the northern point of the shore at the bay's entrance. The squadron anchored off Porto Bello on the evening of November 20, 1739. After a brief artillery duel, the garrison of the Iron Castle raised the white flag and surrendered. It was found to consist of only five officers and thirty-five men. The rest of the three hundred had been either killed or wounded, or had fled during the engagement. The Gloria Castle, which in the meantime had taken up the fight, kept up an ineffectual cannonading until night. The next morning the governor offered to surrender all the fortifications,

---

[1] *Anson's Voyage*, 286 ; Juan and Ulloa, *A Voyage to South America*, ii. 198–204.

provided the Spaniards would be allowed to march out with the honours of war, " receive an indemnity for themselves, the town, and the inhabitants, and be permitted to retain all the ships in the harbour." [1]

The admiral was unwilling to accept the terms proposed by the Spaniards, but required " that the ships with their apparel and arms should be absolutely delivered up to the use of His Britannic Majesty ; but that all the officers, both soldiers and crew, should have three days allowed them to retire with their personal effects." [2] Among the ships surrendered were two Spanish men-of-war of twenty guns each. Other spoils of victory were forty brass cannon, ten brass field-pieces, four brass mortars, and all the ammunition, except one hundred and twenty-two barrels of powder, which was used to blow up the forts. A sum of ten thousand dollars, designed to pay the Spanish troops, was seized and distributed among the troops and the crews of Vernon's ships. Another result of this victory was the prompt release, on the demand of Admiral Vernon, of the factors and servants of the South Sea Company, who had been held as prisoners under the authority of the president of Panama.

The success of this venture stimulated the admiral's ambition to undertake the more difficult conquest of Cartagena, but he recognised that for this task his force was entirely inadequate. If he had been properly supported, he might have accomplished more on the Isthmus ; he might have held Porto Bello, retaining the fortifications intact, taken Panama, and thus have carried out the plan which Anson hoped might be realised. But the attitude of the British government under Walpole made a prompt and energetic conduct of the war impossible ; still, in December, 1740, a large fleet had been assembled in the West Indies, preparatory to an attack on either Cuba or Cartagena. The preference of Vernon for

[1] Quoted by Ford, *Admiral Vernon and the Navy*, 136.
[2] Article 5th, of the Articles of Capitulation.

an expedition against Cartagena appears to have been determinative. This fleet embraced one hundred and fifteen ships, thirty of which were ships of the line, and a force of fifteen thousand sailors and twelve thousand soldiers. By the death of Lord Cathcart, the land forces fell under the inefficient command of General Wentworth; but it has been suggested that the hostility which existed between Wentworth and Vernon was even more disastrous than Wentworth's lack of military capacity.

The city of Cartagena had been fortified by the Spaniards at an expenditure of over fifty million dollars, and it was regarded by them as the main bulwark of their American possessions.[1] It had at that time a garrison of about four thousand men. The British fleet appeared before the town on the evening of March 5, 1741. The new viceroy, Sebastian de Eslava, had arrived the preceding April. The general designs of the British being known, he established himself in Cartagena, and in his capacity as a distinguished soldier took charge of the defence of the city. The attack was unexpectedly successful during the first few days: the fortifications were taken; troops were landed; and the vacated forts were occupied. The admiral, confident of a final and decisive victory, despatched a messenger to England to inform the government of his triumph. This news caused great public rejoicing, and numerous medals were struck, announcing the taking of Cartagena by Vernon. But at this point of the siege, the land forces under Wentworth were successfully resisted by the Spaniards, causing the British great losses of officers and men killed and wounded. Already, moreover, the climate was producing its disastrous effects; and, in want of a proper supply of water, it became necessary to re-embark the troops that had been sent on shore. The destruction had been so rapid, that the general declared that his force of effective men

[1] For a description of Cartagena, with two maps of the bay and the city, see Juan and Ulloa, *A Voyage to South America*, i. 19–47.

in two days had declined from six thousand six hundred to three thousand two hundred. Even many of those who returned to the ships were thereafter unfit for service. The more favourable season, from December to April, was ended, and, with the incoming of the wet season, the ravages of disease increased to such an extent that the admiral was persuaded to withdraw, after a siege of about two months, leaving his task unfinished.

Admiral Vernon thought of his failure as due largely to the inefficiency of the land forces, and in a private letter declared himself "heartily sick of conjunct expeditions with the army." In the same letter, written April 25, 1741, the day after the council of war had decided to return to Jamaica, he said : "As far as depended on the sea to do, or was practicable that way, I carried it to the best end, having entirely destroyed all the shipping, and shall leave all their forts that guarded their harbour entirely demolished ; and I took care to secure by my ships a safe landing for the army as near Cartagena as they could desire, without their having so much as a single musket shot fired at them ; and to land all their artillery, and whatever they desired afterwards. And when they had stayed as long as they cared for, I took the same care of their re-embarkation, without their having a musket shot fired at them, by having my ships well posted to cover them. And as army proceedings are no part of my province, I choose to leave that to their own relation." [1]

The Spaniards did not boast of their defence, but affirmed that "the protection of Heaven was, on this occasion, manifested towards Cartagena." But in the beginning, Vernon claimed that Heaven was on the side of the British ; for, in his premature report sent to England, he says : "The wonderful success of this evening and night is so astonishing, that one cannot but cry out with the Psalmist, 'It is the Lord's doing, and seems

[1] Quoted by Ford, *Admiral Vernon and the Navy*, 163.

marvellous in our eyes.' "[1] But this great apparent success was due to the fact that after the resistance at the castle of Boca Chica, which cost the British fifteen days of fighting and the loss of four hundred men, the Spaniards deliberately determined to withdraw from all outer fortifications and confine their defence to the city. And their procedure was attended with favourable results; for in spite of the greatly superior forces of the British and the unlimited artillery fire, to which they were subjected during nearly two months of resistance, they escaped with only two hundred killed.[2]

With respect to the losses of the British, Spanish writers are less reluctant than English to give definite figures. They affirm that when the fleet departed for Jamaica, it had lost seventeen vessels; that among the officers lost there were seven colonels, three lieutenant-colonels, fourteen captains, and eighteen lieutenants; and that the total loss amounted to about eighteen thousand men.

[1] Letter to the Duke of Newcastle, April 1, 1741, quoted by Mahon, *History of England*, chap. xxii.
[2] Groot, *Historia de Nueva Granada*, ii. 33.

CHAPTER XVII

THE GUIPUZCOA COMPANY

I. The charter of September 25, 1728. II. The beginnings of its trade. III. Popular opposition to the company and the revolt under Francisco de Leon. IV. Prosperity after the rebellion. V. Changes in colonial policy and the dissolution of the Guipuzcoa Company. VI. Venezuela during the activity of this company.

I

THE most noteworthy events in Venezuela during the early decades of the eighteenth century were associated with the history of the Guipuzcoa Company. As already indicated, the Europeans who visited Venezuela in the sixteenth century and the first half of the seventeenth, ranged the wilderness in pursuit of gold and slaves, and in the vain expectation of finding the country of the gilded prince ; and it was not until the middle of the seventeenth century that much attention was directed to agriculture and the pastoral industries. In the course of time, after the immigrants had learned the futility of their search, they found it was less profitable to sell the Indians as slaves than to employ them as labourers. Taking advantage of the favourable condition of soil and climate, they were able to organise an important trade in cacao and hides, which was carried on with the Dutch, who had established trading-posts on the island of Curaçao. This island, settled by the Spaniards in 1527, was taken by the Dutch in 1632, and, under their control, became an important market, where the inhabitants of the mainland exchanged their products for wares

THE GUIPUZCOA COMPANY 345

brought from Europe. The advantages which the Spanish colonists derived from this contraband trade stimulated the agriculture of Venezuela, particularly the cultivation of cacao. But as the Dutch trade in this region increased, that of the Spaniards declined. The high duties and the other restrictions, which were imposed upon Spanish commerce, made it impossible for the Spaniards to compete successfully with the Dutch, whose wares were introduced without duties, and whose shipping was untrammelled by unwise legislation. This contraband commerce increased to such an extent that the government in Spain was persuaded to issue a decree designed to suppress it. It was proposed that the colonists, deprived of their trade with the Dutch, should be supplied with wares sent from Spain. But these wares were burdened with such an enormous duty that their sale was practically impossible in the presence of importations by the Dutch, who not only continued to trade from Curaçao, but also established a post at the site of Puerto Cabello. This post became so important that it " appeared to be a dependency of the colony of Curaçoa rather than a place subject to the government of Spain."[1]   It made, in fact, so successful a resistance to Spain's attempt to re-reduce it to obedience, that the Spaniards were obliged to withdraw, and allow it to continue its lawless course. It was, however, finally suppressed in the beginning of the eighteenth century by the Guipuzcoa Company.[2]

This company was charged with the definite duty of

[1] Codazzi, *Resumen de la geografía de Venezuela* (Paris, 1841), 320; Benedetti, *Hist. de Colombia*, 245.

[2] A writer on the state of the province of Caracas before the establishment of the company, calls attention to its lamentable condition: "Pues siendo una heredad inculta, abandonada, y desierta para España, era sin embargo un rico Patrimonio para los Holandeses, que estaban apoderados, y hechos dueños fraudulentamente de todo su Comercio; y esto con una especie de tolerancia, que parecia formal consentimiento, no menos doloroso, que inevitable en aquel tiempo, tan contrario á los intereses de la Nation."—*Real Compañía Guipuzcoana de Caracas* (Madrid, 1765), 27.

warding off the illicit trade of foreigners from the extensive coast of Venezuela ; and, in consideration of this service, it received the concession of September 25, 1728. Under this grant it might 'despatch its vessels from the ports of San Sebastian and Pasages, as well as from Cadiz ; and they should be exempt from tonnage dues, except such as were made payable, under the decree of October 2, 1629, to the seminary of Saint Elmo.[1]

The treasure confiscated and taken from ships engaged in illicit trade should be distributed : two-thirds should be allotted to the company, and the other third to the officers and the crews of the ships. The king promised to keep the company under his royal protection ; and there were accorded to the officers of the fleet all the prerogatives enjoyed by the officers of the fleet that was dependent directly on the government.[2]

The laws prohibiting trade between the colonies were so far suspended in favour of the company that it might send to Vera Cruz the cacao which it was not able to ship to Spain. All cases concerning this trade requiring a judicial decision might be referred to the governor of Caracas, and from his decision an appeal might be taken to the Council of the Indies. Although the company enjoyed a practical monopoly of this trade, yet the king might create a rival, by granting similar privileges to others in case the company already established did not bring him the desired advantages. The prospect of being obliged to carry on this trade in competition with another company made the existing company careful to meet the expectations of the king. Later, however, the possibility of rivalry was in a measure removed. By the decree of 1742, the privilege of exclusive commerce with at least a part of the territory was granted, and ten years later the region of its exclusive control was enlarged.

After the promulgation of the decree founding the Guipuzcoa Company, a commission was appointed, con-

---

[1] Humbert, *Les origines vénézuéliennes*, 87, note.   [2] *Ibid.*, 87–9.

sisting of five members, who framed a constitution for the company. This constitution established the name of the company as the *Real Compañía Guipuzcoana de Caracas ;* it made provision for issuing the stock, for holding general meetings, for determining the functions of the committees, for fixing the number and powers of the directors, and for calling an annual meeting of the stockholders. The twenty-four articles of the constitution and the eighteen articles embraced in the decree of foundation were sent to the towns of Guipuzcoa, and to the consulate of San Sebastian, for the purpose of inducing persons to subscribe for the stock of the company.[1]

The shares were issued at a par value of five hundred pesos each, and the Crown subscribed for two hundred shares. The subscription books remained open for five years, but private persons appeared to be indifferent to the project, a state of mind probably induced by the failure of an East India Company. Even with the privilege of subscribing extended to foreigners, the company was scarcely able in five years to obtain half of the million and a half of pesos required.[2]

II

·The first important event in the commercial undertaking for which the company was formed was the departure of three ships from Pasages for Venezuela, in July 1730. These were the *San Ignacio*, the *Joaquin*, and the *Guipuzcoana*. In October a fourth vessel, the frigate *Santa Rosa*, was sent to the same destination. When the company had collected the funds needed to equip and man these vessels, it had surmounted only a part of the obstacles in its way. At Caracas it found the

[1] The names of the directors were José Miguel de Vildósola, Domingo Gregorio de Yun y Barvia, José de Lopeola, Juan Antonio de Claesens, and José de Ayerdi.
[2] Humbert, *Les origines vénézuéliennes*, 93.

influence of the Dutch especially powerful in commercial affairs, and the advantages which the inhabitants derived from the contraband trade induced the people and the government to tolerate this violation of the laws. On account of the competition of the Dutch, two years were required to obtain an amount of cacao sufficient to freight one of the ships. The others were obliged to wait three years before they were able to obtain suitable cargoes ; and the maintenance of these vessels and their crews during this period was a considerable item in the expenses of the enterprise. Yet, in spite of all the difficulties encountered, the first two voyages returned to the company an encouraging profit. The total expenses of these voyages, including the purchase price of eighty thousand fanegas of cacao, at ten pesos the fanega, of one hundred and ten pounds each, was 2,861,430 pesos ; while the selling price of the cacao in Spain, forty-five pesos per fanega, amounted to 3,600,000 pesos, leaving a net gain of 738,570 pesos. The favourable results of these early voyages induced the company to establish agencies at Madrid, San Sebastian, Cadiz, Alicante, Barcelona, and other cities, but the annual meeting of the stockholders was held in the hall of the consulate of San Sebastian.

The company grew rich, and during the nine years between 1739 and 1748 gave Spain effective assistance in the war with Great Britain. In 1740 it transported three hundred soldiers with arms and munitions of war to Caracas. It supported Havana with five ships and two regiments of soldiers when that city was besieged by the British. It repulsed the British attack on La Guaira in March 1743, and in 1744 it carried to that port, at the request of Philip V, cannon, arms, and munitions of war of all kinds. During a number of years, the company maintained at Caracas a troop of from six hundred to fourteen hundred men, and employed extensive funds and its credit in the royal service. In addition to these expenses, it suffered the direct loss of eleven vessels. Eight of these were taken by the British, two on the voyage to Venezuela, and six returning to Spain. To replace the ships lost and to provide others to meet the demands of the increasing trade of the company, the shipyards of Pasages and La Guaira were especially active. In spite of the continuing clandestine trade of the Dutch, the quantity of cacao imported into Spain by the company was tripled during the ten years following 1731, and the price fell from eighty pesos per fanega, in 1726, to thirty pesos in 1749. The activity of the company gave an impulse to various branches of industry. The cultivation of tobacco was greatly increased, and the pastoral industries acquired a new importance. To give a further impulse to the economic progress of the country, the company obtained permission to import two thousand negroes, whom it purchased on the African coast from British and French traders. It also established prizes for increases in the harvests of cacao and other products.[1]

The continuance of the company's prosperity depended upon its ability to suppress contraband trade. For this purpose it maintained ten or twelve armed vessels and an equal number of small gunboats, carrying ten or twelve men each. The whole coastguard service cost not less than two hundred thousand pesos annually ; and even with this expenditure it was impossible to prevent the Dutch, who occupied the islands of Curaçao and Buen Ayre, from carrying on with impunity trade with the inhabitants of the mainland.[2]

In obedience to demands made by the company, there was a great increase in the manufacture of arms in the province of Guipuzcoa. Extensive quays were constructed at Pasages, and Puerto Cabello was transformed from a miserable collection of huts occupied by fishermen and pirates into an important seaport town. The rural

[1] Humbert, *Les origines vénézuéliennes*, 107.
[2] Baralt y Diaz, *Historia de Venezuela*, i. 405–412.

district tributary to Puerto Cabello participated in the prosperity of the port.

III

As the company became rich and powerful, it very naturally showed a disposition to dominate all other powers of the province ; and the somewhat tyrannical conduct of its agents drove many persons into an attitude of rebellion. But for more than ten years this popular hostility found expression only in secret conspiracies. Finally, in 1749, Francisco de Leon gathered a body of discontented landowners and peasants under his leadership, and made an open protest against the procedure of the company, and even against the continuance of its functionaries in the country. This protest had much weight, on account of the high character which Francisco de Leon had maintained. He was the founder of the town of Panaquire, was popularly thought to be animated by a spirit of justice, and this view seemed to be confirmed by the fact that he proposed to use only legal means to attain the end at which he aimed.[1]

The popular opposition reached such a point that the director, José Iturriaga, determined to publish a manifesto, October 11, 1749, setting forth the benefits that had accrued, not only to Spain, but also to the colony, from the activities of the company, and at the same time giving an account of the great increase in the production and exportation of cacao that had followed the creation of the company, an increase that had been stimulated by introducing labourers, by loaning capital to persons engaged in agriculture, by encouraging planters to extend their plantations and form new ones, and by improving the facilities for internal commerce. But in spite of the

[1] Rojas, A., *Estudios históricos*, 243 ; Humbert, *Les origines vénézuéliennes*, 111.

director's statement, many of the colonists were persuaded that the domination of the company had not improved their individual condition, particularly when they observed the fall in the price which they received for their cacao. They were not satisfied with making a formal protest, and prepared to organise a force to uphold their interests.

A considerable company, moved by their common grievances, appeared in open revolt, and placed Leon at their head, and proceeded to the capital. Their arrival terrified Governor Castallanos to such an extent that he was unable to decide on any course of resistance. He, however, wrote to the rebel chief, asking for a statement of his pretensions, and called a meeting of the members of the municipal government and the notables of Caracas. This assembly determined to enter into negotiations with the leader of the insurgents through commissioners. In the course of these negotiations Leon made known his demands, which were later definitely set forth in two letters to Governor Castallanos. In the second of these letters he affirmed " that our sole end is the total destruction of the Royal Guipuzcoa Company, intending not only to remove the Basque agents from the factories, but also to banish those who exercise the functions of lieutenants or of ministers of justice, to the detriment of the province." [1] The design of the rebels was not merely to remove the agents of the company, but also to expel from the province all members of the Basque race.

This letter was written on the 20th of April, 1749, and on the same day, between four and five o'clock, Francisco de Leon led his little army into the city, where he took possession of the unoccupied palace of the bishop. His entrance created a panic. The members of the ayuntamiento, who were in session, suddenly closed their deliberations and ran to the residence of the

[1] Rojas, A., *Estudios históricos*, 149–51 ; Humbert, 120.

governor. They assured him of their fidelity, and, joined by a number of ecclesiastics, they continued their discussion the greater part of the night without reaching any decision. The next day negotiations were resumed with Leon, when he assured the commissioners that he did not wish to cause anyone any inquietude or injury, and that he desired only the expulsion of the agents, employees, and all the functionaries dependent on the company. In agreement with the governor, he ordered that sentinels should be placed before the principal public monuments, and that the different quarters of the city should be patrolled, to the end that there might be no violation of public order.

In accordance with Leon's request, a meeting was held on the 22nd of April, under the presidency of the alcaldes of Caracas. It consisted of the members of the ayuntamiento, and more than sixty of the notables of the city. Encouraged by the progress of the insurrection, the assembly manifested great freedom in criticising the conduct of the company, and affirmed that it " continued to disregard the regulations instituted by his Majesty Philip V and his successor Ferdinand VI ; declared that the existence of the company was prejudicial to the interests of the province, and that it was neither advantageous nor desirable that it should be maintained under existing conditions." [1]

Conscious that his pretensions were supported by the inhabitants of the town, Leon wrote to the governor, requesting a statement in legal form that in what he had done he had acted in the name of the inhabitants of the province, and that, although he had entered the city with a considerable body of men, he had done nothing inconsistent with the fidelity which he owed to the king. After some hesitation, the governor finally caused the crier to demand three times in the plaza and other public

[1] Rojas, A., Estudios históricos, Acta de la Assemblea, April 22, 1749, Apéndice, 159 ; Humbert, 122, 123.

places of the city : " In the name of whom has Captain Don Juan Francisco de Leon acted in supporting the cause of the noblesse and the common people ? " And three times the multitude responded : " In the name of all the inhabitants of the province." This reply of the people was officially communicated to Leon, and here began his failure as a revolutionary leader. Caracas was completely in his power ; perfect order had been maintained ; and he believed that what had been resolved would be carried out. He therefore withdrew his troops from the city, and sent his son-in-law, Juan Alvarez de Avila, to Spain to solicit from the king the abolition of the Guipuzcoa Company.[1]

Leon's moderation and his strong sense of justice rendered him unfit to guide a revolutionary movement. He felt that if even his enemies only comprehended his cause they would recognise the legitimacy of his pretensions, and assent to his demands. One may admire the honesty of his belief that all men were just without finding in this quality the virtues of a leader.[2]

While Leon was living quietly on his lands near Panaquire, relying on the promises of the governor, he learned that that officer had fled to La Guaira, disguised as a monk. Leon then went to La Guaira, without an escort, and obtained from Governor Castellanos a confirmation of the promises which he had previously received. In the meantime the governor was playing a double rôle ; while making favourable promises he was plotting Leon's ruin. That he might have evidence of his own good character, he wrote to the ayuntamiento for a detailed statement of his conduct ; and that body replied, embodying in its report an exaggerated laudation of the governor's zeal, valour, and patriotism. When this

---

[1] Humbert, *Les origines vénézuéliennes*, 124.

[2] " No carecia ni de valor ni de seso ; mas para ser caudillo de un levantamiento popular, confió demasiado en la sola justicia de su causa, creyó demasiado en las promesas de los opresores."—Baralt, i. 394 ; Humbert, 111.

certificate had been received, the governor wrote to the king a somewhat lurid account of the insurrection.

Francisco de Leon then, finding that no steps had been taken to remove the agents of the company from Venezuela, again appeared before Caracas with a force of nine thousand men, instead of the eight hundred who had accompanied him on the previous occasion ; and again, with everything in his power, gave up his position of advantage, dismissed his men, and became the victim of the deceitful promises of the governor.[1]

After these events and the arrival of Dr. Francisco Galindo Quiñones, the auditor of the audiencia of Santo Domingo, sent to pacify Venezuela, Francisco de Leon was brought to trial, and the case was in progress when Julian de Arriaga y Rivero, accompanied by fifteen hundred foot-soldiers and a body of cavalry, landed at La Guaira as the successor of Governor Castellanos. With this force Arriaga proceeded to Caracas, in January 1750, and assumed the duties of his new office. Shortly after his arrival in the capital as governor, Arriaga published an armistice, including all those persons who had taken part in the movement to suppress the Guipuzcoa Company and to expel the Basques. But the term of Arriaga's administration as governor was destined to be very brief. The Guipuzcoa Company was displeased that such indulgence should be granted to its enemies, and through its influence Arriaga was promoted from the governorship of Venezuela to the ministry in Spain. Arriaga's successor in Venezuela was Felipe Ricardos, who had been governor of Malaga, and was a creature of the company. Governor Ricardos landed at La Guaira with twelve hundred soldiers in 1751, and immediately took up the work which devolved upon him as governor of the province. He reversed completely the policy of his predecessor, and his administration was characterised at every stage by repression and vengeance.[2]

[1] Humbert, *Les origines vénézuéliennes*, 125.

[2] Rojas, A., *Estudios históricos*, 262 ; Humbert, *Les origines vénézuéliennes*, 127 ; Baralt y Diaz, *Historia de Venezuela*, i. 395.

Ricardos annulled the amnesty proclaimed by Arriaga. The persons who had been opposed to the conduct of the company were now to be prosecuted without pity; and, thinking themselves persecuted, they saw no safety but in union and armed resistance. Francisco de Leon became the leader of the new rebellion, but the circumstances were no longer favourable for insurrection. The new governor, apparently without sentiments of humanity or a sense of justice, supported by a large body of veteran troops, displayed an extraordinary activity, and was not diverted from his purpose by any thoughts of conciliation. Francisco de Leon, finding himself abandoned by most of his former supporters, and a price of two thousand pesos set on his head, fled to the mountains, where, with his son Nicolas, he remained in strict seclusion for two months. He finally came out of his place of retirement and gave himself up on the governor's promise that no harm would be done to him. He returned to Caracas to find his house demolished, and on the site a monument with an inscription announcing that Francisco Leon, rebel and traitor to the Royal Crown, had occupied the house that had formerly stood on this spot.[1]

The trial of Francisco de Leon lasted several months, and on August 7, 1752, he and his son Nicolas were embarked for Spain on the *Santa Barbara*, a ship belonging to the Guipuzcoa Company. Both the father and the son were imprisoned; but the king, needing soldiers to suppress a rebellion in his African colonies, liberated all persons imprisoned for participating in revolutions, on the condition that they would join the army. Francisco and Nicolas de Leon accepted this offer, and, after distinguished service in Africa, Francisco died in Spain.

---

[1] The inscription was as follows: " Esta es la Justicia del Rey nuestro Señor mandada hacer por el Excmo. señor Don Phe. Ricardos The. General de los Exercs. de Su Majestad su Govr. y Capn. General desta prova. de Caracas con Francisco Leon, amo de esta casa por pertinaz, rebelde y traidor á la Real Corona y por ello Reo. Que se derribe y siembre de sal pa. perpetua memoria de su Infa."—Rojas, A., *Fst. hist.*, 268. See Humbert, *Orig. ven.*, 129.

His property which had been confiscated in Venezuela was returned to his son.[1]

IV

With the suppression of the rebellion, the company resumed undisputed power at Caracas. If there was no practical check on its conduct, this was because the king, on account of the distance and the lack of effective administrative agencies, was unable to cause his designs to be executed. The decree of 1751, ordering the general directory of the company to be transferred from San Sebastian to Madrid was an attempt to bring the operations of that body more immediately under the observation of the Crown.[2]

The removal of the principal office of the company was a severe blow for San Sebastian, since it appeared to portend a cessation of benefits which the directory had bestowed upon the city. Another change was effected in the prospects of the company by the order which provided that one-sixth part of the freight capacity of each of the ships of register would be at the disposal of the planters and merchants of Venezuela, and that they might thus ship their cacao directly to Spain without having recourse to the vessels of the company. This provision broke the monopoly, and was thus a step towards the commercial emancipation of Caracas. The inhabitants of Venezuela were further favoured by the decision that the stock of the company should be doubled, and that a part of the new issue should be offered to them. Although the planters and merchants who purchased this stock might pay large sums for freight on their shipments, they would, through the dividends received, have at least some share

[1] Rojas, A., *Estudios históricos*, 270–4; Humbert, *Les origines vénézuéliennes*, 130–2.
[2] The royal order transferring the directory of the Guipuzcoa Company to Madrid is referred to by Humbert, 133, as in *Arch. gen. de Guipuzcoa* (Tolosa), sec. 2, neg. 22, leg. 72, 5th packet.

in the gains of commerce, in addition to the gains of their production.

The company yielded to the temptation to corrupt the assembly that had power to fix the prices of the articles involved in its trade. In alliance with the Dutch of Curaçao, it took part in the contraband trade, and by depriving the mother country of its proper duties, it added to the evils which it had promised to abolish. But the inhabitants of the province, as well as the company, found an advantage in the unlawful trade, and it became increasingly difficult to prevent it. Spain was obliged to acknowledge that here, as well as in other parts of her American possessions, the restrictive system had failed, and Venezuela, during the last quarter of the eighteenth century, shared with the other provinces of Spanish America in the advantages of freedom established by the decree of 1778.

In spite of losses by shipwreck and in the war between Spain and Great Britain, the business of the company continued, at least for a time, to increase, and to shipments of cacao were added large shipments of tobacco and hides. Some features of this increase may be seen in the fact that between 1700 and 1730 the imports of cacao into Spain amounted to 643,215 fanegas, while between 1730 and 1760 they amounted to 1,448,746 fanegas, an increase of 805,531 fanegas. In the eight years between 1756 and 1764, there were imported 2,212,050 pounds of tobacco and 177,354 hides. In the five years following 1769, according to Campomanes, there was a slight diminution of the company's imports: some figures of the imports were, 179,156 fanegas of cacao, 905,200 pounds of tobacco, 75,496 hides, and 221,432 pesos in specie.[1]

[1] Campomanes, ii. 162 ; Humbert, *Les origines vénézuéliennes*, 140. Concerning the cacao of Caracas, Depons remarks : " On sait que le cacao de Caracas a, dans le commerce, une valeur double de celle du cacao des îles du golfe du Mexique, sans en excepter Saint-Domingue.

At first it was the custom to call a meeting of the stockholders every year; this practice was, however, abandoned in 1766, and no general meeting was held until the assembly of 1772, which was convoked by a royal decree.   By a circular letter addressed to the stockholders, they were informed that at the general meeting which had been called for June 1772, an account of the affairs of the company between 1766 and the end of 1771 would be rendered.   This assembly held nineteen sessions, which covered a period of somewhat more than five months. The balance-sheet of the company's accounts showed that, although the amount of the stock had been greatly increased on two occasions, in 1752 and in 1766, the product of the revenues on hand was sufficient to pay the annual interest of five per cent. on the indebtedness, to furnish a dividend of ten per cent., and to leave a considerable surplus, that might be used in liquidating a part of the debts.   A resolution of the assembly provided for a regular annual meeting, and also for informing the king of the proceedings of this meeting.   The king, however, expressed the wish that the general meeting should be held not annually but every second year, to begin on the 15th of June, and to last not more than fifty days.   Touching this recommendation of the king, the company, at a subsequent meeting, expressed the view that, while it believed itself authorised by its charter to act with full freedom in matters concerning its government, it would submit to the wishes of the king.

The company continued to send six vessels to Venezuela annually during the last years of its existence, and to render assistance to the Spanish government when needed, as in the war between Spain and Great Britain, which was declared in 1779.

Il se vend même de 15 à 20 pour cent plus que celui qui se récolte à la même latitude, sur les rives de la fameuse rivière de la Magdelaine (*Voyage*, i. 2).

V

In the sixth decade of the eighteenth century, it was recognised that there was need of a new order of things in commercial affairs, and that monopolies like those represented by the Guipuzcoa Company had ceased to be generally useful. The Spanish colonies, as well as the British colonies, were convinced that greater freedom of trade and better facilities for communication would greatly conduce to their prosperity. Charles III early recognised this aspiration of the colonists, and by an ordinance of August 24, 1764, established a regular postal service between Spain and America. He ordered that for the northern route a packet-boat should leave Coruña for Havana and Porto Rico on the first of each month ; and from these ports articles sent by post should be carried to the continent in smaller vessels.[1]

The packet-boats carried also passengers and freight, and thus furnished to the individual colonists a material extension of their facilities. Another step towards commercial liberty was taken when Charles III, in 1765, extended to all his subjects in Spain freedom to trade with Cuba, Española, Porto Rico, and other islands of the West Indies. A few years later, in 1774, he issued a decree which permitted Peru, Mexico, Guatemala, and New Granada to trade freely with one another; and in 1776 he authorised the formation of private commercial companies, on the sole condition of submitting to the secretary of the consulate of Cadiz a certified copy of the public documents relating to their establishment.[2]

These measures and the publication of the commercial code of 1778 introduced a condition of affairs that left

---

[1] Cárcano, R. J., *Comunicación y transporte en la Republica Argentina*, i. 452 ; Humbert, *Les origines vénézuéliennes*, 146 ; Lafuente, *His. de Esp.*, xx. cap. iii. ; Robertson, *Works*, xi. 99.

[2] Humbert, *Les origines vénézuéliennes*, 146.

no place [1] for companies endowed with monopolies like those held by the Guipuzcoa Company. By a decree of February 15, 1781, this company was deprived of its special privileges, and reduced to the status of a private company ; and four years later, in 1785, after an existence of fifty-five years, the Guipuzcoa Company ceased to exist, or rather was merged in the Royal Company of the Philippines.[2]

VI

In the last years of the period under consideration, the province then known as Caracas attained its complete organisation. It comprised the territory which later belonged to the republic of Venezuela. It became a captaincy-general in 1731, and among its subordinate organisations were the intendencies, corregimientos, and districts governed by alcaldes. The chief officer, or captain-general, as elsewhere in dependencies of the same rank, had also the titles of Governor and president. He held the title of president as the presiding officer of the audiencia, and of all the tribunals except those of commerce and the public treasury. He was not only the head of the

[1] Baralt y Diaz, *Historia de Venezuela*, i. 397.

[2] Humbert refers to the royal decree creating the Philippines Company as existing in the Archives of Passages, Docs., for the years 1780–1803. It is dated March 10, 1785, and bears the signature of the king : *Yo el Rey*, and that of Don Joseph de Galvez. He quotes the following articles relative to the liquidation of the Guipuzcoa Company :

" Art. 4.—Les actionnaires de la Compagnie de Caracas étaient invités, dans le délai de six mois, à présenter leurs titres, et on leur en donnerait un reçu.

" Art. .—Avec les fonds de la nouvelle Compagnie, on paierait les anciens actionnaires, qui d'ailleurs seraient libres de disposer de leurs actions à leur gré ; ils les laisseraient à la nouvelle Compagnie ou on leur en rembourserait le montant.

" Art. 11.—Sur les 32,000 actions (de 250 pesos chacune) émises par la Compagnie, on réserverait d'abord celles que désireraient prendre les anciens actionnaires de la Compagnie de Caracas."—*Les origines vénézuéliennes*, 147.

civil government, but was also the military chief. He might report to the Council of the Indies in criticism of the action of the audiencia, and even make secret inquiries concerning any member of that body suspected of illegal conduct. In cases where the law failed to specify the required action, the captain-general might take such measures as seemed to be demanded by the public welfare. But in this field he was restrained by the consideration of the trial that might follow the close of his term of service. In addition to his administrative and judicial powers, he might appoint various subordinate officers, and fill provisionally certain vacancies which could be filled permanently only by the king.

It was apparently the intention of the makers of the law under which he held office, to cause him to stand apart from the people he governed. He might not engage in business, or enter into close social relations with his subjects. But, like other officers, at the end of his term of office he was subject to the trial known as the residencia.[1]

The territory subject to the captain-general was divided into corregimientos, and in each corregimiento there was a governor, who exercised also the functions of a judge of first instance in civil and criminal cases, and who was assisted by an assessor, or associate judge.[2]

Until 1718 this province remained within the jurisdiction of the audiencia of San Domingo, when it passed under the authority of the audiencia of Santa Fé. But a few years later it was transferred to its original superior, and in 1786 it was brought under the new audiencia of Caracas, whose jurisdiction had the same territorial extent as that of the captain-general, and embraced the districts

[1] Baralt y Diaz, *Historia de Venezuela*, i. 306.

[2] The capitals of the *corregimientos*, or the districts under the jurisdiction of corregidores, were : Caracas, San Sebastian de los Reyes, San Luis de Cura, Valencia, San Juan Bautista del Pao, Nirgua, San Carlos, San Jaime, San Felipe de Fuerte, Nueva Segovia de Barquisimeto, Tocuyo, Carora, Coro, Trujillo, Guanare, San Fernando, and Nuestra Señora del Pilar de Zaragoza y Araure.

of Venezuela, Maracaibo, Cumaná, Varinas, Guiana, and the island of Margareta. In addition to the secular courts, there were other tribunals that took cognisance of ecclesiastical affairs exclusively.

The mass of the people of Venezuela remained in the most profound ignorance. The Indians, the slaves, the labourers, the artisans, or four-fifths of the inhabitants, were unable to read ; for there were very few schools, and those that had been established were found only in the larger towns. Hitherto Spain had furnished little or no support for schools from the royal treasury. The primary schools that existed were supported by the cabildos or by foundations made by private persons for the education of their children.

In Venezuela, as in other parts of Spanish America, the stress laid on the offices of the Church was attended by neglect of the means of instruction in secular subjects ; for the Church here, as elsewhere, seemed to proceed on the supposition that acceptance of its doctrines was a sufficient basis for a high form of civilisation ; and under this impression it was often indifferent to the establishment of any schools except such as were designed to elucidate ecclesiastical doctrines. The first schools of Venezuela were founded to further the special purposes of the Church, The *seminario tridentino*, planned by Bishop Mauro de Tovar, in 1641, was a school of this character. The project to create it remained under discussion for forty-one years, and it was not definitely established until 1682. Later it was proposed to transform the seminary into a university. This measure was opposed by the government in Spain on the ground that it would diminish the import-ance of the university already established at Santo Domingo, to which some of the wealthier youth of Venezuela resorted, while others went to the universities of Mexico and Bogotá. By a decree of December 22, 1721, Philip V permitted the creation of a university at Caracas, and four years later it was inaugurated, in the chapel of the seminary, under the presidency of Bishop Escalona y Catalayud.[1]

For fifty years the university existed in connection with the *seminario tridentino*. The curriculum embraced the usual studies of the Middle Ages : Latin, philosophy, and theology. Some attention was also given to Castillian grammar and the elements of law and medicine. In 1775 the two institutions were separated, and after this the university was considered to be the first corporation of the city, and to have precedence over all other corporations or individual persons in all official ceremonies. Its pretension in this regard was, however, disputed after the establishment of the audiencia in Caracas. In the ceremony of receiving the royal seal, the first place was assigned to the audiencia ; and on learning that this order was to be observed, the university determined to have no part in the cortege. It was the only corporation absent. The university removed the possibility of an evil interpretation of the act by causing a *Te Deum* for the life and prosperity of the monarch to be chanted in its chapel, and by holding a solemn session, in which Fernando Aristeguieta pronounced a eulogy in Latin on the piety and munificence of the king.[2]

In 1761 Colonel Nicolas de Castro made provision in his house for what was called an academy of mathematics and the study of fortifications. It was designed for the officers under his command, and was maintained for seven years, but was discontinued when Colonel Castro was transferred from Caracas to Panama, where he died in 1772. Seventeen years after Castro left Caracas, Padre

[1] Rojas, A., *Estudios históricos*, 310; Humbert, *Les origines vénézuéliennes*, 175.

[2] Rojas, A., *Leyendas históricos*, i. 264–6 ; *Apuntes para los fastos de la Universidad central de Venezuela* (Caracas, 1885) ; Humbert, *Les origines vénézuéliennes*, 180. On the character of instruction in Venezuela and the attitude of the people respecting it, see Depons, *Voyage*, i. 186–96.

Andújar, a learned Capuchin, proposed to occupy a chair of mathematics in the university, and give instruction without compensation, in order " to acclimatise in this country this branch of human knowledge." [1]

The governor acceded provisionally to this request, but desired the approval of the king. The reply of Charles IV was, however, delayed four years, and when it arrived it was found to be a denial of the request, " because His Majesty did not think it desirable that education should become general in America." [2]

The ecclesiastical organisation of Venezuela embraced three bishoprics : that which was founded at Coro and transferred to Caracas in 1636 ; that of Merida, created in 1777 ; and that of Guayana, organised in 1790. The Bishop of Guayana was a suffragan of the Archbishop of Santo Domingo, while the Bishop of Merida was a suffragan of the Archbishop of Bogotá. Both of these became dependent on the Archbishop of Caracas after the creation of that office in 1803. The revenues of the bishops were derived from the tithes, which were subject to a complicated system of distribution.[3]

The military affairs of Venezuela, like all the other affairs of the colony, during the greater part of its history, were neglected by the government in Spain. Viewing the occupation of their possessions in America as a conquest, the Spaniards regarded the colonists as soldiers, and were not disposed to make provision for a military class distinct from the soldier-colonists. It was expected that the settlers would fight their own battles, and that they were equipped to do this is sufficiently shown by the early history of Venezuela, as well as by the occupation of Chile, Peru, and New Granada. When a monopoly of the commerce of Venezuela was assigned to the Welser

[1] Rojas, A., Estudios históricos, 317, 318.
[2] Baralt y Diaz, Historia de Venezuela, i. 414 ; Humbert, Les origines vénézuéliennes, 182.
[3] Baralt y Diaz, Historia de Venezuela, i. 297.

Company or the Guipuzcoa Company, it was expected that the company in possession would provide adequately for the defence of the country ; and it was already recognised that Venezuela was especially vulnerable on three sides : on the northern coast, on the Orinoco, and on the shores of Lake Maracaibo. But it was not until the latter part of the eighteenth century that the Crown found itself under the necessity of constructing fortifications and providing otherwise directly for defence. The Guipuzcoa Company, as we have seen, transported a large number of soldiers to America, and maintained an extensive fleet for the coastguard service. This service was designed rather to prevent contraband trade than to resist assaults by the fleets or armies of foreign nations.

CHAPTER XVIII

THE COLONIAL CITY

I. Some phases of life at Caracas. II. Organisation and activity of the colonial municipality. III. Montevideo and the interference of the governor; Buenos Aires and the place of cities in the colonial system.

I

AT the end of the middle period of Spanish rule in South America, the town of Caracas gave evidence of an ecclesiastical development that had apparently outrun its secular progress. It had fifteen churches and forty hermandades, or brotherhoods. The brotherhood was an association of persons who devoted themselves to the cult of some image, or who, in their collective capacity, performed some other prescribed function in connection with the Church. This body enjoyed the privilege of receiving alms before the church on feast days. The brotherhood Dolores had the exclusive right to ask alms on the day of the execution of a criminal. This it did by going from house to house with the cry : *Hagan bien para hacer bien por el alma del que van á ajusticiar*. Making use of the sum collected, the brotherhood paid for the burial of the body of the person executed, provided certain masses for the repose of his soul, sent a present to his family, and turned the balance into its treasury. Other funds were collected by *santeros*, men who carried a holy image about the city, and received small contributions for the blessing bestowed by the saint represented. The *santeros*, moreover, sold rosaries, relics, and other sacred objects, and returned from their peregrinations not only with a collection of small coins, but also with eggs, bread, and vegetables which the market men and women had given for the privilege of embracing the sacred image.[1]

Each brotherhood had its peculiar fantastic uniform, which differed from those of the other brotherhoods in colour as well as in shape. These groups, with their crosses, banners, and images, formed, therefore, a striking feature of the ecclesiastical processions, which embraced gorgeously robed priests, monks in their distinctive dresses, the members of the ayuntamiento, the officers of the government, and all the other associations of the city. During the days of the great religious fêtes, there was excitement and activity in the streets, which has been likened to the eagerness manifested by the inhabitants of a town on the occasion of a bull-fight. Women appeared on foot, wearing their richest costumes and their finest jewels ; the matrons were followed by their female slaves ; the militia displayed their uniforms and brilliant arms ; " while the first authority of the colony, puffed up with vanity and ignorance, attracted the astonished gaze of the vulgar, whom a smile or a salute filled with joy." [2]

In spite of the quarrels between the clergy and the civil authorities, the Church was able to throw over the life of the city a haze of ecclesiasticism. Even the names of the streets in the eighteenth century appear like the chapter headings of a book of devotion. Those running north and south were called : Encarnación del Hijo de Dios ; Nacimiento del Niño Dios ; Circuncisión y Bautismo de Jesús ; Dulce nombre de Jesús ; Adoración

---

[1] Humbert, *Les origines vénézuéliennes*, 156-8. Some of the names of the religious brotherhoods of Caracas in the middle of the eighteenth century were : Dolores, San Pedro, Las Ánimas, San Juan Nepomuceno, Los Trinitarios, Los Remedios, San Juan Evangelista, Jesús Nazareno, Santísimo Sacramento, Las Mercedes, El Carmen, Santa Rosalia, La Guía, La Caridad, El Socorro, Candelaria.

[2] Rojas, A., *Leyendas históricas*, ii. 83 ; Humbert, *Les origines vénézuéliennes*, 158.

de los Reyes ; Presentación del Niño Jesús en el Templo ; Santísima Trinidad ; Huida á Egipto ; Niño perdido y hallado en el Templo ; Desierto y Transfiguración del Señor ; Triunfo en Yerusalén ; Cenáculo ; Santísimo Sacramento ; Corazón de Jesús ; Oración del Huerto. The streets running east and west had the following designations : Prendimiento de Jesucristo ; La Columna ; Ecce Homo ; Jesú Nazareno ; Cristo crucificado ; La sangre de Jesucristo ; La Agonía ; El Perdón ; El Testamento ; La Muerte y Calvário ; El Descendimiento ; El santo Sepulcro ; La Resurreción ; La Ascención ; El Juicio universal.[1]

The bishop, moreover, asked each family to adopt a patron saint for the house it occupied ; figures of these saints were placed in niches over the doors, and at evening lights were placed before them. Thus the front of each house became a shrine, and at the sound of the angelus the citizens in the streets turned to these figures to recite their evening prayers.

Bishop Madroñero, who had established conspicuous indications of religiosity in the city, acquired a great increase of reputation by predicting the earthquake of October 21, 1766, several days before it occurred. Supported by this augmentation of his authority, he undertook to reduce the pleasures of the city to a Puritan standard. He sought to abolish popular dances, such as the *fandango* and some others which seemed to violate his notions of good conduct. He was especially opposed to the Carnival, and succeeded in suppressing it in spite of a strong popular opinion in its favour. The period of the Carnival had been marked by cruel treatment of animals, by an unusual lack of restraint in the relation of the sexes, and by the reckless squirting, with syringes or squirt-guns, of water of various colours and of various degrees of impurity over the crowds of persons in the

[1] Rojas, A., *Leyendas históricas*, ii., 111 ; Humbert, *Les origines vénézuéliennes*, 168.

streets and over the fronts of houses. Many persons, in order to avoid the objectionable practices of this festival, were obliged to shut themselves up in their houses for a number of days.   This disorder and riot the zealous bishop replaced with representations of religious scenes taken from the Evangelists and the life of the Virgin.[1]

The inhabitants of Cạracas submitted to Madroñero's plans until his death, which occurred in 1769. After this event, the Carnival was re-established with all its ancient practices and a liberal addition of new barbarities. In spite of the puerile character of the exhibitions with which Bishop Madroñero temporarily replaced the Carnival, he undoubtedly exercised a favourable influence on the social customs and practices of the citizens of Caracas. He compelled them to take note of the fact that it is essential to the maintenance of civilisation that society should recognise the difference between desirable and undesirable conduct, and at the same time seek to suppress the one and encourage the other.   The scenes which he caused to be presented, and the music which he provided for the public had more or less influence in promoting the demand, which the theatre, opened in 1787, came to satisfy.[2]

II

Many of the forces that maintained the individuality of the colonies and the provinces operated to preserve the cities as distinct and self-sufficing centres.   Asuncion, Bogotá, Buenos Aires, and Santiago had to manage their local affairs without any reference to one another, and these were the most important affairs with which they were concerned.   They were in a great measure autonomous, because what concerned one city did not involve

---

[1] Rojas, A., *Leyendas históricas*, ii. 131-6 ; Humbert, *Les origines vénézuéliennes*, 171.

[2] Rojas, A., *Leyendas históricas*, ii. 110-115 ; Humbert, *Les origines vénézuéliennes*, 172, 173.

the interests of others. The governors, or corregidores, were accustomed to assume much power in the municipal governments of the cities where they resided. This was a direct interference with the autonomy of the cabildo, or the ayuntamiento, or the local organisation, under whatever name it was formed.

The laws of the Indies, in keeping with their regard for details in general, prescribed the forms to be observed in founding a town. In the English colonies of America the town grew up to meet the needs of the inhabitants of the country ; but in the Spanish colonies the population of the country grew to meet the needs of the towns. The primary plan of the English colonist was to live on the land, and to derive his support from its cultivation. The primary plan of the Spanish colonist was to live in the town, and to derive his support from the labour of the Indians and of such other persons as found themselves compelled by unfavourable circumstances to turn to agriculture or the work of the mines. The Spanish colonial town was created consciously, in accordance with a plan of action predetermined. In most cases the town had an individual founder who went about his undertaking as one might proceed to found a fortress or fix the site of a manufacturing establishment. The English colonial town grew up where it was found, by the experience of many persons, that commercial or other agencies, gathered in a more or less compact community, would be able to be of service to a large number of persons or families. The Spanish founder selected a site, and indicated the place for the principal plaza. Here he erected a monument as a sign of possession and royal jurisdiction. He gave a name to the future city, marked out its plan, distributed the lots, and determined the limits of its jurisdiction. This having been done, all those persons present who were to become members of the municipality signed the act of organisation, and took an oath to support it. The founder then appointed the

alcaldes and regidores, or members of the municipal
council, administered to them an oath, and when the
ayuntamiento, or corporation, was thus installed, the
founder himself took an oath before it. This body,
when organised, exercised legislative and, through its
alcaldes, judicial and executive powers. The members
of the municipal government were in the first instance
appointed, but it was provided that subsequently they
should be elected, and the time for election, the term of
service, and the limits of their authority were already
fixed by a general law.

In some of the larger cities there were officers not
found in the smaller organised towns. In Lima, besides
the two alcaldes and the twelve councilmen, the law provided for a prosecuting attorney, a secretary, a sheriff,
and a legal adviser ; and among the officers appointed
by the cabildo, there was a police magistrate and a *juez
de aguas*. The last-named officer decided all questions
relating to the waterworks belonging to the city and the
suburbs. The fact that a city was the capital of a viceroyalty led to certain unusual forms and practices in the
city government. The viceroy was, for example, president
of the cabildo, and the alcaldes took cognisance of cases
that ordinarily were decided by the governors.

The ancient Spanish charters of municipal liberties
established and guaranteed certain important privileges
or rights : 1. Equality before the law ; 2. Inviolability
of the domicile ; 3. Justice administered by judges elected
either by the people or by their council, except in certain
special cases which fell under the royal jurisdiction ;
4. Participation in public affairs, which was realised by
the election of members of the council by the citizens ;
5. Responsibility of public functionaries. The municipalities established in America did not possess all of
these ancient guarantees. The members of the council
were, however, elected every year, on the first of January.
By royal decree of 1594, it was provided that the inhabi-

tants of the city should elect their cabildos freely, the right to vote being exercised by resident householders of the city, provided they had not shops for the sale of merchandise, in which they were personally engaged. This phase of the constitution of the cabildo, or council, was from time to time modified by the interference of the superior authority. The first cabildo of Buenos Aires was organised by the founder, Garay, who affirmed his right to appoint the members, to indicate the beginning of the year, the end of their service, and also the time when other members should be elected to fill vacancies. The intervention of the governors in appointing municipal officials was in opposition to the will of the king, and the cabildo of Buenos Aires was led to send to him protests against the practice. The governor, moreover, under his right to confirm the result of the elections, sometimes assumed the right to nullify them and order a new election.

The original plan of constituting the cabildos was further violated by the practice of selling the places of members. This was in keeping with the earlier practice of selling offices and titles in Spain. The sale in Buenos Aires was by public auction held in the plaza near the entrance to the municipal building. This practice naturally took away from office-holding all idea of duty, patriotism, or sacrifice for the good of the community. The system of purchasing offices having been established, the purchasers made a business of politics, and were careful that their investments should not be unprofitable. They trampled the laws of the kingdom underfoot, if thereby they could gain a pecuniary advantage. They regarded their personal interest as the only good, and for this they were willing to sacrifice all other interests. "This policy," says an Argentine writer, "violated all notions of good order and administration. By selling offices, the government admitted implicitly that its affairs were exploitable—that they were articles of commerce.

The evil which this tradition has wrought is incredible. It is the root of our political decadence." [1]

There were thus three ways by which one might attain the honour of membership in the cabildo : by appointment, by election, and by purchase at public auction. By whatever way they may have come to their positions, the members enjoyed certain privileges and advantages aside from the legitimate powers of their offices, but the superior authorities did not regard them or treat them with great consideration. The governor not infrequently traversed their will. He might call them to a meeting at an appointed time, direct their debates, or close the discussion when it pleased him. He sometimes sent them as prisoners to their houses or to the prison, when their conduct seemed to him to require punishment. The inhabitants of the city were practically affected only by the acts of these two authorities : the cabildo, or ayuntamiento, and the governor of the province or his deputy. Beginning as civilised camps in a savage wilderness, the question as to the amount of power which the law gave to these two authorities was of little importance. The needs of the common life of the city in its isolation, and not the terms of a charter, determined their action.

In no city should the number of alcaldes exceed two, but the number of regidores, or councilmen, might vary, with the size of the city, from six to twelve. In cases where they were elected, where the posts had not as yet been sold, persons with certain degrees of relationship with the candidates for these places were prohibited from voting for their kinsmen,[2] and the persons elected must be residents of the towns in which they were to serve.

---

[1] García, *La Ciudad Indiana* (Buenos Aires, 1900), 169, 170.

[2] " Mandamos à las justicias, cabildos y regimientos, que no consientan ni den lugar que en las elecciones de oficios se elijan ni nombren padres á hijos, ni hijos á padres, ni hermanos á hermanos, ni suegros á yernos, ni yernos á suegros, ni cuñados á cuñados, ni los casados con dos hermanas, que asi es nuestra voluntad."—*Leyes de Indias*, lib. iv., tit. 10, ley 5.

The election was held annually on the first of January, and in the presence of the governor. By this election the members of the cabildo, or ayuntamiento, were selected and the alcaldes were chosen by this body. The alcaldes exercised judicial power and were invested with this authority for only one year, in order that this honour might be shared by a greater number of the inhabitants, and it was recognised that appointments made for this short period would be less harmful in case the selection resulted in elevating to office an inefficient and unworthy person.[1]

The justice administered by the alcaldes in the city and the surrounding territory subject to its jurisdiction was patriarchal in character. The judge might or might not be able to read and write ; this was not a matter of prime importance, but it was important that he should have the sense to discern what decision would secure essential justice in the usually simple cases that were brought before him. The primitive form of settling petty cases appears to have been satisfactory ; and there was strong opposition to the introduction of a system that would involve the services of lawyers and the consequent emphasizing of legal technicalities. The policy of the king and the Council of the Indies had been to oppose the establishment of lawyers in the colonies, and the colonists themselves entertained the same view. As early as 1613 the cabildo of Buenos Aires had under consideration the advisibility of admitting three lawyers, who had proposed to come to the city. The opinions expressed in the discussion were decidedly adverse to their coming. The treasurer affirmed " that lawyers are not needed in this country, since those who have come to it have only served to excite disturbances between the royal officials and the governors and all the other inhabitants of the town." [2]

---

[1] *Libros Capitularis de Santiago del Estero*, i. 6.
[2] García, *La Ciudad Indiana*, 183.

The ordinary alcalde acted as judge of first instance. From his decision there were three forms of appeal, depending upon the nature of the questions involved. The first appeal was to the cabildo, or municipal council, and might be had when the amount involved did not exceed 6000 maravedis : the second was to the audiencia ; and the third, in Rio de la Plata, was to the governor, from whom the alcalde had received his commission.[1] Here, as at many points in the colonial government, there is observed a mingling of judicial and general executive functions.

The municipal corporations administered the limited funds that were left under their control, cared for the repairing and cleaning of the streets, regulated the price of grain, and inspected the prisons and institutions of charity.[2] They exercised, in fact, general control over municipal affairs, held whatever local autonomy was recognised as existing under the colonial system ; and disposed of the regular revenues of the city. The tribute, however, which was due from persons who were in most respects under the jurisdiction of the city was paid to the corregidor or governor, and the tax called the alcabala was collected by officers of the Crown.[3] In so far as the cabildos acted independently, particularly in managing the revenues, they generally acted not only without foresight, but without ordinary discretion. They were attentive to provide the luxuries, and left the necessities to be secured if there should happen to be a surplus of funds in the treasury. They were wasteful and concerned more with outward appearances than with having the needful things well done. If it was a question between repairing a breach in a street that impeded traffic and paying for fireworks or a bull-fight, the street remained unrepaired, and the celebration was held. But even in the narrow

[1] Estrada, *Historia de la Republica Argentina*, i. 159.
[2] García, *La Ciudad Indiana*, 190.
[3] *Leyes de Indias*, lib. viii. tit. 10, ley 10 ; lib. viii. tit. 5.

field marked out for the municipal corporations by law, they were not independent, whatever might be the position which the law seemed to accord to them. They were often practically subordinated, as already indicated, to the executive officer of the district, called in different parts of the dominion governor, corregidor, or alcalde-mayor, and the relation between the corporation and the governor was a subject of frequent disputes between the two authorities. The corporation, exercising power in civil and economical affairs, came into conflict almost inevitably with the military force that was in the hands of the governor. In some cases " every resolution of the cabildo provoked bitter debates between the military chief and the civil corporation, in which the military usually triumphed, since it was supported by force ; and by this it imposed silence." [1] The cabildo of the town where the governor resided usually suffered most from interference. This is noteworthy in the case of Montevideo, as compared with the three other cabildos of Soriano, Colonia, and Maldonado in Uruguay.[2]

III

In December 1749, José Joaquin de Viana became governor with his residence in Montevideo. According to his instructions, he was subordinated to the government and captaincy-general of Buenos Aires, especially with respect to all military affairs. In political and economical affairs, his government was like that of the other provinces of Rio de la Plata : the gov-

[1] Bauza, *Historia de la Dominación Española en el Uruguay*, ii. 637.
[2] Montevideo was founded under the name of San Felipe y Santiago. The name was given in honour of the reigning King of Spain, Philip V. The beginning was made in 1726 with twenty families from the Canaries. To these were added others from Buenos Aires. A fort was built, and in constructing it, the labour of Guarani Indians was employed, as had been done in Buenos Aires. In 1730, the cabildo was organised, and lots fifty varas square were distributed to the settlers (Zinny, i. xxxii.).

ernor of Buenos Aires might intervene whenever he should decide that laws and regulations touching any point were not followed. He might also remove him from office, if, in his opinion, the good of the public service required such action. In the conflict between the governor and the cabildo, Vertiz, the governor of Buenos Aires, removed La Rosa, and appointed Viana to occupy temporarily the position of governor of Montevideo.[1] The new governor was required to visit the several towns of his province at least once during the term of five years for which he was appointed, but before leaving his capital he was required to notify the governor of Buenos Aires, and to await his reply, in order that the royal service might not be impaired by his absence.

In spite of the satisfaction which the people of Montevideo felt in having a person of rank at the head of their government, their political ideas as civilians were destined to clash with the military ideas of their governor. While Viana was preparing to enter upon the war of the Seven Reductions, he appointed Pedro Leon de Romero as his general deputy. In doing this he had failed to observe some of the provisions of the law which had created the office. Then followed the ordinary civil-military controversy. The people were right, but the governor had the power. The correspondence between the governor and the cabildo was characterised by the incivilities that seem to belong to such a debate ; Romero, however, supported by the governor, continued to exercise his functions. Other governors clashed with the local officials. Governor La Rosa interfered in the affairs of the cabildo, attempting to control the votes of the members, and, failing in this, apprehended them, and ordered them to prison. Pino banished them, and Feliú used the armed force to secure the adoption of resolutions. The struggle, however, did not always turn out to the advantage of the governor. In some instances he was

[1] Bauza, ii. 205.

defeated, and even driven out of the city.   These conflicts
were in many cases the means through which the towns
learned how to defend their autonomy, and acquired
that experience which enabled them to assume an attitude of independence in the later general movement for
emancipation.[1]

In 1530 Mexico was recognised by Charles V as holding the first place among the cities of New Spain, " as
the city of Burgos holds it in our kingdoms." [2]   This
meant that as Burgos held the political primacy in Castile,
a certain precedence in the Cortes over all the other cities,
the same distinction was accorded to the city of Mexico,
among the cities of New Spain.   The personality of the
cities of Spain presented itself for recognition like individual personality in all lands and times.   The king
issued to cities patents of nobility, in essentially the same
spirit as to individual persons.   After this they bore a
coat of arms, and in all official matters they enjoyed a
precedence over cities that had not been thus honoured.
Through a subsequent law issued by Philip II the city of
Cuzco became the political primate " of all the cities and
towns that are or may be in the whole province of New
Castile." [3]

A city sometimes held a meeting that was called an
open cabildo, which was a meeting of the official members
with the people for the purpose of deliberating on public
affairs.   In Montevideo, from its foundation, the inhabitants of the city regarded with great favour open meetings of the cabildo, and in them the imposition of taxes
was always determined, and all important measures touching the general welfare were settled.   In such a meeting
was decreed the political independence of Uruguay.[4]

" To the cabildo is due," as affirmed by Bauza, " the
idea of the representative system and the first glimpse of

[1] Montes de Oca, *Cuestiones constitucionales*, 37.
[2] *Leyes de Indias*, lib. iv. tit. 8, ley 2.
[3] *Ibid.*, ley 4.   [4] Bauza ii. 639.

the division of power. From the time when they took upon themselves the conduct of public affairs, the people observed that not everything depended upon the comprehensive authority of the military chief, and, as a consequence, the rudiments of a system of government more complex than the one-man power began to permeate all minds. Soon the exercise of the right of petition before the cabildos became customary, and from this they advanced to the practice of petitioning the governors. The election of members of the corporation, although carried out in an imperfect way, succeeded in awakening an increasing interest among the citizens, who even if they only contributed to the election as spectators, did not by this fail to show their satisfaction in so far as the act and its result agreed with their views. The conduct of the members of the cabildo will always be a subject for applause, that although authorised during many years by law to elect their successors, they never nominated such as were traitors to the common interests. Thus, by means of these humble and persecuted corporations, public spirit in Uruguay was born, and the inhabitants created a criterion, in accordance with which power should be exercised for the benefit of all in a regulated, equitable, and beneficent manner." [1]

The nucleus of the city of Buenos Aires was the fort. It was constructed not only as a means of defence, but also as a place of refuge for the inhabitants. It was flanked by monasteries, and surrounded by the straw and mud houses of the new town, " where lived the families protected by the soldiers of the presidio, while the men went out to their farms to work, as they might do every day without difficulty." Like the colonists of New England later, the settlers of Buenos Aires lived surrounded by Indians, and were therefore expected to keep arms, and now and then they were called out for review in the plaza.

[1] Bauza, ii. 639, 640.

In laying out the city, Juan de Garay provided that it should extend twenty-four squares from north to south, divided in the middle on the side towards the river by the plaza. It was made to extend back from the river eleven squares. Around this tract which was specially set apart for the buildings of the city, a certain amount of land was reserved as commons, a place for the recreation of the inhabitants. This was designed to be inalienable. Beyond this was the common pasture. The lands surrounding these tracts were early conveyed to private persons for cultivation. The municipal property was thus enclosed by a zone of private property, so that when the population had covered this interior portion, later settlers encountered the high prices demanded by the private owners of the surrounding territory. This led to the illegal occupancy of the lands that had been reserved for the commons. In its growth the city met an obstacle not only in the high price demanded by those who had a monopoly of the available land, but also in the spirit of a dominant class of citizens. This class " was composed of a certain number of persons whose proverbial Spanish pride found in Buenos Aires an adequate and better field for development than in the mother country." [1] They held to the feudal idea, and regarded themselves as the lords and the Indians and creoles as the vassals. This was the fateful idea that very largely contributed to the unfortunate result of Spain's great colonial undertaking. It prevented the growth of a democratic society, without which it is impossible to maintain a democratic government.

The cities were undoubtedly weak; according to Mitre, the " sombra de la sombra de los antiguos cabildos libres de la madre patria," [2] and their administration was often unwise, yet they contained a germ that might have developed into a well-ordered government. Legally the

[1] García, *La Ciudad Indiana*, 74.
[2] *Historia de Belgrano*, i. 62.

people had a voice in the construction of the municipal corporations, and for this reason they might continue to act even if the power of the king were set aside and all the royal officers withdrawn. In the beginning of the period of emancipation, they stood alone between the people and social chaos. The judgment of Sir Woodbine Parish concerning the rôle played by the municipal corporations in this period is worthy of consideration.[1]

" But for the cabildos and municipal institutions," he wrote, " which still existed in most of the principal towns of the interior when the Spanish government was broken up, I believe every semblance of a legitimate authority would have ceased. They retained to a certain extent powers not only for the preservation of the public peace, but for the administration of justice ; and although, perhaps, under the circumstances, they afforded facilities for confirming the establishment of the federal system in opposition to a more centralised form of government, there is no doubt they saved the isolated towns in the interior from worse consequences.

" Those institutions were by far the best part of the colonial system planted by the mother country, and they were framed upon principles of liberality and independence which formed a singular exception to her general colonial policy. I doubt whether those which in most cases have been substituted for them have been so wisely cast, or are so suitable to the state of society in those countries. The people at large were habituated and attached to them, and had they been retained, with some reforms adapting them to the new order of things, they might have been made the very best foundations for the new republican institutions of the country. But the truth was, they were essentially too democratic for the military power which arose out of the change ; they succumbed to that, and the people having no real voice in their new governments, made no struggle to preserve them." [1]

[1] Parish, *Buenos Aires*, 320.

CHAPTER XIX

TRAVEL AND TRANSPORTATION

I. The Inca roads and the Chasquis. II. The principal routes in the south. III. The vehicles of the pampas. IV. Padre Gervasoni's journey. V. The Andine routes. VI. Transportation on the rivers of the south-east.

I

A MORE or less elaborate system of transportation existed in the western part of South America under the Inca régime. It was maintained by couriers, who were trained and practised in their work from boyhood.[1] Stations were established along the principal routes about four and a half miles apart.[2] On the arrival of one courier at a station, another immediately received his charge and carried it on to the next station. It was designed that the stations should be at conspicuous points of the route, in order that the coming of a courier might be known before his arrival, and thus all delay avoided. On some routes the couriers carried a horn, or a shell, which they sounded to announce their coming. The articles entrusted to them they carried on their backs in a bag or pouch made of leather or the hide of an animal.

If the courier bore an oral message, he repeated it carefully to his successsor, thus securing its delivery at the end of the route in the exact form in which it had been received. Sometimes he carried *quipos* as a means of conveying messages from one person to another. The

[1] Acosta, in his *History of the Indies*, Hakluyt, lxi. 409, says: " For this cause there were men of great agilitie, which served as couriers, to go and come, whom they did nourish in this exercise of running from their youth, labouring to have them well breathed, that they might run to the toppe of a high hill without weariness."

[2] Acosta, in Hakluyt, lxi. 425.

quipos consisted of a large cord, from which other twisted cords of different sizes and diverse colours hung like a loose, open fringe, knotted in different ways according to the different ideas or different items of information it was desired to communicate.[1]

[1] For a discussion of this subject, see Larrabure y Unanue, *El Quipu*, in *Monografías Histórico-Americanas* (Lima, 1893), 185–94 ; Acosta, in Hakluyt, lxi. 406. According to Pedro de Cieza de Leon, there were usually two Indians with their wives at each of the stations along the routes. " One of these ran with the news that had to be transmitted, and, before reaching the next house, he called it out to the other runner, who at once set off running the other half-league, and this is done with such swiftness that neither mules nor horses could go over such rocky ground in a shorter time."—*Travels*, Hakluyt, xxxiii. 153. Xeres, in his *Narrative of the Conquest of Peru*, Hakluyt, xlix. 29, refers to the road which " traverses all that land from Cuzco to Quito, a distance of more than three hundred leagues. The road is level, and the part which traverses the mountains is very well made, being broad enough for six men on horseback to ride abreast. By the side of the road flow channels of water brought from a distance, at which the travellers can drink. At the end of each day's journey there is a house, like an inn, where those who go and come can lodge. At the entrance to this road, from the town of Caxas, there was a house at the head of a bridge, where a guard was stationed to receive transit dues in kind from those who came and went ; and no man could take a load out of the town without paying the toll. This was an ancient custom, and Atabaliba suspended it, in so far as it affected the things that were brought for his troops. No passenger could enter or depart with a load by any other road than that on which the guard was stationed, on pain of death."

Of the roads existing in Peru at the time of the arrival of the Spaniards, Alonso Enriquez de Guzman gives some account, stating that Atahualpa " was carried on men's shoulders when travelling, and roads were made five hundred leagues long, and broad enough to allow ten horses to run abreast, the ground being as smooth as the palm of the hand, with a wall on each side, and trees in double rows to keep off the sun " (Hakluyt, xxix. 91). The Inca roads evidently made an impression on Don Alonso, for in a subsequent chapter about Tumbez, he says: " The distance from this place to Cuzco is three hundred leagues, and along the whole way there is a straight, smooth road, passing amongst very lofty, naked mountains, bare of grass or trees. . . . The road is bounded on each side by walls, two yards thick, and six in height. In some parts there are rows of trees which yield a fruit like that of the carob tree. Every three, or at most every four leagues, there is a house which the Indians call *tambo*, but which we, in Spain, should call an inn " (*ibid.*, 95).

The existence of roads corresponding to these descriptions has

The *chasquis*, as the couriers were called, carried not only messages and correspondence, but also articles of food; as fish, game, and fruit from the sea, the forest, or the productive valleys. They ran their courses night or day, so that, by this system of relays, the charge handed over to the courier suffered no delay until it reached the end of its journey. They swam across rivers where there were no bridges ; and, when their way was down the course of a river, they often plunged into the swift current, and, with a large pole or a small log under one arm, were borne rapidly down the stream. In these cases the *quipos* or correspondence in any form was enclosed in a package and bound around the head like a turban. By this system, when the occasion demanded it, as in an emergency like the imprisonment of Atahualpa, information could be sent with great rapidity to the remotest parts of the realm.

The Spanish invaders in Peru and Chile employed the Indians in great numbers as carriers. The hardships and loss of life among the Indians employed in this manner were such as to induce the king to issue decrees prohibiting the use of them as burden-bearers ; but these decrees were without important effect. The Indians were also employed occasionally to carry despatches, but the

been called in question. Prescott, *Conquest of Peru*, i. 457, refers to these roads with less exaggeration than some of the earlier writers.

Dr. Larrabure y Unanue calls attention to the critics who express doubts as to the existence of these roads as described by Cieza de Leon and other chroniclers of the sixteenth century, and finds that these views, published in some cases by persons who had not visited Peru, proceeded either from ignorance or lack of investigation (*Monografías Histórico-Americanas*, 146–8). The geographer, Raymondi, found sufficient evidence of the existence of these roads, virtually in the form described by the chroniclers. In June 1868, near the town of Guadalupe, Department of Libertad, he says: " I came upon a level road, straight and clean, with a little wall on either side ; it was an ancient road, anterior to the occupation of the Spaniards, and in the neighbourhood they called it *Camino del Inca*. I followed this fine road some distance ; it was kept clean and in good condition, in spite of the long time that has elapsed since its construction (*El Peru*, Introduction). See Lorente in *Revista Peruana*, iii. 504.

old system was overthrown, and the new purposes of the Spaniards led communication and transportation along new lines. In place of a systematic service, special messengers were employed to go when and whither they were needed.

II

The most far-reaching change made by the Spaniards in the means of transportation was through the introduction and use of horses and mules. Before the establishment of the new postal system, it was customary to confide correspondence to travellers who might be found ready to make a journey to the place which the sender desired to reach ; or special messengers might be sent, with their expenses paid by the persons taking advantage of their services. The journeys of such messengers were usually made on horseback, the rider generally taking with him three or four horses for a change of mount, and to prevent interruption of the journey by the failure of a single horse. Along many of the early routes there were very few houses or cabins, and the rider was usually obliged to sleep on the ground, either on the open plain or among the mountains. He never took more than five days for the four hundred miles from Buenos Aires to Cordova. Such a messenger was sent to Peru on the arrival of a ship at Buenos Aires from Spain ; and, with the information which the courier brought to them, the merchants of Lima were accustomed to go or to send to Buenos Aires to purchase the newly arrived wares.

The two most notable routes of travel or communication by land in the southern part of the continent were the route from Buenos Aires to Santiago de Chile and from Buenos Aires to Lima. The latter was more used in the colonial period than any other long route in South America. The fact that Buenos Aires was for a long time a closed port made it necessary for the inhabitants of that region to get many articles of commerce from Peru ; and, on the other hand, Portuguese smuggling made it advantageous for the Peruvians to resort to the valley of La Plata for certain articles that could not be procured as cheaply elsewhere. Thus, in the course of time, a line of communication was established across the plains and over the mountains between Buenos Aires and Lima, a distance of somewhat more than two thousand eight hundred geographical miles. In the early decades the journey was made by caravans of explorers or traders over a more or less trackless wilderness, but in 1748 post-houses were established at intervals along the way, at which travellers might obtain horses and carts or carriages. The route passed through Cordova, Santiago del Estero, Tucuman, Salta, Jujuy, Potosi, Oruro, La Paz, Juli, Pucara, Santa Rosa, Cuzco, Abancay, and Huancavelica.[1]   The difficulties, the delays, and the expenses of making this journey or transporting goods were very great ; and in the last decade of the eighteenth century Don Fernandez Cornejo sought to find some way by which they might be lessened. To this end he explored the river Bermejo. In 1790, taking a small vessel and two canoes, and accompanied by twenty-six persons, he passed in forty-four days, without encountering any obstacles, from the mouth of the tributary Centa to the junction of the Bermejo and the Paraguay, a distance of about a thousand miles. The knowledge of the practicability of this route did not cause it to be used ; the communication between Buenos Aires and Lima continued to be maintained by land, notwithstanding the great expense and all the other inconveniences.

[1] The names of all the stations and the distances are given by Wilcocke, *History of Buenos Aires*, 104–18.

III

The vehicles for transportation across the pampas, whether to Mendoza or towards Jujuy were chiefly heavy carts drawn by oxen. The body of the cart was enclosed and covered with a kind of canvas, and had a door in the rear end, and a window for ventilation in either side. The enclosed space was sufficiently high to permit one to stand erect, and was used for baggage, passengers, or freight, according to the demands for transportation. The forward oxen were attached by a long rope or traces to the pole, so that there might be a considerable distance between them and the oxen attached directly to the pole. The reason for thus separating the leaders from the others was to make it possible that, in crossing small streams or narrow swampy places, some of the animals might be on hard ground while the others were passing through the soft places where it would be impossible for them alone to haul the cart. A long light pole with a prod at the end was supended at the balancing point over the tongue of the cart, and by this the driver was enabled to furnish the forward oxen the necessary encouragement.

An ordinary load for a cart on the road to Jujuy was five thousand pounds. The carts on the road to Mendoza were somewhat broader, and carried six hundred or seven hundred pounds more ; for this road lay wholly over the open plain, where it was possible to avoid all difficult places. The distance from Buenos Aires to Jujuy was reckoned as four hundred and seventy leagues, and the charge for freight was about four cents a pound. In case there were passengers, the amount of freight taken was limited in a certain ratio to the number of persons, in order to leave room for them and their baggage. For the journeys across the pampas elaborate preparations were necessary. The caravan carried not only the food

and water required, but also wood for fuel and arms for
defence against assaults of Indians on the way. When
several carts made the journey together, they were accompanied by a number of extra draft animals and of animals
to be slaughtered for food. When the train was in motion,
a mounted guide rode ahead to indicate the way ; and as
the big carts with their immense wheels without tires
moved across the plain, they raised a great cloud of dust,
and their creaking could be heard for miles around. The
capataz, or foreman, rode up and down by the side of the
train to watch the drivers and to see that everything
was kept in order.

IV

In a letter dated August 3, 1729, Padre Gervasoni
describes what he calls his land voyage over the level
country in the winter. In all the journey, he says, he
encountered no hills, nor saw in the distance any mountain
ranges, until after twenty-five days the sierras of Cordova
began to appear. He passed only a few houses, and these
were eight or ten miles apart. They all had hay or grass
roofs, and their walls were made of mud covered with hides.
For half of the way no trees were seen, except a few that
had been planted about the rude houses. All the land
was well suited to cultivation, but no planted fields
were seen until within three miles of Cordova, the few inhabitants being apparently satisfied with their miserable
existence since it did not require them to work.

The disagreeable feature of the journey was the necessity of travelling in the cold weather of July, without
reaching any house in which to take refuge, or fire with
which to warm one's self. The more robust of the passengers
could keep warm by walking, but the others who were not
able to take such severe exercise suffered from cold both
without and within the carts. " What surprised and con-
founded me was to see how the Indians and mestizos

stood it ; for almost all of the drivers were of these classes. Generally they wore no stockings or shoes ; they slept in their clothes, either on the ground on a hide in the open air, or sitting in their seats."

"For food they killed in the afternoon one of the animals that had been driven along with the caravan for this purpose. Each person took the part he wished, fastened it to a pole, one end of which was fixed in the ground, and allowed it to hang over the fire ; and ate it with only the outside scorched. "They put the head of the animal into the live coals, with the hair and skin on, until the skin cracked with the heat, and then they said it was cooked. They observed this same system always. All the Indians had a dispensation from Rome permitting them to eat meat on any day whatever, because they had no other food. The greatest present which one could make to them was a piece of bread, which was a great addition to their meal, and which perhaps they had not had for many years. Their habitual drink was water, and to make it more delicious, they put a certain herb into it, which was sufficient to make me vomit up my intestines.

"Another trial was the water that we drank, which, taken now from a swamp now from a stream, was more mud than water. Nevertheless—would you believe it ?— on the journey I have been quite as well as before, and I recognise it as a special grace of God, who, seeing the great scarcity of labourers in these towns, preserves almost miraculously those who are here. I judge from the little which I have observed of the persons who have accompanied us, that the people, already Christians, live in a most complete innocence ; for in addition to the fact that they are extremely faithful, we have not heard a word or seen anything unworthy of a good Christian. Those who live on these plains are truly in need of spiritual help ; for in all the region we have passed over there are at most three or four parishes, each one of them embracing

some forty or fifty thousand persons. The priests of
Cordova and Buenos Aires, going on their missions every
year after Easter, confess these poor people, celebrate
the communion for them, and teach them the Christian
doctrine ; and they know no other Easter than the arrival
of the priests."

On account of the heat of the sun in summer, it was
found to be more convenient to travel during some part
of the night, at least in the early morning and late in the
evening, resting between ten o'clock in the forenoon and
four o'clock in the afternoon. In some parts of the
journey from Buenos Aires to Mendoza, it was sometimes
difficult to find water when it was needed ; and for this
reason long distances were often covered with only very
brief periods for rest by the way.[1]

V

Transportation over the Andes from Mendoza and from
Salta or Jujuy across the mountains to Upper Peru was
effected by the use of beasts of burden. Helms refers
to the journey through Upper Peru in the following
statement :

" At Salta we changed our carriages for saddle mules,
and thence pursued our way over the highest chain of
mountains on the globe, and on roads the most wretched
and fatiguing, eighteen hundred miles to Lima. It was
fortunate for us that we had entered upon this dangerous
journey at the most proper and favourable season of the
year ; as in our progress across the Cordilleras we were
obliged to ford a number of rapid rivers and torrents
(some of them even thirty different times). In these
torrents, which often suddenly swell during summer, a
great number of travellers perish. In a few hours we
exchanged the very intense summer-heat of the valleys

[1] See Cárcano, *Comunicación y transporte*, i. 99–105.

for the piercing cold of the snowy summit of the mountain—a transition that soon undermines the health of the most robust European. A hectic fever attacks him, or he is seized with the cramp, rheumatism, and nervous melancholy." [1]

This route was extensively used in taking mules from the province of Tucuman to Peru. These animals were purchased in the region about Buenos Aires, Santa Fé, and Corrientes, when they were a year and a half or two years old, and driven to the pastures of Cordova, where they were kept for several months. Towards the end of April or in the beginning of May, great troops of them were formed and moved slowly towards the north, halting by the way wherever there were favourable opportunities for grazing. Arriving at Salta in the month of June, they were kept eight months in the pastures of that district in order that they might be brought into a condition that would ensure their sale at the fair to be held the following February and March in the valley of Lerma.

According to a statement of Bustamante or Concolorcorvo in *El Lazarillo de Ciegos caminantes*,[2] the number

---

[1] Helms, *Travels to Lima*, 17

[2] Bustamante, *alias* Concolorcorvo, *El Lazarillo de Ciegos caminantes desde Buenos Aires hasta Lima*, 1773. New edition, Buenos Aires, 1908. This is an especially important and interesting account of the condition of things along the route from Buenos Aires to Lima in the last half of the eighteenth century. Among the notes made by General Mitre in his copy is found this remark : " Whoever may be the author, the journey is real, and contains data and *noticias preciosas* which can be found only in this work. The traveller was in Montevideo and Buenos Aires in 1749, and gives many details of the condition, customs, and inhabitants of these cities. Critical and humorous anecdotes are scattered throughout the work, and on arriving at Cuzco he inserts four discussions in the form of dialogues between the author and the *visitador* on the condition of the Indians, of whose character he makes a very sad picture."

Helms, *Travels from Buenos Aires by Potosi to Lima* (London, 1807). This is a brief description of Helms' journey made in 1789.

Miers, *Travels in Chile and La Plata*, two volumes (London, 1826). The first volume, narrating experiences during journeys from Buenos Aires to Valparaiso, gives detailed accounts of the condition of the roads and the post-houses in the early years of the nineteenth century.

of mules gathered here annually was sixty thousand. Buyers came from all the provinces of Peru and Rio de la Plata, but the greater part of the animals bought were sent to Peru. Esteban de Urizar Arespacochaga, the governor of Tucuman, wrote to the king, November 24, 1708, that forty thousand mules were taken to that country.[1] This trade with Peru was not especially lucrative, owing to the large expenses of care and transportation. Besides the original purchase price, there were taxes and the very important expense for the wages of a large number of herdsmen. The price at which a mule was sold in Peru depended upon the distance of the selling place from the fair. In this respect the Peruvians living in the extreme south enjoyed a certain advantage over those living farther north. In passing over the level country or along the narrow trails of the mountain passes, the troop was preceded by a bell mare led by a mounted *peon*, and the bell at her neck kept up its monotonous jingle. All the mules followed as if their leader possessed an irresistible attraction. On the plains they constituted a somewhat loose band, but among the mountains they made up a long line, climbing up the steep trail, moving along the mountain side, and descending into the valley. At the end of the journey in Peru, the conditions under which they were used were very unfavourable for the preservation of the animals. The half-savage Indian, who was their keeper, had little interest in them and less knowledge of their needs. They were overworked and inadequately fed, and generally ended their miserable existence prematurely.[2]

[1] " Tan solo de los valles de Salta se llevaban á Potosi, despues que los chilenos abandonaron por el trigo aquella especulacion á fines del siglo XVII, no menos de 60,000 mulas y hasta un million de carneros en cada año " (Vicuña Mackenna, in *Revista del Rio de la Plata*, iv. 86).

[2] Bustamante or Concolorcorvo, *El Lazarillo de Ciegos caminantes*, cap. vi. and vii. ; Cárcano, *Comunicación y transporte*, i. cap. v. ; Markham, *Cuzco and Lima*, 19.

VI

In the great rivers that flow into the Rio de la Plata, the south-eastern part of South America has extraordinary facilities for transportation by water. The Indians who occupied this region were not as skilful navigators as the savage islanders of the south-western Pacific. The difference arose in large measure from the circumstances of the life of the islanders which made skill in navigation necessary, while among the Indians the possession of such skill was only an occasional convenience. The canoe, or dugout, and some form of a raft, or balsa, comprised the craft employed on these rivers by the Indians. The balsa was more frequently used on the Rio de la Plata than any other means for conveying freight and passengers. It consisted primarily of a number of logs or poles lashed together. On this platform a little hut or cabin was sometimes erected as a protection against the sun or rain. A sail was sometimes attached to a mast standing near the middle of the balsa ; sometimes it was attached to two poles, one of which stood on either side of the platform, the two being bent inward and bound together at the top.

Another form of a balsa was made by placing two canoes side by side, a little distance apart, and by laying poles or light beams across them. On these poles or light beams some kind of a floor was constructed, and on this a little hut or cabin was erected. It was on a balsa of this sort that Padre Cattaneo undertook his journey to Misiones in 1729. He had fifteen balsas and about three hundred Indian boatmen. For this voyage the balsas were preferred to other boats, since they were less liable to serious damage in running on the sunken rocks. The boatmen appear to have had good appetites : for Cattaneo wrote that he had seen on the voyage the crew of a single balsa, which consisted generally of twenty-four persons, eat in less than one day a large ox as if it had been a calf, and they did not eat more because they had no more. There were no serious results from this eating, and our missionary explains this fact by affirming that their manner of rowing greatly aided their digestion, since they rowed standing. As the expedition proceeded, they were accustomed to halt for the night, and their first task on landing was to make a little altar out of leaves and branches, on which they placed a figure of the Holy Virgin, one of which was carried in each balsa. As soon as the religious service was ended, they built a fire and made their supper of roasted beef. Then they stretched themselves at length on the ground on the skin of an ox or of a tiger in a circle around a fire. The fire in this case was not for heat, but for the purpose of frightening away wild animals, which, Cattaneo says, had been known to drag off a man so rapidly that he could not be rescued. In the morning, after breakfast and prayers, they returned to their boats and continued till noon, when they halted again for rest and their midday meal. In this manner the days passed agreeably until the middle of the journey, when smallpox appeared among the boatmen. Fourteen of the men of one balsa fell ill at once, and at the same time others here and there in the other boats. Here in the wilderness, three hundred miles from Buenos Aires, and quite as far from the missions, the prospect was without hope of succour ; and the Indians, " as soon as one was attacked by the disease, abandoned him, leaving him on the ground with a bucket of water and a large amount of beef by his side. After three or four days, one went around him on horse-back, always at a considerable distance, to see if the victim was alive or dead. If he was dead, the person making the observation went away immediately, but if he was alive the provision was renewed, and the process was continued until he was well or dead." Here in the wilderness, out of the reach of assistance, they remained until the disease had run its course ; and at the end it was found that of the whole number engaged in the expedition, only forty had escaped contagion, one hundred and seventy-nine had died, and ninety had recovered.[1]

In spite of the fact that it was the policy of the Jesuits to keep the Indians of the missions apart from the Spaniards of other settlements, the existence of the missions helped to increase the river traffic of this region. A certain surplus of products was sent by the reductions to Buenos Aires and exchanged for articles needed in the missions. There was also a movement of passengers more or less extensive between Buenos Aires and the reductions ; and a more or less intimate communication between Buenos Aires and Asuncion and other points along the course of the river. And the interior traffic, both by the rivers and by land, was greatly increased after the promulgation of the commercial code of 1778, which established a large measure of freedom between Buenos Aires and Spanish ports as well as between that city and other Spanish-American ports. This new trade provoked a demand for an improvement of existing routes, and stimulated explorations for the purpose of finding desirable routes that had not yet been used. Many expeditions were sent to explore the Andes with a view of finding a way for carts or wagons across the mountains into Chile. Although carts were used on the road between Buenos Aires and Mendoza, still many articles were carried on the backs of horses and mules. Wine was transported from Mendoza to Buenos Aires in small casks made for the purpose, each animal carrying two, one on either side of the saddle.

[1] Padre Cattaneo's description of this journey is given in a letter of April 25, 1730, written at the reduction of Santa Maria, in the *Misiones*. The part relating to the journey is printed in Cárcano's *Comunicación y transporte*, i. 233–67.

CHAPTER XX

SOCIAL CHARACTERISTICS OF THE SPANISH DEPENDENCIES IN SOUTH AMERICA

I. Europeans, Indians, negroes, and the mixed races. II. Negro slaves. III. Antagonism of Europeans and creoles. IV. General character of colonial society. V. Contrasts of English and Spanish colonial society. VI. Democracy.

I

In the Spanish colonies of America, the Europeans, the Indians, and the negroes represented three distinct races. Besides the representatives of these races, there were various classes with mixed blood. The most important of the mongrel classes were the mestizos, the offspring of the union of Europeans and Indians ; the mulattoes, the offspring of Europeans and negroes ; and the sambos, the offspring of the union of Indians and negroes. The legal and other obstacles that were opposed to the emigration of unmarried Spanish women to America, and the lack of any sentiment hostile to the union of Spaniards and Indians, led to the development of a large class of mestizos, greatly exceeding in number any other mixed class. The same freedom, however, did not exist with respect to the union of the Indians and the Africans. In fact, the government sought to prevent the amalgamation of these races, and prohibited their union by cruel and unusual penalties.

Sambo's contemporaries appear to have entertained a very unfavourable opinion concerning his moral qualities. Depons, writing of him at the end of the eighteenth century, says he " is well formed, muscular, and able to endure fatigue ; but all his tastes, all his inclinations, all his faculties, are turned to vice. The mere name of Sambo signifies in the country a good-for-nothing idler, drunkard, cheat, and even an assassin. Of ten crimes that are committed, eight always appertain to this cursed class of sambos. Immorality is their characteristic. It is not perceived in the same degree either in negroes, mulattoes, or any other race, pure or mixed.[1]

Through the arrogance of the Spaniards, the creoles, persons of pure European blood born in America, came to be regarded as a class by themselves. The character of the creole was developed under very unfavourable conditions. As a child he was turned over to the care of a confidential negro slave, and he remained under this barbarian tutelage for five or six years. Then he passed into the hands of a mulatto instructor, " with whom he neither saw nor heard anything worthy of imitation." He acquired a slave's notion of duty, which recognised little or no spontaneous effort for others, but whose rule of action is the command of the master enforced by the lash. From his teachers he acquired notions of religion that were full of paganism, without the grace and poetry of pagan worship. Outwardly he adapted himself to the forms of civilised life, but his mind was full of the super-stitions acquired from the barbarous companions of his childhood.[2] The Spaniards, who had been born and edu-cated under more favourable conditions, had little sym-pathy with the creole, and apparently concluded that no worthy characters could rise out of his unfortunate circumstances. They regarded him as essentially inferior to themselves, and nothing more was wanting but the ambition of the creole to give rise to a bitter antagonism between these two classes. Through this antagonism the

---

[1] *Travels* (Eng. trans.), ii. 249. " In tutta l'America non evvi nulla di peggio. Il zambo é taciturno, di guardatura o bieca, o malizioza, e di un'indole si perversa, che portale de leggieri al male" (Gilij, *Saggio di Storia Americana* (Roma, 1780–4), iv. 320).

[2] García, *La Ciudad Indiana*, 84.

creoles were ultimately driven into an attitude not only
of social, but also of political, hostility to the Europeans.
The practical expression of Spanish hatred which the
creole resented most vigorously was his exclusion from the
higher offices of the colony in which he lived. Of the 166
viceroys and 588 captains-general, governors, and presidents who had held office in the colonies, in all 754, only
18 were creoles. There was, however, no lack of men of
this class fitted to perform the duties of these offices ;
for many had been educated in Europe, and even those
who had resorted to the colonial colleges were sufficiently
well trained to administer successfully the local afiairs of
the colonies. But they lacked the influence necessary to
obtain these positions. The gravest evil resulting from
this exclusion of Americans was not merely that the
native inhabitants of European descent were deprived of
the privilege of having a part in governing themselves,
but " the moral degradation consequent upon the absence
of all motive to generous exertion, and the utter hope-
lessness that any merit could lead to useful distinction." [1]

But there were some persons who saw clearly that
even the despised creole, using all available opportunities
to improve his standing, would ultimately turn and demand recognition. In a memorial addressed to Philip V,
Don Malchor Macanaz pointed out the effect of this exclusion. He called the king's attention not only to the
injustice of the policy of exclusion, but also to its evil
political consequences.

" As the natives of those, your Majesty's dominions,
are equally deserving of filling the principal offices of
their own country, it appears reasonable that they should
not be divested of all management in their own homes.
I am fully persuaded, that in those countries there are
many discontented persons, not because they are under
the control of Spain ; but because they are cast down,
and tyrannised by the very persons who are sent over

[1] Basil Hall, *Journey*, ii. 237.

to exercise the duties of the judicature.   Let your Majesty give these offices to subjects of that country, and by this means disturbances will be avoided." [1]

In the course of time hostility between the creoles and the Europeans became a noteworthy feature of life in the colonies.   The creoles resented the neglect they experienced under the Spanish government, and made common cause with the mestizos and all the subject classes.   In this manner a line separating one party from another was drawn, leaving the majority on the side of the creole.   This was the breach leading to the struggle which ended in independence.

The Europeans, the Indians, and the negroes, representatives of distinct races, had different antecedents, and consequently different social aims.   The attitude of the Spaniards towards the Indians and the negroes, as well as their attitude towards the creoles, did not indicate that the prejudice of race was to be laid aside.   In spite of the rise of the creole, and the increase of the mixed races, the Europeans were determined to maintain their position as the dominant element in the population.   They "were the lords of the soil, the owners of the mines and the factories, the great political, ecclesiastical, and military functionaries ; they monopolised the riches and the honours.   The Indians were the Pariahs of the colonial régime ; they were overworked in every kind of labour, without ever profiting by the fruit of their toil.   The negroes, in the lamentable condition of slaves, were removed from the protection of the law." [2]

[1] See Walton's *Exposé*, 48.
[2] Oliviera, *La Política económica de la Metrópoli*, 5, 6.

II

As early as 1501 the Spaniards were permitted to take negroes to America, but the decree granting this privilege provided that only such negroes should be taken as had been born under the power of Christian masters. After the introduction of sugar-cane into Cuba in 1506, and the determination of a number of persons to take advantage of the very favourable climatic conditions for its cultivation, negroes were introduced in such great numbers that the colonists feared an uprising. Later in this year further importation of negroes was prohibited ; at the same time permission to marry was extended to those already in the colonies. This prohibition to take negroes to America was subsequently removed, and in 1517 it was required that one-third of those imported should be women. With the increase in numbers the fears that had been entertained of an uprising were seen to be well founded. From the beginning the negroes were the cause of serious social disturbances, and in 1550 they committed great atrocities, and burned the city of Santa Marta. Five years later a negro, calling himself king, headed an insurrection, which was marked by all sorts of crime, and was put down only after strenuous exertions on the part of the authorities. These and similar disturbances led the king again to prohibit taking negroes to the Indies.

It is probable that the brutality of the negro, as displayed on many occasions, had much to do in determining the manner in which he was treated. "No difference was made between a negro and any animal whatsoever. He was a beast of burden that the master disposed of at any time in the same manner as a mule."[1]

[1] Romero, C. A., *Negros y Caballos*, 11. The following advertisements appeared in the *Diario de Lima*, May 16, 1792 :

" *Venta.*—Quien quisiere comprar una criada preñada en dias de parir, bozal, reformada, ocurra, á la calle de Bodegones la primera

By law negroes were prohibited from appearing on the streets of Lima at night, except when accompanying their masters. The penalty for violating this ordinance was a hundred lashes for the first offence, and brutal mutilation for the second offence. A Spaniard meeting a negro at night in the street might take away his arms ; and if the negro dared to defend himself, the Spaniard might kill him. The negro who ran away from his master for a period of six days might be mutilated, and if he was absent for a longer time he might be killed. For even the minor offence of stealing corn, negroes were punished with one hundred lashes for the first offence and mutilation for the second.[1]

The strictest regulations were established to prevent members of the Indian and negro races from living together.[2] The severity of these penalties was not lessened when Pedro de la Gasca assumed full authority over Peru. The disposition of some of the negroes to resume the practices of savagery induced the authorities to offer a reward of from five to twenty-five dollars for hunting down the unruly negroes. If they could not be taken alive they might be killed ; and in order to receive the reward it was only necessary to present the head

casa, donde fué café. Arriba en los altos vive su ama en la segunda mampara."

" *Venta.*—Quien quisiere comprar una pareja de mulas de coche de siete cuartas, bien altas y nuevas, que acaban de llegar de Piura, ocurra á la barbería de la plazuela vieja de San Juan de Dios donde darán razon de su dueño, con quien se tratará del precio en que se venden."

The following advertisements of slaves for sale are taken from the papers of Buenos Aires :

" Se vende, una criada, sana y sin vicios, en cantidad de 300 pesos. En esta oficina darán razon."

" Se vende, una mulatilla sana, sin vicios, primeriza, con leche de cuatro meses. En la casa de Espósitos darán razon."

[1] Romero, *Negros y Caballos*, 12 ; for the ordinances covering these cases, see *Revisto de Archivos y Bibliotecas*, v.

[2] " No podian los negros tener tratos ni contratos con los indios, y el que tuviese manceba india habia de ser castrado, y á la negra que accediese á los requilorios de algun indio, habíanle de cortar las orejas."
—Romero, *Negros y Caballos*, 13 ; *Doc. inéd.*, xviii. 136, 165.

of the negro before the cabildo, or city council. The negroes might not wear fine clothing, silk, or jewels. All persons were forbidden to sell them wine or *chicha*, and they might not ride on horseback. When negroes, either freemen or slaves, died, their bodies might not be carried away in a coffin.

At the end of the century, the king undertook to improve the relations then existing between the Spaniards and the negroes, and on the 31st of May, 1789, he issued an order relating to the education, treatment, and occupations of the slaves in all the Spanish dominions of the Indies. Under this order every owner of slaves was required to instruct them in the principles of the Catholic religion, that they might be baptized; and to this end he should explain to them the Christian doctrine on certain feast days, on which neither the slaves nor their owners should work. All the owners of slaves were required to comply strictly with their obligation to feed and clothe the slaves, as also their wives and children, although these might be free. All the slaves of both sexes, between the ages of seventeen and sixty, should be assigned tasks suited to their age, sex, and strength, and they should be required to work from sunrise to sunset, with the exception of two hours each day, which might be employed in occupations for their own personal advantage. On the feast days, after the mass and the Christian instruction, the slaves might have simple amusements, in which the sexes should be kept apart; and they should be had, moreover, in the presence of the owner or overseer; and they were required to avoid the excesses of eating and drinking, and to conclude their amusements before nightfall. The owners were required to furnish distinct apartments for the two sexes, except in the cases where they were married, and also the necessary beds and clothing; and the sick should be supported by the owner, or sent to the hospital at his expense, and in case of death the owner should bear the expense of burial. The owners were, moreover, required to support the old slaves and the children of both sexes, and they might not set them at liberty without at the same time assigning them perpetual support, to the satisfaction of the prosecuting attorney. The owners might not prevent the slaves from marrying, whether with a slave of the estate to which he belonged or with a slave from another estate. In the latter case the wife should follow the husband, and the owner of the husband was required to purchase the wife. In view of the fact that the owner held a paternal relation to the slave, if the slave failed to fulfil his filial obligation, he might and ought to be given reformatory punishment either by the owner or the overseer; only, however, with imprisonment, fetters, chains, a club, stocks, or lashes, and the lashes might not exceed twenty-five. In case the slave committed a crime against his master, the master's wife or children, or any other person, he should be turned over to the civil judiciary and be subjected to the same trial as a free person. If an owner or overseer should violate any of these provisions, he would be liable to a fine of fifty dollars for the first offence, one hundred dollars for the second offence, and two hundred dollars for the third offence; and if a more severe punishment should be inflicted than that designed by the royal order, the prosecuting attorney should proceed against the owner or overseer who had given the punishment. If the owner or overseer should injure, wound, or kill a slave, he should be subjected to the same penalty as if the violation affected a free person. Each owner was required to make an annual sworn statement as to the number, sex, and ages of the slaves on his estate.

This law, like many others proceeding from the king and council of the Indies, encountered practices too thoroughly established to be reformed by a decree from Spain. It, moreover, came too late to be of great historical significance. The traditions that had been created by centuries of misrule were destined to continue without important abatement until the end. The slave had become a part of the social organism, and convenience or the will of the dominant social factor had determined his place, his treatment, and his uses. In the face of established custom no sudden change was possible. Slaves had often been held for ostentation, and this practice and the desire underlying it could not be abolished with a single stroke. Ladies of distinction wished to be attended by slaves while going to church, and they naturally sought to rival one another in the number of their attendants. They used them as a means of indicating their social standing.[1] But slaves were also employed as a source of profit. The house was a kind of workshop, in which the slaves produced various articles for the market. One hundred or two hundred dollars invested in a slave returned through his labour eight or ten dollars a month. Thus, a gain of from forty-eight to one hundred and twenty per cent. a year was a sufficient profit to maintain the institution in favour. But the impression which the system of slave labour made, as carried out here, whether in the house or in the fields, was essentially the same as that observed wherever in an industrial community slavery has existed. Children growing to maturity in the presence of its practice came to despise work as they despised the position of the only workers they had seen. Add to this the other forms of corruption that were fostered by the association of the youth and the slaves, and it becomes evident that the dominant element in the population acquired a character that unfitted it to lay successfully the foundation of a new society, a character many of the features of which are clearly seen in this latest generation.

[1] Under these circumstances the treatment accorded to the negroes was very different from that which they ordinarily received. The slaves from Africa " are mostly employed in domestic service ; they form a principal part of the train of luxury and are cherished and caressed by their superiors, to whose vanity and pleasures they are equally subservient" (Wilcocke, *History of the Viceroyalty of Buenos Ayres*, London, 1807, 400).

Besides the families that were able to maintain slaves and the slaves who served them, there was another element that constituted a ragged fringe of the society, an element that had ceased to entertain expectations of improvement in its state. It embraced those who were personally free ; but their material condition was not better than that of the slaves. They lived wherever they could find shelter, in huts erected on the unoccupied lands, or wherever there were vacant quarters which they could appropriate. The exploitation by slave labour of all of the sources of profit that had been opened left them no field of enterprise, and their hopeless misery had deprived them of the power to initiate undertakings of their own. Their fate was that of the free poor usually in the presence of a system of slavery.

III

The antagonism between the Europeans and the creoles was hardly less severe than that which existed between groups of different races. The fact that the creoles were of the same blood or of the same family as the Europeans did not seem to abate the hostility. The differences were class differences, and were naturally stronger in the isolated centres of population than in those towns frequented by foreigners. Among the influences tending to maintain the breach between the Europeans and the creoles, Juan and Ulloa found two that were more powerful than the rest :

" The excessive vanity and overbearing manners of the creoles, and the forlorn and penniless condition of the Europeans arriving in Peru from Spain. The latter accumulate a fortune with the aid of relatives and friends, as well as by dint of labour and industry, so that within a few years they are enabled to form an alliance with ladies of distinction ; but the low condition in which the creoles first knew them is not wholly effaced from remembrance ;

and on the first occasion of misunderstanding between the
European and his relatives, the latter expose, without the
least reflection, the mean origin and profession of the
former, and kindle the flames of discord in all hearts.
The Europeans espouse the cause of their injured countrymen, and the creoles that of the native women, and
thus the seeds of dissension spring up, which had been
sown in the mind from the remote period of the conquest." [1]

The pretensions of the creoles were stimulated by the
policy that had been carried out of granting patents of
nobility to certain Spaniards who had taken up their
residence in America. The descendants of these spent
much time in " discussing the order and line of their
descent ; so that it would appear, as it respects nobility
and antiquity, they have nothing to envy in the most
illustrious families of Spain ; and, treating the subject
with the ardour of enthusiasm, they make it the first topic
of conversation with the newly-arrived Europeans, in
order to acquaint them with their noble origin ; but when
this is investigated impartially, we are met at the first step
we take with so many difficulties, that a family can rarely
be found that has no mixed blood, not to mention objections of minor importance. In such cases it is amusing
to observe how they become mutually the heralds of one
another's low birth, so that it is needless to investigate
the subject for one's self." [2]

The vanity of the creoles, moreover, led them to avoid
labour and to refuse to engage in trade. This left them
to a life of inaction and, in many cases, to a life of
vice.

" Hence it is they soon see the end of all that which
their parents have left them, by wasting their money,
and neglecting the cultivation of their estates ; and the
Europeans, availing themselves of the advantages which
the neglect of the creoles affords them, turn them to

---

[1] *Noticias Secretas*, 417.   [2] *Ibid.*, 417.

SOCIAL CHARACTERISTICS 407

account, and amass an estate ; for by engaging in trade
they soon succeed in getting upon a good footing, enjoy
credit, accumulate money, and are solicited for marriage by
noble families ; for the creole women themselves, aware
of the wasteful and indolent habits of their countrymen,
hold Europeans in high esteem, and prefer to be allied
with them." [1]

Through the antagonism of the Europeans and creoles
arising from these and other circumstances, the social
life of the cities of Peru was marked by tumults and bitterness of spirit. Under conditions " where they might pass
the most agreeable and tranquil life that could be desired," [2] they led a wretched existence, kept in a state of
perpetual commotion by uncontrolled passions.

IV

Observing colonial society generally, and not merely
as it appeared in the dependencies of Spain, it is seen
that from whatever nation Western colonies proceed,
they are all found to have similar features, and, in case
of growth, pass through common stages of development.
They are all socially stagnant for a time, while the
societies from which they issued continue their development unimpeded. In fact, a colony separated from the
mother country may be likened to a branch cut from a
tree and planted in the soil. The branch in many cases
will take root and grow ; but in the beginning there will
be a period of stagnation in the growth of the severed
branch, while the tree will continue its growth without
interruption. Ultimately, under favourable conditions,
the branch developing new roots will acquire a vigour
of growth exceeding that of the old tree. This period
of temporarily arrested development determines certain
features of colonial society, and of the society of the independent nations into which the colonies may grow.

[1] *Noticias Secretas*, 418, 419.   [2] *Ibid.*, 422.

408 THE SPANISH DEPENDENCIES

After decades of a separate existence, even after a colony has grown into a populous and cultivated nation, the language, the customs, and many of the external forms of life will recall the ancient days of the mother country; will recall characteristic features of the parent nation as it was at the time of the separation. The mother country will have continued its growth, and in the course of this growth forms of speech, peculiarities of institutions, and features of national customs will have become antiquated and dropped, while in the colony, where growth has been arrested, these changes will not have been made. The history of the colonies planted in America by European nations furnish illustrations of this general rule of colonial development.

The illustrations presented by the languages are, perhaps, the most familiar. The peculiarities of the French which continues to be spoken in Canada, or of the English of the United States, show survivals from those languages as they were spoken in Europe two or three centuries ago. In this manner there has been preserved in the speech of America a certain archaic quality, which by a process of uninterrupted growth has passed out of the languages of the mother countries. These linguistic survivals are a minor indication of a psychological difference that exists between the descendants of the colonists in America and their kinsmen in Europe, whose ancestors did not emigrate. The peculiarities of American speech were increased in the course of time by the adoption of elements which were unknown in Europe—elements made necessary by the new circumstances, and by the new conceptions arising out of these circumstances. A language adopted and used is a powerful factor in determining one's psychological attitude. The Chinaman, for example, who learns thoroughly the English language and uses it for many years passes through an important mental transformation. The language has brought to his mind new conceptions and modified his intellectual

SOCIAL CHARACTERISTICS

horizon. In like manner, by using a language with important survivals and more important additions, the mind of the American has come to have a different content from the mind of the European. This mental peculiarity of the colonists and their descendants was an element in the foundation of American society. It is the basis of a social difference which separates America from Europe.

Another element in the basis of a society, or of a community, is the peculiar expectations entertained by the persons who have been drawn together, and under which they live. These expectations constitute an important force in the growth of the character of the community. The colonists of the New World became mentally unlike their kindred who remained in Europe, partly because their minds were dominated by expectations peculiar to the emigrant, and partly because in their new environment their minds embraced hopes and expectations which had no influence on the members of the Old-World communities. Under the influence of different expectations, furthermore, the characters of the several colonies were differentiated The very marked difference that existed between the community of Potosi in the seventeenth century and a community of New-England colonists was in part due to the different expectations entertained in the two cases. The English who came to New England expected no other fate than to be obliged to gain their living from a hard and unfruitful soil. They accepted this fate with stoical resignation. Adventures into unknown regions did not allure them with promises of extravagant rewards. Neither within the limits of their colonial possession nor by expeditions abroad did they expect to acquire great wealth that would enable them to live in another country. Here in the land of their exile they took up the task of rearing their children, and making whatever provision they might for the coming generations. The fact that they expected their lives and the lives of their descendants to be spent in America made them solicitous for the future of their communities. This difference was not altogether a matter of nationality; for when the youth of New England went to California in 1848 and 1849, they made communities that were strikingly like that of Potosi in its most flourishing years.

V

The Spaniards who migrated to the New World had somewhat more extravagant expectations, particularly in the early decades, after the exploits of Cortes and Pizarro. The marvellous spoils gained through these expeditions unsettled the minds of later explorers and colonists. The expectation of acquiring immense wealth, as it had been acquired in Peru, made the slow gains and comparative poverty of agricultural life seem entirely unsatisfactory. Even when the delusions of the early adventurers were exposed by more or less thorough explorations of the continent, the search for mines to exploit took the place of the search for an Indian prince to plunder. Under these extravagant expectations society was slow in assuming a normal form. Large numbers of the colonists expected, with quickly acquired wealth, to be able to return to Spain and live in independence. These hopes drew attention away from the ordinary occupations of a settled society, and made the inhabitants careless of many things essential to social stability and prosperity.

Another element that was fundamental in English and Spanish colonial society was the sentiment of protest. This was favoured and stimulated by absence from a previous environment and emancipation from ancient traditions. The appearance of this sentiment was later in the Spanish than in the English colonies. But after it appeared its growth was more rapid in the south than in the north. Some of the English colonies were in an attitude of revolt from the beginning, even before they left England ; while in the Spanish colonies this sentiment appeared especially among the creoles, the mestizos, and the Indians ; but only after they had discovered that the policy of the Spanish government was to confer power and privileges almost exclusively on men of Spanish birth. It was, moreover, significant for the later condition of the society that the earliest phases of the protest against Great Britain concerned the Church, or the ecclesiastical side of the State. This involved the most vital sentiment of the age. But no such religious antagonism existed between Spain and her dependencies. Those profound emotions of religious hostility which troubled the hearts and minds of the inhabitants of New England were never aroused in the Spanish colonists. In the case of the Puritans, these emotions became a transforming power. Under their influence the New Englander became a man apart, spiritually as well as geographically separated from the majority of those of his own blood in England. He ceased to be attracted by the things his ancestors had admired. He repudiated whatever his race, in the course of its progress, had invented to adorn and embellish civilised life. He was unlovely, but he was strong. He went to his work and to his worship in the same spirit of grim determination.

No such complete breach with their immediate past appeared in the lives of the Spanish colonists. It is true that in the course of time they acquired certain characteristics different from those of their kin in Spain, but this difference was due to their environment and their attitude towards an alien race rather than to any new and profound spiritual emotions. The alienation of the colonists of New England was in large part a religious revolt, and their new religion became the corner-stone of their social structure. In the establishment and administration of the Spanish colonies, on the other hand, persistent and successful efforts were made to preserve unadulterated and unbroken the religious traditions of Spain. The worship that was set up in the English colonies was without controlling traditions. There was, moreover, no power to hold separate communities to a prescribed form. The principle of liberty was here applied to the most fundamental feature of their life, and this made its application logically necessary and inevitable in politics, and in all the departments of the social organism and of social conduct. On the other hand, the recognition of external authority and the restraining force of tradition in the ecclesiastical affairs of the Spanish colonies gave the principle of governmental protection in them great prestige, and provided a hindrance to the rise of any other determining force in their social affairs. In the Spanish colonies, there was thus no religious liberty to give countenance and support to political liberty.

The preservation, in the Spanish colonies, of the ecclesiastical traditions of Southern Europe sanctified the spirit of absolutism, which the Church represented. It made it difficult for the colonists to conceive of public power except as an emanation from a superior independent authority ; and against this preconception the idea of a government by the people made only insignificant progress during two centuries and a half of the colonial period. But the preservation of these traditions was attended with certain advantages. Not disturbed by any shock of religious separation, the Spanish colonists were able to bring to the New World the artistic sense which the Church had assiduously cultivated. In spite of their isolation and the rudeness of their environment, they retained an appreciation of artistic forms ; while the English colonists of the north apparently lost their artistic sense in their devotion to the severe morality and the unpoetic worship of Puritanism.

This contrast is revealed in many of the externals of life in the two cases. The meeting-house of the English colonists was undoubtedly adapted to their economical condition, but it was not an artistic object ; indeed, the presence of objects of decoration having an artistic quality would have been considered desecration. The Spaniards, on the other hand, came to America as thoroughly dominated by the artistic traditions of Europe as were their countrymen who remained in Spain. A manifestation of this sense is seen in their architecture. The patios of the old Spanish-American houses were in many instances masterpieces of artistic construction. Many of the churches, even in those features that had their origin in America, show not only a survival of European tradition and a strong artistic sense, but they also reveal the existence of an original creative power. A manifestation of this artistic sense of the emigrating Spaniards may also be seen in the magnificent church edifices that arose in the Philippine Islands in defiance of all the vagaries of oriental architecture.

But the most important element in the foundation of English and Spanish colonial society was the spirit of democracy. This was an element in the society even where it did not entirely determine the external form of the institutions. In some places, particularly in the northern English colonies, it encountered no effective hindrance to its expression in the forms of the social organisation. Here were the most favourable conditions for its manifestation. Here each head of a family held independently a certain amount of property ; and there were only unimportant differences among the amounts held by different persons. There was neither lord nor vassal ; and the government of the mother country seldom intervened. The equality of material possessions made inevitable a large measure of social equality. The opportunity to become economically independent rendered all men ambitious to be independent. The practical maintenance of the European relation of superior and inferior was, therefore, for the time being made impossible by the absence of any large class of persons willing, and compelled by circumstances, to continue in the position of dependents. Government takes its practical form from the form of the society in which it is established, possibly disregarding the terms of the organic law. In these northern colonies society had assumed a democratic form—that is to say, there was equality of material possessions, there were few outward manifestations of superiority, and there was a general spirit of public co-operation. Under these circumstances the local governments, which were created, generally without external compulsion, necessarily assumed a democratic character.

VI

The democracy of colonial society did not arise from a desire for equality; for there appears to be no such desire in the human mind. What men desire is not equality, but superiority. This is the force that is manifest in all efforts of political ambition; in the struggles for economic achievement; and in all the devices and expenditures for social advancement. If men desired equality as a good in itself, they might easily find it in the ranks of the hopeless and unambitious, by simply abandoning effort. It is not a desire for equality that has produced democracy; nor does such a desire offer a force on which it is possible to rely for the preservation of democracy. The social history of Switzerland through several centuries furnishes an illustration. The spirit of democracy and the forms of democratic government have survived in the Forest Cantons, where the population has continued sparse, and where there is no great inequality of wealth. But in those cantons where some persons have become rich while others have remained poor, or where material conditions have permitted social differentiation, the aristocratic spirit has appeared and supplanted the spirit of democracy.

The democratic spirit has found obstacles in the way of its development wherever society has grown away from the simple life of independent agriculturists. The spirit of the southern English colonies, with their slaves and the consequent separation of classes, was rather aristocratic than democratic. Moreover, in the Spanish colonies the forces preventing the rise and dominance of the democratic spirit were stronger than in the English colonies. They were the product of a peculiar Spanish inheritance, and of the conscious effort of the Spanish authorities to make Spanish colonial society like the society of Spain. The creation of a titled aristocracy ; the discrimination against the creole with respect to all the important offices of government and the Church ; and the personal concessions made to powerful leaders who established colonies or resided in America, introducing a form of feudalism, were all hindrances to the development of the democratic spirit. The existence of extensive mining and industrial undertakings, where the employment of large numbers of dependent Indians brought labourers as a class into disrepute, emphasized the lines of class distinction, and made practical democracy for the time being impossible. But in the course of time the exclusive policy of the Spanish government with respect to political offices and economic privileges created an opposition party, a party of the unprivileged, within which the essential equality of the members provided conditions favourable to the rise of the democratic spirit.

The rise of the class embracing the creoles, the mestizos, and the more cultivated Indians determined the fate of the dependencies. The mestizos and the creoles created whatever public opinion was developed in the eighteenth century. They became the democratic part of the population, and stood over against the aristocracy as represented by the titled nobility and the high officials in the Church and in the State. Their presence and their influence explain why, in emancipated Spanish America, republics were established, when, with rare exceptions, both the military and the civil leaders, and all the holders of privileges, sought the foundation of American monarchies. In each of the several colonial divisions they formed the nucleus, and were the creators, of the republics.

INDEX

Cochabamba's tribute revolt, ii. 333

Coche, pearl-fisheries, i. 31

Code of 1778, ii. 395

Coimans, slave-trader, ii. 265

Colb in the Chagres, ii. 260

Colegio, of Santa Tomas, ii. 96; Mayor del Rosario, ii. 97; of Monserrat, ii. 141; in Santiago del Estero, ii. 155; Maximo at Cordova, ii. 156

Colmenares on the Atrato, i. 11

Colonia (town), ii. 256

Colonial city, ii. 366–381; society, general view of, ii. 407–416

Colonists of Las Casas, i. 34; as soldiers, ii. 364

Columbus, third voyage of, i. 2; governor of Santo Domingo, i. 4; opposition to, i. 4; charges against and trial, i. 4; at Cadiz, released by Ferdinand's order, i. 5; fourth voyage, i. 5

— Diego, objects to Ojeda and Nicueza, i. 6

Comendadores, ii. 43

Commerce of Peru, ii. 184, 185

Comet of 1577 portends Drake, i. 363

Commissary-general (proveedor) of the Casa, i. 253

Commissaries in Chile, i. 336

Comogue, i. 10

Compulsory service of Indians, i. 320; Toledo on, i. 323

Comuneros of Paraguay, ii. 310

Concepcion abandoned and sacked, i. 353; audiencia at, i. 361

Concolorcorvo, *Ciegos Caminantes*, ii. 391

Concordia limiting power of Inquisition, i. 334, 378

Concubinage among the clergy, ii. 313

Conditions of work in the mines, ii. 48

Conduct in the churches, ii. 219

Confession, abuses of, i. 369

Conflicts, political - ecclesiastical in Paraguay, i. 202; with Araucanians, ii. 111

Confradias of Indians, ii. 218; ii. 236

Conquest, Mexico and Peru, influence of, i. 121; individual's power of, in Paraguay, i. 194

Conspirators against Bastidas, i. 47

Constituciones of 1556, i. 282, 284, 290

Consulado of Lima, ii. 68–70

Contineo, slave-trader, ii. 265

Contraband trade of Buenos Aires, ii. 129

Controversies, society favourable for, i. 377; parties to, i. 377–379

Conversion of Indians, difficulties of, i. 319; Barros Arana on, ii. 237

Copiapó, reached by Valdivia, i. 177

Cordova, founded, i. 199; ii. 38; seat of university, ii. 41

— Nueva, founded in New Granada, i. 301

— Diego Fernandez de, succeeds Esquilache, ii. 70

— Pedro de, friar, i. 205; inquisitor, i. 329

— y Coalla, Juan Fernandez de, succeeds Saavedra in New Granada, ii. 93

Corillo, Luis, death of, i. 22

Cornejo explores the Bermejo, ii. 386

Coro, founded by Ampués, i. 58; after Ehinger's death, ii. 68, 69; under Navarro, i. 73; after von Hutten's departure, i. 76; descent of governorship, i. 77; after eighteen years, i. 78

Corral, Francisco del, i. 318

Corregidores, of natives, i. 299; not to hold soldiers, i. 314; and tribute, ii. 318; and trade monopoly, ii. 319

Correspondence by post, i. 390, 391

Corrión in conflict with Potosi, ii. 19

Cortázar y Azcárate, inquisitor at Cartagena, i. 347

Coruña, bishop of Popayan, i. 318

Cosa, Juan de la, i. 2, 7

Council of Castile, i. 231, 232

— of the Indies, revoked Federmann's election, i. 71, 230–234, 264, 270, 337; in ecclesiastical affairs, ii. 225

Court, ecclesiastical, ii. 222

Council, general of Church, ii. 222; national, ii. 223; provincial, ii. 86, 224; of Trent, ii. 224

Countess' powders, ii. 77

Cozumel, bishop of, ii. 211

Creoles and luxury, ii. 204; their training, ii. 397; excluded from office, ii. 398, Creole-European hostility, ii. 399, 405;

Martinez y Vela, ii. 9, 11, 12
Massacre of San Espiritu, i. 190
Maté, trade in, ii. 205
Matienzo, Juan, i. 318
Maynas acquired by Peru, i. 274;
  Jesuits in, ii. 178
Mazeta, Jesuit, ii. 123, 143
Mediation of Bobadilla, i. 114
Medina, Gaspar de, of Tucuman,
  ii. 38
Melo's expedition, i. 50
Mena, executed, ii. 309
Menacho, bishop of Panama, i.
  291
Mencia, i. 311
Mendoza, A. Hurtado de, viceroy,
  i. 312; character of his rule, i.
  312; restrictions, i. 313
— Antonio de, first viceroy, i.
  268; arrives in Lima, i. 302;
  death, i. 303
— Diego, admiral, i. 191; fleet
  leaves San Lucas, 1534, i. 191
— Garcia Hurtado de, governor
  of Chile, i. 313, 353; his military
  force, i. 354; hypocrisy towards
  Aguirre, i. 355; campaign
  against Araucanians, i. 357;
  viceroy, 1590, i. 386; Quito
  riots, i. 388; sends Zurita to
  Tucuman, ii. 27; policy in Chile,
  ii. 49
— Gonzalo, governor of Paraguay, i. 198
— Pedro de, at Buenos Aires,
  i. 190
— town, founded, i. 355
Meneces, leader of royalists, i. 310
Mental unlikeness of Europeans
  and Americans, ii. 409
Mercado, death at Mompox, i. 156,
  276
Mercado y Villacorta, governor,
  folly as to Bohorquez, ii. 134;
  transferred to Buenos Aires, ii.
  138; and the Dutch ship, ii.
  138-9
Merced, the order of, in Santiago,
  ii. 237
Merchant ships, i. 262
Merchants, who held to be, i. 257
Mercury in mining, ii. 23
Mesa, B., and bishopric, ii. 210
Messengers mounted, ii. 385
Mesta, i. xvii.
Meta reached by Ordaz, i. 40;
  Jesuits in the Meta, ii. 101
Metals, precious, used by Incas,
  ii. 2

Miguel, the negro king, i. 81;
  attacks Barquisimeto, i. 82
Militia against the Pijaos, ii. 82
Mill, first in Chile, ii. 44
Miller, Jan, burnt for Protes-
  tantism, i. 330
Mines and Indians, ii. 48; of
  Upper Peru, i. 385; of Potosi,
  ii. 1
Mining placer, ii. 45; more
  profitable, ii. 316
Mint at Lima, i. 199, 200
Missions, futility of, ii. 229; of
  Casanare, ii. 102, 103; of Paraguay, ii. 143; traffic with, ii.
  395; under Buenos Aires, ii. 307
Mission to Paraguay, by Anglés,
  ii. 283
Mita under Toledo, by Matienzo,
  i. 322; at Potosi, ii. 7; to be
  abolished, ii. 64, 177; and free
  labour at Huancavelica, ii. 317
Mitre on the cities, ii. 380
Mogrobejo y Robles, archbishop,
  i. 381
Mompox, Santa Cruz de, founded,
  i. 145
Monastery, first in South America,
  1513, i. 32; in Tierra Firma
  destroyed, i. 33; of San Lorenzo
  el Real, printing privileges, i.
  374; "Desert," ii. 83; attractions of, ii. 230
Monasteries in Lima, ii. 201;
  multiplied, ii. 204; only with
  King's consent, ii. 207, 214-16;
  elections in, ii. 226; permission
  to construct, ii. 225-7
Monastic quarrels, ii. 185
Monclova, viceroy, ii. 200, 254;
  on Portuguese encroachments,
  ii. 256; on degrees for mestizos,
  ii. 257
Monks as parish priests, ii. 213-
  216; 229-231
— when not allowed to emigrate,
  i. 259; manner of life, ii. 313
Monopoly in trade with America,
  i. 235; of the post, i. 261, 388-
  391
Monroy, Alonso de, in Chile, i. 179
Montalvo, Lope de, i. 74, 75;
  led force to Bogotá, i. 76
— Jimenez de, president of audiencia after Esquilache, ii. 71
Montaño, sends oidores to Spain;
  executed, ii. 278
Monte Carmelo, Anson's capture,
  ii. 337

DATE DUE
